Christian Higher Education in the Global Context:
Implications for Curriculum, Pedagogy, and Administration

Christian Higher Education in the Global Context:
Implications for Curriculum, Pedagogy, and Administration

PROCEEDINGS OF THE
INTERNATIONAL CONFERENCE

International Association for the
Promotion of Christian Higher Education

15–19 NOVEMBER 2006
GRANADA, NICARAGUA

HOSTED BY
UPOLI
Polytechnic University of Nicaragua

Nick Lantinga, Editor

DORDT COLLEGE PRESS

Cover design by Amanda Niewenhuis
Layout by Carla Goslinga

Copyright © 2008 by IAPCHE

Fragmentary portions of this book may be freely used by those who are interested in sharing these authors' insights and observations, so long as the material is not pirated for monetary gain and so long as proper credit is visibly given to the publisher and the author. Others, and those who wish to use larger sections of text, must seek written permission from the publisher.

Printed in the United States of America

Dordt College Press   www.dordt.edu/dordt_press
498 Fourth Avenue NE
Sioux Center, Iowa 51250
United States of America

ISBN: 978-0-932914-78-1

The Library of Congress Cataloging-in-Publication Date is on file with the Library of Congress, Washington, D.C.

 Library of Congress Control Number: 2008930289

TABLE OF CONTENTS

Nick Lantinga
    Preface   1

Nick Lantinga   5
    Opening comments

OPENING KEYNOTE

Nelly García Murillo   9
    Christian higher education in a global context:
    Implications for curriculum, pedagogy, and administration

BANQUET ADDRESS

John Hulst   21
    Highlights of IAPCHE's history

TRACK 1 "HOW CAN CHRISTIAN HIGHER EDUCATION BRIDGE THE GAPS BETWEEN COMPETING CULTURES/WORLDVIEWS?"

B. J. van der Walt   33
    How to explain and evaluate cultural differences
    from a Reformational-Christian perspective

Clinton Stockwell   53
    Fundamentalisms and the shalom of God:
    An analysis of contemporary expressions of
    fundamentalism in Christianity, Judaism, and Islam

Cristian Buchiu   71
    Response to Clinton Stockwell

Daniel S. Shishima   75
    Response to Clinton Stockwell

Moshe Rajuili   77
    Developing a curriculum, employing a pedagogy,
    and an administration of Christian higher

education that addresses competing worldviews
in Southern Africa

Adrian A. Helleman   93
    Response to Moshe Rajuili

Peter Tze Ming Ng   97
    Response to Moshe Rajuili

José Ramón Alcántara-Mejía   101
    Transculturizing the humanities in
    Christian higher education

Douglas G. Campbell   113
    Response to José Ramón Alcántara-Mejía

R. Ruard Ganzevoort   117
    Teaching religion in a plural world

Musa A. B. Gaiya   125
    Response to R. Ruard Ganzevoort

Elisabeth Hulscher   129
    Response to R. Ruard Ganzevoort

TRACK 2 "WHAT CAN CHRISTIAN HIGHER EDUCATION DO TO PROMOTE EDUCATIONAL WELL-BEING?"

Faith W. Nguru   135
    What can Christian higher education do
    to promote educational well-being in Africa?

Susan S. Hasseler   151
    Response to Faith W. Nguru

Lizette F. Knight   155
    Productive pedagogy among Asian learners

Margaret Edgell   177
    Response to Lizette F. Knight

T. Stephen Tangaraj   179
    Response to Lizette F. Knight

Darrel W. Hilbrands   181
    The task of redeeming the educational
    process in Mexico

Susheila Williams   197
    Response to Darrel W. Hilbrands

Doug Blomberg   199
    New wineskins: Subverting the "sacred story"
    of schooling

David MacPherson   215
    Response to Doug Blomberg

Samson Makhado   219
    Response to Doug Blomberg

TRACK 3 "HOW DOES CHRISTIAN HIGHER EDUCATION CONNECT KINGDOM CITIZENSHIP TO SPECIFIC REGIONAL ISSUES AND CRISES?"

Henk Jochemsen & Johan Hegeman   223
    Equipping Christian students to connect
    kingdom citizenship to issues in today's societies

Sergio Saavedra Belmonte   241
    Response to Henk Jochemsen & Johan Hegeman

Tom Larney & George A. Lotter   251
    The parental role in establishing Christian values as
    the starting point of kingdom citizenship in an
    African (South African) context

Perry L. Glanzer   265
    Response to Tom Larney & George A. Lotter

Stan L. LeQuire   269
    Response to Tom Larney & George A. Lotter

J. Emmanuel Janagan   273
    Impact of Christian higher education in bringing social change in the life of Dalits in South India

Samuel P. Ango   287
    Response to J. Emmanuel Janagan

John Hiemstra   291
    Response to J. Emmanuel Janagan

Jeffrey P. Bouman & Lauren Colyn   295
    Ways that the pedagogy and philosophy of service-learning can be useful in teaching students in international contexts.

Ken Bussema   311
    Response to Jeffrey P. Bouman & Lauren Colyn

Premalatha Dinakarlal   315
    Response to Jeffrey P. Bouman & Lauren Colyn

Research Expo

M. Elaine Botha   319
    Metaphor and embodiment: New perspectives on cognition and meaning

Closing Keynote

Joel Carpenter   337
    Christian higher education as a worldwide movement

Nick Lantinga & Anne Maatman   353
    IAPCHE: Where we are today

Contributors   371

PREFACE

IAPCHE's seventh international conference provided many surprises for the 145 delegates from 34 countries. The process of arrival itself found most of us moving through structures of glass and steel to Granada, Nicaragua, a sleepy Spanish colonial town of wood and terra cotta. We moved from our own church affiliations into a time of work and worship with brothers and sisters from a great variety of church affiliations spanning the historic divisions of the faith. Many traveled from economic powerhouses and rapidly industrializing societies to one of the poorest nations in the Western hemisphere. What could we expect from such a conference in such a setting and with such a variety of people?

The specific venue and, for many, a new association raised further questions. The venue was named after St. Francis, the 13th century reformer who insisted on charity, poverty, and delight in God's creation. The open architecture and the classic arches of the bell tower suggested our communion with the saints across the centuries. We were pleased that Amanda Niewenhuis (Dordt College, USA) emphasized the bell and its tower in our conference logo, reproduced on the cover of this volume. Although for more than 30 years the Association had echoed John Calvin's insistence on the great scope of creation—extending to every domain of life—many of the delegates had little familiarity with IAPCHE.

Right from the beginning of the conference the staff at UPOLI, the Polytechnic University of Nicaragua, welcomed delegates and provided hospitality beyond all expectations. From airport transfers and meals, to excursions and cultural presentations, Tomas Tellez (Director for International Relations, UPOLI), UPOLI's Committee for Local Arrangements, and dozens of student ambassadors clearly demonstrated a great level of care for all the delegates. Tellez also provided the critical link between these many hands and the work of Anne Maatman, (IAPCHE Director of Operations) who coordinated the international inputs from the IAPCHE office on the campus of Dordt College. Such actions, demonstrating a spirit of community, began to answer in deed the questions many had already formulated.

Underlining our commitment to working together with scholars from around the world, we conducted the conference in both Spanish and English. This meant that many members translated abstracts, manuscripts, brochures, biographies, and the conference schedule. We are especially grateful to the following persons for their translation work: Corinne Hentges, Socorro Woodbury, and their students (Dordt College, USA); Darrel Hilbrands and students (*ILMES*, Mexico); Diana Gonzales and students (Northwestern College, USA); Tomas Tellez and the UPOLI staff; Sid Rooy (IAPCHE Latin American regional advisor); Lindy Scott (Wheaton College, USA); Tom Soerens (*UNELA*, Costa Rica); and Rob Suwyn (Unity Christian High School, USA). We carried this commitment into the conference itself with simultaneous translation during all of the plenary and track sessions.

Rector Emerson Sandoval (UPOLI, Nicaragua) welcomed the delegates and officially opened the conference; Jerjes Ruiz (UPOLI, Nicaragua) began with a Bible study, "The Temptation of Christ, Temptation of CHE." Although limited space prevented publication in this volume, we are grateful to Ruiz, Blanca Cortes (*Centro Intereclesial de Estudios Teologicos y Sociales,* Nicaragua), Alexandre Brasil (*Universidade do Rio de Janeiro,* Brazil), Marcelino Bassett (*Centro Intereclesial de Estudios Teologicos y Sociales,* Nicaragua), and Alicia Winters (*Universidad Reformada,* Colombia) for Bible studies that reminded us daily of our profound unity in Christ.

Nelly García (*Universidad de Costa Rica*) began our conference discussions with the keynote theme: *Christian Higher Education in Global Context.* After that evening's banquet, John Hulst (IAPCHE Executive Secretary Emeritus) reviewed several *Highlights of IAPCHE's History* in order to introduce the Association to the many in attendance who had little knowledge of what we had accomplished during more than 30 years of networking and related activities.

After the conference opening, we moved from our broad theme to three specific tracks. Scholars from all five IAPCHE regions began the discussions:

Track 1: "How does Christian higher education bridge gaps between competing cultures/worldviews."

Track 2: "What can Christian higher education do to promote educational well-being?"

Track 3: "How does Christian higher education connect kingdom citizenship to specific regional issues and crises?"

Delegates spent the following two days pursuing these three themes more closely in concurrent track discussions.

After several papers and responses in the track discussions, delegates began the fourth day by meeting in regional strategy sessions. In this way delegates who had attended different track sessions could weigh the relative importance of the track discussions for their own region, be it Africa,

Asia/Oceania, Europe, Latin America, or North America. These regional reports, presented to the whole conference on the closing day, contributed to a strategy session for IAPCHE's efforts worldwide.

The conference included two other components—the Research Expo and Institutional Conversations. We were delighted to inaugurate the Research Expo, a forum that provided the opportunity for delegates to give and receive examples of integrally Christian scholarship in specific disciplines and then display in poster form that work for the duration of the conference. Although we would have liked to include many of the more than 50 Research Expo papers in this volume, we have limited the sample to one paper by Elaine Botha (Redeemer University College, Canada). Carl Zylstra (Dordt College, USA) facilitated Institutional Conversations, a roundtable discussion on the ways in which cross-cultural conversations can make institutional leaders more effective in their home culture and institution.

In the closing keynote, *Christian Higher Education in Global Context: Where Do We Go from Here?*, Joel Carpenter (Calvin College, USA) built on the variety of conference conversations in the tracks, regional sessions, Research Expo, and institutional round table.

Having edited these proceedings I need to address two final items. First, we greatly benefited from the editorial assistance of Helen van Beek (Dordt College, USA) who typed in revisions, formatted, and organized this manuscript—from headers to footnotes. We are also grateful that Jo Faber (Dordt College, USA) donated many hours to assist with copyediting.

Finally, I am struck by the ways in which our conference reflected the context in which we met and demonstrated IAPCHE's identity and purpose. Like the architecturally unified city of Granada, we all came out of a commitment to the orthodox Christian faith, a faith with deep historic roots. And Granada's buildings also came in a vibrant variety of colors: lime green next to orange, across the street from pink. So too the members of IAPCHE come from a colorful variety of church affiliations, geographic and institutional settings. And yet we come together to consider centrally important issues for Christians committed to higher education. I pray that the essays included here, like the buildings in Granada, convey the vibrant and faithful spirit of **IAPCHE Congreso Internacional 2006.**

—Nick Lantinga
IAPCHE Executive Director

OPENING COMMENTS

Nick Lantinga

Soon after I assumed my responsibilities with IAPCHE in 2002, I began to speak of the need for an academic community of trust. While completing our doctorate studies my wife and I had witnessed the consequences of distrust.

Why such distrust? After all, the Berlin wall had fallen just before we began our graduate studies—indeed, I had read Francis Fukuyama's famous article on "The End of History" just before visiting various graduate programs. Fukuyama argued that the world was emerging from its violent cycle of thesis-antithesis-thesis. The grand ideological conflicts that brought about world wars and cold wars would soon be behind us. Surely, it was reasonable to hope that there could be trust among the victors.

Who were the victors, exactly? If the struggle was between the West and the East, then the clearly the West won. At least that was the picture provided by Bernard Lewis and Samuel Huntington who highlighted the importance of civilizations and their inspiring religious communities. However, the West resembles not so much a civilization as an orphanage.

The image of an orphanage comes to mind when reflecting on Western higher education, particularly the multiversity. When these institutions held to a relatively consistent and coherent understanding of the world and the human place within it, they were called universities. Multiversities, by definition, cannot agree upon any commonly accepted organizing principles. This is in part why free speech conflicts with campus speech codes, advocates of multiculturalism battle orthodox feminists, and so on. A multiversity is a university that has grown into incoherence.

For some, this incoherence is seen as an advance in civilization. I for one sympathize with post-modern thinkers who refuse to partake of the 20th century's bitter fruit. After all, there were many in the cult of rationality who aided and abetted the rise of such monstrous irrationalities as national socialism and communism. The suspicion of grand metanarratives arises for good reasons.

However, this explanation does not fully account for the multiversity, for the multiversity has grown markedly since the fall of communism. It seems to me to make better sense to recall that modern philosophy began with Descartes' suspicion that the world was ruled not by God but rather by an evil demon. Further, the best way to respond to this horrible suspicion was to doubt everything. As Hannah Arendt pointed out, "I doubt therefore I am" comes before the more famous "I think therefore I am." Thus the multiversity, where we are taught to suspect everything, provides a hyper- (not post-) modern soil from which we harvest thorny fruit.

What do we have to offer in this context? From the beginning of my tenure, I have repeated a theme from IAPCHE's founding: we need to work in a community of trust. Here I want to mention just two items that have been central in sustaining IAPCHE as a community of trust.

First, we have repeatedly emphasized our common project. As we express in our purpose statement: we seek to serve Jesus as Lord. Abraham Kuyper, the 20th century Dutch theologian, statesman, pastor, and writer famously said: "There is not a single square inch in all of human existence over which Christ, who is Lord over all, does not proclaim: 'This is Mine!'" As members of the academic community, we must not be afraid to follow our Lord not only to the ends of the earth, but also in every area of study.

Second, this common project arises out of our common faith—what C.S. Lewis described as "mere Christianity." We all believe that God created a world with humanity fit perfectly within it, that we rejected that perfection, that God's son has come to reclaim the world, and that until Jesus comes again the Spirit calls us to faithfulness in all of life. Our common project of humble service arises from our common faith, which includes a common recognition of our need for grace.

Third, this recognition of need requires gratitude. Often this comes in the form of patience. We are often tempted—all right, I am often tempted—to become frustrated when poor judgments, flawed research and irritable colleagues keep us from all that God promises. Richard Mouw encouraged Christian scholars to find a square inch on which to serve and then be prepared to suffer. We can suffer—indeed many of us here have suffered much—with confidence in our faithful God.

Patience and suffering are not the only ways to demonstrate gratitude. Sometimes we can publicly demonstrate our gratitude to those who have worked long and hard at their task. So I ask you to join me in gratitude to the conference committee that established the conference themes; to the many agencies, individuals, and institutions who have given generously to support this conference and the travel costs for many delegates; to Tomás Tellez and the Committee on Local Arrangements at UPOLI for preparing for our conference with diplomatic and organizational expertise; and to the many people who helped with the task of translation so that we can come together in conversation here this week.

These efforts to advance our common project proceeded from our common faith and from gratitude to God. May we continue to build on their examples during this coming week, thinking together in ways that demonstrate that we are not orphans but rather fellow brothers and sisters adopted by our Father God.

CHRISTIAN HIGHER EDUCATION IN A GLOBAL CONTEXT: IMPLICATIONS FOR CURRICULUM, PEDAGOGY, AND ADMINISTRATION

Nelly García Murillo

Translated from Spanish by Alicia Hines

Globalization is the context in which we must reflect on all of our tasks—academic-professional, psychosocial, familial, religious, environmental, daily life, or whatever other issue we face.

We used to live in a small community, but now it is global and this change has multiple consequences. It has been said, and I am sure that we all agree: "we do not live in a season of changes, but rather in a change of seasons." Faced with a world that seems too complex from time to time, what is our reaction? Are we concerned with understanding it, or do we assume the attitude of the ostrich and hide our heads in the sand? Have we asked such a question? How should we respond?

I invite you to reflect on the characteristics of this historical moment that, as we know, has been given the name "postmodern." In my understanding, there is no consensus about how to define it.

Faced with the difficulty of finding a satisfactory definition, let us explore some attempts by institutions and authorities that are qualified to do so.

UNESCO has characterized postmodernism as a time of uncertainty, where fear and uneasiness are the factors that are common to all of us. It is characterized by "presentism": What is important is today because we cannot count on tomorrow. In addition, we live in a world of sensation. So much so that parents, along with educators, artists, merchants, and communicators, are concerned about offering varied and fast options if they want to capture their audience. Brian McClaren, a Christian leader in the United States, said a few weeks ago in the *Universidad Bíblica* in San Jose, Costa Rica, that children, adolescents, and adults now have available "weapons of mass distraction." These allow us to "kill" time without feeling so bored. Lisbeth Queseda, head of the Office of Civil Rights of Costa Rica, in an appearance before a Commission of the Legislative Assembly, characterized the present culture in the following terms:

> We are moving toward a culture that has changed the means into the end itself. It has left the person behind as a cause and an end of all of the activity of the institutional system. It is about a culture that changed wellbeing into "well-having."

This apparent play on words helps us to think about how the values of our societies have changed. We are taught to love people and use things. Often however, even among self-proclaimed Christians, there are those that passionately cling to things and use people, for example those that preach the "Prosperity Gospel." The struggle between being and having that was raised several decades ago by Erick Fromm is still valid. The most wonderful commandments, to love God above all things and to love one's neighbor as oneself, remain and have even greater significance now.

Many experts point out that poverty continues to grow in and between countries, and not only in the Third World. No doubt, this has many causes, but among them is the unjust distribution of resources with the increasing asymmetry between the rich and poor. Logically, this situation brings about perplexity, resentment and anger, as well as tension, anger and violence. Evidence of violence can be seen in street children, assaulted women, gangs, traffic accidents, suicides, and murders.

La Nación, the Costa Rican newspaper, on September 25, 2006, had the following article, *Violencia sin control. Grupos de Exterminio*, (Violence out of Control. Extermination Groups), that mentioned some groups in Guatemala, Honduras, and El Salvador that carry out what is called "social cleansing" and concludes, "In Honduras, since 1998 there have been more than 3,300 young people under the age of 23 that have been killed in alleged acts of social cleansing." Sometimes it seems that the only news that we hear is bad news. Could it be that nothing else happens in our countries?

The phenomenon of immigration is another characteristic that distinguishes our context. People have always moved for various reasons: to flee from an imminent threat like war; to find food; in search of better options for life like work, education, health, adventure; and many other reasons. The existence of this type of relocation today has several alarming characteristics. Since many people are moving to other places, it is important to be aware of potential dangers and the possibility of failure that they have to achieve their goals, knowing beforehand that there are barriers that are almost impossible to overcome. Through varied means of communication and from the stories of survivors, we hear about the thousands of people that die trying. They die from hunger, cold, heat, accidents, violence, and from merchants' deceitful promises to cover large sums of money with the promise of helping immigrants cross the border. These groups include many children, as well as women who embark on difficult journeys in search of sustenance for children who often die in their mothers' arms. The suffering does not end when they reach "the promised land" where they are taken as prisoners and are searched for their papers. Upon returning "home," they still do not have any hope or any belongings. This situation exists in many places, but currently the situation is particularly distressing for the thousands of Sub-Saharan Africans who are struggling to get to the Canary Islands, Spain, and other coastal European locations. How appalling! Desperation can be seen in the faces of the people that have made every effort to improve their lives. When they find out that they are going to be deported, some say, "Now I will not be able to keep the promise that I made to my mom to send her money for the family's sustenance and to buy back the cows that she sold to pay for my trip." The destination countries in the European Union are frustrated and concerned about these situations. A wall is being built on the border between the United States and Mexico that will prevent undocumented immigrants from crossing in hopes of reaching *El Dorado*. In Costa Rica, this phenomenon is seen in the exploitation of immigrants, especially those from Nicaragua. There are many corrupt acts that happen like granting fake permits for profit, paying smaller salaries to immigrant workers, and avoiding paying social taxes for healthcare and retirement.

In the 21st century, as people are seeking greater equality, there is increased awareness about the difficulties that women have experienced throughout history. Women and children are among the poorest of the poor. Women constitute 70 percent of the world's poor, as cited by Elsa Támez in her book, *La sociedad que las mujeres soñamos*. In some societies, women are not considered worthy to deserve educational opportunities. In fact, they often receive discrimination at work. For the same working day and the same type of work, women are paid less just because they are women. Furthermore, many women suffer oppression, violence, and sexual harassment by their bosses, co-workers, husbands and other men.

In Latin America and the Caribbean, the violence in the home has increased in the last few years. And in macho societies where unemployment rates are high, men's frustrations are taken out upon the women, women's frustrations are taken out upon their sons and the boys' frustrations are taken out upon the little girls. The dream is to break the vicious cycle of violence, which is impossible if the socioeconomic situation is not seriously considered. (Támez, 1979)

Our abusive relationship with nature explains many of the natural disasters that affect us today: global warming, droughts, floods, the hole in the ozone layer, water shortages, trash, lack of energy for cooking and working, and excessive heat and cold. We see nature as an endless resource that we can exploit for maximum profit. This all seems to indicate that we humans are not aware of the fact that we are part of nature that God created for our wellbeing, and that the abuses that we commit against the creation directly and negatively affect us. We forget that we were called by God to care for the earth and cultivate it.

Today many people lack water, an essential resource, which translates into famines, disease, and death. Experts say that the wars of the 21st century will be over water. If wars are currently being fought over oil, it will be more serious to undertake struggles over water, without which we cannot live.

This problem is tackled in various movies like *Si le Vent Souleve les Sables* (*If the Wind Lifts the Sands*) by the French film director Marion Hansel, based on the novel written by Marc Durin Valois. Hansel refers to her work in these terms: "It is a universal story. I wanted the whole world to be involved. Durin himself remembered that 1.5 billion people around the world lack water" ("Drama Africano a la Pantalla", 2006). The book that Al Gore, former vice president of the United States, just wrote led to a documentary. This documentary, *An Inconvenient Truth,* has caught the attention of many people. It is a warning about global warming, the result of the greenhouse effect in the atmosphere, produced by the indiscriminate burning of combustibles. It also warns about the serious effects that global warming has on atmospheric phenomena, which will hurl all of humanity toward an eco-catastrophe and back again like a boomerang, which will end life and its different expressions.

It is true that what we have alluded to is tragic and evil, but people are starting to act positively, which gives hope.

Technological advances in the last decades let us communicate more efficiently. Just a few years ago, we could not have imagined such fast communication. How great it is that available technology allows us to communicate instantly with people on different continents! It also lets us learn about events that occur in distant regions. Above all, knowledge of this information can build empathy, solidarity, and advocacy for those who suffer most.

What would happen if we were not able to learn about the disasters that provoked the war between Israel and Lebanon or about the aftermath of tsunamis, earthquakes, hurricanes, and floods? People around the world are still reacting to the pain that our neighbors in Nicaragua, New Orleans, Sudan, Ethiopia, Palestine, and other communities have suffered in the last few years.

How do we then orient Christian higher education in a way that organizes curriculum, methodology, and the school administration in such a way that the true objects of these educational concerns, the students themselves, are taken into consideration? If we do not dialogue with our context, we are dancing with danger, not only of being irrelevant, but also of being unable to offer necessary training to students who should be enabled to move forward in a world that is constantly becoming more complex. Moreover, if we cannot reach this goal, what is our role as Christian educators?

Educators like Simón Rodriguez (Simón Bolívar's teacher), José Martí, Gabriela Mistral, Carmen Lyra, Mariano Fiallos Gil, Paulo Freire, Omar Dengo, Joaquín García Monge, and other excellent Latin American teachers have reiterated that education is an act of love and that it is formed in the dialogue between teachers and students with their environment. Along with the formal education that we have, we need to be conscious of a life-long informal education that includes the participation of many others. Families, friends, books, neighbors, the media, and political and sports leaders sometimes have a greater educational influence than those called to be educators.

Today, people declare that education is a dialogue as if the idea were a novelty, but this type of pedagogy was already practiced by Socrates in ancient Greece and by Jesus in his ministry in Judea, Galilee, and Samaria. Jesus' followers Peter, Paul, and Luke also joined in.

Dialoguing, besides being a pedagogical strategy, demonstrates an attitude of honesty, transparency, and humility on the part of the professor. The professor recognizes that he or she does not know everything or have the absolute truth and that he or she has to learn from the people with whom they are in dialogue. Is this not what God was communicating when he said, "Not many of you should presume to be teachers, my brothers, because you know that we who teach will be judged more strictly. We all stumble in many ways" (James 3:1-2a).

What is the Christian's responsibility, then, as an educator, student, administrator, parent, communicator, businessperson, carpenter, mechanic, engineer, lawyer, or religious leader in a sad world where discouragement and confusion reign? How do we re-encounter a love for the world that God made for us? This question was asked a few weeks ago by a Brazilian theologian in a meditation in the *Comunidad Cristiana Emaús* in San José, Costa Rica. The theologian, Silvia Regina de Lima, reflected on the kingdom of God in her meditation. She pointed out that the reign of God has a place in history. *The time has come.* It is the time of God. The reign of God is near. We cannot fully comprehend it, but it is near. This reign of God is proclaimed by a Christian community that undertakes life in the kingdom of God. The kingdom of God is present in social and religious organizations. It has a liberating presence in people's lives and has a political impact. To proclaim the kingdom of God is to propose another way of doing things. The kingdom of God is a different proposition than the image of God. It is presented like a seed that is fruitful and can make a difference. God is the fire that is under the coals, and with his action, he can create a strong reaction in the world. This revolution can be seen in the life of service of the Christians who have been told to practice what is right, not only with their friends, but also with their enemies. By doing this, Christians accomplish what Jesus taught in the beatitudes (Matthew 5) and in many other passages like Mark 1:14-15.

For a true dialogue to exist, the participants must listen to each other. Often what happens is that teachers, professors, and all educators find themselves driven to speak, speak, and keep on speaking, because they consider it their responsibility to provide information to their students. Frequently, they do not take the time to see if the students are interested in what they are saying or if they are daydreaming. The Argentine writer, Julio Cortázar, used to say that for this reason, the fantastic or the unreal is much more real than reality and through what we imagine, we can find profound truths. As we question what constitutes an academic dialogue, we should keep in mind that speaking is not the same as communicating. How often do we find ourselves voiceless in a dialogue because no one is listening to what the other person is proposing? Sometimes we think that taking a few minutes to listen to the other person is a waste of time, when we could be able to provide more information to the students. We are faced with a problem that has to do with what we understand as the function of the educator in the process of teaching and learning. Is this really your mission to provide information? Moreover, if the information can be found through other means, what is left for you to do?

Several remarkable teachers have made well-known statements that give us key ideas to understand better the function of the professor. One such teacher is Joaquín García Monge. Through his work as the Director of the *Revista Repertorio Americano* magazine, García Monge kept Latin America alive in the minds of many in the first part of the 20th century. This teacher used a well-tested metaphor, "to teach is to give the soul wings." I understand that he used the word "soul" to condense all that, which characterizes human beings, who are unique and indivisible. Therefore, an integral and humanistic formation is required that takes into consideration all of the different facets of people: the rational, the affective, the feeling, the will, and the spiritual. Jesus Christ taught us to see people as whole beings, not having false dichotomies. Another famous educator, Simón Rodriguéz, Simón Bolívar's teacher, stated in reference to education, "that which does not make one feel, is of no interest; that which is of no interest, is not understood." In the process of teaching and learning, we should appeal to the whole human being. We should also concern ourselves with making the discussion appeal to the emotional, because we know that this can motivate the rest of the person. If we manage to motivate the student to have a desire to learn, we have achieved a fundamental part of our mission. A principle in education says this: "nobody can teach anyone anything (if they are not willing); people learn when they are motivated to do so, when they want to." Therefore, we deduce that an educator is a facilitator that provides the conditions in which the educational process can be achieved. In many instances, the parents take this role without realizing it. This challenge is an opportunity for service and a gift from God for people that facilitate learning. The educator should be an alert, inquisitive, observant person who loves his or her work and who is prepared to invest a great deal of time in personal preparation. He or she should be comprehensively trained and have up-to-date knowledge based on research. No one can give that which he or she does not have. Students catch their professors' interest from the first moment. If the professor is apathetic, or unenthusiastic, he or she is not going to light the spark needed for the student to want to learn. The educational process runs the risk of becoming cold or even boring. In Costa Rica, the students have coined the phrase to describe this type of professor: he is a "yawn."

Albert Einstein spoke many times about the importance of knowing how to raise questions that create a desire to learn. We can ask the questions of ourselves, of others, or of the context in which we live. Possible questions include: Who am I? What am I doing in the world? What is the meaning of my life? Why should I have relationships with others? Who is my neighbor? May I use natural resources for only my personal benefit? Who is God? Why would he want to relate to me? Why does evil exist? Who created it? Why is there so much violence in our time? And the questions continue—leading to other questions and the search for answers.

Jesus was called the Teacher from Galilee. Why? What did he teach? Did he have compassion on those with whom he spoke? How did he resolve the problems that were posed to him, for example, the multitude that was hungry after hours spent listening to him? How did he explain the miracle of multiplying the loaves and fish? Did he take into account the context in which he carried out his mission? Why was it necessary in that time and in that place to wash feet as a demonstration of love and consideration?

I know that some presenters will delve deeply into related subjects of the main theme in this conference. I would like to finish my part with two simple charges from Latin America: first, to all of the Latin Americans that are meeting here and, second to all of our friends and neighbors that are representing other countries.

To the Latin Americans, I remind you that we have dignity because we are God's children, created in his image and his likeness. Nicaragua is a beautiful place where we can appreciate the God-given ability to be creative human beings. This is a land of poets, singer-song writers, painters, sculptors, skilled artisans, and artists. I must mention Rubén Darío, the poet that dared to start the first clearly Latin American movement, Modernism, and with it, its own way of writing that did not take on foreign characteristics. I hope that we have the opportunity to know other outstanding writers, not just Central Americans, but globally recognized authors, like José Coronel Urtrecho, Ernesto Cardenal, Gioconda Belli, Sergio Ramírez, and others too numerous to count. In the same way, each country from the so-called Third World represented here, has valid reasons to be grateful to God for the talents he has distributed around the world.

Latin America history has been difficult because some people came to Latin America saying that they represented God, but, in reality, they selfishly made us slaves. These people also made us believe that we were children of the treachery, which seems to have soaked deeply into the conscience and personality of our communities, to the point that we feel unworthy of God's grace. Thank God that along with the conquistadors and gold prospectors, people also came to Latin America that wanted to claim the Good News of salvation and wanted to share what they had learned from their experience with God. (Bartolomé de las Casas is an example.) Today, Latin America is a region where we are learning to live together: indigenous, blacks, mixed-race, *zambo-mosquitos*, Asians, and many other mixes unimaginable in the past. The Mexican philosopher Leopoldo Zea used to say that Latin America is the best-prepared continent to succeed in this globalized world because we have the experience of having interacted with very diverse cultures, a factor that is very relevant in this time. Of course, there are other factors that do not work well for Latin America like the idea that foreign relations should be modeled like markets, where everything is the product of supply and demand.

For many decades, the dominant religious vision in Latin America was that described by Juan Mackay in his book *El otro Cristo español (The Other Spanish Christ)*: Christ was hidden in great and beautiful cathedrals, but the people did not have access to him. The Peruvian novelist, José María Arguedas refers to that Christ and his followers in his book *Los ríos profundos (The Deep Rivers)*.

Because of the faithfulness of many Christians from around the world, including several educators, Latin Americans were able to know God who is the light, the way, the truth and the life. He has lived among us in mud shacks and rickety homes made out of cardboard, as well as in huge condominiums, schools, universities, coffee fields, banana plantations, lakes, volcanoes, and markets. He has reached to the heights and depths of our continent, to the plateaus, rain forests, wet high lands, and deserts. The security of knowing that we are his children allows us to grow, and for this reason, we can move forward toward the consolidation of his kingdom.

In our churches, we sing the song *Gente Nueva* that goes like this:

> Gente nueva, creadora de la historia
> Constructora de nueva humanidad,
> Gente nueva que vive la existencia
> Como riesgo de un largo caminar.[1]
>
> (New people, authors of history
> Builders of a new humanity,
> New people that risk their lives
> To forge a new path.)

We are a diverse people with a mission that derives from being pro-

---

[1] Celebremos Juntos. San José, Costa Rica: Seminario Bíblico Latinoamericano, 1989, núm 75.

fessors at the service of the kingdom, in a continent that cries out for justice, peace and a concern for the creation.

Now this message for our friends from the so-called first world, members of economically powerful countries, and keepers of cutting-edge scientific and technological knowledge: the love of God drives us to tell you that, like Paul, we know that by the grace of God, we are what we are and that his grace has not been in vain among us.

The Colombian writer Gabriel Garcia Márquez, winner of the Nobel Prize for literature, gave an address when he was in Stockholm. In the speech, he asked the more powerful peoples of the world to let us make mistakes, if necessary, in order to find our own way and to not have to spend another hundred years in solitude. Be our ambassadors, and being the Christian educators that you are, tell your countries that we can learn a lot from other people and cultures. Internationalizing the curriculum of our schools, our teaching methods, and the way we manage our educational tasks should show that God is at the center of our lives. We cannot ignore the outcries of millions that live in helplessness, poverty, fear, violence, and loneliness, as they also have the right to an education that allows them to develop the talent and potential that God has given them.

José Míguez Bonino (1999), the Argentine Christian leader, in his book *Poder del evangelio y poder politico* (*The Power of the Gospel and Political Power*), calls us to a deeper reflection. This is what he says,

> God commissions us work for "a full life"—fertility, growth, vigor, and fullness. Our responsibility is to defend the fullness of human life, humanity's access to the world's good resources, the possibility of growth and expansion, the cultural mandate to govern animals and things; and to defend the dignity of humans made in the image of God. This "fulfilled Adam" is the object and goal of our mission. (p. 61)

As Christian educators, we can indeed have hope in God's work in people and Christian communities. In Isaiah 65:17-19 it says,

> Behold, I will create new heavens and a new earth . . . be glad and rejoice forever in what I will create, for I will create Jerusalem to be a delight and its people a joy. I will rejoice over Jerusalem and take delight in my people; the sound of weeping and of crying will be heard in it no more.

Is this not what we all yearn for?

Dear colleagues in Christian higher education, let us remember the tools that technology provides us. These advances should be used to increase awareness and to act Christianly in the world where we live, declaring the kingdom of God.

We cannot delay our commitment to include in our university's curriculum those topics that include respect for all forms of life and for all human beings. It is necessary to be aware that we are partly responsible for the environment. For this reason, we should denounce society's aggressive consumption that causes the emission of gases and the green house effect, the hole in the ozone layer, and planetary consequences associated to accelerated climate changes, global warming, and the consequences of ultraviolet rays on the health of the ecosystem.

We need to remember that our vocation as educators is founded in the truth and knowledge of our discipline, historical reality, and the diligence and enthusiasm with which we serve. We remember that it is based on humility as we relate to one another in our collegiate environment, in the strength of Jesus' love, and in the grace that he gives us.

As Christians committed to higher education, we need to renew our call to serve young people. We can do this by joining in fraternity and solidarity in the context of a changing of seasons in which the coming generation will develop.

In conclusion, the final message is for everyone present here, for those from the North and the South and for those from the East and the West; it is a message of solidarity of communion and love that fills our lives of service to the kingdom of God and that allows us to sing Psalm 133 together:

> How good and pleasant it is when brothers and sisters live together in unity! It is like precious oil poured on the head, running down on the beard, running down on Aaron's beard, down upon the collar of his robes. It is as if the dew of Hermon were falling on Mount Zion. For there the LORD bestows his blessing, even life forevermore.

May God, our Lord and Savior, allow us to be the salt and light in our universities. May he allow us to fully achieve the objectives of this conference, that each and every one of us would be able to respond to his or her call as obedient servants that want to say, "Here am I Lord, send me!"

References

Bonino, J. M. (1999). *Poder del evangelio y poder político: La participación de los evangélicos en la política en América Latina*. Buenos Aires: Ediciones Kairós/FTL.

Drama Africano a la pantalla. (2006, September 25). *La Nación*. Retrieved from La Nación newspaper database.

Támez, E. (1979). *La sociedad que las mujeres soñamos*. San José, Costa Rica: DEI.
Violencia sin control. Grupos de exterminio. (2006, September 25). *La Nación*. Retrieved from La Nación newspaper database.

HIGHLIGHTS OF IAPCHE'S HISTORY

John Hulst

I am pleased to be here and to have an opportunity to speak to you. I know many of you and hope to become acquainted with the rest.

However, I want to begin my address this evening by making an apology—an apology to Bennie van der Walt. Six years ago, at IAPCHE Conference 2000, I asked Bennie to give a speech following the opening banquet at which we celebrated IAPCHE's 25th anniversary. Knowing that it would be difficult on a warm summer evening to hold the attention of people with full stomachs, I suggested that he keep the speech short, tell a few stories, and insert a bit of levity. Bennie did all of this with great success; but I realize now what a difficult assignment that was.

I have been asked to speak to you—following a delicious meal—regarding the history of IAPCHE. To begin with, dealing even superficially with IAPCHE's history would take far too long. Therefore, to stay within the time limit that has been set, 30 minutes, I decided to focus on the "highlights" of that history. However, even with this limitation, I soon realized that I could not do this alone. I needed help from others who were also acquainted with IAPCHE's history. For this, I decided to contact IAPCHE's regional advisors—each of whom has become a friend—asking them to share their thoughts concerning one or two significant moments in IAPCHE's 30-year history.

I mention this, not only because these advisors have been helpful to me in preparing this address, but also because each has played an important role in the development of IAPCHE's history and in giving shape to our Association. I want to recognize each of them in the following order:

1. From Africa, Bennie van der Walt, who from the beginning in 1975 at Potchefstroom University for Christian Higher Education, South Africa, has been a committed and compassionate advocate in the region of Africa and other regions as well.
2. From Asia/Oceania, Bong Ho Son, Seoul National University,

South Korea, who has been a humble but powerful voice for quality in Christian higher education (CHE), all the while, making us aware of our responsibility to the poor and needy.
3. From Europe, Natalia Pecherskaya, St. Petersburg School of Religion and Philosophy, Russia, the first member of the Association from Russia, who has been instrumental in making us aware of the serious conflict between secular and Christian higher education.
4. From Latin America, Sidney Rooy, until recently from the Biblical University of Latin America, Costa Rica, the lone representative from that region at the 1975 Potchefstroom conference and a participant ever since in Association activities. He is undoubtedly the person largely responsible for the fact that we are holding this 2006 international conference in Latin America.
5. From North America, John Vanderstelt, Dordt College, the United States, the first executive secretary of IAPCHE and one who has had much to do with formulating and articulating the kingdom perspective and vision that characterizes our Association to this very day.

To all of these I personally and we, as an Association, owe a great debt of gratitude for their contribution to the work of Christian education as well as their help in preparing this address. Still, what you are about to hear reflects my perspective on IAPCHE's history, and I take full responsibility for the omission of any individuals or events that should have been included.

Now to the highlights. All of the advisors agreed that Highlight #1 is the beginning of our Association in 1975 at the Potchefstroom University of Christian Higher Education in South Africa.

I was not privileged to attend that initial gathering. However, I do recall a meeting prior to 1975 at Dordt College with J. Christi Coetzee, who had been commissioned by Potchefstroom University for Christian Higher Education (PUCHE) to travel throughout the world to consult with likeminded institutions and persons about the possibility of an international conference of Reformed institutions of CHE. The result of Coetzee's efforts was the first meeting of the International Conference of Institutions of Christian Higher Education (ICICHE), September 9-13, 1975, attended by 140 participants from 19 different countries.

Those who were present at the conference reported that there was much conflict felt and expressed, especially over the issue of apartheid in

South Africa, reflected also in the policies of PUCHE. Still, in spite of the conflict, at least two things stood out at this conference. First, there was the clear desire to establish an international academic community. As Bennie van der Walt (1976) observed, "we listened together, thought together, sang together, prayed together, differed together, relaxed together, and struggled together for the coming of the kingdom of God" (p. 413). Second, there was a commitment to carry on the work of CHE, not in isolation but in relation to issues present in contemporary societies and cultures, such as the issue of racism.

These two themes, a desire for community and a commitment to academic work related to contemporary society, have characterized our Association throughout its history, and, we trust, will continue to characterize our communal activity as we move into the future.

Highlight #2 has to do with the organization of our Association. Already in 1975, there was an indication that the Association begun in Potchefstroom should continue, in some form, into the future.

The first conference suggested "an alliance of institutions for CHE." The second conference in 1978 at Calvin College, Grand Rapids, Michigan, rejected this suggestion in favor of a loose "affiliation . . . beneficial for the institutions involved" (Vanderstelt, 1999, p. 2). It was not until the third international conference in 1981, at Dordt College, Sioux Center, Iowa, chaired by Klaas Runia, from Kampen, the Netherlands, that the Association was formally organized as the International Council for the Promotion of Christian Higher Education (ICPCHE).

In 1987, at the fifth international conference in Lusaka, Zambia, an important organizational change took place in our Association. Instead of functioning solely as an Association of institutions of CHE, we became an Association of Christian scholars—working in Christian and non-Christian institutions—supported, also financially, by Christian institutions and individuals committed to the promotion of CHE throughout the world. (I will comment further on this under Highlight #4.)

This brief review of our Association's organizational history may seem insignificant; but in reality, it reflects our struggle to develop and maintain our identity as an organization seeking, as our mission statement indicates, to serve Jesus as Lord by fostering, worldwide, the development of integral CHE through networking and related academic activity.

Two additional items are worthy of note in connection with the initial organization of IAPCHE in 1981. First, to make clear its continuing commitment to confront difficult contemporary issues, such as apartheid, the Association adopted the following statement:

> To promote Biblically-grounded, critical analysis of distortions of the truth in the contemporary world—special attention should be given to those ideologies prevalent in today's society, such as secularism, Marxism (including its theory and practice of class struggle), capitalism (including the oppression that results from faith in economic growth and power), racism (including institutionalized forms of racial discrimination such as apartheid), nationalism (as the idolizing of national self-interest), and militarism (including trust in armaments for national security); and to distortions of truth, such as rationalism (including the idea of the autonomy of reason), scientism (including the idolizing of scientific method), and historicism (including the relativity of norms) which are encountered primarily within the context of scholarship. (ICPCHE, 1982, p. 268)

This statement reflects a commitment, which remains with the Association to this very day.

Second, the organizing conference in 1981 ended with Paul Schrotenboer, executive secretary of the Reformed Ecumenical Council (REC) and later executive secretary of IAPCHE, presenting the following statement, which was officially adopted by the conference:

We have now been provided with an effective vehicle to facilitate the work of an international movement of Christian scholarship. Time will tell if it is an effective means. There are no tried and tested ways. We face an uncertain future in this respect. Any mistrust that was there was quite understandable. But it was regrettable, nevertheless, and we must work to overcome it.

Therefore, these three things:
1. We should give one another all the help we can, and surely the benefit of the doubt. . . . We must trust one another to carry out the terms of the agreement.
2. The Council will have to demonstrate that it is trustworthy.
3. The Council will need your encouragement, your support, and your prayers (Schrotenboer, 1982, pp. 279-280).

The Council (ICPCHE) about which Schrotenboer spoke no longer exists; but the call to trust one another, to work and to pray together, is as meaningful in 2006 as it was in 1981.

Highlight #3 involved a crisis, which occurred at the international conference in 1984, and which I have decided to highlight because it reflects the early fragility and strength of our International Association.

Prior to the August 15 opening of the 1984 conference in the Netherlands, the Council held its annual meeting. Representatives of the *Belydende Kring*, an anti-apartheid group from South Africa, received permission to meet with the Council. At the meeting, they registered a complaint against the presence of five conference registrants from South Africa, claiming that allowing these five persons to participate in the conference would be viewed as supportive of the apartheid policies of the South African government. Further, they indicated that, if these five persons were not dismissed from the conference, they and those they represented would leave the conference in public protest.

The Council responded by noting that, since the five persons in question had indicated their personal opposition to apartheid, the Council should not and would not dismiss them. They also urged the *Belydende Kring* contingency to remain at the conference, assuring them that their presence and participation would be welcome. That the *Belydende Kring* representatives were not satisfied with the response soon became apparent. They were given permission to make known and explain to the entire conference the reasons for their complaint. Nevertheless, at a certain point, they stood and walked out of the conference hall; and there were a few others who, for various reasons, left with them. The immediate appearance of the media clearly indicated that their departure had been planned and publicly announced.

Some have observed, and rightly so, that this was the most difficult conference in the history of IAPCHE. I have personal recollections of this difficult moment, since I was serving as chair of the Council and of the conference at that time. Henk Verhuel, rector magnificus of the Vrije Universiteit of Amsterdam and chair of the conference hosting committee rushed up to me and said that if I did not do something the conference would be brought to a premature conclusion and the entire Association could be broken up. Obviously, there was nothing that I, or Verhuel, or any single individual could do at that point. Nevertheless, eventually with the blessing of the Lord and the direction of the Holy Spirit, the conference resumed its meetings and consideration of its theme, "The Critique and Challenge of CHE." The Association has continued to this very day—even though, as we shall soon see, there were other challenges.

In the end, the conference in Breukelen, the Netherlands, not only came to its scheduled conclusion, it was also able to pass significant resolutions affirming its stand in opposition to apartheid; appealing to PU-CHE to open its doors "unconditionally to all people who desire CHE;" and encouraging the Council, in its planning for the next international conference, to arrange for the establishment of "an Association of individual Christian scholars and educators" (ICPCHE, 1987, pp. 170-171).

It is in connection with this last item that we move to consider Highlight #4, which has to do with IAPCHE becoming an Association of individual scholars.

It must be clear to you by now that the first ten years of our Association were marked by conflict and that much of that conflict was between institutions. The Council realized that it was limited in its ability to resolve these institutional differences; but, at the same time, it did not want these differences to jeopardize the progress being made in the development of a Reformational Christian academic community. Therefore, with the encouragement of the previous conference and under the leadership of Peter De Vos, Calvin College, the Council recommended to the 1987 conference in Lusaka, Zambia that a new constitution be adopted. The recommendation proposed, among other things, naming the organization the International Association for the Promotion of Christian Higher Education (IAPCHE) and making the organization an Association of individual scholars and educators, supported by institutions of CHE (IAPCHE, 1990).

Given its theme, "Rainbow in a Fallen World: Unity and Diversity of CHE Today," the conference in Lusaka—even though held in a very tense international political situation, which again had to do with the issue of apartheid—provided an excellent context for considering these important adjustments in our organization. The adjustments were approved recognizing the diversity reflected by the five regions—Africa, Asia-Oceania, Europe, Latin America, and North America—and emphasizing the unity provided by our shared commitment to the lordship of Jesus Christ over all of life and learning.

The results of these organizational changes were mixed. On the one hand, the changes enabled the Association to maintain its base of support, including financial support; to avoid the negative effects of institutional differences; to serve the needs of scholars in both Christian and non-Christian institutions; and, in the words of Paul Schrotenboer, "to maintain its Reformational roots, while reaching out to the broader Christian academic community."[1] On the other hand, the change raised questions for supporters of the Association, especially supporting institutions. What does institutional membership mean? Why should we support an Association of individual scholars? How do we benefit from institutional membership in IAPCHE?

In part because of these questions, for the next ten years the Associa-

---

1 It was repeatedly emphasized that to be "Reformational" is to reform all of life and learning according to the Word of our Lord Jesus Christ.

tion struggled. A number of excellent regional conferences were held—the first in 1991 in Harare, Zimbabwe—but there were no international conferences. Several institutions, including theological schools, withdrew their support or allowed their membership to lapse. In addition, individuals in the various regions began to wonder about the need or importance of continuing their participation in the Association.

All of this led to Highlight #5, which occurred at the turn of the century.

In 1996, the Executive Committee, with a few select advisors, met in Grand Rapids, Michigan, to reflect on the past and to consider the future of IAPCHE with its dwindling membership, its critical financial situation, and its executive secretary, Paul Schrotenboer, struggling with terminal cancer. Having been invited to attend this meeting, I recall being encouraged by the fact that the question was not so much, "Should we continue?" but assuming that we should, "How should we continue?"

How should we continue? We decided to declare an interim period, during which the Association would simply maintain the organizational status quo—including the membership of the current board. Reflecting on what had been learned from experiences, a new mission statement was developed, which sought to clarify the nature and purpose of the Association and to answer the question as to why individuals should participate in and institutions should support the Association. The mission statement read:

> The IAPCHE is a network of scholars and educational institutions seeking to provide leadership for the Christian community by encouraging and supporting joint Christian Reformational scholarly activity throughout the world.[2]

The year 2000, the turn of the century, was set as the year for the next international conference. It was the intention that, at this time, papers would be presented describing the challenges in each of the Association's five regions and that a long-range plan for the 21st century would be placed before the conference for its consideration.

It was further decided at this meeting to accept the resignation of Paul Schrotenboer, for reasons of health, and to appoint me to serve as executive secretary—an appointment which I accepted with some hesitation because I had just retired from the presidency of Dordt College. As the new executive secretary I was instructed, among other things, to visit the various supporting institutions, primarily to consult with board

---

2 IAPCHE Executive Committee, Board of Governors Meeting, Grand Rapids, MI, September 6, 7, and 9, 1996, Article 32.

members, associate members (institutions), and regular members (individual scholars) concerning their reactions to the new mission statement; and to develop, in consultation with others, a strategic long range plan for the first ten years of the 21st century—for presentation to the next international conference set for the year 2000.

International Conference 2000 met on the campus of Dordt College, Sioux Center, Iowa, August 12-16, with 100 delegates from all five regions in attendance. The theme of the conference was "Challenges for CHE in the 21st Century." During the first part of the conference, representatives from each of the regions described the challenges facing CHE in the 21st century. In the second part, ways of meeting these challenges were considered. It was unanimously decided that IAPCHE should continue into the 21st century, according to the mission statement previously distributed and discussed. It was further decided to develop and present to the board for its approval a ten-year plan describing how the Association would proceed into the future.

As a result of this planning process, a new purpose statement was adopted.

> The purpose of IAPCHE, an organization of individuals and institutions, is to serve Jesus as Lord, by fostering worldwide the development of integral CHE through networking and related academic activity. (IAPCHE, 2002, p. 309)

Approval was also given to a statement describing what IAPCHE means when it speaks of CHE as, on the one hand, seeking "to understand its entire task in the light of God's inscripturated revelation," and, on the other hand, desiring "to serve the larger Christian community as it seeks, through Spirit-directed faithful witness, to bring the healing power of Christ to bear on all areas of life." (See appendix A.)

A number of exciting projects were considered. Three of these projects are supported and promoted by IAPCHE to this very day. First, the Institute for Christian Studies in Toronto proposed the development and implementation of a Faith and Learning Network, an electronic bibliographic system that would make Reformational materials available to students and scholars in each of the Association's regions. Second, John Van Dyk, of the Center for Educational Services at Dordt College, presented a proposal whereby institutional members of IAPCHE would assist in the training of Christian teachers for elementary and secondary schools around the world. Third, Harry Fernhout, of the Institute for Christian Studies, proposed the development of a Christian Academic Studies Certificate, "an international effort to identify and deliver a graduate level program of study that will provide participants with grounding in integral Christian scholarship" (IAPCHE, 2002, p. 311-312).

Finally, while it was acknowledged that the Association should maintain a central office for its Secretariat, a commitment was made to the development of IAPCHE's perspective and program in each of the five regions. This, too, is an effort, which the Association continues to promote not only by way of regional conferences, but also by the establishment of committees or boards able to give attention to regional issues and needs.

Given the decision to continue into the 21st century, it was agreed that an international conference should be held every five years. We are just one year off—it is 2006—but we are in the right place, Nicaragua. Already in 1979, the hope was expressed that the next international conference would take place in Latin America. For a variety of reasons, some of them logistical, although there have been a number of regional conferences throughout Latin America (four of them), this is the first time that this hope for an international conference is being realized, which means that we are about to participate in what could be Highlight #6, an international conference in Latin America under the theme "CHE in Global Context."

Perhaps the theme sounds a bit arrogant. However, it is not arrogant, because that is in fact what we are, an Association of individuals and institutions promoting CHE throughout the world, that is, in a global context. For that reason, some have said that this promises to be the first international conference that reflects what IAPCHE is really all about.

As we, 145 delegates from 34 nations prepare for participation in this conference—the largest in IAPCHE's history—there are a number of things that call for our attention.

First, we must carefully review the conference theme: "CHE in Global Context: Implications for Curriculum, Pedagogy, and Administration." Under this theme, there are three questions confronting us, i.e., how does/can CHE 1) bridge gaps between competing cultures/worldviews? 2) promote educational well-being? and 3) connect kingdom citizenship to specific issues and crises?

Early on, I served as advisor to the conference program committee. When this theme and these tracks were proposed, my initial response was that this was going to be too much. Since then I have changed my mind. This is just right. At this conference, we have an opportunity to be what we are, what we claim to be, and to reflect on how we can carry out the work of CHE so that we may be a blessing to one another, to our schools, to our countries, and to our world—which, of course, belongs to God.

Second, we must give thanks to God for the opportunity to gather in this place. We give thanks to God for the good direction given by the IAPCHE board with George Monsma as chair. We give thanks for the excellent work of the conference and hosting committees. We give thanks for the devoted leadership provided by the Secretariat consisting of Nick Lantinga, executive director, and Anne Maatman, director of operations. In addition, we give thanks to God for all of you and the institutions of which you are a part. What a blessing that we may meet here together!

Finally, as was noted at the first international conference, 1975, in Potchefstroom, South Africa, we must never forget the importance of listening together, thinking together, singing together, praying together, differing together, relaxing together, and struggling together in the power of the Holy Spirit and in the name of our Lord Jesus Christ.

References

IAPCHE. (1990). Constitution of the International Association for the Promotion of Christian Higher Education. In *Rainbow in a fallen world: Unity and diversity of Christian higher education today* (pp. 259-269). Sioux Center, IA: Dordt College Press.

IAPCHE. (2002). Long-Range plan for IAPCHE 2001-2010. In B. D. Cedja, J. Hulst, & D. B. Lumsden (Eds.), *Christian Higher Education,* 1(2-3), 309-313.

ICPCHE. (1982). International Council for the Promotion of Christian Higher Education. In J. C. Vanderstelt (Ed.), *The challenge of Marxist and neo-Marxist ideologies for Christian scholarship* (pp. 268-272). Sioux Center, IA: Dordt College Press.

ICPCHE. (1987). Statements I-VI of 1984 conference. In *Critique and challenge of Christian higher education* (pp. 170-171). Kampen: J.H. Kok.

Schrotenboer, P. G. (1982). Comments at the end of the last business meeting of the third international conference of institutions for Christian higher education. In J. C. Vanderstelt (Ed.), *The challenge of Marxist and neo-Marxist ideologies for Christian scholarship* (pp. 279-280). Sioux Center, IA: Dordt College Press.

van der Walt, B. J. (1976). First international conference for Christian higher education, review and preview. In *Christian higher education: The contemporary challenge* (pp. 407-418). Potchefstroom, South Africa: Institute for the Advancement of Calvinism.

Vanderstelt, J. C. (1999). Breve historia y visión de AIPECS. In S. Rooy

(Ed.), *Educando como Cristianos en el siglo XXI* (pp. 183-190). Alajuela, C. R.: Imprenta Grafos.

Appendix A

IAPCHE Statement on Christian Higher Education
Adopted at Conference 2000

1. **What is Christian higher education?**
   Christian higher education encompasses all educational endeavors at the tertiary or undergraduate and graduate level, in which all facets of created reality, especially human life, are explored and examined in an advanced and more detailed manner than they are in primary and secondary education.

2. **On what foundations should Christian higher education be developed?**
   In distinction from its non-Christian counterparts, Christian higher education assumes a recognition of:
   a. The operation of religious commitments controlling all educational and research processes.
   b. A desire to perform its entire task in the light of God's inscripturated revelation.
   c. The presence of God's Word and Spirit to, respectively, structure and guide created reality; consequently, any concepts of neutrality and/or relativism are rejected.
   d. The distortions of disobedience and its repercussions in all educational and research activities.
   e. The call to redemption and restoration, not just abstract analyses and descriptions of impersonal research.
   f. The importance of a local and global community of competent and effective educators and researchers concerned with developing integrated academic programs and providing serviceable insight in their areas of specialization for the benefit of society.

3. **What is the purpose of Christian higher education?**
   The unique purpose of Christian higher education is:
   a. To deepen our understanding of the world and human life in it,
   b. To design steps that address and seek to correct distortions in all of life,
   c. To prepare students and other members of the academic community for knowledgeable and competent discipleship in an increasingly complex world and culture,
   d. To serve the larger Christian community as it seeks, through Spirit-directed faithful witness, to bring the healing power of Christ to bear in all areas of life.

HOW TO EXPLAIN AND EVALUATE CULTURAL DIFFERENCES FROM A REFORMATIONAL-CHRISTIAN PERSPECTIVE

B. J. Van Der Walt

Abstract
This paper investigates the difficult problems of explaining and evaluating cultural diversity. The introduction presents the need for such an explanation as well as problems in comparing different cultures. Secondly, the paper explains why cultures can be so different, according to the basic Biblical ideas of creation, fall, and redemption. Such an approach enables one, in the third place, to tackle the sensitive question of evaluating other cultures fairly instead of falling into the traps of either cultural ethnocentrism or cultural relativism. Fourth, the question is discussed how to decide what is acceptable or unacceptable in specific cultural behaviour. To further indicate the practical value of intercultural (or comparative) philosophy, the final part of the essay briefly compares African and Western modes of thought in order to indicate how (especially tertiary) education can be "Africanised."

Introduction: current interest and the need for reflection
I write this paper from a broad Biblical philosophical/theological perspective. It will therefore not go into the details of the curricular, pedagogical, and administrative considerations that can assist us in addressing conflicts between cultures. I do encourage discussion of these more practical issues during the sessions of track 1. I also hope—as the African proverb goes—that what I have to say is not so low (elementary) that the intellectual "giraffes" amongst you will not be able to get something to eat, and neither too high (philosophical) that the small "antelopes" cannot digest it. My paper does not explicitly discuss competing worldviews. However, worldviews are the religious or directional "soul" of every cul-

ture. The two can be distinguished, but not separated. I will also not go into the differences between various Christian worldviews (and cultures). My own viewpoint (in agreement with IAPCHE's basis and aims) is that, as Christians, we should be involved in order to transform (our own and other) cultures. I do not agree with the following Christian worldviews: the Christian simply *accommodating,* the Christian *against,* the Christian *above,* or the Christian *alongside* culture or the world.

How can Christian higher education bridge the gaps between competing cultures? Before we enter into all kinds of details of curricular and pedagogical nature, we as Christian lecturers as well as our students have to know *why* cultures are sometimes so different, to learn *how* to evaluate these differences, and to decide *what* is acceptable or unacceptable in our own culture or another culture. By way of an example, I will indicate how traditional African culture and modern Western culture may mutually enrich each other in the field of (Christian) higher education. It may help you to approach your own cultural context. As an introduction, we first have to explore briefly the current interest in comparing cultures in order to concentrate on two key problems.

For thousands of years a great variety of cultures has blessed the world. Except for more informed people, like travellers and scholars, many people were not aware of the great diversity of ways in which human beings responded to God's cultural mandate (Genesis 1:28; 2:15). Increasing globalisation changed this situation. Very few cultures today develop in isolation. Globalisation implies the spread—all over the world—of Western science, technology, politics, and economics. It is therefore a multifaceted process (van der Walt, 2006, p. 92) and not merely economic in nature. In addition, the social, intellectual, moral, religious, and cultural life of many nations is transformed. This has both positive and negative consequences.

Globalisation, furthermore, is not always a peaceful process. Already in 1996, Huntington wrote *The Clash of Civilizations.* Recently Saul (2005) draws attention to the collapse of globalisation. Non-Western countries are not simply accepting Western cultural domination, but reaffirm their own cultural heritage and identities—even in violent ways.

That especially the American so-called "cocacolonization" and "macdonaldisation" of the world is increasingly questioned, is evident from inter alia the following publications by Chomsky (2003, 2005, 2006), Fallows (2006), Hardt (2004), Shadid (2006), Soderberg (2005), and Suskind (2006). According to Barber (2002), who opposes Jihad with McWorld, the rebellion against the market-driven Western world was, among other things, an example of a reaction against the expansive drive of American culture. Jacobs (2005) even predicts a dark age ahead.

Against this background the interest in intercultural knowledge—both for its academic as well as practical value—is growing. A few examples from a large number of publications may serve as confirmation. Already in 1946, Benedict tried to describe the patterns of Japanese culture, as did Hall & Hall (1987). In order to improve business, Saccone (1994, pp. 23-70) summarised the typical characteristics of Korean culture. Clotaire (2006) uncovers the "cultural codes" of the Americans, as well as other nations, to assist the USA in selling its products elsewhere. Also for commercial purposes, South African books by Boon (1996), Christie, Lessem & Mbigi (1994), Lessem (1996), and Mbigi & Maree (1995) try to explain the difference between Western and traditional African cultures.

Not only has the business world realised the need and value of cross-cultural knowledge. To a greater or lesser extent, it is happening in all domains of life. Its theological-missiological relevance is, for example, evident in the works of Adeney (1995, pp. 106-124), Hesselgrave (1991), Hiebert (1998), Mayers (1987), and Lingefelter & Mayers (1986). In Reformational thinking interest in this field is growing. Examples are Brugmans (2002) and Griffioen (2003) from the Netherlands. In Griffioen (2006), a renewed interest in Chinese culture is also evident. In different publications (van der Walt, 1999; 2001; 2003; 2006) I have struggled, as another Christian thinker, with the cultural differences between traditional Africa and the modern West.

These examples—from a vast and growing amount of publications—clearly indicate that intercultural understanding and communication have become a topical issue. Is it possible to add something new to the worldwide discussions? Most publications do not discuss or deal with two important problems satisfactorily. In the first place, writers do not explain *why* cultures differ, but simply accept it as a fact. Secondly, they do not deal with the sensitive issue of *how to evaluate* cultural differences, but simply accept their own or the foreign culture as normative. To provide a tentative answer to these two vital questions, and to try to do so from a Reformational-Biblical perspective, is the main aim of this paper. However, one should be aware of the difficulties and even dangers of such a venture.

Rüsen (2005, pp. 267-269) provides a summary of the following dangers also mentioned by many other authors: because intercultural comparison touches the field of cultural identity, it is often involved in a struggle for power and domination. This is especially the case in respect to Western dominance and non-Western resistance against it. An epistemological difficulty is that every comparison is done in the context of a pre-given culture, viz. that of the investigator or scholar. Comparison of cultures therefore presupposes (often hidden) norms. Their distance or proximity to such norms is the measure for cultures. In most cases, the norm is one's own culture (ethnocentrism). However, it is possible to evaluate one's own culture with norms adopted from other cultures. A typology of cultural differences is methodically necessary as an hypothetical construct, but it should try to avoid the tendency to substantiate or reify cultures, in other words to treat cultures as if they are static units which can be neatly separated from each other. A typology usually stresses the differences and not the similarities between cultures. It therefore runs the risk of oversimplification and overgeneralisation.

With these warnings in mind, I will attempt to explain why cultures differ. The answer to this question will also influence the way cultures should be evaluated.

Why cultures differ

The emphasis on the Biblical revelation about the creation, fall, and redemption of reality is a key element of a Reformational worldview (Colson & Pearcey, 1999; Walsh & Middleton, 1984; Wolters, 1985). These basic concepts (formation, deformation, and reformation) can also provide an explanation for the great variety in the cultures of the world (Van den Toren, 2005, pp. 2-5).

The Reformational tradition asks special attention for the so-called creational mandate or cultural mandate given by God to all human beings in Genesis (Wolters, 1985). In Genesis 1:28 they are instructed to fill the earth and subdue it, and according to Genesis 2:15 they should take care of the Garden of Eden. This mandate is not limited to agriculture, but to all of creation: the creation of languages, simple tools and sophisticated technology, all kinds of human relations, the arts, sciences, etc. Christ's great commission (Matthew 28:19-20) should be understood as a reminder of this original, all-encompassing mandate and not—as often the case—only narrowly as a mandate to proclaim the Gospel "to win souls for Christ."

God gave humankind clear norms, like stewardship, care, love, etc., but never a precise blueprint to fulfil the cultural mandate. He expects human beings to be creative. The creational mandate makes room for genuine cultural variety. Cultures vary because God's creation can legitimately be shaped differently; human creativity varies widely; and environmental contexts vary.

A careful study of the first eleven chapters of Genesis confirms the fact that God's intention was not that there should be only one culture, but the development of many different responses to his mandate. After the flood, Noah's descendants "were scattered over the earth" (Genesis 9:19). In Genesis 10, a "table of nations" is given and it is repeated (10:32) that "the nations spread out over the earth." This automatically entails cultural variation. Different environments require different tools, forms of agriculture, languages, and social structures.

In the account of the tower of Babel in Genesis 11, we read (11:4) that the people rebelled against God because they did not want to be "scattered over the face of the whole earth." God, however, confused their language so that they could not understand each other. In Genesis 11: 8-9 it is stated twice. "So the Lord scattered them from there over all the earth." Therefore, what happened at Babel should not be understood only (or primarily) as God's punishment. He used the confusion of language as a means to pursue his original plan of cultural diversity. God intended the development of different ethnic groups (nations), each with its own culture.

Not every form of culture or every cultural practice is acceptable. Already Genesis 3 records the sad story of the fall of Adam and Eve. They became disobedient to God, rejecting his norms for life. Because culture, in essence, means answering God's mandate according to his norms (cf. below), sin deeply affects every aspect of culture. Thus, the development of the full potential of creation was stunted. The essence of the fall was that Adam and Eve no longer wanted to be God's image bearer (*imago Dei*), or his representative, fulfilling their cultural calling. They wanted to be *sicut Deus*, like God (Genesis 3:5b), gods themselves. This furthermore implies that they rejected God's laws to become autonomous (a law unto themselves). From then on evil and wickedness increased. (Genesis 6:4) The fact that the creation has to be developed according to God's norms (given in creational revelation)—to be able to obtain the goal He as Creator had in mind for his creation —was ignored. Finally, the people became so corrupt that He decided to wipe them out from the face of the earth (Genesis 6:11-12).

In the light of creation and fall, Van den Toren (2005) identifies the following three reasons for cultural diversity:

(1) legitimate cultural variety that shows the creativity of (man as) the image of God and glorifies the Creator; (2) cultural variety that results from not

yet fully attaining the potential of creation; and (3) cultural variety that is a result of lack of respect for the (God) given structures of creation and thus an expression of disobedience and rebellion to the Creator. (p. 4)

Apart from the perspectives of formation (creation) and deformation (the fall), cultural diversity can also be viewed from the perspective of reformation (or redemption). As the word "reformation" indicates, humanity's cultural mandate can again be redirected according to God's will.

At Pentecost (Acts 2:6-12) different peoples from various regions heard the apostles proclaiming the Gospel in their own languages. Note that this miracle was not necessary for communicating the Good News as most, if not all, the Jews and the proselytes from the surrounding countries present on that day could speak the lingua franca (Koine Greek) of those days. We, therefore, have to look for a more profound, symbolic meaning behind this miraculous event. In my view, it indicates that in the new dispensation the Gospel should be proclaimed, heard, and expressed in one's own language and pattern of thought. Pentecost legitimises the contextualisation of the Good News of redemption and recreation in different cultural "clothes." The Spirit of God acknowledges and respects cultural diversity as developed during all the previous centuries since Babel. In spite of their unity in faith (Acts 2:42-47), church members did not expect believers to return to one language as was the case prior to Babel. Without giving up their unique cultural identities, people of all cultures should experience the liberating power of faith in Jesus Christ. This trend continued throughout history. For example, the New Testament itself was written in a different language (Greek) than the Aramaic spoken by Jesus and his disciples.

The emerging church experienced great difficulty with respect to the cultural diversity amongst its members. Finally (Acts 15), it was decided that Christians from a Hellenistic cultural background should not be required to embrace the cultural aspects—not even the important ceremony of circumcision—of the Jewish religion. During the subsequent history the Gospel entered and changed many different pagan cultures: from Jerusalem to Samaria, Ethiopia, Damascus, Antioch, Rome, Northern Europe, North America, Latin America, Asia, and Africa.

That this development of multicultural Christianity was not simply God's concession to history is also clear from the book of Revelation. When history concludes at the consummation, God will not *undo* cultural diversity. On the contrary, it will be *appreciated* on the new earth: the glory and honour of the nations will be brought into the New Jerusalem (Revelation 21:26). Note that verse 27 adds that nothing impure (sinful) will enter the new creation. Only good cultural products, "the *honour* and *glory* of the nations," will be acceptable. Good culture has eternal value. Not only will humankind accept their cultures, but also the different nations will retain their distinctive identities. Revelation 5:9 and 7:9 mention *every* language, tribe, people, and nation. The conclusion is that the revelation in the creation story, that God loves cultural diversity, is confirmed in his plan for the recreation of the world.

In the light of Scripture, cultures differ because (van der Walt, 2001, pp. 12-15): (1) God intended his cultural mandate to be answered in a variety of ways; (2) the creativity of humankind varies; (3) God wanted human beings to develop the whole earth, with different environments and challenges to survive; and (4) the sinfulness of mankind can retard the development of creation. Different cultures over-emphasise different relationships, like the relationship to the self, as is the case in Western individualism, or the relationship to the other, as in African communalism. One will never stop creating culture because the fall did not change the nature of the human being (as God's representative on earth, responsible for its development). What changed was the direction of his/her cultural activity—done in either disobedience or obedience to God's norms. Christ's redemption enables believers to transform culture (Romans 12:2). The Word of God promises that such a transformed culture will become part of the new creation.

Two (bad) ways of evaluating cultural diversity
The reasons for cultural diversity already provide ways of evaluating it. Christians evaluate culture in different ways. (See Niebuhr's classic *Christ and Culture* [1951] and also recent works like Brugmans [2002] and Verbeek [2005].) Apart from the Reformational way, we should be aware of how cultures are evaluated when the Word of God is not employed as the norm. Two ways of evaluating cultural diversity should be rejected: ethnocentrism and relativism (Griffioen, 2003, pp. 196-201). A critical look at both theories with an alternative follows.

In the past cultural evolutionism placed all cultures on a single line of development, beginning with so-called primitive or simple cultures towards modern or more complex cultures. Proponents of this viewpoint usually spoke about "culture" (singular). Culture was according to them not influenced by differences in place and time. Each culture has to climb the developmental "ladder." Western culture was regarded as superior to other cultures, because it was believed to be the most highly developed civilisation. This evolutionistic viewpoint was also applied to Christianity—it was regarded as the highest religion. Accordingly, Christian mission was often viewed as the export of the Western form of Christianity to the "uncivilised" non-Western world. Western culture became the norm for the judgement of every other culture.

Note that the West did not always evaluate "primitive" cultures negatively as something underdeveloped or backwards. Some scholars adhered to a romantic viewpoint: because the so-called primitive cultures represent the original beginning, the ideal of the West should be to return to the state of the "noble barbarian or savage." Such a perspective, however, boils down to reverse ethnocentrism: Western culture is evaluated according to the norm of "primitive" culture. A present-day Afro-centric reaction against Euro-centrism will also be a form of ethnocentrism and therefore equally unacceptable.

According to both the creation story in the Bible, as well as the prophecies about the recreation, cultural diversity *as such* is not something to be lamented or eradicated. God himself did not want us to develop a monolithic culture. Cultural diversity can be something good that enriches us and therefore has to be appreciated. This implies a clear rejection of ethnocentric viewpoints. Griffioen (2003, p. 162), however, makes a distinction between negative ethnocentrism and positive ethnocentrism. He describes the first as when *universal* meaning is attached to a *specific* culture with the result that it is regarded as the *norm* in the comparison of different cultures. Positive ethnocentrism is the natural fact that one takes pride in one's own culture.

Cultural relativism was a justifiable reaction against cultural evolutionism. Especially cultural anthropologists became aware of the great variety in cultures and accordingly did not speak about "culture" (singular) any longer, but about "cultures" (plural). They believe that humankind should not arrange cultures *hierarchically*, from lower to higher. They exist *alongside* each other and are—in spite of great differences—equal in value. This viewpoint is therefore of the opinion that, as each culture is "true" on its own terms, one culture does not have the right to evaluate or judge another. Cultural habits have to be accepted as long as a particular culture condones such practices.

The implication of this viewpoint is that culture—any culture—is above critique. There can be no argument about a statement like "this is how we behave in our culture." One could only reply by saying, "Obey what your culture prescribes." Such an attitude, however, makes people captives to their own culture.

Together with the rejection of cultural evolutionism, clear norms for evaluating different cultural customs also disappeared. Because it is difficult—impossible—to maintain such a "neutral" point of view, cultural relativism (at least in its radical form) does not have many advocates left.

Today emphasis is placed on the dynamic, heterogeneous nature of a culture as well as the fact that, in creative ways, people adapt to different situations. Culture is not regarded as "a thing" (the so-called reification of culture), but as a way of life. No approaches, however, could solve the problem of relativism.

The relativist viewpoint is clearly unacceptable to Christians who believe that God's revelation contains "supra"-cultural norms. According to his will human sacrifices, slavery, the burning of widows together with their deceased husbands, the caste system, the pursuit of a "master race," loveless capitalism and many more are sinful practices. We can appreciate cultural diversity only to the degree that it conforms to God's norms and his goal for creation. Because of the sinfulness of human beings, this is seldom the case. Even when conduct is labelled as "Christian," we cannot accept every behaviour and practice as a genuine expression of Christian discipleship.

A Christian approach to evaluating cultural diversity

According to many Christian anthropologists (Onvlee, 1973) and philosophers (Buijs, Blokhuis, Griffioen & Kuiper, 2005); Griffioen (2003, 2006), God calls human beings to answer to him and his revelation. Every culture (not only those created by Christians) is fundamentally a religious response to a divine calling. The human cultural answer has to obey God's norms or principles for different areas of life or societal relationships. Human beings have to positivise or concretise these divine norms according to God's central commandment of love toward himself and his fellow creatures (Matthew 22:37-40).

Onvlee (1973) correctly states that, in spite of the fact that *each* culture is dignified in its own way, *no* culture is so good that it can be accepted as a norm to measure other cultures because of the fact that *no* culture is a fully obedient response to God's norms (cf. Romans 3:10-12). Therefore, one should clearly distinguish the *divine* norm from *fallible* ways. Cultural variety is an indication of the various ways people—correctly or wrongly—apply God's norms in their lives.

Such a "third way" of viewing culture provides an alternative to both cultural evolutionism (ethnocentrism) and cultural relativism. It rejects (negative) ethnocentrism, because one may not judge another culture according to one's own fallible response to God's calling. It also rejects the relativist idea that one should withhold any judgement about culture. Both one's own and the culture of another person either obey or disobey God's fundamental norms.

From the preceding it is clear that culture cannot be isolated from either one's religious orientation towards God (or an idol in his place) or from the various societal institutions. Mouw and Griffioen (1993, p. 17) and Griffioen (2003, pp. 13, 98, 171; 2006, p. 7) therefore distinguish between the following three kinds of plurality or diversity: (1) the religious (or directional), (2) the structural (or associational) and (3) the cultural (or contextual). These three should be distinguished but cannot be separated.

Structural diversity (the diversity of different societal relationships) expresses deep-seated religious and worldview convictions. Viewed from the side of one's religious commitment, religion shapes the different societal relationships like marriage, the family, school, business etc. Augustine already indicated this in the following way: (1) every human being serves either the true God or an idol in his place; (2) human beings look like or bear the image of the God/idol they serve; (3) they create a societal life according to their own image of being human. How societal life is structured (3), reveals how humans view themselves (2), and ultimately which God/god they serve (1). Different religions are also the "heart" or motivating force behind all cultures. In addition, the reverse is true: specific culture shapes religious convictions. Summarised: every ethnic group combines the religious and structural dimensions into a unique cultural configuration.

The religious, structural, and cultural dimensions should be distinguished and acknowledged. Cultural relativism, for example, ignores the truth claims of opposing religious directions. (This, of course, does not imply a neutral viewpoint, because relativists believe in their own perspective.) At the same time, the religious element should never be separate from the structural and cultural element; the structural should not be isolated from the religious and cultural aspects; and the cultural cannot be viewed correctly when it is separate from religion and the structures of society.

In a nutshell: in the (1) cultural (2) the structural is opened or developed in (3) different (religious) directions. The cultural is one facet of one's all-encompassing response to God's calling.

Because we today live in the time after the fall and Christ's redemptive work, we experience a mixed situation. On the one hand, horrible consequences of the fall are evident. On the other hand, clear signs of God's grace are visible. O'Donovan (2000) correctly states:

> No culture is best. No culture is right in everything. There are things in every culture that the sincere Christian must reject because they are not pleasing to God. There are also beneficial things, which can be learned from every culture. (p. 15)

One can be grateful because every culture—also one's own—contains something good and one should be humbled, because every cultural activity—including one's own—contains defects and needs reformation in the light of God's revelation (van der Walt, 2001, pp. 12-15).

Dealing with a mixed situation in the same culture and between cultures is clearly not easy. Producing clear-cut answers is difficult, because the spiritual *direction* of a culture (its obedience or disobedience to God's norms) cannot always be clearly *located* in specific cultural behaviour or structures. For example, we cannot simply say that the extended family system in traditional African societies (different from the Western nuclear family, consisting only of a father, mother, and children) is the ideal. Neither can we regard it as simply wrong. Depending on different socio-economic circumstances (a rural, agricultural economy or a modern money economy)—the structural element—it can either assist the family or a couple or financially ruin their marriage.

The reason why it is so difficult to decide what is good and what is not, is that since the fall the human heart itself is divided. From this deep-seated origin of all we do (the directional), good and bad permeate every cultural activity. The apostle Paul bemoans the fact that he does not do the good he strives after, but rather does the bad things he tries to evade. In trying to solve this complex issue, Van den Toren (2005) distinguishes between degrees with an upper and a lower limit. The upper limit is the ideal situation for which we should aim.

> This is a situation in which all cultural variety . . . reflects the rich potential of cultural creativity given with creation and on the other hand respects the structures of creation and the reality of redemption as given by God. (pp. 5-6)

The lower limit is decided by asking this question: What sort of cultural variation can be accepted that still can be legitimately identified as "Christian?"

To explain what he has in mind with his lower limit, Van den Toren employs as an analogy the concept of heresy. We regard a practice or doctrine as a heresy when it undermines one's Christian identity, understanding, and practice of Christ's redemption. In a similar way, Christians have to ask themselves which truths and cultural practices are essential to their call to be a Christian. When true Christian behaviour becomes endangered, one reaches the lower limit.

Van den Toren realises, however, that Christians do not live as individuals in isolation from the rest of society. In their private and ecclesiastical life, they may still be able to stay above the lower limit, striving towards the upper limit. Nevertheless, in our growing multicultural, multireligious, and secular societies it will be very difficult, if not impossible, to adhere to God's criteria. According to him, dialogue between the different cultures and religions is the only way to solve this problem. Christians and people of other faiths have, for example, to discuss how marriage and family life, the workplace and government have to be organised.

Van den Toren is of the opinion that such an honest dialogue may also be insightful for Christians, because their surrounding culture may imprison Christians. People of other faiths and cultures may even remind them about the need to respect the God-given order for creation!

The basis for this kind of intercultural dialogue is that all ways of organising life—whether acknowledged or not—are responses to God's creation ordinances or norms. In his "general" revelation in creation, God speaks not only to Christians, but also to every human being, revealing his ordinances for the different spheres of life. Not only Christians, but all human beings can understand that mutual fidelity is the norm for married life, that justice is the norm for politics (the state), that care is the norm for family life, that honesty is required in business, etc. From perceiving the (good) order *in* creation, we can conclude to God's order *for* creation.

These divine creational ordinances or structural principles are *constant*. The way in which they are given shape in different cultures usually *varies*. Stated differently: the human *form* that cultures acquire in a specific culture should not be identified with the divine *norm*. This fact explains the great cultural variety and emphasises that it should be positively appreciated (Griffioen, 2003, p. 173). At the same time, it reminds every culture that its form (shape) should continuously be reformed according to the divine norm. People of different cultures will therefore have to decide through dialogue what cultural practices open the inherent potential of reality and what cultural practices stunt or destroy that potential.

The perspectives developed on the preceding pages provide general criteria for the evaluation of cultures. Most cultural ideas and practices cannot be compared to either red "stop!" lights or green "go!" lights. They will occur on different levels or degrees, either closer to the ideal or closer to failure. Instead of a general judgment like "this is absolutely beautiful" or "this is totally wrong," we should study every cultural concept and behaviour carefully and weigh it on the scale of God's infallible directions. Studying and evaluating cultures in the light of God's revelation provides a "third way," transcending both ethnocentric cultural imperialism and relativism. Obeying God's will liberates, enriches, and empowers every culture!

Western and African modes of thinking
Following the contours of the African mode of thought is not easy. There are significant cultural differences between the different ethnic groups and regions in Africa, which may not be ignored. Yet it is possible to identify general features and to speak of *African* thought (cf. O'Donovan, 2000, p. 21; van der Walt, 2003, pp. 187-188; and Wiher, 2003, pp. 428-431). The most important differences are summarised in the following table (van der Walt, 2006, pp. 210-211):

THE WEST	AFRICA
A. The aim/direction/focus of knowledge	
1. Scientific-technical control of visible reality	Magic-ritual manipulation of the spiritual world
2. Focused on knowledge of universal regularities	Focused on the individual, concrete phenomena
3. Conceptual direction—concepts are important	Relational direction—relationships are important
4. Knowledge for the sake of better insight in matters—epistemology important	Knowledge for the sake of the right actions—ethics is important
B. The nature of the one who knows	
5. Emphasis on the individual—individual autonomy	Emphasis on the person in the community—socially sensitive
6. Contextually independent	Contextually bound
7. More progressive—open for new ideas	More bound by tradition—less readily accepts new ideas
8. Independent-critical attitude	Inclined to mere reproduction of facts

C. The knowing activity or process	
9. Hearing is important—auditory way	Seeing is important—visual way
10. More rational	More intuitive
11. More intellectual and clinical	More emotional
12. Dualistic—faith and other presuppositions may not play a role in the process of knowing	Integral—presuppositions involved in process of knowing
D. The nature of the object of knowledge	
13. Material things	Spiritual powers and forces
14. Distance between one who knows and object of knowledge	One who knows more involved with the object of knowledge
15. Natural causes and laws that regulate things	The spiritual (supernatural) causes that determine events
16. The object of knowledge seen as more static	The object of knowledge seen as dynamic
E. The characteristics of the result of knowing (knowledge)	
17. Abstract knowledge, distanced from reality	Concrete knowledge, nearer to the object of knowledge
18. Analytically reduced knowledge of subdivisions	Synthetic, integral knowledge in which the whole object and its relations are involved
19. Systematic—organised according to a clear categorical framework to form a pattern or system	Seemingly unsystematic—details not systematically connected according to a logical framework
20. Step-logic: one thought is built logically on the previous with a clear-cut conclusion; more rigid—judgements are either right or wrong; more geared to differences than to similarities	Block-logic: central theme is often repeated without a clear-cut conclusion; more flowing and linked together (and-and style); more geared to analogies and similarities than to differences
F. How knowledge (truth) is transmitted)	
21. Without mincing matters	In a circumspect, indirect way

How do these two ways of knowing interact? The Western way of teaching from the colonial period did not take into account the traditional culture and mode of thought of the people of Africa (cf. Bowen, D. N., 1984, pp. 2-7). Africans regarded this type of education as too abstract and academic, too focused on memorization, and geared towards examinations. Because of these foreign educational methods they could not give their best. Bowen then attempted to ascertain the cognitive styles of African students and to find suitable teaching styles.

"Cognitive styles" simply means (cf. Bowen, D. N., 1984, p. 20) how one takes note of one's environment, obtains information and creates meaning from it. Many factors are involved in this process including culture, background, experience, and family. Knowledge of cognitive styles is particularly important in education, for they determine: (1) the interests of learners and students, preferences for certain kinds of reading matter and even choice of occupation; (2) learners' academic development; and (3) the best way of learning for students and how teachers/lecturers teach.

In order to determine cognitive style, Bowen uses a "field-dependent" and "field-independent" approach. She chose this method because in her opinion it is the method most applied—also in teaching (cf. Bowen, D. N., 1984, pp. 23-26). The difference between "field-dependent" (fd) and "field-independent" (fi) has to do with how the person acquiring knowledge experiences the field, domain or object of knowledge. A person for whom the subdivisions of the field fuse, thinks fd (in a more holistic manner), while a person thinks fi if he/she clearly distinguishes the subdivisions (therefore thinks more analytically). An fd person is more dependent on his environment and (external) social relations, while an fi person thinks more individualistically and autonomously. The former is more person-oriented, while the latter is more clinical and task-oriented. Fd learners are greatly dependent on the structuring and guidance of their teachers, while fi persons can and want to learn more independently.

African students tested (91 percent) fd with some disciplinary variety (theology 97 percent, and government schools 83 percent) and regional variety (100 percent in Nigeria and 84 percent in Kenya) and gender differences (women are more fd than men) (Bowen, D. N., 1984, p. 123). These psychological tests confirm the comparative table above (6.1).

Bowen recommends 26 new teaching strategies that better meet Africans' way of thinking and learning. Limited space permits only three examples. First, provide overviews of the work and material to be learned. Second, avoid individual competition between students and encourage students to study in groups as far as possible. Third, because African students are visually oriented, employ different types of reading work, the use of an overhead projector, films, videos, slides, illustrations, role play, field work, and other concrete experiences are far more suitable and therefore also more effective (Bowen, D. N., 1984, pp. 111-117). From the other point of view, Buconyori (1991) also uses the fd-fi method for his research and his results agree with Bowen's.

Further, although Buconyori appreciates the fact that Bowen and others recommend teaching styles, which are more suitable to the learning styles of students from Africa, he believes that this is not sufficient to improve the situation of education in Africa. Earlier research did not indicate what could be done to improve the reasoning faculty of African students (Buconyori, 1991, p. 179). He does not mean that Africans cannot reason, but that they are not strong in independent analytical thought (like Westerners). They are inclined to memorise prescribed matter almost mechanically and reproduce it in tests (cf. Buconyori, 1991, p. 5). They experience difficulty with analysis and critical evaluation to reach logical conclusions (cf. Buconyori, 1991, p. 106).

This state of affairs does not correspond with the main aim of higher education and study, namely to convert learners into thinkers (cf. Buconyori, 1991, p. 50). Modern education, apart from linking with the traditional culture, should also stimulate a more Western independent analytical mode of thought.

How can teaching strategies be devised which would connect with the cognitive styles of the Africans and yet promote independent reasoning faculties? From among numerous strategies Buconyori (1991, p. 185 et seq.) suggests, I mention seven. First, dovetail one's teaching with the visual orientation of the students. Second, present factual knowledge in such a way that it does not promote parroting but reflection. Third, help the student focus on the most salient aspects of the subject and identify the real problems. Fourth, stimulate creativity in the forming of new ideas by working cooperatively in groups and not through competition between individuals. Fifth, encourage analytical thought by classifying the learning matter, discovering differences and similarities, determining relations and patterns, and discerning main thoughts from less important ones. Sixth, encourage the integration of new knowledge with existing knowledge. Finally, demonstrate the practical use of independent, analytical thought.

African and Western modes of thought

In certain cultures, different gifts develop better than in others. These gifts also include the cognitive gifts—the gifts of knowing by means of which people attempt to understand reality and make sense of it. Knowledge of reality may, however, be acquired in different ways (a person *knows* more than that which he can *logically know*), and articulated and transmitted in different ways. The different cultures (from the East, Africa, and the West) are a clear proof of this.

Fortunately, learning is no longer regarded as listening, reading, memorising, and writing. Already in the sixties Arnheim (1969) emphasised that thinking requires more than the formation of concepts. It calls for the unravelling of relations, for the disclosure of elusive structures. A work of art is interplay of vision and thought, of visual thinking.

More than twenty years ago, Gardner (1983) already pointed out that we should differentiate between kinds of intelligence. Not only people who can work with words and numbers are "intelligent." People can for instance also learn by means of visual images, bodily action, social intercourse, and in a technical way. These other types of learning styles do not mean that the person is *less* intelligent, but merely intelligent *in a different way*.

> More recently, Olthuis and others have stressed the same point: reasoning is only one of the ways in which we engage (i.e. know) the world.... Knowing is ... multidimensional.... We also know by touch, by feel, by taste, by sight, by sounds, by smell, by symbols, by sex, by trust—by means of every modality of human experience. (Olthuis, 1997, p. 6)

Conclusion: A challenge

I have approached that which Olthuis and others explain in a systematic fashion (the theory of modalities as devised by Reformational Christian philosophers like Dooyeweerd, Stoker, and Vollenhoven) in this paper from a cultural-philosophic view. To get real knowledge of God's creation, we need all the different capacities (functions or modalities)—not merely the logic-analytical. Since in some cultures some of these functions are better developed than in others—and are even over-emphasised—they once more draw the attention of another culture to that which it has neglected.

Mutually acknowledging cultural pluralism is therefore the correct approach. A strictly Eurocentric, or Orientalistic or Afrocentric orientation is no longer appropriate in education in the fast integrating world of the 21st century.

Apart from being mutually *acknowledging* this cultural pluralism should also be mutually *correcting*. If correction can take place in the light of God's Word—which transforms every culture—the result can be even richer and more liberating.

References

Adeney, B. T. (1995). *Strange virtues: Ethics in a multicultural world.* Downers Grove, IL: Intervarsity Press.

Arnheim, R. (1969). *Visual thinking.* Berkeley: University of California Press.

Barber, B. R. (2002). *Jihad vs. McWorld: Terrorisme en globalisering als bedreiging voor democratie.* Rotterdam: Lemniscaat.

Benedict, R. (1946). *The chrysanthemum and the sword: Patterns of Japanese culture.* Cambridge, MA: Riverside Press.

Boon, M. (1996). *The African way: The power of interactive leadership.* Wynberg: Struik.

Bowen, D. N. (1984). *Cognitive styles of African theological students and the implication of these styles for bibliographic instruction.* Ann Arbor, MI: University Microfilms International.

Bowen, E. A. (1984). *The learning styles of African college students.* Ann Arbor, MI: University Microfilms International.

Bowen, E. A., & Bowen, D. N. (1984). *Mapping booklet: cognitive style inventory for African students.* Florida: Florida State University (Unpublished manuscript).

Bowen, E. A., & Bowen, D. N. (1986, January-March). Theological education and learning styles in Africa. *World Evangelical Fellowship Theological News,* 5-10.

Brugmans, E. (Ed.). (2002). *Cultuurfilosofie: Katolieke, reformatorische, humanistische, islamitische en joodse reflecties over onze cultuur.* Budel: Damon.

Buconyori, E. A. (1991). *Cognitive styles and the development of reasoning among younger African students in Christian higher education.* Ann Arbor, MI: University Microfilms International.

Buijs, G., Blokhuis, P., Griffioen, S., & Kuiper, R. (Eds.). (2005). *Homo respondens: Verkenningen rond het mens-zijn.* Amsterdam: Buijten & Schipperheijn.

Chomsky, N. (2006). *Failed states: The abuse of power and the assault on democracy.* New York: Henry Holt.

Chomsky, N. (2003). *Hegemony of survival: America's quest for global dominance.* New York: Henry Holt.

Chomsky, N. (2005). *Imperial ambitions: Conversations on the post-9/11 world.* New York: Henry Holt.

Christie, P., Lessem, R., & Mbigi, L. (1994). *African management.* Randburg: Knowledge Resources.

Clotaire, R. (2006). *The culture code: An ingenious way to understand why people around the world live and buy as they do.* New York: Broadway Books.

Colson, C., & Pearcey, N. (1999). *How now shall we live?* Wheaton, IL: Tyndale House.

Fallows, J. (2006). *Blind into Baghdad: America's war in Iraq.* New York: Random House.

Gardner, H. (1983). *Frames of mind.* New York: Basic Books.

Griffioen, S. (2006). *Een weg gaan: Cultuurfilosofie tussen west en oost.* Budel: Damon.

Griffioen, S. (2003). *Moed tot kultuur: Een aktuele filosofie.* Amsterdam: Buijten & Schipperheijn.

Hall, E. T., & Hall, M. R. (1987). *Hidden differences: Doing business with the Japanese.* New York: Doubleday.

Hardt, M., & Negri, A. (2004). *Multitude: War and democracy in the age of empire.* London: Penguin.

Hesselgrave, D. J. (1991). *Communicating Christ cross-culturally.* Grand Rapids, MI: Zondervan.

Hiebert, P. G. (1998). *Antropological insights for missionaries.* Grand Rapids, MI: Baker Book House.

Huntington, S. (1998). *The clash of civilizations and the remaking of the world order.* London: Touchstone.

Jacobs, J. (2005). *Dark age ahead.* New York: Random House.

Lessem, R. (1996). *From hunter to rainmaker: The South African business sphere.* Randburg: Knowledge Resources.

Lingenfelter, S. G., & Mayers, M. K. (1986). *Ministering cross-culturally.* Grand Rapids, MI: Baker Book House.

Mayers, M. K. (1997). *Christianity confronts culture.* Grand Rapids, MI: Zondervan.

Mbigi, L., & Maree, J. (1995). *Ubuntu: The spirit of African transformation management.* Randburg: Knowledge Resources.

Mouw, R., & Griffioen, S. (1993). *Pluralisms and horizons: An essay on Christian public philosophy.* Grand Rapids, MI: Eerdmans.

Niebuhr, H. R. (1951). *Christ and culture.* New York: HarperCollins.

O'Donovan, W. (2000). *Biblical Christianity in modern Africa.* Carlisle: Paternoster Publishing.

Olthuis, J. H. (Ed.). (1997). *Knowing other-wise: Philosophy at the threshold of spirituality.* New York: Fordham University Press.

Onvlee, L. (1973). *Cultuur als antwoord.* (Verzamelde opstellen van prof. L. Onvlee uitgegeven ter gelegenheid van zijn tachtigste verjaardag.)

's-Gravenhage: Nijhoff.
Rüsen, J. (2005). How to compare cultures? The case of historical thinking. *Koers,* 70(2), 265-286.
Saccone, R. (1994). *The business of Korean culture.* New Jersey/Seoul: Hollym.
Saul, J. R. (2005). *The collapse of globalization and the reinvention of the world.* Toronto, ON: Penquin.
Shadid, A. (2006). *Night draws near: Iraq's people in the shadow of America's war.* New York: Henry Holt.
Soderberg, N. (2005). *The superpower myth: The use of and misuse of American might.* New Jersey: John Wiley & Sons.
Suskind, R. (2006). *The one percent doctrine: Deep inside America's pursuit of its enemies since 9/11.* New York: Simon & Schuster.
Van den Toren, B. (2005, August). *Christ and cultures: towards a Christian theology and ethics of multiculturalism.* Paper presented at the International Symposium of the Society for Reformational Philosophy, Hoeven, the Netherlands.)
van der Walt, B. J. (2001). *Afrocentric or Eurocentric? Our task in a multicultural South Africa.* Potchefstroom, South Africa: Institute for Reformational Studies.
van der Walt, B. J. (1999). *Kultuur, lewensvisie en ontwikkeling: 'n Ontmaskering van die gode van die onderontwikkelde Afrika en die oorontwikkelde Weste.* Potchefstroom, South Africa: Institute for Reformational Studies.
van der Walt, B. J. (2003). *Understanding and rebuilding Africa; From desperation today to expectation for tomorrow.* Potchefstroom, South Africa: The Institute for Contemporary Christianity in Africa.
van der Walt, B. J. (2006). *When African and Western cultures meet; From confrontation to appreciation.* Potchefstroom, South Africa: The Institute for Contemporary Christianity in Africa.
Verbeek, G. (2005). *Recht in overvloed: Gerechtigheid en professionaliteit in de ontmoeting tussen arm en rijk.* Budel: Damon.
Walsh, B., & Middleton, J. R. (1984). *The transforming vision: Shaping a Christian worldview.* Downers Grove, IL: Intervarsity Press.
Wiher, H. (2003). *Shame and guilt: A key to cross-cultural ministry.* Bonn: Verlag für Kultur und Wissenschaft.
Wolters, A. (1985). *Creation regained: Biblical basics for a Reformational worldview.* Grand Rapids, MI: Eerdmans.

FUNDAMENTALISMS AND THE SHALOM OF GOD: AN ANALYSIS OF CONTEMPORARY EXPRESSIONS OF FUNDAMENTALISM IN CHRISTIANITY, JUDAISM, AND ISLAM

CLINTON STOCKWELL

Each semester in Chicago, I introduce the students that I serve to a particular text of scripture, Jeremiah 29:7. The text reads as follows: "But seek the welfare (shalom) of the city where I have sent you into exile, and pray to the Lord on its behalf, for in its welfare (shalom), you will find your welfare (shalom)."

The context for the verse is that ancient Israelites found themselves as captives and exiles in a foreign land. This people faced several choices. They could flee, and attempt to leave Babylon and try to make it back to the homeland, a fate that they managed to achieve 70 years later. They could rebel, and try to take over the political apparatus in the city, though they had little means to do so. Third, they could remain in the city as exiles, and do as Jeremiah suggested, live in and seek the peace and welfare of the city where they were exiled.

For Jeremiah, the pursuit of shalom was the goal for the ancient Israelite exiles. Though the Israelites of Jeremiah were exiled and captive in the ancient city of Babylon, they were encouraged, even mandated, to seek the peace of the city, for in its peace, they would find their peace. In short, it was in the collective interest of the ancient Israelites to seek the peace of the city where they resided, for their peace was interconnected with the peace of the whole. So, shalom implies interconnectedness, a certain interrelationship with a city (and society as a whole) and with other peoples who represent different histories and cultural traditions.

A *shalom* society means that peace is not only the norm, but it is the essence of social and political practice. It means that those less fortunate, including the "widows and the orphans," the "strangers and the aliens," and the "poor and oppressed" (all Biblical categories) are attended to. In short, rather than fleeing the city, Jeremiah implored that the exiles settle in the city, plant vineyards, build houses, raise families, celebrate marriages—to live in the city as "resident aliens" or perhaps as "situated exiles."

Several individual authors have written rather extensively about shalom as a Biblical ideal. These include, Jack L. Stotts (1972); Roger S. Greenway (1978); George W. Webber (1979); Nicholas Wolterstorff (1983); Bruce W. Winter (1994); Cornelius Plantinga (1995, 2002); and Mark R. Gornik (2002). These writers, among others, recognize that shalom and the call to pursue the peace of the city and of society in general is a mandate. Plantinga (1995) argues that shalom captures the ultimate intention of a God-willed society. Shalom is "the way it's supposed to be."

> They [Old Testament prophets] dreamed of a new age in which human crookedness would be straightened out, rough places made plain. The foolish would be made wise, and the wise, humble. They dreamed of a time when the deserts would flower, the mountains would run with wine, weeping would cease, and people would go to sleep without weapons on their laps. People would work in peace and work to fruitful effect. Lambs could lie down with lions. All nature would be fruitful, benign, and filled with wonder upon wonder, all humans would be knit together in brotherhood and sisterhood; and all nature and all humans would look to God, walk with God, lean toward God, and delight in God. (pp. 9-10)

Christian fundamentalism in the U.S.
In February of 2006, I had the fortune of attending a conference on: "The Psychology of Fundamentalism," in Chicago. It was sponsored by the Chicago Institute for Psychoanalysis. While recognizing the positive features of conservative religion, this conference nonetheless explored the impact of the extremes inherent in fundamentalism, particularly in the Muslim and Christian worlds. But even in the conference description, there was some latitude on the word's meaning:

> Religious fundamentalism is one of the most powerful forces in the world today. In some ways, fundamentalism improves people's lives. For many individuals, their strict religious beliefs give them a sense of meaning and encourage them to be caring and benevolent. But for others, fundamentalism can have dire consequences for adherents, as well as for those deemed "enemies" of the belief system.

Historically, "fundamentalism" described a unique historical movement in U.S.-based evangelical protestantism. Humphreys and Wise (2004) describe how in the U.S, fundamentalism was a reaction to emerging cultural trends in the US culture. The leaders of fundamentalism in America included a variety of scholars, including Gresham Machen, James Orr, and B. B. Warfield. They were not dispensational premillennialists. Warfield and A. A. Hodge were actually postmillennial. Warfield believed that evangelical work in the present would usher in the coming Kingdom. They represented a variety of theological perspectives, though Warfield and Machen were influenced by "Scottish Realism," or the "common sense philosophy" that gave 19th century Protestants confidence that they could discuss and argue via reason for the truth of scripture and for the God-hypothesis. Others, such as R. A. Torrey and A. T. Pierson were dedicated to evangelism and Protestant missionary activity.

Despite its diversity, as a late nineteenth century and early twentieth century movement, fundamentalism was a reaction to higher criticism, modernism, evolution, and theological liberalism (Sandeen, 1970). In its first use, "fundamentalism" was not viewed in a pejorative manner. It would be like stating what was essential, fundamental or necessary to the faith. It was assumed that evangelical Christians would be in wide agreement. The fundamentals included the inspiration and authority of the scripture, the belief in mircles, the virgin birth of Christ, and the deity of Christ. For the first group of fundamentalists, it was enough to believe simply in the return of Christ.

The name fundamentalist was derived from a 12 volume collection of essays written from 1910-1915 by 64 British and U.S. scholars and ministers, called *The Fundamentals*. By 1919, this group founded the "World's Christian Fundamentalists Assocation." After World War I, the confidence that Protestant missions would lead to world conversion, or the belief that progress and the march of the Gospel would bring on a millennial kingdom was on the wane. With the violence of the Great War, Protestants were skeptical that any social gospel would make a difference in the world. John Nelson Darby's dispensationalism and premillennialism began to take hold among those who called themselves fundamentalists. "In the 1920s, simple belief in the Second Coming of Christ qualified as fundamental, but in the 1930s one might have to believe in Christ's pretribulational and premillennial Second Coming" (Weber, 1990, p. 464). Premillennialists believed that the world was getting worse, and that the world systems would collapse into the battle of Armageddon, and the true believers would be raptured just before the Great Tribulation. Revivalists like Dwight L. Moody or Billy Sunday sought to save individuals for heaven, and were less concerned about making the world better for the here and now. Further, the Scopes Trial led to the 1920s "fundamentalist controversy" where fundamentalists militated against evolution and therefore, presumably, against science.

Scholars in the post World War II era like Ernest Sandeen or Norman Furniss saw in fundamentalism a pervasive anti-intellectualism. Fundamentalists also seemed to adopt a social ethic that decried movies, Hollywood, public drinking, smoking, card playing, loose morality, sexual perversion, and anything that seemed to challenge a literal interpretation of the Bible. George S. Marsden argues that the central characteristic of fundamentalism historically was its vigorous anti-modernism (Marsden, 1980). In the 1970s, evangelical scholar Francis Schaeffer argued that "secular humanism" was a grave threat to Protestant orthodoxy. Schaeffer went on to place the "pro life" (anti abortion) issue centerstage for conservative evangelicals. Schaeffer was militantly against abortion, and argued that abortion stemmed from "secular humanism" (Schaeffer, 2005).

Fundamentalists in the post world war II era embraced dispensational premillennialism, and this version achieved academic respectability at the Dallas Theological Seminary. Theologians who gravitated to Dallas placed dispensational premillennialism as the centerpiece of fundamentalist theology. Hal Lindsay, a graduate of Dallas, popularized dispensational premilllennialism in his book, *The Late Great Planet Earth* (1970). In 1980, the President of the Dallas Theological Seminary, John F. Walvoord, wrote a book, *Armageddon: Oil and the Middle East Crisis* (1980). In this book, Walvoord argued that Armageddon would occur in the Middle East, and this war would be the result of an international conflict over oil. Other professors at the Dallas Theological Seminary, like J. Dwight Pentecost, championed the writing of Biblical prophecy. In the past ten years, the authors of *Left Behind: A Novel of the Earth's Last Days*, Timothy F. LaHaye and Jerry B. Jenkins (1986) reintroduced "Bible prophecy" to a wide reading audience that has gone beyond the conservative evangelical reading public. Terms like "rapture," "millennium," "antichrist," or "second coming" are now part of popular religious lore. The "Left Behind" series now has twelve volumes and is a huge best seller.

Today, many fundamentalists have been on the forefront of the so-called "culture wars" in America, insisting that Christians should become involved politically to save America as a Christian land. Hallmarks of religious fundamentalism include the pro-life movement, Christian home-schooling, a belief in American exceptionalism, and a foreign policy that is determined in no small part by the particular reading and interpretation of Bible prophecy and the end times as advanced by Dallas Theological Seminary. While the bogeyman of American fundamentalists today is "secular humanism," fundamentalist writers link several issues together

> By the 1970s they had identified new enemies and supported new causes. They organized to oppose secular humanism, the decline of traditional values, feminism, legalized abortion, homosexuality, and the elimination of prayer in public schools. They even revised the old anti evolution crusade by sponsoring legislation to provide equal time for what they called "creation science." (Weber, 1990, p. 465)

Dogmatic believers sometime question the validity of science, demonize those who disagree with them, and some may adopt violence to advance their views or to react to threats. In the American Heritage Dictionary, there are two definitions of fundamentalism. Definition number one states that fundamentalism is a "protestant movement characterized by the literal truth of the Bible." Definition two states that fundamentalism is "a movement or point of view characterized by rigid adherence to fundamental or basic principles." Fundamentalism often combines literalism with absolutely certainty, what Roy A. Clouser calls the "encyclopedic assumption," the belief that scripture, and fundamentalist intepretations of it, reveal truth on every conceivable topic.

Michelle Goldberg, author of *Kingdom Coming: The Rise of Christian Nationalism* (2006), thinks that Evangelicals are perhaps 30 percent of the total US population, but that only 10-15 percent (half or less than half the total) are "fundamentalists" in the way she uses the term. Still, she argues that this group has a disproportionate influence on the U.S. government, and she is particularly concerned about what some have termed "dominion theology," reconstructionism, theonomy, and apocalypticism that together comprise a movement she calls "Christian Nationalism." This group is adverse to any form of pluralism, and believes that the doctrine of the separation of church and state is a contrivance to keep "fundamentalists" out of power. And note, what Goldberg is describing is not extreme sects such as the KKK or the various "Christian identity" movements, but rather evangelicals with power who are impacting US domestic and foreign policy. In another recent book, *American Theocracy*, Kevin Phillips notes how fundamentalist leaders have had a strong influence on George W. Bush's presidency, especially with respect to domestic policy (environment) and foreign policy (the invasion of Iraq and the single minded support of Israel) (Phillips, 2006). For these writers, fundamentalism has had a disproportionate effect on US government, particularly with respect to US foreign policy.

Jewish fundamentalism:
Zionism and the birth of a Jewish state in Israel

Fundamentalism is found in each of the great world religious that stem from the patriarch, Abraham. Judaism is divided into three main groups, Conservative, Orthodox, and Reformed Judaism. However, none of these groups should be confused with Zionism. Zionism is the Jewish nationalist movement that focuses on the rebirth and renewal of the nation state of Israel in the land of Palestine. Modern Zionism emerged in the late 19th century in response to the persecution of the Jews in Eastern and Western Europe. According to the Anti-Defamation League, Zionism "continues to be the guiding nationalist movement of the majority of Jews around the world." Further, it is probably true that most US residents support the Jewish state. There are many who have strong connections to a successful state for economic and political reasons. Also, many evangelical Christians or Christian fundamentalists' support for Zionism derives from their view of Bible prophecy and adherence to premillennial eschatology. These include "Christian Zionists" who are convinced that the restoration of the Jewish state is the fulfillment of prophecy (Merkley, 2007).

The origins of Zionism may be traced to Moses Hess (1812-1875) and Theodor Herzl (1860-1904). Herzl is the more significant figure. Theodor Herzl moved to Vienna in 1878 and received the Doctor of Laws from the University of Vienna. He first encountered anti-semitism while studying at the University of Vienna, and this experience colored his life. In the play, *The Ghetto* (1894), assimilation to the secular or Christian civilization was rejected as a solution. In 1894, Captian Alfred Dreyfus, a Jewish officer in the French army, was accused of treason. Herzl witnessed mobs crying "death to the Jews" in France. As a result of this experience, he began to argue that the only solution was for Jews to immigrate to a land that they could call their own. Herzl later published the book, *The Jewish State* (1896) to argue that the solution to the Jewish problem was not individual, but national and political. This was the birth of "Political Zionism."

The term "Zionism" comes from the hill of Zion, where the original temple of Jerusalem was situated. Zionists seek to establish a Jewish homeland with geographical boundaries. However, Zionism includes several orientations: "spiritual and cultural; work ethical; Marxist; and

Orthodox Jewish." The central motif is the notion of founding a homeland for the Jewish diaspora, which was in exile to Babylon, Europe, and the world since the sixth century BCE. Other motifs in Zionism include the expectation of Messiah, socialism (Kibbuttzim), nationalism, and Jewish religious identity. Zionists appealed to European powers to support a nation state in Israel. Early Zionism in Herzl's time was secular in nature, and looked for a nation like other nations.

Zionism in Palestine
Although not all Zionists are fundamentalists or racists, it is clear that Zionism reflects the convergence of two dangerous forces, fundamentalism and nationalism. Jewish historian and Zionist supporter Solomon Grayzel critiques the convergence of such forces in the Arab world, even as he minimizes it among Zionists. Grayzel (1968) critiques Islamic fundamentalism as follows:

> But nationalism's usual concomitants are racialism and religious uniformity. Consequently, the struggle for independence was everywhere accompanied by anti-Jewish words and acts, the excuse being that Jews were Zionists and therefore anti-Moslem. Ancient Jewish communities were broken up as a result, and obstacles were placed in the way of exiled Jews going to Israel. (p. 818)

Grayzel argued that the state of Israel was necessary because of the resurgence of Arab nationalism. At the very same time that a Jewish state in Israel was being considered, Jewish people in Arab nations such as Iraq, Tunisia, Morocco, Algeria, and other places were repressed due to Arab and African nationalism. Following the holocaust in Europe and liberation from colonialism in Africa and the Arab world, more persons were forced to migrate to Israel.

Not all Jews of course accept Zionism, and not all accept a Zionist interpretation of history such as one finds in Grayzel. In recent times authors like Israel Shahak and Norton Mezvinsky, *Jewish Fundamentalism in Israel* (1999, 2004); Ian S. Lustick, *For the Land and for the Lord: Jewish Fundamentalism in Israel* (1988); and most recently Gershom Gorenberg, author of *The End of Days: Fundamentalism and the Struggle for the Temple Mount* (2000), and *The Accidental Empire: Israel and the Birth of the Settlements, 1967-1977* (2006), have called into question the legitimacy and the impact of Zionism, especially Zionist fundamentalism.

For these authors, most Jews are not Zionists, and most Zionists are not fundamentalists. Zionism in this perspective is viewed as a skewed reinterpretation of Judaism and has been a chief force of destabilzation in the world. Shahak and Mezvinsky argue that Jewish fundamentalism in Israel is not as well known as Arab fundamentalism, which is virtually identified with terrorism; or Christian fundamentalism, which is influenced heavily by a literal interpretation of Bible prophecy and the end times (Boyer, 1993; Weber, 2004). Yet, Jewish fundamentalism is just as deadly and disturbing and is a major contributor to destabilization in the Middle East and the world at large. When Yitzak Rabin was assassinated by Yigael Amir in 1995 in Israel because the former "wanted to give Israel to the Arabs," Rabin's death was applauded by a minority in Israel as necessary for the sake of "true" Jewish religion. Such violence illustrates the danger in religious fundamentalism as a movement that focuses on preserving an ideal version of the past. "The basic principles of Jewish fundamentalism are the same as those found in other religions: restoration and survival of the 'pure' religious community that presumably existed in the past" (Shahak & Mezvinsky, 1999).

Shahak and Mezvinsky go on to describe characteristics of Jewish fundamentalism. These include a messianic tendency, oppositon to human freedoms, especially freedom of expression in Israel, support of occupation of Arab lands, support of discriminating policies versus Palestinians, the repression and oppostion to democratic values, and the condemnation of homosexuality and lesbianism. Further, Jewish fundamentalism has adopted an extreme form of Biblical literalism, arguing that the destiny of Israel requires Israeli control of all lands from the Suez Canal to lands West and South of the river Euphrates, including the Sinai Peninsula, Jordan, Lebanon, most of Syria, much of Iraq, and Kuwait (Brownfield, 2000). Christian fundamentalists (Christian Zionists) share the views of Jewish fundamentalists. They believe that it is Israel's destiny to control these lands as natural frontiers, and that the repression of Arabs and "sexual deviants" is consistent with a theocratic state. Not only do Jewish fundamentalists strive for religious purity and for geographic expansion, but they also believe in religious, moral, and racial superiority. Beliefs in superiority feed policies that discriminate against Muslims, alternative sexualities, and non-Jewish people.

Perhaps the most radical of fundamentalist groups in Israel in the post 1967 era is the *Gush Emunim*. The Gush Emunim (Block of the Faithful) is a right-wing ultranationalist, religio-political movement. It was formed in March 1974 in the aftermath of the Yom Kippur War of October 1973. A major focus of the Gush Emunim was to support and establish Jewish settlements on the West Bank of the Jordan River. From 1977-1984, the Likud Party (of Menachem Begin) gave Gush Emunim resources to develop settlements on the West Bank. This group believes that the West bank is part of Biblical Judea, and along with Samaria, constitute the lands of ancient Israel. Because Gush Emunim believes in "the literal truth of the Bible and total commitment to the precepts of modern secular Zionism, it may be called Zionist fundamentalism" (Sprinzak, 1986, p. 4). Zionism was historically a secular movement, but the Gush Emunim succeeded in combining the idea of a nation-state with religious fundamentalism.

Adherents to Gush Emunim ideology are opposed to democracy and to the rule of civil law. Like fundamentalists in Christianity and in Islam, this group appeals to a "higher" religious ideology. They believe that their interpretation of the Torah transcends democracy and the laws of a secular state (secular humanism again). Officially, democracy is acceptable as long as it can be practiced in the context of Zionism, but if the two polities collide, Zionism takes precedence. Zionists are willing to tolerate a civil society in the interim, but in the end, like other fundamentalist movements, they look to a theocratic state ruled by a strict interpretation of the Torah.

Today the political and spiritual principles of the Gush Emunim are prevalent in Israel. For Sprinzak (1986), "it would not be erroneous to speak today of the invisible kingdom of the Gush Emunim, which is acquiring the character of a state within a state" (p. 19). In 1978, Amana, Gush Emunim's official settlement organization, was established. Amana was able to gain political support from Menachem Begin, and Ariel Sharon worked with Amana while aggressively pursuing a "creeping annexation" of "Biblical" lands (Sprinzak, 1986, p. 23). However, Gush Emunim was never completely happy with Likud, because it perceived Begin and Sharon as too secular, lacking Gush's religious perspective.

Lustick believes that Jewish fundamentalism is wider than the Gush Emunim. However, he concedes that the Gush Emunim captures the basic force and ideology of Jewish extremism in Israel. He writes that for all practical purposes, contemporary Jewish fundamentalist ideology in Israel is "the ideology of Gush Emunim" (Lustick, 1988, chapter IV). Jewish fundamentalism is grounded in several basic beliefs, including the sanctity of the land of Israel, its low view of Muslims, Israel's isolation rationalized as proof of its chosenness, and divine providence.

Among the core beliefs for Jewish fundamentalism is the acceptance of the "abnormality of the Jewish people." Lustick notes that Leo Pinsker and Theodor Herzl argued that the Jews should become like other nations, a nation within other nations. This was essentially a secular solution to a global political problem. The solution for Herzl was not to assimilate but rather to establish a homeland. Jewish fundamentalists go beyond Herzl by arguing that Jews should not seek a process of normalization as a national culture. Jews should embrace their own abnormality, and their own peculiarity. Key to this understanding is the notion of chosenness and exceptionalism. For Zionists, Jews are unique; they are not normal, and they are endowed with a unique destiny, distinct from every nation that has ever existed. For Jewish fundamentalists, their religious values could not be found in civil society or even in reason, but in a "theonomous scale rooted in the will of the Divine architect of the universe and its moral order . . ." (cit. Lustick, 1988, IV, p. 2).

Jewish fundamentalists eschew the vain search for normalcy. Rather, they see themselves as unique, special carriers of the divine purpose of redemption for themselves and for the earth as a whole. Their ideology supports not only national defense but military aggression if it means that their destiny is to be fulfilled. "It is this intimate connection between what is felt as transcendentally imperative and what is perceived as one's personal, political duty, that is the distinguishing mark of a fundamentalist political vision" (Lustick, 1988, IV, p. 11).

The danger of the fundamentalist mind is its conviction that reality is bound to follow ideology and not vice versa. Facts can therefore simply be disregarded. For Jewish fundamentalists, the Palestinians do not exist, the Arab countries do not count, world public opinion is rubbish, and the U.S government is merely a nuisance. The only reality that counts is Jewish redemption, which is imminent—to be realized by a massive *aliyah*, the negation of the Diaspora, and the building of the Third Temple. Throughout Jewish history there have been true believers like Gush Emunim who were convinced that the Messiah was at the door. Fortunately these messianic believers were in most cases few and isolated. Their messianic vision was not translated into operative political programs. However, this may not be the case with Gush Emunim (Sprinzak, 1986, p. 31).

Muslim fundamentalism in modern Palestine
Most Muslims are not fundamentalists, and even fewer are committed to a terrorist program. Neither is Islam a homogenous religion. For, not only are there Sunni, Shia, and Sufi groups in Islam, but there are many others. Also, Islam has historically evolved in very different ways responding to the divergent national contexts where Islam is found. So, Islam in Turkey is very different from Islam in Iraq, Iran, Jordan, Syria, or Egypt. Each of these countries has experienced a very different historical evolution of Islam.

Islam means to surrender to God, Allah in Arabic. It rejects polytheism. The word Islam is a derivative of the word, *salaam*, which means peace in its fullest sense. Salaam means freedom from all harm, so that the greeting, *assalumu aliakum* wishes the recipient peace, and specifically health or freedom from harm or danger. So, like Christianity and Judaims, rightly understood peace has an important meaning for Islam. Historically, there are numerous examples of Islamic tolerance regarding Christians and Jews as fellow "peoples of the book." The history of conflict between the world religions is not the only story of the relationship between them.

Like Christian and Jewish fundamentalists, Islamic fundamentalists believe that the problems of the world are the result of secularism. They believe that the path to peace and justice occurs only by returning to the original message of Islam. Islamic fundamentalists hold to a high view of moral purity, and are scandalized by Western permissive attitudes toward dress, sex, food, and material consumption. Many are resentful of Western presence and interference in the Middle East, particularly over oil reserves in Arab lands. Many also allege that the United States in particular sides exclusively with Israel, and has had a one-sided foreign policy against Arab interests. Fundamentalist Islam rejects the equality of men and women. It rejects secularism and rejects the doctrine of the separation of church and state. This is similar to fundamentalism in Christianity and Zionism. Further, some Muslim groups reject the right of Muslims to leave their religion, including in particular the acceptance of Christianity or any other non-Muslim religion. In some countries, it is against the law to proselytize or to even practice a non-Islamic religion.

Perhaps the most significant religious symbol of fundamentalist conflict among world religions is the Temple Mount in Jerusalem. Muslims believe that the Temple Mount is holy, as it was the place where Muhammed ascended. Christian fundamentalists believe it is holy, because, after the building of a new temple, Christ will return to the site. Jewish fundamentalists believe that the Temple Mount is holy, and that a new Third Temple must be built for the Messianic age to begin (Weber, 2004, p. 18). Jerusalem is a place of Messianic dreams and expectations. Gershom Gorenberg (2000) writes that such millennialist expectation is a prescription for violence.

> For redemptive Zionists, physically possessing Hebron, Jericho, Shiloh, Old Jerusalem, and the Temple Mount proved that the final act was under way. Watched through a very different theological lens, the conquest had the same meaning for premillennialist Christians in front-row seats. Both literalism

and the false hope of history's end fed the enthusiasm. Those two fallacies were joined with a third ancient error: That God could be owned by owning a place. (p. 248)

To Islamic fundamentalists, Israel is an alien body in the heart of Arab and Muslim worlds and the vanguard of Western hegemony in the Middle East. If the establishment of Israel in 1948 was the first major event in the recent Palestinian-Israeli conflict, the second event was the 1967 war and the defeat of a coalition of Arab nations by Israel. The occupation of Jerusalem and the West Bank has led to the wholesale displacement of Palestinians. Muslims believe that this has happened because of the impact of secularism on Muslims, and the failure of Muslims to unite and embrace true Islam.

A third event was the Islamic revolution in Iran in 1979. This is perhaps the most significant event in the rise of Islamic fundamentalism. The revolution in Iran demonstrates a successful development of Islam as a viable alternative to Western secularism. Iran has also provided the rest of the Muslim world with a model of what it means to be a Muslim-controlled state. In the 1970s, a fourth factor was the decline of the effectiveness of the Palestinian Liberation Organization (the PLO). The PLO failed to achieve an independent Palestinian state, and it failed also in uniting more moderate Muslims against Israeli settlements—what Goshem Gorenberg calls an "accidental empire" (Gorenberg, 2002). Abu-Amr writes that the PLO's "consequent evolution from ideological purity to political pragmatism created an ideological vacuum that was soon filled by [radical] Islam, the only available alternative" (Abu-Amr, www.palestinecenter.org, nd).

A fifth critical historical event in Palestine was the emergence of the Palestinian popular uprising in 1987, called the intifada. The intifada, for Abu-Amr, has been the most important factor in the rise of Islamic fundamentalism. The intifada defined Islam as a nationalist, political movement of resistance against Israel. Its political objectives became organized in the charter of Hamas, and have been characterized often by violent resistance to Israeli settlements with the goal of liberating Palestine from Israeli control. Abu-Amr argues that Jerusalem and the Muslim religious sites (including the Temple Mount) are holy, and that Palestinians must control these sites. Writes Abu-Amr (1995):

> Israel's declared insistence on considering a "united Jerusalem" as the eternal capital of Israel is likely to complicate efforts at finding a common denominator between the Palestinians and the Israelis regarding an acceptable agreement on the city . . . . Jerusalem may continue to be an issue of se-

vere contention between the two sides . . . . If control over Arab Jerusalem, and definitely over Muslim religious sites, is not granted to the Palestinians, the Arabs, or the Muslims, the city will remain a source and a symbol for Muslim resentment, indoctrination, mobilization and perhaps agitation and struggle.

John L. Esposito (2005) calls Islamic fundamentalism "Islamic Revivalism" and outlines its "ideological worldview" as follows:
- Islam is a total and comprehensive way of life. Religion is to be integrated to politics, law, and society.
- The failure of Muslim societies is due to its departure from the straight path of Islam and its acceptance of Western values and secularism.
- Renewal of society requires a return to Islam, the Quran, and the teachings of the prophet Muhammed.
- Western inspired civil codes must be replaced by Islamic law.
- Although Westernization is condemned, science is not, although science is to be subordinated to Islamic beliefs and values.
- The process of Islamization requires a struggle against corruption and social injustice (jihad) (p. 165).

Esposito notes that Islamic fundamentalism often goes beyond even these tenets to urge adherents to fight Zionism, the Western crusader mentality, and to move toward establishing an Islamic system of government. As such, a jihad against unbelievers is warranted, even necessary, and Christians and Jews are generally regarded as "infidels" because of their connections with Western neo colonialism and Zionism. A major goal is to rid Muslim lands of these forces of colonization (Esposito, 2005, p. 166).

Conclusion

Fundamentalisms of all faiths share some similar characteristics. They reject modernism and with it, secularism. They seek to return to a former utopian era and to the root teachings of their faith. As a result, fundamentalists yearn for a previous era, even a state that returns to "conventional, agrarian gender roles, putting women back in their veils and into the home" (Armstrong, 2002, p. 166). In more extreme forms, fundamentalism attempts to replace secularism with some form of theocratic state, be it Zionism in Israel, Sharia law in Islam or "Christian nationalism" in the U.S. Moreover, fundamentalists seem to share a literalism and an encyclopedic breadth when it comes to the interpretation of a sacred scripture. They seek clarity and certainty when certainty is illusory. They tend to believe that only a particular "chosen" group of people can interpret scripture in the right way. As Gorenberg (2000) points out, such literalism is not only dangerous, but could turn out violently, particularly for groups who are disappointed that a timeline for the end times has not materialized, and as a result they may believe that it is up to them to help the process along.

> We live in a time when extremism is confused with religious authenticity, and not just in Protestantism. Purveyors of "literal" readings of sacred books claim to represent old-time religion, unadulterated by modernity. Yet literalism, apparently a mark of a conservative, is often the method of millennialists who look forward to an entirely new world. They place prophetic texts at the center of religion—and insist that the words must be read as factual, tactile accounts of the future. (p. 245)

Fundamentalism is a widespread phenomena. Although as a movement, it began in the United States with the "fundamentalist controversy" of the early 19th century, fundamentalism as a religious ideology described here has been around since tribal and prehistoric times. While not all Jews, Muslims or Christians are fundamentalists, and not all fundamentalists are violent, fundamentalism is nonetheless a powerful and pervasive force in the world today.

In 1893, Chicago hosted the World's Parliament of Religions. It was perhaps the first time that Hindus, Muslims, Christians, Jews, Zoroastrians, and others met and discussed their distinctivnesses and similarities under one roof—peacefully and civilly. Among the attendees was one Mohammed Alexander Russell Webb of New York City. Granted, he was an American Muslim, but nonetheless he perhaps raised a standard for all of the world's religions and for all the world's peoples to emulate.

> We should only judge of the inherent tendencies of a religious system by observing carefully and without prejudice its general effects upon the character and habits of those who are intelligent enough to understand its basic principles, and who publicly profess to teach and follow it. If we find that their lives are clean and pure and full of love and charity, we may fairly say that their religion is good. If we find them given to hypocrisy, dishonesty, uncharitableness, and intolerance, we may safely infer that there is something wrong with the system they profess. (Mohammed Webb, cit. Hansen, 1894, p. 524)

The Shalom of God as described in the Old Testament strives for similar goals. Shalom in the Old Testament describes a peace that is interconnected with prosperity, and this prosperity ideally extends to all members of a society. Today, in response to the conflicts that exist between religions and other social groups, we desperately need a theology and a worldview that can somehow foster a respectful meeting of peoples across boundaries and ideologies with the charitableness that Imam Webb describes.

If shalom means peace, prosperity and well-being for each constituent member, including the immigrant (sojourner/alien) or the the poor (widow and orphan), then to what extent can any nation-state measure up to the standard of God's shalom? The Torah demands that the most vulnerable be protected, and this protection extends particularly to the most vulnerable of any society (usually widows and orphans, certainly women and children). The great text regarding the judgment of the nations found in Matthew chapter 25 in the New Testament is an expression of this standard. There, the question is whether or not a nation-state has provided for the thirsty, the homeless, the hungry, the sick and the imprisoned. Shalom is therefore the standard by which nations are judged.

A "shalom" society is a society where even the visitor is protected, where even the "alien" and the "enemy" can prosper. Shalom means that all peoples can come to the table to dine and share gifts with one another. The Old Testament notion of shalom is not just a good idea, but it could be a norm and a standard for all nations, especially for those who represent the Abrahamic religions. For Cornelius Plantinga, Jr, shalom is therefore not merely a plausible norm for society. Rather, Shalom is "the way its supposed to be."

References

Abu-Amr, Z. (1995). The significance of Jerusalem: A Muslim perspective. *Palestine-Israel journal.* Retrieved September 11, 2006, from http://www.pij.org/details.php?id=646

Armstrong, K. (2002). *Islam: A short history.* New York: Modern Library.

Boyer, P. S. (1992). *When time shall be no more: Prophecy belief in modern American culture.* New York: Harvard University Press.

Brown, C. (General Editor). (1976). *The new international dictionary of New Testament theology, volume II.* Grand Rapids, MI: Zondervan.

Esposito, J. L. (2005). *Islam: The straight path.* New York: Oxford University Press.

Esposito, J. L. (2002). *What everyone needs to know about Islam.* New York: Oxford University Press.

Goldberg, M. (2006). *Kingdom coming: The rise of Christian nationalism.* New York: W.W. Norton.

Gorenberg, G. (2006). *The accidental empire: Israel and the birth of the settlements, 1967-1977.* New York: Times Books.

Gorenberg, G. (2000). *The end of days: Fundamentalism and the struggle for the Temple Mount.* New York: Oxford University Press.

Gornik, M. R. (2002). *To live in peace: Biblical faith and the changing inner city.* Grand Rapids, MI: Eerdmans.

Grayzel, S. (1968). *A history of the Jews: From the Babylonian exile to the present.* Philadelphia: Jewish Publication Society of America.

Greenway, R. S. (1979). *Apostles to the city: Biblical strategies for urban mission.* Grand Rapids, MI: Baker Book House.

Hanson, J. W. (Ed.). (1894). *The world's congress of religions: Addresses and papers.* Philadelphia: W.W. Houston.

Humphreys, F., & Wise, P. D. (2004). *Fundamentalism.* Macon, GA.: Smith & Helwys.

Kimball, C. (2002). *When religion becomes evil: Five warning signs.* San Francisco: HarperCollins.

Lustick, I. S (1988). *For the land and the Lord: Jewish fundamentalism in Israel. Council on Foreign Relations.* Retrieved August 21, 2006, from www.sas.upenn.edu/penncip/lustick/index.html

Marsden, G. M. (1990). Secular humanism. In D. G. Reid, R. D. Linder, B. L. Shelley & H. S. Stout (Eds.), *Dictionary of Christianity in America* (p. 1069). Downers Grove: Intervarsity Press.

Marsden, G. M. (1980). *Fundamentalism and American culture: The shaping of twentieth century evangelicalism, 1870-1925.* Grand Rapids, MI: Eerdmans.

Marty, M. S., & Appleby, R. S. (Eds.). (1994). *Fundamentalisms observed (The fundamentalism project).* Chicago: University of Chicago Press.

McIntire, C. T. (1990). Secularism/Secularization. In D. G. Reid, R. D. Linder, B. L. Shelley & H. S. Stout (Eds.), *Dictionary of Christianity in America* (pp. 1069-1070). Downers Grove: Intervarsity Press.

Muilenburg, J. (1961). *The way of Israel: Biblical faith and ethics.* New York: HarperCollins.

Philips, K. (2006). *American theocracy: The peril and politics of radical religion, oil, and borrowed money in the 21st century.* New York: Viking.

Plantinga, C. Jr. (2002). *Engaging God's world: A Christian vision of faith, learning, and living.* Grand Rapids, MI: Eerdmans.

Plantinga, C. Jr. (1995). *Not the way it's supposed to be: A breviary of sin.*

Grand Rapids, MI: Eerdmans.
Sandeen, E. R. (1970). *The roots of fundamentalism: British and American millenarianism, 1800-1930*. Chicago: University of Chicago Press.
Schaeffer, F. A. (2005). *A Christian manifesto*. Wheaton, IL: Crossway Books.
Shahak, I., & Mezvinsky, N. (1999). *Jewish fundamentalism in Israel*. [Electronic version]. Retrieved August 31, 2006, from www.geocities.com/alabasters_archive/jewish_fundamentalism.html?200631
Sprinzak, E. (1986). *Gush Emunim: The politics of Zionist fundamentalism in Israel. American Jewish committee: Institute of Human Relations*. Retrieved September 7, 2006, from www.geocities.com
Stotts, J. L. (1973). *Shalom: The search for a peaceable city*. New York: Abingdon Press.
Webb, M., (1894). The influence of social condition. In J. W. Hanson (Ed.), *The world's congress of religions: Addresses and papers* (pp. 523-531). Philadelphia: W.W. Houston.
Webber, G. W. (1979). *Today's church: A community of exiles and pilgrims*. Nashville: Abingdon Press.
Weber, T. P. (1990). Fundamentalism. In D. G. Reid, R. D. Linder, B. L. Shelley & H. S. Stout (Eds.), *Dictionary of Christianity in America* (pp. 461-465). Downers Grove: Intervarsity Press.
Weber, T. P. (1987). *Living in the shadow of the second coming: American premillennialism, 1875-1982*. Chicago: University of Chicago Press.
Winter, B. W. (1994). *Seek the welfare of the city: Christians as benefactors and as citizens*. Grand Rapids, MI: Eerdmans.
Wolterstorff, N. (1983). *Until justice and peace embrace*. Grand Rapids, MI: Eerdmans.

RESPONSE TO CLINTON STOCKWELL

Cristian Buchiu

In *Bowling Alone: America's Declining Social Capital* Robert Putnam argues that the social capital of the United States is eroding and as a result, Americans are increasingly disengaged from political participation (Putnam, 1995). He grounds his thesis on the observation that while the number of people in bowling leagues has decreased, the number of individuals bowling has continuously increased. The phrase "bowling alone" has since become shorthand for the atomization and fragmentation of civil society. Putnam subsequently summarized the reasons for the erosion of civil society with a general rule: as modern society becomes more and more atomized, and as we are invited to rely less and less on cooperation with others, we tend to stay out of associations and participate less directly in the life of the city (Putnam, 2000). However, Putnam was not the first to notice the atomization and civic fragmentation in modern contemporary societies. It is commonplace to all those interested in a social analysis grounded in moral ontology that despite modern technical advancements, a certain sense of ethical and social void caused by careless individualism and ravenous consumerism pervades modern society. Many are tempted to argue that despite all its shortcomings, the past offered to humanity values that are now harder to proclaim. It is relevant to notice that this is the precise point from where fundamentalist rhetoric usually springs.

Professor Stockwell addresses this question in the historical part of his study. I agree with him that fundamentalists, while living in the world today, attempt to build a world that resembles the pastoral golden days of yore: "fundamentalisms of all faiths share some similar characteristics: they reject modernism and with it, secularism", as they "seek to return to what they believe to be the root teachings of their faith. As a result, they yearn for a previous era," and we know that some of them even seek a powerful state that would summon the undisturbed peace and perfection of the idyllic beginning of the world. Further, fundamentalists claim that the Golden Age can be reinstated by revolutionary and artificial means. Indeed, as Professor Stockwell points out, "the danger of the fundamentalist mind is its conviction that reality is bound to follow ideology and not vice versa."

Today more and more people, dissatisfied with the shortcomings of modern society and lacking participation in those particular communities of memory and meaning from which modernity developed, turn to the all-inclusive rhetoric of fundamentalists and reject modernity altogether. Fundamentalists take advantage of these dissatisfactions with a discourse rhetorically constructed to switch indiscriminately between categories of ideal and real, using elements of their faith to draw utopian, disembodied, and immaterial pictures of an unrealizable, perfect society. Fundamentalists of all religions accept only the faults of today, never the flaws of the past. Much of their social appeal comes from the precision with which they crystallize our most disheartening intuitions about the world.

However, to social analysts, there is always an exit. Putnam has been criticized for perpetuating the myth that the 1950's were the Golden Age in the United States. This claim is not completely accurate. It has been argued for instance that by ignoring such field studies as the *Middleton Studies* (Lynd & Lynd, 1937), Putnam missed the ways in which communities manage to "humanize" modern technology. The Middleton studies examined the social effects of radio, which turned out to be harmless on society in the long run. Similarly, today the web-blogging communities throughout the world are changing the political and social landscape of community involvement. The Internet, blamed for provoking social fragmentation and isolation, was tamed and turned into a huge public sphere, fully connected to the life of the city. Such developments suggest that new social relations in new social contexts tend to replace older dynamics in ways not clearly visible or evident. For example, no modern liberal democracy has been consumed by unsolvable social strife or unstoppable political or economical decay (Fukuyama, 1992).

The "shalomification" of society cited by Professor Stockwell seems to seek a city similar to that foreseen by Fukuyama, where peace and welfare are the fundamental values in society. It is especially comforting to know that sociological theories can be translated into a language of values, and that there is a close connection between larger historical processes and the moral values and imperatives of religious traditions we share. Nevertheless, how does one deal with societies where fundamentalism appears to become more and more entrenched?

Fukuyama (2006) recognizes four substantial challenges to his scenario of a peaceful post-history. The first challenge, which is equally shared in Professor Stockwell's paper, is Islam and particularly Islamic fundamentalism (by extension any religious fundamentalism used for political ends). Fukuyama is not convinced that Islam is necessarily hostile toward democracy, but rather builds on Alfred Stepan's observation that the so-called Muslim exception is rather an Arab exception (Stepan, 2003). Fukuyama (2006) also believes that radical Islamism "is best understood as a political ideology" which "emerges precisely when traditional cultural identities are disrupted by modernization and a pluralistic democratic order that creates a disjuncture between one's inner self and external social practice" (p. 378).

In general, fundamentalist groups tend to be born through the clash between modernity and religion. Note a temporary dimension linked with this process: usually duration of the religion's exposure to modernity is in inverse ratio to the intensity of the radical rhetoric it spawns. In Fukuyama's (2006) view, the greatest peril in overcoming this challenge might come not only from the fundamentalists themselves, but also through the lack of "moderation and good judgment" from world political leaders, "something that is not automatically guaranteed by the modernization process itself" (p. 379).

In conclusion, if we strive for "shalomification," then we must take into account the warning of Professor Philip Jenkins (2003):

> By any reasonable assessment of numbers, the most significant transformation of Christianity in the world today is not the liberal Reformation that is so much desired in the North. It is the Counter-Reformation coming from the global South. And it is very likely that in a decade or two neither component of global Christianity will recognize its counterpart as fully or authentically Christian. (p. 221)

The future has never ceased to be open and still has a lesson or two to teach us.

References

Fukuyama, F. (2006). After the end of history. In F. Fukuyama, *The end of history and the last man* [with a new afterword] (p. 432). New York: The Free Press.

Fukuyama, F. (1992). *The end of history and the last man*. New York: The Free Press.

Jenkins, P. (2003). *The next Christendom: The coming of global Christian-*

ity. New York: Oxford University Press.

Lynd, R. S., & Lynd, H. M. (1929). *Middletown: A study in American culture*. New York: Harcourt Brace.

Lund, R. S., & Lynd, H. M. (1937). *Middletown in transition: A study in cultural conflicts*. New York: Harcourt Brace.

Putnam, R. (1995). Bowling alone: America's declining social capital. *Journal of Democracy*, 6(1), 65-78.

Putnam, R. (2000). *Bowling alone: The collapse and revival of American community*. New York: Simon & Schuster.

Stepan, A. C. (2003). An 'Arab' more than a 'Muslim' democracy gap. *Journal of Democracy*, 14(3), 30-44.

RESPONSE TO CLINTON STOCKWELL

Daniel S. Shishima

Preliminary Remarks
I found this paper very interesting and educative. It represents the work of a well-researched scholar. The paper has discussed a contemporary burning issue in religious circles.

Summary of the paper
The paper is an analysis of the cultural current in the US and the world at large. It has vividly discussed the rise of fundamentalisms in the United States and the world over. Stockwell identifies and discusses four dominant ideological movements: fundamentalism, nation-alism/imperialism, secularism, and pluralism.

Stockwell analyzes fundamentalisms in three religions using the concepts of Shalom and the Torah. All four ideological movements merge into one—fundamentalism.

Comments
Fundamentalism is a worldwide issue. In Nigeria, fundamentalism is practised by Christianity and Islam. African religion does not practise fundamentalism, at least in the open.

In Christianity, fundamentalism is practised in different ways especially by religious groups called the Pentecostal churches. Pentecostals believe in the Pentecost out-pouring of the Holy Spirit. These churches believe the Spirit is still manifesting itself on people practically and openly. The Pentecostals are also called Hallelujah churches because of their frequent use of the word more than orthodox churches such as the Catholics, Baptists, Methodists, and the NKST.

The Pentecostals express fundamental tendencies in the way they preach. They believe that only in their churches can one get salvation. They do not relate well with members of other churches believing that such people are non-believers. In extreme cases, they do not even go to the hospital when sick. They believe in faith healing. The Pentecostals preach only prosperity and success. If you are poor or sick it is because you are a sinner. Otherwise, for the Pentecostals, a righteous person cannot be poor or sick.

The Muslims also play fundamentalist tendencies in Nigeria. All political appointments in the country have religious undertones. The Muslims believe that their members must occupy all important political positions. Also, several attempts have been made to introduce Sharia law as the only legal system for Nigeria. In some states such as Zamfara, Sharia has been successfully implemented. This has brought a lot of untold hardship on Christians there. Not only that, during their mosque sessions Muslims blocked major streets in cities causing traffic problems. Thus, fundamentalism is not only in the US but also in the world over.

Comments on the paper
X-raying fundamentalism in Christianity, Judaism, and Islam in the US and the world over is a worthy exercise. In fact, the paper has tried to achieve this. However, I think it would be better to reduce the scope of the paper to either one religion or at most two for a vivid analysis of the issues of fundamentalism in the world.

Consequently, I suggest that the title of the paper should read: "Fundamentalisms and the Shalom of God: An Analysis of Contemporary Expressions of Fundamentalism in Christianity and Judaism" or "Fundamentalism and the Shalom of God: An Analysis of Contemporary Expressions of Fundamentalism in Islam."

Furthermore, although your recommendation of Shalom of God for a solution to the problem of fundamentalism worldwide is good, it would be better to suggest a term similar to Shalom, which is more universal. The word peace is similar and applies to almost all religions so it is better to stress the word peace whether it is called Shalom as in Christianity or Judaism, or Salaama in Islam, or Bem in the Tiv religion, or Asomdwee in the Ashanti religion.

Conclusion
This paper has discussed a vital contemporary issue, which is a problem to most societies, the world over. The solution advanced, if properly adopted, would minimise religious fundamentalism in the world and usher in peace and harmony. The paper is recommended to all Christians, Muslims, Jews, and indeed all religious groups.

DEVELOPING A CURRICULUM, EMPLOYING A PEDAGOGY, AND AN ADMINISTRATION OF CHRISTIAN HIGHER EDUCATION THAT ADDRESSES COMPETING WORLDVIEWS IN SOUTHERN AFRICA

Moshe Rajuili

Introduction
It is a privilege and a great honour for me to have been invited to lead the discussion on how Christian higher education (CHE) could bridge the gaps between competing cultures/worldviews in Southern Africa. The part of the globe we are focusing on in this paper is made up of fourteen countries located south of the equator (as defined by the Southern African Development Community [SADC] trade, industry, and investment review).

In the North is the Democratic Republic of Congo and South Africa is the southern most member. Geographically, the area is roughly equal to continental United States. The population of this part of the globe is in excess of 200 million. Formally established through a treaty signed in 1992, the countries that form the SADC have as their primary aim economic integration, which will hopefully lead to a single currency for the region and a common market pact by 2015. As with the rest of the African continent, Southern Africa is characterised by a multiplicity of indigenous languages and competing cultures. The lingua franca's of this region are Kiswahili, Portuguese, English, and French.

In this paper, I will first explore representative samples of primal worldviews found in the sub-continent. I will seek to find why is it that they continue to play such a critical role in people's lives today. Secondly,

I will determine the extent to which CHE curricula could engage competing worldviews so that people in the region are mutually enriched rather than paralysed by differences. Methodologically, does CHE seriously consider issues raised by andragogy and an African approach to teaching? Finally, I will look at some adjustments that could be made in the administrative arrangements of CHE in the region in order to bridge the gaps between competing worldviews.

Common worldviews in Southern Africa

As a geographical entity, Southern Africa is very diverse in terms of its history, economy, and the cultures of its inhabitants. In this regard van der Walt (1978, p. 20) notes, "all Black people in Africa do not have the same world and life view and there are also white Africans and Africans of other colours who do have their own world and life view." Whereas earlier researchers (Callaway, 1970; Tempels, 1949; Willoughby, 1928) could with a measure of accuracy write about the African worldview, it is extremely difficult at this time to generalise about Africans and even about African culture.

Several factors contribute to this difficulty. First, the people of this region are spread over a geographic area approximately five thousand kilometers from north to south and the same distance at its widest point if we include Madagascar. According to Naidu & Roberts (2004, p. 1), the region is a plateau edged by many escarpments, cliffs or steep slopes. Its inhabitants are isolated by impenetrable terrain and the modern means of fast and effective communications are still inaccessible to the majority of its inhabitants.

Second, people of European, American, and Asiatic descent were introduced to sub-Saharan Africa by missionary pioneers such as Moffat, Livingstone, and many others (Latourette, 1975). The new arrivals introduced their own religious and social cultures. Others still regard themselves as Europeans or Americans after two hundred years and more of being in Africa. That is not to imply that the new arrivals disturbed what was once a tranquil monocultural environment. There never was one. Within each of the national entities there existed various languages and worldviews sometimes leading to violent encounters. However immigration, together with the fact that the native worldviews were marginalised and at times uprooted[1] as heathen and backward, has resulted in the exis-

---

1 Dachs (1973:59) cites Roger Price, a missionary who exhibited his ethnocentric ignorance of the African worldview when he advocated "the complete breaking up of the tribes (Batswana) ending the petty tyrannies of chiefs and chieflings and the semi-communistic ways of tribal life."

tence of competing, sometimes diametrically opposed positions.

Third, within the same country there are often clear fault lines between the urban and rural, rich and the poor, Christians and traditionalists. The differences are accentuated by a widening generation gap and ideological differences between men and women. All of the above categorisations result in a multiplicity of worldviews that stubbornly defy any attempt at reducing them to some monolithic African belief system.

Having said all of that, there remain some common religio-cultural motifs in the sub-region. These are in turn informed by various understandings of the world and the realities of our contexts. The African Renaissance project and the Negritude that preceded it are bold attempts at enabling us to understand our African reality. I will use AmaZulu[2] as a case study, convinced that their worldview and the challenges that they face are not too different from those encountered by other Bantu peoples in the SADC region.

The concept of a creator God

African cosmology acknowledges the existence of a supreme being or God who is the creator and sustainer of the universe. Prior to the arrival of missionaries, this God was known in the different countries as *Mwari, Modimo, Imana,* and *Mulungu*. AmaZulu referred to God as *uMvelinqangi*—variously translated as The One who came out first, the first outcomer, one who emerged first before the origin of all things. As the prior source of being, *uMvelinqangi* was believed by AmaZulu to have emerged (*wadabuka*) from a bed of reeds whose locale is shrouded in mystery, *ezindzulwini*. He was also referred to as *uQili* or the Wise One, or *uMdali*, the Creator. All that Zulu sages could confirm was that *uMvelinqangi "wa vela lapho abantu badabuka khona ohlangeni"*—that *uMvelinqangi* emerged or broke off from the reeds where all humans come from. This view of God, considered alongside other[3] appellations of him as the creator and the powerful one belie the common assertion that Africans cannot think in abstract terms.

Smith et al. (1961, p. 109) notes that AmaZulu used abstract expressions such as *uDumakude* or the one who thunders since long far off times—from the beginning—to convey God's power. Furthermore, they

---

2 AmaZulu, erroneously referred to as Zulus, are the largest ethnic group of between six to seven million people found mainly in the South East coast of Southern Africa in a province of KwaZulu-Natal.
3 Berglund (1976:36) adds expressions such as uMpande, which he says, is formed from a stem meaning a root. Also uNsondo or someone whose good actions are repeated over and over again like a wheel in motion.

referred to God as, *uMabonga-kutuk'izizwe-zonke,* The One who roars so that all nations are struck with terror. This happens, according to Berglund's informants, when the male thunder, *elenduna,* murmurs at some distance and then becomes louder and louder as it approaches. "This kind is not feared but looked upon with awe and respect" (1976, p. 37). The female thunder, *elesifazane,* on the other hand, was believed to be caused by *uMvelinqangi* when he was in a good mood. This is the type accompanied by lightning and heavy rainfall.

Smith cites Father Wanger as saying that in his (Wanger's) encounter with AmaZulu, he came across other hard-to-explain expressions even among AmaZulu themselves for God, such as *Icibi-eli[n]omnqwazi-pezulu.* The probable meaning of this expression is that God is "the immense ocean whose circular head-dress is the heavens (horizon)." Other titles of God, such as *uZivelele,* He who came of himself into being, led Wanger to conclude that AmaZulu had "a God-name more philosophical and theological, more precise, and significative than any European people can boast of" (Smith et al., 1961, p. 109).

Recently, contact with Western philosophies, the rise of Eastern religions along the east coast of Africa, plus a general ignorance of the primal worldview have resulted in urbanised Africans developing a different concept of God. Eastern religions subscribe to an impersonal God, while secularism flatly denies the existence of the supernatural (Halverson, 1996). Belief in God has not been removed but has taken on new meanings. According to Meiring (1996, p. 13), some people in the region say that the God of Africa is an impersonal force, experienced as *deus otiosus,* uninvolved divinity or *deus absconditus,* the concealed remote God. Next to God in order of importance, are the ancestors.

The ancestors

Among AmaZulu, *uMvelinqangi* was believed to be too far removed in time and space to be approached directly by living beings. Consequently the people who were qualified to approach *uMvelingangi* were (1) departed members of their community who had (2) distinguished themselves by leading upright and exemplary lives, (3) died at a ripe old age, (4) left offspring, and (5) whose *izibongo* (praise names) were known. These ancestors were believed to have formed a hallowed company of the gods of the people and were known as *amathongo, amadlozi, izinyanya, izithuzi.* Ancestors were believed to have a more privileged access to *uMvelinqangi* than their living descendants did and could thus act as intermediaries between the family units and God.

Despite their privileged position as mediators, ancestors possessed limited healing powers.[4] Two of Maboea's informants, Sibeko and Sihlangu (2000) maintain that:

> God is still accepted as the only God responsible for their (i.e. traditional Africans) welfare and success. Traditional healers believe that healing, protection, success are not possible if God does not so desire . . . it is clear that they know that the power of healing is not vested primarily in medicines used. It is God's power that ensures protection and brings about healing. (p. 25)

A careful study of African languages shows that ordinarily ancestors were not worshipped. In support of this contention, and in relation to Batswana, Setiloane (1968) argues that:

> Africans, unless they have grown to internalize the "Westerners" views of themselves, strongly resent the suggestion that they worship *Badimo*.[5] They argue that the European word "worship" does not properly convey the same meaning as that "service" (*tirelo*) which they perform in relation to their ancestors. That service which is rendered to *Badimo* is in fact of the same quality and level as that rendered to one's parents while they are living. In Setswana: *"re direla Badimo"* . . . (we fulfill all proper duties to the ancestors) but *"re rapela Modimo"*, we pray to God. (p. 18)

To complete the picture, I hasten to point out that there is a very thin line that differentiates veneration from worship of ancestors. Their mediatorial function can and does become an end in itself. Many people in Africa do appeal to ancestral spirits for protection and good fortune (Lapointe, 1995). Among some Christian people, there seems to be little or no difference between the ancestral cult and the veneration of the saints.

The concept of time

The question of time management is a subject of constant debate in Africa. Many westerners and some Africans such as Mbiti (1969) maintain that Africans do not have a concept of chronological time and of the future. This view is supported by Meiring (1996, p. 12), who states that for Africans "life is lived in the here and now, while the future will be important when it becomes the present. There is thus little concern with making provision for the future." However, a careful study of African proverbs and sayings point in a different direction. Basotho have a saying that *koekoe ea morao e tloha le sepolo* (if you are slow on the uptake

---

4 See also Vilakazi, A. (1964). Zulu transformations: A study of the dynamics of social change. Pietermaritzburg: Shuter & Shooter.
5 Badimo is a Setwana and Sesotho expression for Ancestors.

you will be injured). AmaZulu have sayings such as *isisu esihle esibonwa yilanga* (do not use up everything today, remember there is a future), and *ungiza akazaleli* (procrastination yields no fruit).[6]

Long before the arrival of westerners in Africa, time keeping was highly prized. When a king or some important dignitary summoned a meeting, subjects dared not be late or else they would be fined heavily. On the home front, a young woman's worth was traditionally based on her ability to be up at dawn and have food ready by daybreak.

It is nevertheless true that with urbanisation and Christianisation there has grown a measure of laxity with regard to punctuality. Could it be that early church planting efforts, where a lone missionary who serviced many preaching points and would inevitably arrive late at the next venue, conveyed a wrong idea that late arrival at a church meeting is excusable? Over the years there has developed a common saying among African Christians that *uMfundisi ulindwa ngeculo* (keep on singing until the minister arrives).

The place and role of women
Both tradition and modern African worldviews allows little room for meaningful female leadership. Global statistics tell us there are numerically more women than men, yet patriarchy remains unchallenged. Naidu and Roberts (2004),[7] commenting on labour trends and unemployment patterns in Southern Africa, note that in the formal sector gender concerns have not been adequately mainstreamed into policy formulation and programme implementation. It is thus not unusual for major gatherings of African leaders, nationally and internationally, to be dominated by men and for women to form a pitiful minority often relegated to some dark little corner out of which they strain hard to extricate themselves. At times women contribute to their own oppression and marginalisation through uncritical acceptance of patriarchal culture. Petty jealousies or the so-called "pull her down syndrome" delays their emancipation. More importantly, within the church, not all Christians are agreed on how equality before the Lord works itself out in practice.

A holistic worldview
The African worldview precludes the compartmentalisation of life into secular and spiritual and the discrimination of people on the basis of

---

6 See also Nyembezi, S., & Nxumalo, O. E. H. (Eds.). (1966). Inqolobane yesizwe. Pietermaritzburg: Shuter & Shooter.
7 See Naidu, S., & Roberts, B. (2004). Labour trends and unemployment patterns in Southern Africa.

material possessions or educational achievements. This holistic view of life finds expression in greetings, which are always in the plural form. When an African meets another and asks, "How are you?" the "you" is plural. The respondent will go on to tell the story of his/her life, their well being and that of the family; the weather and state of the harvest will be thrown in for good measure to complete the picture. Moila (2000a, p. 39), agreeing with Tsele (1994), Moyo (1999), and Kinoti (1991), attributes the African holistic approach to their belief that "all things belong together by virtue of having been created and being sustained by a supreme being."

A holistic worldview means that individual morality cannot be easily separated from communal norms. Positively this means Africans had—and some still do have—ready access to external checks and balances thus reducing stress levels. Negatively it means the entrepreneurial spirit is severely curtailed. The unwillingness to take individual and unpopular decisions is aptly illustrated by the following African fable regarding the origin of death as retold by Rajuili (2004):

> Belief in immortality is based on an old African legend, with many local variations, that after God had created human beings, he sent a slow animal, AmaZulu say it was a chameleon, *unwabo* to tell human beings that they would not die or if they died, they would rise again.
>
> A second animal, *intulo* or a lizard was sent with the same message but in its haste to deliver the message, it altered it to say that human beings would die one day. It reached its destination and delivered the wrong message. When the sluggish first messenger arrived, death had set in, and AmaZulu were not open to receive the original message saying *sesibambe elentulo* meaning, we have decided to hang on to the first message received, a message of death. (p. 179)

Beyond social intercourse and communal ethics, the holistic worldview finds expression in African hospitality and mutual support when members of a community exchange gifts during betrothals, marriages, initiation, mourning, and other social gatherings (Moila, 2002a, p. 4).

Leadership styles and election patterns
A study of the post-independence history of SADC countries shows that the leadership styles of some of the presidents are characterised by intolerance to criticism from political opponents, a desire to live in material comfort, centralisation of power, and a selective recognition of the rule of law. The self-aggrandizing leadership style can be ascribed to bad lessons copied and internalised during the colonial period. It does result from a

feeling of being indispensable. Yet in other instances a dictatorial disposition could be due to a failure to distinguish between Western style democracy with its periodic elections and traditional leadership styles where the incumbent such as a king or headman holds on to power indefinitely. In church and Christian organisations this type of dictatorial behaviour often leads to splits and political upheavals in the wider society.

Therefore, given the multiplicity of worldviews outlined above and the fluid nature of many societies within Southern Africa, institutions of CHE would do well to individually and corporately develop curricula that are contextual and a pedagogy and administration structures that are flexible to allow for growth.

A contextual curriculum
There is abundant evidence that in recent years the worldviews of people in the sub-continent are undergoing important changes. With those changes, the people in the region are confronted by the juxtaposition of a numinous worldview in a secular environment; abject poverty in the midst of wealth; and the desire to solve African problems using African solutions, when for many countries the dependency syndrome remains strong. In that environment, we do well as Africans to note Eisner's (1985) conviction that "there is no single conception or aim for education that is suitable for everybody in all places forever" (p. vi). As African educators in the region, we do need to develop a curriculum that engages the critical issues that face us at this time in our history. Such a contextual curriculum, while addressing the pressing needs of the sub-region, should not be so reductionist that it fails to learn from other contexts and also take seriously the people involved and the content of the theological education in which they are involved (Pazmino, 1995).

A contextual curriculum is evaluated periodically. Cole's (2001, p. 36) suggestion is that such an assessment should be a collaborative effort of faculty, past and present students, and parishioners. Data collected from the community should be used by faculty to define curricular values. The beauty of this approach is that it is in line with the African worldview where consensus is prized in establishing norms and values.

Secondly, bear in mind that all curricula, contextual or otherwise, consist of explicit, implicit, and null elements. The explicit curriculum is the one outlined in the published school literature. It does not always account for everything that a school teaches. There is also an implicit curriculum, which, according to Eisner, has a more powerful and long lasting effect on the learner. The null curriculum represents what the school omits (Eisner, 1985, pp. 87-88).

Eisner's threefold curriculum has relevance for CHE in Southern Africa. In order for the church and the academy to fulfill its mandate to make disciples of all nations in the region and beyond, the explicit curriculum has to be a well-rounded one, engaging the head, warming the heart and strengthening the hands. The implicit curriculum ought to be instrumental in leading people in general, and in some cases theological students, to accept Jesus as Lord and Saviour of their lives.

However, in order to address the cultural gaps in the region, the null curriculum is one that needs closer examination. At its meeting in Bangui in September 1990, the Theological Christian Education Commission of the Africa Evangelical Alliance encouraged graduate schools to identify the needs of the church in Africa.[8] At that time, four broad categories were singled out—spiritual formation, the Christian home, Christian fellowship and accountability and, finally, the church and its relation to society.

It is my contention that such a curriculum omits some of the critical challenges that face the church in Southern Africa today. By contrast, the Nairobi Manifesto[9] is a more seminal document that balances piety with present as well as future challenges. With the unemployment rate increasing from 18.6 million (31 percent) in 1986 to 50.9 million (59 percent) in 2000 within the SADC region (Naidu & Roberts, 2004, p. 15), I would like to think that curricular offerings on the theology of work would help to counter the perception among many graduates and pastors that hard physical work is unfashionable and lowers one's dignity. Whereas work and economics were integral parts of 16th century Reformed theology, classical education, with its emphasis on cognition, has devalued work. This is very different from Biblical revelation where the God of the Bible is seen hard at work. Jesus and Paul did not shy away from manual work and neither did many of the apostles.

Similarly, a curricular offering on the theology of beauty might help instill a greater sense of pride in what are frequently drab church buildings and college campuses. The themes of beauty and excellence do not seem to feature prominently in college curricula. By contrast, God saw everything that he had created and was pleased with its beauty and per-

---

8 See Taylor-Pearce, J E. M. (1993). Contextual Framework for Theological Education, pp. 16-31 in V. B. Cole, R. F. Gaskin, & R. J. Sim (Eds.), Perspectives on leadership training.
9 The Nairobi Manifesto is a summary of the findings of a Consultation on Re envisioning Theological Education in the 21st Century. Over a hundred participants met at the Nairobi Graduate School of Theology in January 1998.

fection (Genesis 1:28). The Psalmist marvels at the fact that he is wonderfully and fearfully made (Psalm 134:14).

I am not convinced that our CHE curricula address the dependency syndrome adequately. At best, the subject is consigned to little footnotes in courses on church administration or missions. At worst it is left out altogether since "the natives still need us" and they, in turn, seem satisfied to hold up the begging bowl for a few extra morsels from overseas. Here we have a classical example of competing worldviews that mutually reinforce each other. Should courses on overcoming dependency, drinking from our own wells as it were, not take precedence over rarified discourses on such things as Martin Heidegger's philosophy of being?

Another serious omission in the curricula of many schools is a Biblically based course on gender studies. As stated above, women are the backbone of many of our churches in the sub-region, yet they do not hold any meaningful leadership positions except in independent churches (Ngada & Mofokeng, 2001, p. 47). Could the primal worldview of members of these independent churches enable them to remember that in traditional societies, especially the matrilineal ones, women were honoured and respected? Despite numerous resolutions on gender equity, many of the historic churches still find it difficult to allow women meaningful roles in leadership structures. Reflecting on this reluctance, Kapua asserts that women are often encouraged "to take minor positions that reflect our traditional roles, such as teaching in Sunday school, visiting the sick and the bereaved, raising funds (but having no control over them), cleaning the church, and cooking and serving food" (2002, p. 351).

Next, what about a fully-fledged seminary course on the church and HIV/AIDS? A global summary of the HIV/AIDS epidemic showed that in December 2002, 29.4 million or 70 percent of people living with HIV/AIDS were found in sub-Saharan Africa. (UNAIDS, 2002) Since the first infections were noted twenty years ago, the disease has now surpassed malaria and tuberculosis as the leading cause of death with an estimated 3.1 million adult and children's deaths in 2002. Unless urgent interventions are put in place, ambitious political and economic plans for the region will be severely hampered.

What are even more worrisome are various attitudes towards HIV/AIDS. There are those, even among the leadership of the church, who will neither teach nor preach on human sexuality lest they breach cultural norms. Others maintain that HIV/AIDS is the means by which God punishes promiscuous people. Still others have simplistic solutions to the pandemic maintaining that one just has to pray and abstain from extra-marital liaisons.

In response to the challenge of HIV/AIDS theological educators gathered in Kenya and in South Africa. At the Kenya meeting in June 2000,[10] twenty participants from fourteen nations were urged to develop a HIV/AIDS curriculum for their respective colleges. Three years later, a much larger group met in Pietermaritzburg, South Africa to share their HIV/AIDS intervention strategies as well as chart the way forward for a relevant HIV/AIDS curriculum. It was at that meeting that a Kenyan participant summed the purpose of the gathering by saying, "If you are not addressing the things that eat your people, you are not relevant."

It is, however, all too possible for seminaries to design a contextual curriculum that is subsequently taught in racially segregated centers. This approach is often justified on the basis that different students have different learning styles. The homogenous principle of church growth could also account for racial segregation in theological colleges. While not wanting to deny anyone their freedom to choose whom they will associate with, curriculum designers in Southern Africa need to remember that from the very beginning, the church was multi-cultural. Its leadership was drawn from the entire Mediterranean region and was made up of Jews and Gentiles, males and females.[11] Genuine inter-culturalism, which has gone beyond tokenism, should result in intercultural churches and societies where members will be enriched by perspectives different from their own.

Methodology

We turn next to consider the most appropriate methodologies that could be used as a vehicle to teach a contextualised curriculum. Because many churches in Africa grew out of wayside Sunday school classes meeting under a simple structure or even a tree, pedagogy, useful then and appropriate now for instructing children, tends to be indiscriminately applied in adult settings with disastrous consequences.

Unlike in Europe and North America, where the average age of college students is in the early twenties, African students tend to be much older, bringing with them a greater life experience to their tertiary education. Freire, Mezirow, Daloz, and other theorists of andragogy maintain that when adults return to higher education, the role of the teacher or mentor is to challenge the students to examine their assumptions and

---

10 This meeting was sponsored by MAP International, World Council of Churches and UNAIDS

11 Acts 11, 13; Galatians 3; Romans 16.

formulate new and more developed ones. That being the case, the different worldviews that characterise the SADC region are more likely to be addressed by an andragogical methodology.

Another very powerful didactic method that commends itself in this region is the use of proverbs and riddles. This teaching method was used in the past to convey information and change lives. A skillful use of riddles meant that the person being instructed became emotionally involved in the education transaction. Their pre-conceptions were challenged and they were open to new possibilities of truth. Furthermore, they developed problem-solving abilities, which are sorely needed in multicultural environments. The gospel narratives show how our Lord used parables, similes, and hyperbole to change people's attitudes. CHE instructors would do well to make greater use of such a methodology to transform the lives of their students.

Verbal communication does achieve some of the desired educational results. However, in a pre-literate environment such as is the case in many parts of the sub-continent, music, and dance are powerful communication media.

> For us liturgical music is much more than just singing a hymn after the reading or the sermon or the prayers. It is the experience of being caught up in a rhythm that possesses you so that you not only sing the praises of the Lord spontaneously and in harmony, but your worship of God expresses itself at the same time in bodily movements like swaying, dancing, clapping or humming. It is a total experience that unites you with the others in the group in an all-embracing movement of the Spirit. (Ngada & Mofokeng, 2001, p. 41)

Traditionally when regiments went to war, they maintained their unity of purpose in song. Women folk cheered them on by ululating. Even today African preachers, unless they have been too westernised, almost sing their sermons as do poets or praise singers who herald the arrival of a king or some important official at a public ceremony. The three-point sermon with sub-headings does not have the same effect of exciting and uniting African people from divergent social backgrounds and economic strata as does music and dance.

Moila (2002b, p. 22) agrees with Booth that African religion is learnt through involvement and assimilation. Booth maintains "this process of absorption and participation forms almost unbreakable habits in the child which are strengthened through wider participation and greater influence throughout youth and adult life." In traditional settings, children and young people were taught through active participation in domestic chores and cultural practices.

By contrast, a greater portion of the three or four years of study at seminary and Bible colleges is taken up with professors dispensing knowledge. Students pride themselves in the amount of books they have read. The driving force behind this highly cerebral approach to education is demands of national and international recognition. It was in response to this trend that Barth, cited in Banks (1999, p. 215), issued his famous diatribe in which he paraphrased Amos 5, saying of many theological institutions:

> . . . I hate and despise your lectures and seminars, your discussions, meetings, and conventions. For when you display your hermeneutic, dogmatic, ethical, and pastoral bits of wisdom before one another and me, I have no pleasure in them: I disdain these offerings of your fatted calves. Take away from me the hue and cry that you old men raise with your thick books and you young men with your dissertations . . . .

Africa certainly needs to produce more scholars but the greater need, at present, is for Biblically literate practitioners. Dissertations should be expressions of a grounded theology produced by students who learn by doing. Learning by doing is a methodology that Scripture constantly emphasizes.

Administration

We now turn to the third component of the intervention strategy, a flexible administration. Has the time not come for some of the limited financial resources of higher education institutions to be deployed in producing theological texts in the vernacular? How much longer should our region have to wait before the training and use of female leaders in church and seminary become a reality? Is the residential model, inherited from western, middle-class paradigms, still relevant in the face of a church that is growing rapidly, at least numerically? On average, the population of the different SADC countries has doubled in thirty years (Kritzinger-van Niekerk & Pinto Moreira, 2002). Can the sub-region afford the luxury of numerous denominational schools, each struggling to survive on limited personnel and financial resources? Are we seriously preparing our graduates to be hands-on people who will function effectively in the market place?

Africa is the only continent where higher education is taught in foreign languages. The standard argument that is often put forward is that there are no good theological resources to prescribe in the vernacular. Recently, I raised the issue of vernacular instruction with the CEO and registrar of a predominantly black university, whose theology department is about to close. The reply I got was that isiZulu would limit graduates' participation in a global economy. If that were true, I thought to myself later, why is it that Asian, Scandinavian, South American, Russian, and other graduates are making their mark in the global arena? I am inclined to think that the real reasons for not moving ahead with vernacular instruction, which scholars like Sanneh, Bediako, and others have been calling for, is that African scholars have far too many irons in the fire. Secondly, instruction in foreign languages accommodates the needs of the expatriate missionary. The overall result is that schools in the South continue to import books at exorbitant cost. Unless there is change, we in the sub-region will continue answering many questions that nobody is asking.

Women Hold Up Half the Sky—Women in the Church in Southern Africa (Ackerman & Mashinini, 1991) seeks to show that women are not mere adjuncts to the history and struggle for justice in Southern Africa. Until very recently[12] the contribution that African women made to our Christian heritage has not been widely acknowledged despite the fact that in some countries 70 percent and more of church members are women and children. Not so long ago Africa witnessed the election of the very first female president in Liberia. Gradually the belief that women's place is in the kitchen is being challenged in business and in politics. Sadly, the church and theological education planners have very grudgingly repositioned themselves to address gender issues. As long as our significant CHE appointments continue to be the sole preserve of men and as long as research grants are distributed by gender, the cultural gaps due to and sustained by patriarchy and intolerance will persist. Urgent administrative adjustments need to be made before theological graduates become social misfits.

Administratively it is easier to run a residential school than a distance education programme. In the former case, there is an added bonus when a school belongs to a particular denomination. The school day starts and ends at pre-determined times. Time tabling presents few hassles and financial support is easier to find. In a sense, all the ducks fit nicely in a row.

However, the world from which students come and to which they return defies any neat categorizations. On the one hand, the urban students are drawn from a multi-cultural, impersonal, fast-paced, noisy en-

---

12 See also Phiri, I., Govinden, D. B., & Nadar, S. (Eds.). (2002). Her-stories: Hidden histories of women of faith in Africa. Pietermaritzburg: Cluster.

vironment that is very different from the serene locality of many of our colleges. On the other hand, rural students, having been introduced to a comparatively easy and more attractive, leafy locale for extended periods, will naturally find it difficult to return and minister in their rural homes.

The Lord did call on his disciples to come ye apart and rest awhile,[13] but that did not necessarily imply three or more years of isolation in ivory tower settings. If we are to reach the teeming masses of the sub-continent with the Gospel, should we not establish a few strategically placed residential colleges that are linked to several sites of delivery located in the city, the informal settlements, mines, suburbia, and rural communities? Administratively such an arrangement will present a logistical nightmare. Thankfully, modern communication methods by radio, television, and e-mail can be used to supplement the written texts and face-to-face encounters.

In conclusion, three points can be made. Southern Africa is a vast region with a multiplicity of worldviews, which change slowly. In order to act as change agents and minimise the cultural divide, theology students need exposure to a contextual curriculum that creatively deals with the pressing needs of people in the various countries of the sub-region. That will be best facilitated when education planners put into operation flexible administrative structures.

References

Banks, R. (1999). *Reenvisioning theological education.* Cambridge: Eerdmans.
Cole, V. B., Gaskin, R. F., & Sim, R. J. (Eds.). (1993). *Perspectives on leadership training.* Nairobi: Nairobi Graduate School of Theology.
Cole, V. (2001). *Training of the ministry: A macro-curricular approach.* Bangalore: Theological Book Trust.
Dachs, J. A. (1973). Christian missionary enterprise in Sotho-Tswana societies in the 19th century. In A. J. Dachs (Ed.), *Christianity south of the Zambezi, 1.* Gwelo: Mambo Press.
Eisner, E. W. (1985). *The educational imagination: On the design and evaluation of schools programs* (2nd ed.). New York: Macmillan.
Halverson, D. C. (Ed.). (1996). *A compact guide to world religions.* Minneapolis: Bethany House.

---

13 Mark 6:31. In fact, no sooner had the disciples been by themselves in the boat that the crowds ran ahead to meet them at their next destination!

Kritzinger-van Niekerk, L., & Pinto Moreira, E. (2002). *Regional integration in Southern Africa: Overview of recent developments*. Washington D.C.: World Bank.

Latourette, K. S. (1975). *A history of Christianity: Volume II, A.D. 1500-A.D. 1975*. New York: HarperCollins.

Makobane, M., Sithole, B., & Shiya, M. (Eds.). (1995). *The church and African culture*. Conference papers of a seminar held from February 21-22, 1995. Lumko: Mazenod Press.

Mbiti, J. S. (1969). *African religions and philosophy*. London: Heinemann.

Meiring, P. (1996). *A world of religions: A South African perspective*. Pretoria: Kagiso.

Moila, P. M. (2002a). *Challenging issues in African Christianity*. Pretoria: CB Powell Bible Centre.

Moila, P. M. (2002b). *Getting the message heard: Essays in contextual theology*. Pretoria: CB Powell Bible Centre.

Naidu, S., & Roberst, B. (2004). *Confronting the region: A profile of Southern Africa*. Cape Town: Human Science Research Council Publishers. Retrieved September 4, 2006, from www.hsrcpress.ac.za

Pazmino, R. W. (1995). Designing the urban theological education curriculum. In E. Villafane, B. W. Jackson (Eds.), *The urban theological education curriculum* (pp. 13-22). Vocational Papers. Roundtable 1 held on June 4, 1995, in Boston, Massachusetts.

Phiri, I. A., Govinden, D. B., & Nadar, S. (Eds.). (2002). *Her-stories: Hidden histories of women of faith in Africa*. Pietermaritzburg: Cluster Publications.

Smith, W. et al. (1961). *African ideas of God*. London: Edinburgh House.

Southern African Development Community (SADC). *Official Southern African Development Community (SADC) trade, industry and investment review*. Retrieved September 11, 2006, from http://www.sadcreview.com/

van der Walt, B. J. (1978). *Horizon: Surveying the route for contemporary Christian thought*. Potchefstroom, South Africa: Potchefstroom University for Christian Higher Education.

RESPONSE TO MOSHE RAJUILI

Adrian A. Helleman

The need for Christian higher education (CHE) in Africa is greater than almost anywhere in the world. In a continent that is now about 50 percent Christian (Johnston & Mandryk, 2001, pp. 19, 21), and in a country like Nigeria, where signs for churches can be found every 50 meters or so along major roads in cities and towns, the number of people who need seminary and university training is growing exponentially. Moshe Rajuili's timely paper addresses some of the issues that CHE faces in, especially sub-Saharan, Africa.

Let me begin by underlining the importance of worldviews. As in many other parts of the world, "traditional," "Christian," "Muslim," and "secular" worldviews compete, change, and combine throughout Africa. For Christians or Muslims, a Biblical or qur'anic worldview is sometimes superimposed on the traditional one, with a secular worldview added as well. As I discovered many years ago, it is much easier to change a person's religion than worldview. Religion is directional in nature. Conversion, as the etymology makes clear, involves a "turning" toward God away from that which is not-God. In contrast, a worldview is part of the structure of created reality and thus participates in its fallen character. Shifts from one worldview to another are often slow, since they are deeply rooted for most people.

CHE has a crucial role to play in working out a Biblical worldview. In a 1998 paper titled *Is There Hope for Africa*, Joel Carpenter (p. 19) observes, "more converts alone will not make a difference in this suffering continent." What is needed, he adds, ". . . is the engagement of Christianity with aspects of traditional African outlooks and values. However, in many settings, Christian faith operates at one level, while some of the deep structures of traditional values remain untouched." Across the continent, he continues, many community workers and leaders stress that "deeper Christian conversion, which makes for a renewing of minds . . . is the key to social, economic and political progress in Africa" (cit. Hulst, 2004, pp. 19-20).

Such an engagement must deal with many of the traditional African concepts that Rajuili mentions. For example, "God" and "ancestors" are both important for African Christian scholars, as a burgeoning literature on these concepts proves. But this literature also shows that not all scholars agree on their usefulness for contextualization. The concept of "time" is controversial as well, as the growing critique of John Mbiti and others clearly illustrates. Western Christians can learn much from the holistic aspect of the African worldview. Similarly, many Westerners have individualized faith and neglected the Biblical idea of community. Africans derive their identity from community, although this sometimes becomes distorted into collectivism. Africans, however, can learn much from Westerners when it comes to women and leadership styles. CHE needs to promote the issue of women not only through the curricula but also by encouraging more women to engage fully in the life of the universities or seminaries. As Rajuili affirms, these concepts are important for formulating CHE curricula.

Leadership and HIV/AIDS are two other important issues. Throughout Africa, one can find the "big man" syndrome. It is evident not only in the state but also in the church, where many pastors neglect the servant model of leadership that Jesus Christ displayed. On the contrary, they demand a large house, fancy car, and other trappings of success. Nigeria may be one of the few countries where people enter the Christian ministry in order to become rich. The false "prosperity gospel" has played a key role in fostering such expectations. CHE should indeed do more to change the attitudes toward HIV/AIDS. CHE ought to promote abstinence and faithfulness, as is already happening in the University of Jos' graduate-level program on HIV/AIDS.

In addition to the issues that Rajuili mentions, CHE should also deal with the environment and corruption. In Africa, it is easy to excuse misuse of the environment as an issue that only the West needs to address, since it is largely responsible for much of the global warming and can afford to pay for the necessary cleanup. That excuse must be rejected. China will soon overtake the United States as the world's biggest producer of greenhouse gases, while India is not far behind ("The heat is on," 2006, p. 9). Similarly, on the problem of corruption it is inappropriate for African countries to blame their former colonial masters entirely more than forty years after gaining independence. This is akin to a grownup man, when caught stealing, blaming his parents and society for a lifetime of crime.

These are all important curricular concerns that CHE should address. A contextualized curriculum is not enough, however; an appropriate pedagogy is also required. New teaching methods that make use of proverbs, riddles, music, and dancing will need to be developed, as Rajuili suggests. I also agree with him on the importance of learning by doing. For example, when I taught at a seminary in Philippines, students were required to be involved at the same time in church work, and I was involved in supervising both students and an emerging church. Students must not only learn by doing but also do something with what they learn.

However, I am not convinced that teaching at the tertiary level should be done in the vernacular, as Rajuili and an impressive list of African scholars advocate. In Nigeria, for example, more than 490 languages are spoken, although 96 percent of the population uses one of 21 major languages (Johnston & Mandryk, 2001, p. 488). Because this multiplicity of languages exists in much of West Africa, there is no other viable alternative to using English in universities and seminaries. The use of vernacular languages, while appealing to students, would pose almost insurmountable barriers to faculty not competent in those languages. It would also isolate African universities and seminaries from dialogue with the rest of the world. Already many Nigerian students have no reading ability in any European language other than English, while in theology there is little or no literature available in any vernacular language. Therefore, I seriously doubt that the use of vernacular languages will improve university-level education in Africa.

Finally, I question Rajuili's assertion that the implicit curriculum of a school "ought to be instrumental in leading people . . . to accept Jesus as Lord and Saviour of their lives." I hope that I have not misunderstood him on this crucial point. If I have, I beg his indulgence. I do want to point out, however, that a Christian school through its curriculum, pedagogical methods and administrative style should witness to the triune God who created this world, redeemed it in Christ and is renewing it through the Holy Spirit. For me, as someone who comes from the Kuyperian tradition, the purpose of Christian education at any level is not primarily evangelistic, in the sense of converting people to Christ. Evangelism is the task of the church, not only as an institution but also as a body of believers. The school can and must witness to God, but it is not intended primarily for evangelism. In Nigeria, if I may use it as an example, I may teach the Christian faith openly, but I am not allowed to proselytize. Muslims, for one, would be very upset if I did try to do that. That does not mean that I must leave Christ outside the classroom, in contrast to secular universities in North America, but even with the greater openness that I enjoy in Nigeria, I am not permitted to try to convert my students to the Christian faith.

In conclusion, I want to express my appreciation to Rajuili for a thought-provoking paper. He has raised many significant issues, even if I cannot agree with him on every one of the solutions he proposes. May God richly bless our efforts to promote his kingdom in the area of CHE!

References

Carpenter, J. (1998). Is there hope for Africa? In J. Hulst (Ed.), *Christian world view and scholarship* (pp. 19-20). Melbourne, Australia: Amani.

Johnstone, P., & Mandryk, J. (2001). *Operation world: 21st century edition*. Waynesboro, GA: Paternoster Publishing.

Rubingh, E. (1969) *Sons of Tiv: A study of the rise of the church among the Tiv of central Nigeria*. Grand Rapids, MI: Baker Book House.

The heat is on. (2006, September 9). *The Economist*, p. 9.

RESPONSE TO MOSHE RAJUILI

Peter Tze Ming Ng

I would like to express my sincere gratitude to Moshe for his most informative and stimulating paper. He has given us a clear picture about the situation in Southern Africa, especially in describing the African worldviews—the concept of God, time, and the role of women in African communities. His suggestions for developing a contextual curriculum, employing an andragogical methodology, and seeking a flexible administrative structure are all very proper and insightful. Indeed, while I was reading the paper, I could think of many parallel situations in Asia.

I first draw your attention to some abstract thinking about globalization (a more Northernized or Westernized way of reflection), then I shall come back to respond with more concrete remarks (a more African or Asian way of response). Moshe's paper reminds me of the ideas of a Canadian sociologist of religion, Peter Beyer, who wrote about religion and globalization. In *De-centering of Religious Singularity: The Globalization of Christianity as a Case in Point* (Beyer, 2003, pp. 357-386), Beyer mentioned "the factor of cultural otherness" as one crucial factor in the globalization of Christianity in its confrontation with other non-Christian cultures. This is precisely what we can find in South Africa. Indeed, this has been a common experience of most of the missionaries in Africa and Asia in the past centuries. The first reaction of the missionaries was to identify non-Christian cultures as "pagan cultures or superstition," but nowadays we are more ready to respect and appreciate all these local cultures, especially when we are more concerned with our educational agendas. Another well-known historian of Christian missionary movement in Africa, Andrew Walls (2002), has also reminded us to be open to the diversity of cultures in a global context and he says that ". . . by cross-cultural diffusion it (Christianity) would become a progressively rich entity" (pp. 9-10). Hence, we need to take a more *open* attitude towards African cultures and trust that they may in turn enrich our faith.

Now I shall respond to the paper with more concrete remarks. Moshe's suggestions for engaging competing worldviews in Southern Africa include, exploring a contextual curriculum, developing an andragogical methodology, and employing a flexible administrative structure. For me, a contextual curriculum is an *open* curriculum. It is open for constant review, or as Moshe says, "evaluated periodically." It should also get more people involved in curriculum development and assessment. I admire the African culture of seeking "consensus" as a prized commodity in establishing norms and values. I am also excited to see that there could be "the null curriculum" which represents what the school omits. Contextual curriculum is open to new elements and any missing elements therein.

As for methodology, I must say I do not know what the word andragogical means. I cannot find the word in my dictionary, but I can guess its meaning. (Perhaps it would be something of the heart/mind, analogically or anthropologically, it would typically be an African way of apprehension.) Anyway, it must be an *open* methodology, which can accept all kinds of methodology available. Besides the ones mentioned by Moshe, I would treasure also the use of story-telling, self-discovery method and any structured sharing of experiences. The most important thing is that the students are totally involved, learning not only with their mind, but also their bodies and hearts, which would eventually bring along the transformation of their whole lives. We are told that African people are holistic in preaching and worship. I admire much of what our African brothers and sisters have regarding liturgical music, singing sermons, and dancing services. They surely would remind us that we need to be holistic, in not only exploring curriculum and methodology, but in the administration of Christian higher education.

Finally, a flexible administration is also an *open* one. The reference to *Women Hold Up Half the Sky* reminds me of exactly the same phrase we have in Chinese. I am sure it is true all over the world. In fact, women are holding up more than half the sky—say in many of our universities now. (While being a visiting fellow at Cambridge University in the fall of 2005, I was amazed to find that they had a brilliant and capable chancellor who is a woman, and she was launching a worldwide financial campaign to raise money for the 800th anniversary of Cambridge University. She went to Hong Kong in April of 2006, to meet their alumni in the Far East. She really was an energetic president.) Moshe is right in pointing out the need to provide more resources for training female faculty and staff. In China, we are proud to say that we already had women ordination in our Anglican church in China in 1940s. We had our first women president in Christian higher education in China in the 1920s, i.e. almost eighty years ago. Dr. Wu Yi Fang received her Ph. D. degree from University of Michigan, USA in 1928. She did not wait for her graduation ceremony but was immediately called back to China to become the first Chinese woman president at Ginling College in Nanjing, China. Surely, our female colleagues can do as much as we do and even better. I shall fully support the suggestion of a flexible administrative structure, which is open to those who are capable, regardless of gender, social and racial heritages.

In conclusion, I may quote a paragraph from a paper I presented at an Asian consultation and workshop in 2004 on the study and teaching of Christianity as a worldwide historical movement. The paper was entitled *Teaching Christianity in a Global Context in China* and in the final paragraph, I (2005) wrote the following:

> Indeed, the Christian movement is one, global and worldwide movement, drawing people from different parts of the world. The people are many yet they are one in Christ. However, in teaching Christianity in a global context, we are also struck by the fact that there are so many peoples from so many different parts of the world. Such a variety of peoples reminds us of St. Paul's letter where he says, "For the body is not one member, but many" (Corinthians 12:14). Though we are one body of Christ, yet we belong to different parts of the same body. This imagery of "the body of Christ" helps us understand better the meaning of teaching Christianity in a global context. For though the Christian (global) movement is one, it is comprised of many different (local) parts; and the Christian universal faith embraces a variety of particular representations. It is in this way that we need to develop an open-ended approach to the study of Christianity globally. The teaching should be in such a way that it is not to create another form of indoctrination, but instead should *open* up a new horizon for our students to appreciate the readings of a variety of local narratives. (p.125)

References

Beyer, P. (2003). De-centering of religious singularity: The globalization of Christianity as a case in point. *Numen, 50*, 357-386.

NG, P. T. M (2005, November). Teaching Christianity in a global context in China. *Quest,* 4(1), 125.

Walls, A. (2002). *The cross-cultural process in Christian history.* Maryknoll, NY: Orbis Books.

TRANSCULTURIZING THE HUMANITIES IN CHRISTIAN HIGHER EDUCATION

José Ramón Alcántara-Mejía

Translated from Spanish by ILMES

I would like to begin with a generalization that is true in my country but may not be in other countries, so that my presentation may generate a wider sense of what is occurring in other universities in the "Humanities." I believe the phenomenon of globalization has meant a disciplinary movement in the institutions of higher education in the two-thirds world. In order to compete in the global economy in the area of the hard sciences, the universities of these countries have concentrated their resources in the productive economic and technological fields, the technical or administrative areas, and to a certain degree the social sciences for what they contribute to the others, leaving the humanities, and also to a certain degree the arts, with minimal support. Another possible explanation, besides the purely economic, is that the humanities have lost their relevance. In effect, the humanities had been thought of, since the middle of the 20th century, as the place where a type of knowledge was generated that gave identity and supremacy to Western Culture. Nevertheless, at the end of the last century, it was already evident that this role was being assumed by the economic structures that began to dictate what was relevant in university studies. Universities reallocated funds to newly formed disciplines, such as cultural studies, which assumed from a sociological perspective the task that was previously assigned to the humanities.

Therefore, this paper attempts to respond to this question: Is it true that the humanities have lost their relevance, converting themselves into an appendage of what is today called cultural studies, and can Christian institutions of higher learning follow this example; or can the humanities, under a distinct paradigm from critical theory, add something new to the construction of a Christian worldview that responds to the challenges of the 21ˢᵗ century?

In order to respond to this question allow me to sketch the historic development of the humanities as a preface to its present role. I believe that it is well known that before the fall of the Roman Empire, the reintegration of Western Culture was a task assumed almost exclusively by the Western Church. Therefore, it was natural that the Roman educational system would be retained and that it would persist during the Middle Ages until the Renaissance. The reason for maintaining this scheme was its usefulness to found an education oriented towards preaching. In this process, the discursive arts (grammar, rhetoric, and dialectic) were grouped under the name of *trivium*, in whose nucleus the incipient presence of Scholasticism can be perceived (Baldwin, 1928).[1] Poetics was assimilated by Rhetoric, then that was incorporated into Dialectics, which was simply a collection of literary fragments of classical models whose usefulness was essentially to be a source of preaching illustrations.[2]

In addition, we know that in the 5ᵗʰ century, in a treatise on the arts, Martianus Capella observed that dialectics demanded a central place in the *trivium* indicating that theology had begun to demand a more precise oratory instrument. Several centuries later, dialectics had become the fundamental tool of Scholasticism, and therefore, the foundational element of the *trivium*[3] (Baldwin, 1928, pp. 156-178).

The movement of the so-called literary disciplines outside of theological discourse occurred with the appearance of cathedral schools, where the education formerly located in the monasteries was concentrated. Education turned more cosmopolitan, and the preservation of

---

1 See also Curtius, 37ss.
2 It is significant to observe the successive places that these three arts have in the development of the trivium, which reflects the slow dominance of the formation of Scholasticism over eloquence. At the beginning, rhetoric held a preponderant place over philosophy to the degree that dialectic was considered part of rhetoric; but quickly grammar acquired a status similar to rhetoric until it was completely taken over. Given that oratory began to be at the service of dialectic, it passed to a secondary status in grammar since it was more important in the formation of the monastic scribes who in the Middle Ages were occupied with the preservation of Latin Scholasticism and of copying the Sacred Scriptures. See Baldwin, Medieval 91.
3 Change in emphasis toward the dialectic is seen in the 11th Century when previously unknown parts of Aristotle's Organon were incorporated into it. Therefore, the place of rhetoric is even more restricted so as to convert itself into a mere stylistic treatise, with which it ceased to be a dominant instrument in education. This is evident in Hugo de San Víctor (1096-1141), and in Metalogicus of John de Salisbury (1159), where we see the predominance of logic over rhetoric, which is finally assimilated into the grammar. St. Bonaventure (1221-1274) reduces the rhetoric even more to ornatus. By then poetics was frequently confused with rhetoric, which was also assimilated into grammar.

the Sacred Texts was converted into a monastic task. In this context appeared the association of scribes, the educators of the nobility and the newly birthed bourgeoisie.[4] With the passing of time, the scribes took over primary education and modified it in order to create what is called the *Studia Humanitatis*, what educators began to call Humanities.

The formation of new nobility and the new bourgeoisie required a restructuring of the medieval system of education, and this began with rescuing the scholarship and eloquence of the classical authors. The classical models acquired their own value; philological studies, oratory, and Greco-Latin historical moral treatises were converted into the basis of humanist education and as the model of conduct. All of these were aspects that the Church had neglected in favor of a theology that was more speculative and impractical in the new social and political reality of the Renaissance.

Humanism and the humanities emerge, then, as an alternative course to scholastic thought, poor preaching, and a decadent Christian life, even in the same monasteries (Kristeller, 1965). As we know, the humanism of the Renaissance is manifested later in the Enlightenment and from there to modernity. However, Stephen Toulmin (2002) questions a vision of modernity that is rooted only in 18th Century rationalism, as understood by Habermas, and traces the origins of modernity to the 16th century, when "writers like Erasmus of Rotterdam, François Rabelais, William Shakespeare, Michel de Montaigne, or Francis Bacon" (p. 45) already manifested a change toward a modernity mentality. We might add the cluster of humanistic Christians that began the Reformation, like Luther and John Calvin, or those like Francisco de Vitoria, Antonio de Montesinos, and Bartolomé de las Casas, who attempted to give another interpretation to the American conquest and others, like Mateo Ricci, who gave form to a more open and profound vision to the sense of culture in his efforts to evangelize in the Orient.

Toulmin traces a humanist current that, together with the development of an enlightened rationalism, remained active in Western thought as a critical attitude towards the excesses of rationalism. For example, Toulmin points out that the effects of enlightened modernity are manifested through the movements of oral to written, from particular to universal, from local to general, from temporal to non temporal, and from the feudal lords to the Nation States. However, the humanist perspective, including the Christian perspective, valued orality, the particular and the

---

4 See Smalley, B. (1978), 37ss.; Kristeller, P.O. (1965) 83-106; Colish, M.L. (1968) 161 ss.

local, and maintained the predominant role of history and art as instruments of knowledge and as political directives. Such an attitude lives with rationalistic perspectives and both characterize the development of the modernity. As Toulmin (2002) adds: "what is not clear is that these two traditions are seen from the beginning as competitive instead of complementary" (p. 77). Toulmin (2002) concludes:

> The key characteristics of the modern age had two distinct intellectual beginnings. The first is owed to Erasmus and the rest of the humanists of the Renaissance, who lived a time of relative prosperity and created a culture noted for sobriety and religious tolerance. The second beginning is owed to Descartes and the rest of the rationalists of the 17th century, who reacted to the economic crisis of their time—in that which tolerance was considered a failure and that religion was defended with the sword—renouncing the modest skepticism of the humanists and looking for "rational" proofs that would underpin our belief in a certain neutrality in regards to all of the religious positions. (p. 124)

One can observe in Toulmin's analysis that the humanist perspective always maintained a critical attitude toward rationalism and was precisely the ferment that at the end of the 19th century and the beginning of the 20th put the modern enlightenment in crisis.

The year of 1914 signaled the crumbling of the European enlightenment and the Nation-States that started the First World War. Enlightenment parameters were questioned at the same time in the fields of the arts, philosophy, science, and theology. Evidence of this is the beginning of vanguardism; but it would be simplistic to indicate that the vanguards were the only or the most significant group to question the Enlightenment. Humanism, in contrast to the anti-rationalistic criticism of the vanguard, maintains the role of reason as a critical instrument of the same enlightened rationality. The great pillars of modern humanism, from Blaise Pascal to Paul Ricoeur, without leaving behind Goethe, Nietzche, Marx, Freud or Einstein, although well fed by the Enlightenment were also intelligent critics of it. Because of this I believe that it is important in the critical discourses of postmodernity that the presence of humanism is also identified, which at the same time recognizes the validity of postmodern criticism. Far from realizing a negative criticism, it has proceeded to rearticulate its vision from a humanistic perspective.

One representative voice of Christian postmodern humanism is Nicholas Wolterstorff, who in 1983 asked, "How should a Christian insert himself into the present social order?", and proceeds to cite Lucien Goldmann, a Marxist thinker, who writes:

> The essential Augustinian truth and dialectic materialism is what we should

believe in order to understand reality and to act in a humanistic and efficient way, and it is for this reason there is no autonomous and independent Marxist or Augustinian ethic. (cited in Wolterstorff, 1983, p. vii)

It is interesting to note that Goldmann refers to what is today a neomarxist vision that is re-envisioning the Christian tradition as a positive cultural ferment. In effect, Wolterstorff, as with Goldmann, believes in molding beliefs according to the principles that come out of the same belief, and to mold is to create culture from a worldview, call it Christian or Marxist.

Therefore, it is evident that a Reformed perspective that is fueled by 16th century Christian humanism, views the transformation of social structures as an implicit process in the cultural imperative of Creation. That is, the task of human beings is to create cultures. Such cultures, however, are also expressions of diversity and difference, of the reality of the other, whose difference is precisely a fundamental element of itself. Such differentiation is the contribution of the Reformation to the diversity in forms of being, principally in the account of Christian communities, but also in the account of nations. It is the application of the Pauline paradigm of the Body whose real existence is only possible when the different parts that constitute it maintain that difference, and thus contribute to a healthy functioning of the whole.

It is here that the worldviews generated in the Renaissance differ most radically. While the secular humanist view constructed its belief that reality can only be integrated by reason, which was the beginning of enlightened rationalism, the Christian humanists formulated an *integrative* reality more than an integrated one with a Creation model and the metaphor of the Body. However, it has been the Enlightenment belief in rational integration that has given birth to what Wolterstorff (1983) calls world systems, with which world empires and world economies are distinguished.

> A world empire would be a culturally diverse group that besides having a unique and complete economy has a unique and final political authority (an authority that can weaken itself to the point of almost disappearing in certain areas of the group). In contrast, a world economy would be a culturally diverse group that possesses a unique, complete economy more than a final political authority. (p. 27)

However, in reality, Wolterstorff adds, the distinction between a World economy and a World empire is a question of degree. This, I believe, is evident at the end of the 20th century and the beginning of the 21st century. However, it is the logical rationalist who has advocated for a global economy that has acquired the characteristics of Imperialism; economic power substitutes for political power, and the homogenization of cultural diversity occurs outside of economic processes, especially those directly related with the market. For our purpose, the importance is that in both cases cultural diversity does not affect the system as such. To say it in another way, cultures are homogenized, which means that the distinctive traits serve the Empire or the economy.

Therefore, education is one of the instruments of homogenization. It is not necessary to prove that one of the most powerful instruments of empire has been the imposition of an educational system whose purpose has been to provide a common worldview to the cultures that constitute the empire. A careful analysis of this process in postcolonial studies has demonstrated that the education curriculum has had the tacit purpose of homogenizing culture into one dominant Western worldview. The already classic textbook of Edgar Said, *Orientalism*, postulates the creation of the fiction that we know as "Orient" to justify the supremacy of the fiction of "Western," just as the conquistadores of the 15th century created the fiction of "America" to justify the fiction of the supremacy of Europe, as indicated by the Mexican scholar Edmundo O'Gorman. In the 21st century, the fiction of the "Axis of Evil" is located in the Orient, to justify the "axis of goodwill and Western democracy."

The reductionism of cultural diversity for imperial and economic ends, a practice that has acquired global traits from the Renaissance, was always a way to justify imperial conquests (using the term "barbarians" is another example). Therefore, beginning with the Renaissance and the mediation of secular humanism that evolves into the Enlightenment and modernity, the empire finds its rational justification reinforced with an educational model: the humanities. The humanities, therefore, acquired from their beginnings traits that were imposed by "Western" culture and they were converted into a model that was imposed upon the curriculum of the colonies. In this way, they were privileged with Western cultural devices: literatures, the arts, philosophies, and ethics that were reproduced in the colonial cultures, marginalizing and silencing the local cultures.

At least in Latin America it is clear that even after the processes of independence, the ideological imposition of the Empire continued to manifest itself in national educational curriculums that, although timidly, began to incorporate their own cultural elements. The practice has continued up to today.

The secular humanist model is one that has evolved in postmodernity. The supposed postmodern critique of the Enlightenment seems to be an attempt to renew Anglo-/Euro-centered thought in order to establish its hegemony more firmly. Postmodernity has turned against the inheritance of the Enlightenment but has tried to make the turn towards a type of neoclassicism, evident in postmodern architecture. The result has been a secular neo-humanism, or post-humanism, that has at the same time pretended to dismantle the great narratives that have sustained it in order to maintain a position of power in the political, social, and economic systems. However, to do this, secular postmodernity finds itself in a position whose frailty is evident. If we take the description that Terry Eagleton (1996) makes of post-modern aesthetics, we can see an implicit critique of enlightened rationalism; but at the same time, it is not difficult to connect this project with the global system fomented by a market economy.

> Postmodernism is a style of thinking that suspects classical notions of truth, reason, identity, and objectivity of the ideal of universal progress and emancipation, of unique reference marks, of grand narratives or of the ultimate basis of explanation. Against such norms of the Enlightenment, it sees the World as contingent, without basis, diverse, instable, undetermined, as a group of disunited cultures and interpretations, that cultivate a certain degree of skepticism about the objectivity of truth, history, and norms of given natures and of the coherency of identities. (p. vii)

The paradox in this position is that the suspicion is authentic because the system constructed by the Renaissance, the Enlightenment, and Modernity, is founded on the Utopia of cultural homogenization that ignores imperial and economic manipulation of that same Utopia for its own purposes. Today, postmodernism as an aesthetic and as an ideology has accepted the reality of a global market economy and of an imperial system that requires an ambiguity of the rules (social, esthetic, ethic) for its expansion and from there an apparent exaltation of multiculturality—but only with economic ends.

The attempt to retrieve what is left is what in western curricula is called cultural studies. Born because of the crisis that the humanities experienced after the sixties and under the influence of post-colonialist thinking, cultural studies, in their most perverse form, became what Terry Eagleton (2003) has called "Culturism."

> Culturism is a form of reductionism that sees everything in terms of culture, in the same way that the economist sees everything in economic terms. As a result, it feels uncomfortable with the truth that we are, among other things, material or animal objects, and in their place insist that our material nature is culturally constructed. (p. 162)

This form of culturalism is the expression of the importance that anthropology had acquired in the seventies and served as a basis, together with sociology, for the fusion of the humanities with the social sciences in what we now call cultural studies. Naturally, much is positive in this process. However, it is important to note that the locus of this transformation continues to be Western, and therefore would be another form of the "Orientalism" that Said described in the seventies.

The critique of this development is found in Neomarxism that in reforming itself, does not vacillate to incorporate Christian categories. For example, in the text cited by Eagleton, all of the chapters dedicated to morality or ethics that are absent in post-modern proposals, the English Neomarxist critic frequently returns to the Biblical model, with many references to the Old Testament, to Jesus and Paul, and to the concepts of justice and compassion that religious fundamentalism has neglected.

The most significant critique of secular humanism is its failure to incorporate an analysis of the economic, political, and social consequences of its educational system. One that not only does not comprehend the role that it has played in the development of the global economic and imperial systems, but also it is not able to see that its post modern version, cultural studies, continues to be an instrument that globalizes an economic and political system. From there Eagleton (1996), whose emphasis on the embodiment of ethics approaches very closely the Christian concept of incarnation, points out that "for some cultural thinkers, ethics should be elevated from the banal field of the biological to something more enigmatic and mysterious" (p. 174). For that, Eagleton calls attention to an educational approach that promotes a transformation necessarily linked to a different vision from the marginalized cultures.

One must remember that Christian humanism, especially the type that the Reformation embraced, also conceives the cultural mandate as a process in which the process itself as well as its result should be governed by Biblical principles of compassion, justice, and peace understood as Shalom, that is to say, as integration. Unfortunately, as Wolterstorff points out, this tradition has manifested itself as a vision that, even though it emphasizes creation and affirms the importance of human liberty through the cultural mandate, does not develop a perspective of liberty as self-determination, as liberation theologies propose. (What we might say in passing is that liberation theologies lack in turn a perspective that includes the cultural mandate.) The reason could well be that the Reformed model became ensnared in the imperial and economic aspects of a secular humanist education system. This is not the place to examine the role of missionary projects and the establishment of educational institutions that, far from encouraging educational models appropriate to local cultures, dedicate themselves to reproduce, often in a violent and imposing form, the imperial model.

Maybe this would be the moment to think in terms of a true transformational model, one that would begin with local cultures, recognizing that these also respond to the Biblical mandate of configuring their own identity as creators of culture with their own cultural devices. Further, Western culture only can recognize itself when it incorporates in its worldview other perspectives, as the Body is only a true body when it incorporates the other members in a relation of cultural, social, and economic equality.

What, therefore, does a transcultural education project signify? I believe that it is too soon to say. Without doubt, it should begin by criticizing its own history, and be open to be transformed by other cultures. What does a transcultural Christian educational project mean? I believe that Christ gives us the model to follow—incarnation. Not only should we make education a center for the study of foreign cultures, as frequently occurs in the Western world, but also a space in which cultural exchanges are facilitated, as much with academics as with students.

From a Christian perspective, a globalized Christian higher education (CHE) cannot follow the economic-imperial model that only legitimizes the Western model. From here transcultural experiences achieved in the West serve only to assimilate students and academics from other cultures to the already established system and send them to perpetuate it in their own cultures, as has occurred with great frequency even in Christian educational institutions. On the contrary, a Christian perspective values and legitimizes other cultural points of view. This might include encouraging an official established institution from other cultures and combining their approaches with one's own, so as to understand other ways of perceiving the world. This is the incorporation of the other within our own body to enrich us, that is, to make us truly human according to the incarnational manifestation of Christ, in whom two or more peoples are converted in only one humanity, but with members that maintain their own identity.

CHE in the 21st century must retain cultural transformation as an imperative, but not for economic (pragmatic) reasons, but because there is *integrating* Biblical-theological sustenance whose essence is the belief that every culture, with its differences, is exactly what makes the world a manifestation of the Kingdom and Body of Christ.

References

Agustín de Hippo. (1956). *De doctrina Christiana*. Obras completas. Vol. 15. Madrid: Biblioteca de Autores Cristianos.

Alcántara Mejía, J. R. (1995). El concepto de poscolonialismo en los estudios literarios contemporáneos. Unpublished manuscript. *III Coloquio de investigación en las humanidades*. Universidad Iberoamericana.

Alcántara Mejía, J. R. (2002). *La escondida senda: Poética y hermenéutica en la obra castellana de Fray Luis de León*. Salamanca y México: Universidad de Salamanca and Universidad Iberoamericana.

Auerbach, E. (1979). *Mimesis: La representación de la realidad en la literatura occidental*. México: Fondo de cultura económica.

Baldwin, C. S. (1928). *Medieval rhetoric and poetic*. New York: Macmillan.

Brown, F. B. (1983). *Transfiguration: Poetic metaphor and the languages of religious belief*. Chapel Hill: University of North Carolina Press.

Colish, M. L. (1968). *The mirror of language: A study on the medieval theory of knowledge*. New Heaven: Yale University Press.

Dussel, E. (1999). *Postmodernidad y transmodernidad. Diálogos con al filosofía de Gianni Vattimo*. México: Universidad Iberoamericana.

Eagleton, T. (2003). *After theory*. New York: Basic Books.

Eagleton, T. (1996). *The illusions of Postmodernism*. Oxford: Blackwell.

Goldmann, L. (1964). *The hidden God: A study of tragic vision in the "pensées" of Pascal and the tragedies of Racine*. In N. Wolterstorff, *Until justice and peace embrace* (p. vii). Grand Rapids, MI: Eerdmans.

Jameson, F., & Zizek, S. (1998). *Estudios culturales. Refelxiones sobre el muticulturalismo*. Buenos Aires: SAICF.

Jauss, H. R. (1982). *Aesthetic experience and literary hermeneutics*. Minneapolis: University of Minnesota Press.

Kristeller, P. O. (1965). The modern system of arts. In P.O. Kristeller, *Renaissance Thought II* (pp. 162-227). New York: HarperCollins.

O'Gorman, E. (1984). *La invención de América*. México: F.C.E.

Ricoeur, P. (1974). Hermeneutics and Structuralism. In P. Ricoeur, *The conflict of interpretations* (pp. 25-96). Evanston: Northwestern University Press.

Said, E. W. (2002). *Orientalismo*. Madrid: Debate.

Smalley, B. (1978). *The study of the Bible in the Middle Ages*. Indiana: Notre Dame University Press.

Thiselton, A. C. (1980). *The two horizons: New Testament hermeneutics and philosophical description with special reference to Heidegger, Bultmann,*

Gadamer and Wittgenstein. Grand Rapids, MI: Eerdmans.

Toulmin, S. (2002). *Cosmópolis. El trasfondo de la modernidad.* Barcelona: Península.

Touraine, A. (2000). *Crítica de la modernidad.* México: FCE.

Velasco, J. M. (1996). *Ser cristiano en una cultura posmoderna.* México: Universidad Iberoamericana.

White, H. (1978). *Topics of discourse: Essays in cultural criticism.* Baltimore: John Hopkins University Press.

Wolterstorff, N. (1983). *Until justice and peace embrace.* Grand Rapids, MI: Eerdmans.

Zizec, S. (2002). *El frágil absoluto o ¿Por qué merece la pena luchar por el legado cristiano?* Valencia: Pre-Textos.

RESPONSE TO JOSÉ RAMÓN ALCÁNTARA-MEJÍA

Douglas G. Campbell

Dr. Alcántara offers us some significant insights that deserve both careful consideration and further discussion. Of primary importance, in my view, is his observation "that the humanities have lost their relevance." He attributes this loss of relevance, in part, to several shifts in educational methodology which have taken place since the middle of the twentieth century. So, instead of being seen as culturally central the humanities have been relegated to a minor role within culture generally and academia in particular. He goes on to observe that Christian higher education can choose this path, which relegates the humanities to a minor role, or it can choose an alternative, which takes into account a Christian worldview.

What I am most fascinated by is the view Dr. Alcántara credits to Nicholas Wolterstorff and Lucien Goldman, that "believing in the reality of a certain form is essential to mold it according to the principles that come out of the same belief, and to mold is to create culture from a worldview." In other words, belief (which is defined as acceptance) is the basis for the shaping of culture. Reason, on the other hand is not a worldview; it is a method of thinking about nature and culture, a means for understanding but not a means of shaping culture. Therefore, belief is a step beyond reason. When we use reason, we analyze, look for causes, and work towards human understanding of whatever it is we confront. However, until we believe, until we accept (and reasoning may be part of this path towards acceptance), we cannot begin to act, to shape, or to form.

However, one views belief and reason, what is disconcerting is Dr. Alcántara's observation that whether or not culture is based on belief in a worldview, or on the methodology of reason, cultural homogenization is the result. Therefore, there is a problem of importance that Christians in higher education needs to confront.

What then can be done to create an educational system that does not perpetuate this seemingly inevitable homogenization? Dr. Alcántara suggests that we elevate the role of "local cultures" in a way that follows the Biblical mandate and is not misperceived as supporting cultural imperialism. Secondly, that more emphasis should be placed on the metaphorical approach to understanding intercultural interactions. The specific metaphor he suggests is the metaphor of the body, which models a more egalitarian understanding. This understanding recognizes the value of all parts of the body, or all cultures large or small, rather than allowing fist, or brain, or heart, or stomach to dominate.

Dr. Alcántara's desire for Christian institutions to remove themselves from the practice of cultural dominance and assimilation is imperative given the fact that Western culture, though it may dominate Christianity financially and academically, plays a much smaller role in the world. Alternatively, in Lamin Sanneh's (2003) words: "What is at issue now is the surprising scale and depth of worldwide Christian resurgence, a resurgence that seems to proceed without Western organizational structures, including academic recognition . . ." (p. 3). Thus, if Christians who come out of Western culture want a seat at the table they need to listen to the non-Western voices from within the body of Christ; and they need to do so with humility and grace. We Western Christians seem to have forgotten how to wash the feet of non-Western Christians; we have lost, if we ever had it, our ability to take on the role of the servant and listen to what other Christians have to teach us.

We also need to understand that a variety of points of view, including a variety of local points of view is part of a healthy dialogue, a dialogue with different and sometimes divergent points of view. As Philip Yuen-Sang Leung (2004) put it in relation to his own cultural experience: "Differences and debates between different groups of Chinese Christians should not be viewed as entirely negative. Arguments and differences are natural and sometimes necessary in a vibrant, creative, and energetic culture or faith system" (p. 107).

My own experience confirms much of what Dr. Alcántara presents. My background is art and art history. A recent trend in art departments in universities and colleges is that art history, admittedly an art history that has been focused primarily on Western cultures, is now being replaced with the study of material culture. So cultural studies are gaining prominence; but the emphasis is still on Western cultures at the expense of local cultures. So clearly, the emphasis on cultural studies is not one that counters the tendency towards homogenization. In more traditional art history, the tendency to homogenize is also dominant, especially in relation to art history survey courses. In such courses, the mainstream of art history is the major focus, so Florentine art of the Renaissance is studied in depth because Florentine art fits within the concept of the mainstream. On the other hand, Sienese art is mostly ignored because it does not fit within what is considered the mainstream. This mainstream model "assumes that one style or conceptual model for art must dominate the artistic arena within each particular time and place" (Campbell, 2002, p. 2). This mainstream approach in art history also dismisses many "local cultures" that do not fit into major trends.

In closing, I must say that I wish Dr. Alcántara had spent more time in outlining his vision for a true "transformational model." He makes it clear that the current academic paradigm will not work, since assimilation has been the typical result of academic pursuits in higher education. His use of the metaphor of the "body of Christ" offers great promise. I hope too that he will also focus on the trinity, which manages to combine three individuals into one, with no loss to any part's unique and individual identity. Both concepts offer the possibility of true dialogue, true intimacy, and true oneness. Without such metaphors to guide those committed to Christian higher education, parts of the body will remain stunted and misshapen and the "body of Christ" will remain weak and disunited.

References

Campbell, D. G. (2002). *Seeing: When art and faith intersect.* Lanham, MD: University Press of America.
Leung, P. Y. (2004). Conversion, commitment, and culture: Christian experience in China, 1949-99. In D. M. Lewis (Ed.), *Christianity reborn: The global expansion of evangelicalism in the twentieth.* Grand Rapids, MI: Eerdmans.
Sanneh, L. (2003). *Whose religion is Christianity? The Gospel beyond the west.* Grand Rapids, MI: Eerdmans.

TEACHING RELIGION IN A PLURAL WORLD

R. Ruard Ganzevoort

Introduction
How does Christian higher education (CHE) bridge gaps between competing cultures or worldviews? That is the question governing this track of the program, and I feel privileged to add my views to that discussion. As context is essential to any argument, I will start by saying that I come from a Western-European Dutch background. You may know that the Netherlands is sometimes referred to as the most secularized country in the world, but it holds in fact a rather average median position on the Western-European scale. Everything depends of course on the definitions used. If we follow the most recent World Values Studies (1999-2004) and look at self-report as a religious person, we find that the Dutch rank 44 on a list of 70 countries with still 61.4 percent responding affirmatively. On the question how important God is in the person's life, the Dutch score five on a ten-point scale, which places them on a low position 72 on a list of 84 countries. When we ask whether participants belong to a religious denomination, however, the Netherlands joins Japan, China, Estonia, and the Czech Republic as the only countries where non-members outnumber members. On the most recent national poll, 64 percent call themselves non-members, and of the members, only 38 percent are regular churchgoer (Becker & De Hart, 2006). Overall, it is safe to say that my country is not particularly religious.

That is, however, not the only thing to be said. Of all countries in the WVS, we score second highest for the percentage of adherents to non-denominational churches besides our 24 percent Protestants and 49 percent Roman Catholics. The number of Muslim believers is around 3 percent but still growing. Invisible in these figures is the fact that some 5 percent of the Dutch population consists of Christian migrants that belong to Roman Catholic parishes or form independent congregations with a strong ethnic background (Euser et al., 2006). Finally, there is some adherence to alternative religious traditions, although this is rather limited.

The picture is more complex when we look beyond the statistics and ask what religion means to people and how it relates to their lives. Then we find among church members a wide diversity of religious experiences, beliefs, and practices. Some of these are supported or indeed prescribed by the church to which they belong. Others are officially incompatible with a Christian conviction, but are nevertheless found among Christians.

I am not claiming that this is a unique phenomenon for the Netherlands. On the contrary, in many countries of Africa, Asia, and Latin and South America, we will find examples of the like. My point is that this has not often been accounted for in our theological thinking on pluralism. When theologians speak of pluralism and interreligious dialogue, they usually refer to competing worldviews or practices on the societal level and encounters between official representatives of the world religions. My claim will be that every classroom in the Netherlands is religiously pluralistic; indeed that many people are engaged in an interreligious *dialogue intérieur*. I will first discuss the concept of deinstitutionalization as an alternative to secularization theories, and relate deinstitutionalization with religious pluralism on different levels. The second part of my paper will deal with the development of religious identity in a plural context and with the implications for education.

Deinstitutionalization
Until recently, the religious context of western countries was usually described with concepts like secularization. Because of processes of modernity, rationalization, and individualization would eliminate religion's role as a sacred canopy, an overarching frame of reference. According to sociologists like Casanova (1994), this entails three different elements. First, differentiation entails increasing the distinction between different domains of life, like labour, family, leisure, consumption, politics, and so on. In all these domains, religion is no longer the fundamental dimension that holds everything together. Instead, it has become but one subsystem among many. Second, religion is reduced, not only in terms of church membership and religious activity, but much more in terms of a desacralization of the world. The domain of the sacred loses ground to the rational and the secular. This process of desacralization is not alien to Christianity but has actually been stimulated by it, especially by Protestantism. Third, in privatization, religion recoils into the private sphere and plays a much smaller role in the public domain. These three processes have been observed in many countries, especially—but not only—in the

western world. In every country, a unique constellation of these three processes is found.

More recently, the monopoly of secularization theory has waned. Some sociologists nowadays claim that we live in a time of desecularization and especially deprivatization (Berger et al., 1999; Casanova, 1994). Religion has become more important in societies, but it is less clearly connected to traditional religious institutions like churches and mosques. Instead, we find a strong religious impetus from commercial sources, the media, popular culture, and so on. To call that desecularization would miss the fact that religion is not reinstated as the ground for all existence, but remains one isolated domain of life. Secularization is a continuing phenomenon, but it is complemented by other tendencies. Desecularization and deprivatization can be observed as well, but not as if, the processes are simply reversed.

The common factor in both secularization and desecularization is the diminution of the impact of religious institutions. That was the case in secularization, but it is a prominent feature of desecularization as well. When religion plays an increasing role in present day society, it is not necessarily the church that embodies this role of religion. Cinema, pop music, commercials, schools, political parties, and new spiritual groups have taken the seat that was left vacant. Both processes thus are part of the larger phenomenon of deinstitutionalization, which affects not only religion, but also politics and labor unions. In a consumerist society, people will use what they need from whatever source, and form their own bricolage.

The concept of deinstitutionalization thus captures both secularization and desecularization. It is a concept directly connected to institutionalization and reinstitutionalization. The nucleus of religion is not sought in this institutional dimension, important as that is, but in human devotion, the individual and collective relations with the sacred. Throughout the ages and in different contexts, devotion has been institutionalized in various structures and organizations, and these structures have eroded in other times. Religious traditions can thus be seen as the processes of taming this lived religion or "wild devotion" as some call it. By taming devotion, the anarchistic tendency of human devotion is curbed, and checks and balances are applied that turn religion into a social force that sustains society (Ganzevoort, 2006).

In the process of deinstitutionalization, devotion is withdrawn from the powers of the institutions. A direct consequence of that is an increasing pluralism. When every individual creates his or her own religion, blending traditional elements of the institutionalized religion with material from other sources, the result will never be identical. This can be called a form of enculturation of the Christian faith, but it happens at the level of individuals and groups as much as it happens at the level of societies. In the process of developing one's religion, individual factors become more important than institutional ones. Pluralism thus results from deinstitutionalization, but at the same time, it stimulates deinstitutionalization: if one's context is pluralized, it is more difficult to reserve all plausibility for only one religious institution.

Let me go even one step further. This understanding of deinstitutionalization and the accompanying religious pluralism is found not only on the level of societies, groups, and between individuals. It is also found within the individual religious identity. At least in our context, persons develop their own personal religion and use material from very different sources. This personal religion is then given shape in the context of a wide variety of mutually exclusive life domains. The direct consequence of this is that many people do not form a consistent, monolithic religious identity, but a patchwork construction of bits and pieces. If we ask people about their religious affiliation, they still may answer in terms of the official tradition to which they belong, but that does not mean that they follow the teachings of the church and organize their lives accordingly. Roman Catholics may distance themselves from the moral teachings of Rome and Protestant churchgoers may be active in alternative healing practices like Reiki or practice Zen-meditation.

Education and identity
My point is this. If we ask ourselves how CHE can bridge gaps between competing cultures or worldviews, then we should address this issue at all the levels of pluralism. Competing cultures or worldviews are found at the level of society, but they are also found in the classroom and within the individual student. Even if we teach in a relatively homogeneous population, we encounter a plethora of views and practices that call for an interreligious dialogue. Even when in individual coaching or pastoral counseling we work with an interreligious *dialogue intérieur*. The various voices of the self compete and converse with one another like voices in a polyphonic novel (Ganzevoort, 1999). They represent different truth claims, and we try to bring these together in an effort to build an inhabitable world. To achieve that, it is not adequate to look for consensus or harmony; we need to explore the conflicts much deeper.

At this point, it is useful to discuss three types of teaching religion as models for education in a pluralist world. I will apply these models not only at the levels of society and classroom, but also to intrapersonal plurality. One can opt for teaching from a religious point of view, for teaching detached from religious points of view, or for teaching dialogically, between religious points of view. These types are called kerygmatic, liberal, and communicative-communitarian respectively (Altena & Hermans, 2002). The kerygmatic type is usually located in a context that is thought to be monoreligious (Sterkens, 2001). One religious tradition is dominant, and the pedagogic aim is the internalization of that tradition. The normative basis is the truth claim of this one religious tradition. This type does not really acknowledge plurality, but lives on the assumption of an absolute revealed truth. Other religions are taken into account as competing or indeed misleading traditions. On the individual level, it holds religious convictions that do not leave room for variance. Alternative viewpoints are automatically seen as dangerous and therefore should be rejected.

The liberal type is located in a multi-religious context. It takes its starting point in the conviction that all religious traditions are equally valuable. Detached from a particular tradition, the educator aims to provide knowledge about various religious options. The normative basis is religious relativism. On the individual level, this type allows conflicting parts of one's religious identity to function alongside each other without being integrated, or even without being contrasted with one another. This model is in fact dominant in the Netherlands, but in recent years, it has lost much of its appeal. Instead of creating the promised harmony and mutual understanding, it yielded indifference and lack of communication. In a society of increasing interreligious tension, this type proved unable to address the strong religious motivations that people may have.

The communicative-communitarian type focuses on interreligious dialogue. This is no detached observer's point of view, nor a monolithic defense of the faith. Instead, the aim is to develop competence in dialogue (Vroom, 2006). Plurality is taken as the starting point and considered an opportunity for mutual enrichment. Here the educator works with the religious plurality in the classroom, and the coach or counselor tries to bring out the competing views and practices rather than harmonize them. Conflicts are seen as the possibility for growth for all and an enrichment of the particulars of each tradition. That means that each participant is challenged to deepen existential involvement with his or her own religious tradition. On the intra-individual level, it means that we do not harmonize different religious views or practices in our lives, but instead highlight their contrasts. This allows us to enter into a real dialogue that demands us to take seriously the various perspectives and engage with a particular Christian perspective ourselves. Between the monolithic self and the multiple personality, there is a polyphonic self.

In my opinion, teaching religion in a plural world should take this third approach. Neither the proselytizing dogmaticism of the monoreligious model, nor the neutralizing liberalism of the multireligious model does justice to plurality and to the meaning of religion. In the interreligious dialogical model, we accept and strengthen the religious commitment of each participant, we highlight the differences as well as the parallels, and we seek forms of accommodating each other in order to build a peaceful society. However, this should not only take place on a group level. Bridging gaps should start within the individual. To function in an interreligious, plural world, we have to acknowledge the plurality within ourselves.

That is not just a pragmatic consideration. It has to do with the nature of religious identity. Practical theologian Henning Luther (1992) has claimed that the idea of a fixed and stable identity is misleading. It can only be achieved if we renounce grief over what we have lost in the past, hope for what might come in the future, and the pain and joy of meeting other persons. True identity, Luther states, should be an open identity. This is all the more the case when it comes to religious identity for to build a fixed identity would mean renouncing transcendence. Such a strong identity may include a clear commitment to convictions and norms of a specific tradition, but that is more fundamentalism than religiosity. Open religious identity builds on receptivity, transcendence, and the awareness that God can meet us every day in a new way (Ganzevoort, 2004).

Conclusion

As a theologian and educator, I take my starting point in the plural world that students and I live in. It is this plural world that also lives in our own hearts. We have to come to grips with this plurality instead of seeing it as a fundamental threat to our religion. Learning to live with plurality is not opposed to developing a religious identity. On the contrary, it may help us to rediscover the open nature of religious identity.

References

Altena, P., & Hermans, C. A. M. (2002). Vorming van religieuze identiteit in een pluriforme samenleving. In C. A. M. Hermans (Ed.), *Participerend leren in debat* (pp. 113-138). Budel: Damon.
Becker, J., & De Hart, J. (2006). *Godsdienstige veranderingen in Nederland*. Den Haag: SCP.
Berger, P., Sacks, J., Martin, D., Weiming, T., Weigel, G., Davie, G., & An-Naim, A. A. (1999). *The desecularization of the world: Resurgent religion and world politics*. Grand Rapids, MI: Eerdmans.
Casanova, J. (1994). *Public religions in the modern world*. Chicago: University of Chicago Press.
European Values Study Group and World Values Survey Association 2006. EUROPEAN AND WORLD VALUES SURVEYS FOUR-WAVE INTEGRATED DATA FILE, 1981-2004, v.20060423. Análisis Sociológicos Económicos y Políticos (ASEP) and JD Systems (JDS), Madrid, Spain/Tillburg University, Tilburg, The Netherlands/Zentralarchiv fur Empirische Sozialforschung (ZA) Cologne, Germany.
Euser, H., Goossen, K., De Vries, M., & Wartena, S. (2006). *Migranten in Mokum. De betekenis van migrantenkerken voor Amsterdam*. Amsterdam: Vrije Universiteit.
Ganzevoort, R. R. (1999). Stemmen van het zelf en rollen van God. Fragment en identiteit in religie en pastoraat. *Praktische Theologie*, 2(1), 3-23.
Ganzevoort, R. R. (2004). Receptivity and the nature of religion. *Journal of Empirical Theology*, 17(1), 115-125.
Ganzevoort, R. R. (2006). *De hand van God en andere verhalen: Over veelkleurige vroomheid en botsende beelden*. Zoetermeer: Meinema.
Luther, H. (1992). *Religion und alltag. Bausteine zu einer praktischen theologie des subjekts*. Stuttgart: Radius Verlag.
Sterkens, C. (2001). *Interreligious learning: The problem of interreligious dialogue in primary education*. Leiden: Brill.
Vroom, H. M. (2006). Godsdienstige vorming en religieus pluralisme in het onderwijs. In S. Miedema & G. Bertram-Troost (Eds.), *Levensbeschouwelijk leren samenleven* (pp. 187-200). Zoetermeer: Meinema.

RESPONSE TO R. RUARD GANZEVOORT

Musa A. B. Gaiya

Nigeria, with a population of more than 120 million, is about half Muslim and half Christian. Nigeria is certainly a pluralistic society. It was because of this obvious pluralism that the Nigerian constitution provided for the separation of function between the state and the church in society. It means the state is not the church and vice versa. They are distinct institutions. The pertinent clause is section 10 of the 1999 constitution, which says, "The government of the Federation or that of a State shall not adopt any religion as a state religion." This is not the same thing as secularism as we have it in parts of Europe and America where the church (religion) is disestablished and government does not involve itself in religious matters. The Nigerian situation is different because government can and does regulate and assist both Muslim and Christian religious establishments. Unlike Europe, Nigeria's religious landscape is still institutional. Institutions control teachings and behaviour rather than, as stated by Ganzevoort, "cinema, pop music, commercials, schools, political parties, and new spiritual groups" as in Europe.

Also unlike the Netherlands, Nigeria is a religious country. Some of the religious conflicts that occur in Nigeria are actually struggles for religious space. The churches and mosques are so full on Sundays and Fridays that in some cities the roads are taken over to accommodate the overflow of worshippers. However, the two major religions in Nigeria, Islam and Christianity, have not been on friendly terms for almost three decades. The area of intense conflict is the Northern part of the country home of perhaps the largest population of Muslims in Africa. This part of Nigeria has experienced many eruptions of violence due mainly to religious differences between Christians and Muslims (Boer, 2003).

In my opinion, inter-religious conflicts can be ameliorated through theological training that helps build bridges of peace. The present curriculum for the study of Islam in Nigeria's theological schools is inadequate because it is narrow. Topics selected are those that would aid student to evangelise Muslims. It cannot prepare students to face the contemporary challenges of Muslim and Christian relations. Issues of Christian and Muslim relations are generally neglected; pastors are not encouraged to teach cordial relations between Christians and Muslims; evangelical theologians in Nigeria often do not understand the Muslim worldview; and "bridge building" is often not taught. I recently met a leader of a mission church and stressed the need for open-minded dialogue between Christians and Muslims to reduce the tension and conflict due to mutual hatred, suspicion, and misunderstanding. He retorted, "What do you mean by dialogue? The only dialogue we can have with Muslims is to tell them of the need to receive Jesus as their personal saviour or they go to hell!"

Christian and Muslim relations in Africa have been studied by many scholars (Center for Religious Freedom, 2002; Kasfelt & Tvillinggaard [Eds.] 1997; Kenny, 1979; 1996; Ostien and Nasir, [Eds.] 2005; Sanneh, 1996, 1997; Uwazie et al., [Eds.] 2000; Yakuba, 2001). However, these studies do not see that theological education can help deal with the crisis in Muslim Christian relations.

Christian and Muslim relations, at least in Nigeria, have become very complex and require a fresh understanding by Nigerian theologians. Thus, curriculum change may be needed so that dialogue and mutual understanding between Christians and Muslims are emphasised. This way pastors trained to understand and relate well with Muslims will in turn preach mutual understanding to their flocks. I agree with Ganzevoort, that communicative-communitarian curricula can help bridge gaps existing between religious groups. However, for theological education in Nigeria, the pendulum should swing between what Ganzevoort calls "kerygmatic" and "communicative-communitarian" approaches. This is because dialogue, open dialogue, if done with sincerity of purpose can lead to conversion. However, the main purpose of dialogue is to reach an understanding not conversion.

The three major evangelical theological schools in Northern Nigeria were established more than twenty years ago: Baptist Seminary, Kaduna (established in 1948), Theological College of Northern Nigeria (established in 1968), and ECWA Theological Seminary, Jos (established in 1980). All three schools teach the basics of Islam: its history, theology, and practices. ECWA Seminary and Baptist Seminary go on to treat Muslim evangelism. ECWA Seminary's Islam course description reads:

> This course is an introductory study of the historical and theological development as well as the philosophy of Islam. Attention is given to an overview of the Muslim culture, its beliefs and practices, and the strategies or Muslim

polemics against Christianity as a background for stimulating evangelism and Christian apologetics. (ECWA, 2004, p. 4)

The priority in this course is evangelism. This would serve a perfect description of courses provided by Islington and Moody Bible Institute, two famous institutions for the training of missionaries in the nineteenth century. A doyen of the history of Christian missions in Nigeria, E. A. Ayandele (1966), reports how missionaries who were so trained were disillusioned when they realised the difficulties in converting Muslims:

> The missionaries, called the Sudan Party, expected very quick results, for Brooke had calculated that within six months much of Northern Nigeria would be converted–Not a single convert was made. One by one, the Sudan Party fell off, either by resigning or being invalided home or by dying. Not even Brooke's apparently invincible idealism could withstand the reality of facts. As he saw his vision collapse like a house of cards, his letters conveyed gloomier and gloomier forebodings. Early in 1892 he wrote, "the long gathering political troubles seems coming to a head, and I greatly fear that we may be on the verge of a general Muhammedan rising." (pp. 121-122)

Only the Theological College of Northern Nigeria has a course on Muslim and Christian relations, which reads:

> The following will be covered: a study of Muslim attitudes to Christ and Christians; a study of scriptures from classical sources (Qur'an traditions), medieval sources (chazal, Ibn Arabi, Gospel of Barnabas, Ibn Hazn for example), and modern sources with special reference to Muslims in Nigeria; a study of the early Muslim-Christian dialogues in the Christian sources; medieval attitude (especially in Spain and the Reformation); the modern missionary movement; a study of conversion with special reference to West Africa, but compared with other parts of the world; the history and meaning of dialogue. (TCNN, 2002, p. 49)

This is an improvement, but does not deal with the contemporary relationships between Nigerian Muslims and Christians, which to my mind requires tact and the cultivation of friendship. Theological education should be tailored toward helping pastors through their preaching to be peace builders not instigators of violence.

The call this paper is making is the modeling of theological curriculum in Nigeria to help recipients of such education face the challenges of Muslim and Christian relations in Nigeria today.

Conclusion

Theological education in Nigeria should be modified to face the new challenges in Muslim evangelism. Pastors and teachers should serve as peace builders in a society that has gained notoriety for religious and sectarian violence.

References

Ayandele, E. A. (1966). *The missionary impact on modern Nigeria 1842-1914: A political and social analysis.* London: Longman.
Boer, J. H. (2003). *Nigeria's decades of blood, 1980-2002.* Belleville, ON: Essence Publishing.
Center for Religious Freedom. (2002). *The talibanization of Nigeria: Sharia law and religious freedom.* Nigeria: Freedom House.
ECWA Theological Seminary. (2004). *Academic catalogue 2004/2005.* Jos: JETS.
ECWA Theological Seminary. (2005). *Course description 2005/2006.* Unpublished.
Kastfelt, N., & Tvillinggaard, J. (Eds.). (1997). *Religion and politics in Africa and the Islamic world.* Copenhagen: University of Copenhagen.
Kenny, J. (1979). Christian-Muslim relations in Nigeria. *Islamochristiana, 5,* 171-192.
Kenny, J. (1996). Shariah and Christianity in Nigeria: Islam and a 'secular' state. *Journal of Religion in Africa, 26,* 4.
Ostien, P., & Nasir, J. (Eds.). (2005). *Comparative perspective on Shariah in Nigeria.* Ibadan: Spectrum Books Limited.
Sanneh, L. (1996). *Piety and power: Muslims and Christians in West Africa.* New York: Orbis Books.
Sanneh, L. (1997). *The crown and the turban: Muslims and the West African pluralism.* Oxford: Westview Press.
TCNN. (2002). *Catalogue 2002-2006.* Bukuru: Theological College of Northern Nigeria.
Uwazie, E. E., Albert, I. O., & Uzoigwe, G. N. (Eds.). (2000). *Inter-Ethnic and religious conflict resolution in Nigeria.* New York: Lexington Books.
Yakubu, M. A., Kani, A. M., & Junaid, M. I. (Eds.). (2001). *Understanding Sharia in Nigeria.* Ibadan: Spectrum Books Limited.

RESPONSE TO
R. RUARD GANZEVOORT

Elisabeth Hulscher

Introduction
First and foremost, I would like to say that as far as the aims of education are concerned, I wholeheartedly agree with Ruard Ganzevoort that a contribution to peace, dialogue, and reconciliation is of the utmost importance.

In his paper, Ruard Ganzevoort addresses the question how higher education bridges the gap between competing religions. Although in my field of higher education I am involved in bridging the gap between competing cultures, for both of us our main objective is teaching pluralism.[1]

There are two issues raised by Ruard Ganzevoort that I would like to go into:
1. The complex picture of plurality
2. Teaching plurality geared to professional duties

The complex picture of plurality
To further explore and explain the complex picture of religious plurality as described by Ruard Ganzevoort, I think Sander Griffioen's model of plurality (Griffioen, 1992; 2006) may be helpful as an alternative to Ruard Ganzevoort's concept of deinstitutionalisation and reinstitutionalisation.

Griffioen makes a distinction between directional plurality, differences arising from different value orientations; structural plurality, the diversity of all structures making up human society; and contextual plurality, the general context that both reflects and influences the lives of large groups or communities of people.

---

[1] I would like to distinguish between plurality, the state of people of different races, religions and beliefs living together in the same society, and pluralism, the principle that people of different races, religions and beliefs can live together peacefully in the same society. I see the former as a factual description and the latter as a view.

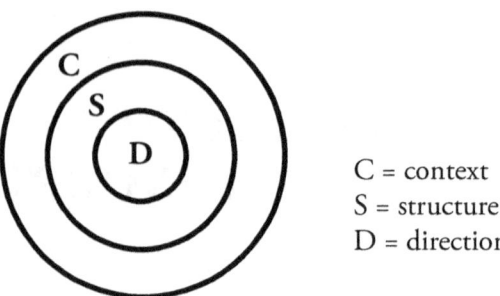

C = context
S = structure
D = direction

When this model is applied to religious plurality, a distinction could be made between religious direction (value orientations/faith), religious structure (e.g. religious institutions), and religious context (general context).

According to Ruard Ganzevoort, when theologians speak of plurality they usually refer to competing worldviews and practices on the societal level and encounters between official representatives of world religions. In Griffioen's model, this would be the level of structure. Ganzevoort's "*dialogue interieure* of the polyphonic self" would be on the level of value orientations/faith, direction. The context refers to the society in which we find ourselves, including commercial sources, the media, and popular culture all of which offer a strong religious impetus. In my view, all three forms of plurality interact with each other.

The complex picture of religious plurality described by Ruard Ganzevoort, according to this model, shows decreased importance of a particular structure, namely religious institutions, which are being replaced by other structures, e.g. new spiritual groups. Further, the context (e.g. commercial sources, the media etc.) seems to have an increased impact on structure.

The picture also reveals the increased importance of direction, value orientations that have become more individualized. I would like to further explore this particular form of plurality by discussing Trompenaars' theory of cultural plurality (Trompenaars, 2001). Trompenaars argues that value orientations must be seen on a continuum. The categories on the continuum, e.g. ranging from individualism to communitarianism are not mutually exclusive. This means that individual value orientations are different, and where you find yourself on the continuum may vary depending on the situation. Moreover, in principle each culture shows the total variation of its human components (Trompenaars, 2001), which may cover a broad spectrum. I think this is also true for religion. According to Trompenaars, we need to realize that most cultural differences are within ourselves, even if we have not yet recognized them. This would be in line with Ganzevoort's concept of intrapersonal plurality.

What is very important in Trompenaars' view, and I agree with him, is that value orientations tend to be taken for granted and, because of their very nature, have usually disappeared from our conscious awareness. However, for that very reason they tend to be most influential. This means that becoming aware of one's own value orientations, and the differences with other value orientations, is absolutely essential. It is also a challenge to any Christian who wants to be a homo respondens, a human being responding deliberately and intentionally to the calling of God, his/her fellow human beings and the world (Glas, 2005).

According to the Dutch Christian philosopher Gerrit Glas, man reveals and develops his identity by responding. Our identity is defined by that which makes us a person in the most profound sense of the word, that is, our response to the calling of God, our fellow human beings, and the world. We will never know exhaustively who we are and therefore our identity will never be "finished" (Glas, 2005). In that sense I agree with Ruard Ganzevoort that our identity will always be open-ended, because we must respond to the calling all our lives.

Teaching geared to professional duties
Rather than teaching, as Ruard Ganzevoort does, I would like to take learning as the starting point for my teaching strategy. At our university, we formulate professional duties in terms of professional competencies. A competency integrates knowledge, skills, and attitude in actual performance. Business and human resources graduates are required to be competent at dealing professionally with a person from a different culture. Incidentally, in business, diversity management is considered to make a contribution to the realisation of company goals, and this may be something we could learn from business!

Our students are expected to acquire transcultural, or you might also say, transplural competence. In line with Trompenaars' theory (Trompenaars, 2001) they will have to be aware of their own culture, be able to understand and respect other cultures and be motivated to try and reconcile the differences by looking in a different culture for something to enrich their own. Key words are awareness, respect, and reconciliation. From that point of view, as I see it, the only appropriate teaching strategy would be Ruard Ganzevoort's third option of dialogical teaching between point of view. According to cross-cultural psychological research

(Oldenhoven, 2002) competencies needed in this respect are open-mindedness, sensitivity (or cultural empathy), social initiative, flexibility and emotional stability. Research has shown that these competencies are best developed by learning from experience.

To stimulate learning, a powerful learning environment is essential. De Corte defines a powerful learning environment as "a good balance between discovery learning and personal exploration on the one hand, and systematic instruction and guidance on the other, always taking into account the individual differences in abilities, needs and motivation between students" (cited in Dochy, Segers & De Rijdt, 2002, p. 19). For that reason, besides instructing and guiding them, we expose our students to a cultural learning experience in both national and international contexts.

The pedagogy followed, along with instruction and guidance, includes self- and peer-assessment of transcultural competencies, defining learning goals, awareness of basic assumptions/value orientations, personal experience of a different culture (national or international), and a reflection paper on the learning experience. There is a special emphasis on what could be learned from a given culture that would enrich its own learning.

Conclusion

The answer to the question how Christian higher education bridges the gap between competing cultures or worldviews must include teaching different forms of plurality, and encouraging transplural competency. The ultimate goal would be for every student to become a "homo respondens," able to respond to the calling of God, fellow human beings, and the world and in doing so develop their identities and use their unique talents to serve God and His kingdom.

Awareness, respect, and reconciliation in the service of pluralism and of the Lord!

References

Dochy, F., Segers, M., & De Rijdt, C. (2002). Nieuwe ontwikkelingen: De assessmentcultuur. In F. Dochy, L. Heylen, H. Mosselaer (Eds.), *Assessment in onderwijs: Nieuwe toetsvormen en examinering in studentgericht onderwijs en competentiegericht onderwijs* (pp. 11-32). Utrecht: Lemma.

Glas, G. (2005). Homo ipse, homo idem - Over de menselijke identiteit.

In G. Buijs, P. Blokhuis, S. Griffioen & R. Kuiper (Eds.), *Homo respondens* (pp. 49-57). Amsterdam: Buijten & Schipperheijn.

Griffioen, S. (2006). *Een weg gaan*. Budel: Damon.

Griffioen, S., & Mouw, R. (1992). *Pluralisms and horizons*. Grand Rapids, MI: Eerdmans.

Oudenhoven, J. P. (2002). *Cross-culturele psychologie*. Bussum: Coutinho.

Trompenaars, F., & Hampden-Turner, C. (2001). *Riding the waves of culture*. London: Nicholas Brealy Publishing.

WHAT CAN CHRISTIAN HIGHER EDUCATION DO TO PROMOTE EDUCATIONAL WELL-BEING IN AFRICA?

FAITH W. NGURU

Introduction
In the last thirty years of IAPCHE's existence and more particularly in the last twenty years various Christian scholars have spoken and written with conviction regarding the potential that the African continent has for Christian higher education (CHE) (Carpenter, 2005; Fowler, 1991; Hulst, 2004; Kinoti, 1997; van der Walt, 2000). In their analysis of the African situation, however, they have recognized the great economic, physical, political, and religious challenges that face the development of such education.

The conference theme: *CHE In Global Context: Implications for Curriculum, Pedagogy and Administration* provides an appropriate umbrella under which to discuss the issues confronting educators in their efforts to promote educational well-being. Concisely, we believe that CHE is like the long awaited 'savior' of the educational enterprise, regardless of the many challenges and problems confronting the continent. According to van der Walt (2002), these include inadequate funding, undue government interference, a burgeoning student population, inadequate attention paid by society to the plight of the universities, and duplication instead of cooperation among universities.

This paper will summarize the genesis and development of higher education on the continent with a special reference to Kenya. It will seek to demonstrate how the African Christians both in the churches and in institutions of higher education, have over the years contributed their resources towards Christian education.

Today, international agencies, including UNESCO, OECD, and the World Bank, national governments and the leadership of higher education institutions have all recognized the need for improved managerial effectiveness in order to make the best possible use of the available resources to meet the changing needs. The current developments in the establishment of new public and private universities in the region provide a context from which to discuss the well-being of education that depends on the people (learners), teachers, curriculum, methods of teaching, administration of the institutions, and the eternal or kingdom value of knowledge and praxis.

Historical overview of the development of higher education in Africa

Since independence, most countries have experienced a remarkable expansion of higher education that has made a major contribution to the development of their human resources. The current demand for expansion in this sector results from the success the countries have made in the last four decades. Despite the apparent success, there have been major constraints and shortcomings that have a strong bearing on future development of higher education. One of the major challenges of the transformation of the sector is how to overcome the legacy of the past while affirming positive elements of that heritage. Looking back to the past four decades, one can perceive that higher education in general, and public universities in particular, have gone through three critical phases in their development. These phases are closely intertwined with the socio-economic and political developments in the various countries. These developments have had a bearing on the growth of CHE, particularly in Sub-Saharan Africa.

The first phase revolved around intense discourses on what kind of university was appropriate for a country emerging from colonialism. This phase was common to most African countries that were emerging from colonial domination. The search entailed building a consensus on the nature and orientation of university education. The emerging consensus pointed towards the concept of a "development university" that was to spearhead the process of de-colonization and overcoming the legacies of foreign domination while making a major contribution to nation building efforts. In particular, the universities had a major role to play in Africanization and development in general. This was a period of high expectations. Hence, the idea of a development university gained wide acceptance in Africa and had strong state support and involvement. At this point, historically, there were very few institutions of Christian higher learning apart from Bible schools. The only Christian university or institution of higher learning could be found in Southern Africa.

The second phase witnessed a process of politicization, tight state control, and repression of students and staff in institutions of higher learning. This was not unique to universities as civil society organizations underwent similar experiences. In Kenya, for example this period was marked by decline in economic growth and the introduction of structural adjustment policies. This phase was characterized by political tension, constrained academic freedom, and decline in government funding for research and infrastructure, such as libraries in the public universities. Contrary to the prevailing context, this was a period of phenomenal expansion of higher education in most countries. Additionally the establishment of legal bodies, such as the Commission for Higher Education, to oversee the establishment of private universities also occurred during this period. Kenya was the first country to establish private institutions. It was followed by Benin, Senegal, Tanzania, Uganda, Ghana, Mozambique, Cameroon, and others. Today, there are more than 100 private universities in sub-Saharan Africa; more than half of these have arisen since 1990 (ADEA Newsletter, 2005). However, private universities remain small and still only account for a small part of the total number of students who qualify for university education.

The third phase is characterized by the expansion of democratic space. During this period, the universities have undertaken reforms and innovations in response to both internal and external pressures. Measures have also been taken to increase access to women. Public universities have diversified funding through the admission of self-supporting students to meet the growing demand for professionals in the countries. In Kenya, for example, this has led to an expansion of facilities and programmes closer to the clients in various parts of the country. While this has widened access to university education, it has accentuated concerns for quality, relevance, and equity.

Reforms in higher education today
The Association of African Universities (AAU) is an international, non-governmental organization, which serves as a principle forum for consultations, the exchange of information and cooperation among higher education institutions in Africa. It has also spearheaded reforms in higher education. Currently it has 195 members from 44 African countries cutting across the five sub–regions, the major linguistic groupings and the educational traditions in Africa, with Arabic, English and French as its official languages. The AAU, which includes some institutions of Chris-

tian higher learning, consult regularly on key issues affecting higher education in Africa such as:
1. The processes of differentiation (mission, curricula, fields and levels of study, governance and size among others) and articulation (student and staff mobility and collaboration);
2. Embracing different delivery methods thanks to the spread of new information and communication technologies;
3. Opening up and adapting to the international higher education sector, owing to the rapid expansion of cross—border education.

Education at a global level, especially higher education, is emerging as a profitable commercial venture and industry. There is fierce competition among institutions of higher education to attract foreign students in their own countries and to open campuses in other countries to generate income and profit. How can CHE institutions provide a different model? Can they rise against the spirit of the age and collaborate among themselves by sharing scarce resources?

In Kenya, the Nairobi Fellowship of Theological Colleges (NFTC) used to play a coordinating role for theological colleges and one Christian university. Recently the vice chancellors of Christian universities and theological colleges have established a new organization known as Kenya Fellowship of Christian Universities and Colleges (KFCUC). We trust that this body will provide the necessary Christian leadership in reforming CHE. Further, the newly established Centre for the Promotion of CHE in Africa (CPCHEA) should involve KFCUC in providing leadership for the whole continent. It is only in this way that the problems and weaknesses highlighted by van der Walt (2002) can be overcome: academic mediocrity, malpractices, irrelevant curriculum, institutional politicization, severe poverty among students, frustrations among lecturers and the lack of models of excellence

In many African countries, progress towards Universal Primary Education (UPE) is stimulating the demand for education among families and communities. Mamadou Ndoye (2005), the Executive Secretary of the Association for the Development of Education in Africa, notes that unlike conventional analyses of human capital, arguing that individual and social returns of primary education are greater than that stemming from higher education, recent studies conducted in African countries tend to show that higher education helps to reduce poverty, drive technological advances, and increase labour productivity. New research suggests that investments in tertiary education will be important for promoting faster technological catch-up and improving a country's ability to maximize economic output.

Although enrolment rates in tertiary education in Africa are relatively low compared to the rest of the developing world, high unemployment among university graduates and the brain drain syndrome seem to indicate an oversupply of higher education. This sets up a paradox; can Africa at its current stage of social and economic development absorb the number of higher education graduates or is the quality and relevance of education flawed? These questions are pertinent to those concerned about CHE. Can the graduates from such institutions provide a form of Christian leadership that can transform society and bring hope? Can they prayerfully contribute policy recommendations from their stations of work and accelerate the development process?

Some people advocate limiting access to the summit of the educational pyramid in order to align it more closely with the structure of the job market. Others believe the problem is not quantitative but rather related to academic specialization, curriculum design and an approach to higher education that makes little effort to respond to national economic needs and local demand. We propose that an increase in the number and quality of Christian students and scholars will have an impact on the traditional pyramid.

Christian religious education in Africa

In the past, religious education was called "Bible Knowledge" or simply "Religion." Its history dates back to when missionaries established the first secondary or post-primary schools. One of the principles on which the educational system was based was that religious training and moral instruction should be accorded complete equality with secular subjects (Mkena, 2004). Because missionaries owned most of the schools founded, the teaching of religion occupied a place of prominence in the school's curriculum.

Without any clearly stated aim, apart from preparing candidates for higher school certificates, the syllabus rested at the cognitive level, requiring merely the possession of knowledge and facts of Bible passages. The syllabus seemed not to relate in any way to the needs and experience of the African child. In many circles, there is a growing feeling that religious education ought to be "open-ended," implying that religious education should give children a religious view of life and then allow them freely to make up their minds about how that view will express itself, both in belief and practice. This type of reasoning is contrary to Scripture and does not provide a truthful, firm base on which to build.

Since the takeover of schools in the early 60s and 70s, religious education is no longer accorded such a prominent position in the school curriculum. This change occurred particularly at the primary level, which is the base of our educational system. Even at former missionary schools, where teachers had always dealt with this subject, they now began to shirk their responsibility. At a certain point, it appeared that only specialists would be handling religious education. Religious education continued to be taught at the secondary level, but fewer and fewer students pursued it at the university level. This resulted in fewer academics being admitted to the Department of Religion in the public universities, leading to a dearth of professionals to advance CHE and Christian education in our churches.

Church growth in Africa
The 20th century has witnessed the unprecedented growth and spread of Christianity across Africa south of the Sahara. For example, there has been intensification of African initiatives in evangelism and church planting. Students of missions and church history have noticed Africans' increased receptivity to the gospel when it is communicated effectively in relation to traditional worldviews and cultures. The rise of theological associations across the continent, often stimulated by the ecumenical movement; the expansion of evangelicalism, Pentecostalism and charismatic renewal movements globally; and the advances in travel, and communications technology that enhance opportunities for evangelism and discipleship are evidence of great growth. The relevance of the Christian faith to life in modern Africa is another factor. As a result, Africa is now acknowledged as a heartland of the gospel and a central zone of theological activity in the world. Therefore, an appreciation of African Christianity is imperative for the ongoing development of Christian thought worldwide (Daystar University, 2006).

Further, according to Carpenter (2005) the African influence on the world Christian scene is growing. Africans increasingly lead Christian agencies and shape Christian thought. Leadership for the World Council of Churches and the World Alliance of Reformed Churches are a couple examples. Africa is fast becoming a heartland for world Christianity (see also Bediako, 1996).

The church with all its challenges has a vital stake in the existence and encouragement of institutions of higher learning. Cornelius Plantinga (1998) of Calvin Theological Seminary, observed,

> The main trouble with secular higher education is that it cannot provide a Christian student with the help she needs to form a truthful view of the clash between [the kingdom of Christ and the kingdom of "this present darkness."] Secular higher education today is full of a kind of moral relativism in which this clash does not even matter. (p. 6)

The church, working together with Christian scholars on the continent therefore has a great shepherding role to play.

Christian education growth in Africa
In Kenya, for example we have many private primary schools that describe themselves as Christian schools. Christian entrepreneurs have taken up the challenge to fill the gap in the public schooling system and have established private Christian primary schools or academies. Some have gone further to establish Christian high schools, which could provide students for the growing number of Christian universities. As mentioned earlier, most secondary schools were taken over by the government from the sponsoring mainline churches leaving a vacuum in the development of a Christian worldview among students.

Newly formed churches have come up with schools that take the Christian education mandate very seriously. An example of this is the Logos primary school of the Nairobi Chapel. Apart from the fact that these types of schools are found in the urban areas and are quite costly they contribute toward the well-being of Christian education. However, the question remains, are these schools really propagating a Christian worldview or are they Christian by name only? Are they completely Christian or do they incorporate Christianity in some of their activities? Paul wrote in Philippians 1: 15-18 that some indeed preach Christ from envy and rivalry but others from good will. What mattered to him was that Christ was proclaimed.

However, proprietors and educators need to be challenged that ultimately there is little point in attending a school that calls itself "Christian" if it does not approach all truth as being from God. This is a potential strength as well as a challenge to Christian schools. A Biblical worldview will see God as the source of truth in all the subjects taught. This may be difficult for that fiercely competes for recognition through their students' performance in national examinations.

The third group is the parents who are either home schooling or establishing schools that use various Christian curricula. The current generation of educated Christians believes that education and children are twinned ideas. Not only does the kingdom of God belong to those who would accept it as children but that God also values children and will punish those who lead them astray. Greene (2003) asserts that it is most urgent for the very preservation of the church that parents become more concerned about the overall education of their children [so that it is] "in the discipline and instruction of the Lord" (Ephesians 6:4b). He laments that people who profess to belonging to the body of Christ seem oblivious to the magnitude of the crises brought about by the technological invasion of the home by television and the Internet. In his view, Christian schooling at home or in a Christian school "ceases to be a luxury and becomes an irreplaceable bastion for the communication of the faith to the next generation" (Greene, 2003, p. xiii). If more and more Christians on the continent could be persuaded to view education in a similar manner, the well-being of Christian education would be further enhanced.

CHE in Africa

CHE, though very small in the continent, has great potential. This is because existing and newly formed primary and secondary Christian schools create a market and a need for CHE. The public universities also do create a market because students can come from these universities and move to the Christian universities to further their education in either masters or doctoral studies. The Akrofi—Christaller Memorial Centre for Mission Research and Applied Theology in Ghana and Nairobi Evangelical Graduate School of Theology are some of the institutions offering doctorates in areas that are beginning to impact CHE in Africa. Their graduates are serving in churches and Christian universities.

In the last 15 years, there has been a marked growth in the number of institutions offering Christian education; particularly in East Africa, many Christian universities have been established in the last five years. In the region, there are both denominational and interdenominational universities. In Kenya, for example, we have Kenya Methodist University, African Nazarene University, Baraton University, Kabarak University, Scott Theological College, St Paul's United Theological College, Pan African Christian College, Nairobi Evangelical Graduate School of Theology (to become African Christian University), and four other Christian universities await registration by the government. In Uganda, we have Uganda Christian University, Martyrs University, Uganda Pentecostal University among others, and in Tanzania we have Mt. Meru Baptist University, Tumaini University, University of Arusha, and University of Ruaha among others. In Southern and Central Africa we have Potchefstroom University for Christian Higher Education (in South Africa), New

Africa University (Zimbabwe), the Christian College of Southern Africa (Zimbabwe), and Hilltop University at Mkar (Nigeria). Ghana has a Pentecostal University and several other Christian schools.

For any of these Christian institutions to impact Christian education they have to clearly identify and articulate what makes them distinct in the world of higher education. According to Jim Mannoia (1999) there are practical, pedagogical, and theological reasons why this sharpened focus is essential. Christian colleges can and must discover their genius given that CHE has both intrinsic and instrumental values, which help students, not only become a certain kind of person, but also teach them to do certain kinds of things.

According to Mannoia, these values should forcefully shape an institution's goals. In his view, colleges are required to help their students go beyond both dogmatism and scepticism to what he calls critical commitment. Christian colleges ought not to be content to produce dogmatic graduates with "all the answers" who have never risked asking the questions. Nor should they be content with graduates who have asked all the questions but like the sceptical products of most secular institutions have embraced relativism and abandoned hope that there even are answers.

The integration of faith and learning demands the best disciplinary competence and—at the same time—a commitment to bring that competence to bear on "real world" problems. Such problems inevitably integrate multiple disciplines, values and learning, and theory with practice. Graduates of such institutions are best placed to wrestle with the spiritual and material conditions of the continent and the world.

Higher education's worldview

In arguing for a distinction between the church and the kingdom of God, Lont (2004) states that the opportunity for CHE guided by leaders imbued with the Christian world view/life system (i.e. teachers, administrators, governing board members and a Christian support community including the church) is the challenge of every age. To meet that challenge requires that these deeply committed leaders provide an area for teaching, learning and scholarship that has a stability born of purpose and is marked by performance.

A recent survey by Daystar University among youths in churches revealed that a large majority would choose a Christian University against a secular one. However the type of courses offered in most of the Christian universities are not necessarily the ones most young people are interested in pursuing. The well-being of Christian education will be improved when Christian institutions of higher learning can provide training in professions such as medicine and technology.

Tools for Christian educational well-being
The well-being of Christian education on the continent needs to be understood in context. Beginning with the colonial experience, the missionary enterprise, the growth of local forms of Christianity and the high-level energy of its scholars and entrepreneurs one recognizes the threads in a multicoloured tapestry that has great potential.

B. J. van der Walt (2004) recognizes a group of African Christians who adhere to a holistic, world-transformative worldview. However, there are four dysfunctional types of Christianity on the continent. First, Ecclesiastism confines Christianity to converted individuals and established churches. It lacks a broader kingdom vision. Second, escapist Christianity flees the harsh realities of the "outside" world. Escapism manifests itself in different sub-types (often imported from overseas), like an apocalyptic Christianity or a gospel of prosperity. Third, secularism prevails when people think and behave as Christians in their personal or church life, but in every other area of life, they are lost. More and more African Christians do not see any relevance in the Gospel for the real and burning issues on our continent- they have capitulated to a secularist religion, living as if God does not exist. One of the basic reasons for this is the lack of a clear, Biblically inspired philosophy of society. Finally, pietism regards Christian faith as individual piety, not necessarily trying to escape the harsh realities of life, but trying to solve or deal with them without God's revelation.

To address the challenges, that come from a dualistic worldview, and to encourage the Christians who recognize an oneness in all spheres we propose the following five tools for promoting educational well-being.

First, we need suitable texts. The newly published Africa Bible Commentary (2005) written by seventy African scholars is a testimony of the value of and need for Christian Education on the continent. Educational well-being for the millions of believers in Africa will be well on its way if the commentary is properly used in institutions of higher education. In the first foreword John Stott states, "Its foundation is Biblical, its perspective African, and its approach to controversial questions balanced." Similarly, we believe that such descriptions are necessary for the type of Christian education that would contribute to the spiritual and socio-economic development of the people of Africa.

The second foreword by Aboagye-Mensah brings to our attention the need for an appropriate tool or basic texts for teaching the Christian faith given that one of the greatest challenges facing Christians in Africa is the means of "sustaining the numerical growth while ensuring that the faith of the Christians is firmly grounded in the revealed and written word of God."

Second, we need solid studies in philosophy. Philosophy is one of the basic disciplines. Historically it is the discipline from which all other branches of scholarship developed, and there is the opinion that all other disciplines somehow have philosophical points of departure. It is important that Christian scholars in the continent grasp basic philosophic ideas that would lead them to pursue wisdom regarding basic concepts like reality, humankind, society, nature, culture, value, and knowledge. A careful understanding of African philosophy will enhance philosophical thoughts from other ages and societies.

According to J. J. Venter (2004) the duties of a scholarly philosopher are:

- To give academic form to our life view in such a way that avenues to wisdom are opened up to the reader or student.
- To study the "wisdom" of other thinkers.
- To point to the underlying philosophies and worldviews in culture, politics, art etc.
- To point to the roles of philosophy and worldview in other academic disciplines.

Further the Bible says, "that the fear of the Lord is the beginning of wisdom," using wisdom in the sense of living practically in God's presence. In a Christian university, this is important. Believers and unbelievers can be found in the same institutions yet facing similar experiences. The difference will be seen in how each person responds. The duties of any university, especially in a time when information is abundantly available, are to impact intellectual knowledge in such a way that it will lead the student and reader to wisdom, and to criticize the intellectual ideas which may close the way to wisdom.

Third, we must adopt a relevant curriculum. Daystar University, Nairobi has been providing CHE for the last 30 years. The recently launched Master of Theology in African Christianity is an example of the way in which Christian scholarship is being encouraged in the continent. The purpose of the programme is to provide theological formation and to promote research for the expansion of God's kingdom in the pluralist world especially in Africa. This programme focuses on African Christianity in view of the prominent place it holds in world Christianity today.

In keeping with African epistemology and ontology the programme will endeavour to take a holistic approach. It aims at nurturing and equipping students for ongoing personal formation, ecclesial reformation and social transformation. It seeks to assist students in identifying and articulating significant elements of development of Christianity in Africa. The aim will be to foster an increased sense of African Christian identity, an enhanced ability to engage rigorously with theological issues in the African context and a deeper commitment to accountability for authentic Christian witness. This new programme seeks to respond to the needs of the continent as well as provide a theological basis for faith and action. It builds on the faith of the learners while challenging them to excel in their scholarship. Development of similar curricula addressing other areas would contribute significantly to the well-being of Christian education.

Fourth, we must develop well-trained educators and teachers. Apart from the curriculum, the pedagogy, and institutional management, the teacher is critical to the well-being of education. Our recommendation would be for the establishment and strengthening of departments of education in the Christian institutions of higher learning. As an alternative the current online courses provided by the IAPCHE Christian Academic Studies Certificate project would be highly recommended.

A recent directive by the Tanzanian president is very encouraging. He has authorized any qualified student who wishes to be trained in education to apply to any university, private or public and receive government funding for the training. This will again provide a great opportunity for potential Christian educators.

Finally, we must improve the management of Christian institutions of higher education. In managing the institution of higher learning, several concepts need to be placed under the Lordship of Christ. Academic freedom and university autonomy, perhaps of primary importance, are essential to the advancement, transmission, and application of knowledge. In practical terms, academic freedom and university autonomy relate to the protection of the university from day to day direction by government officials, over the selection of students, appointment and removal of academic staff, determination of the content of university education, control of degree standards, determination of size and rate of growth, establishment of the balance between teaching, research and advanced study, the selection of research projects and freedom of publication, and allocation of recurrent income among the various categories of expenditure.

A second concept that needs to be placed under the Lordship of Christ is relevance. To ensure sustainability an education system needs to be balanced. It must be capable of producing students at different levels with qualifications that respond to labour market needs, generating a steady supply of skilled workers, professionals, and leaders.

Concepts like accountability, effectiveness, and efficiency all have this place in CHE. The resources in the university should be dealt with stewardship in mind. The leaders are accountable to their supervisors who are ultimately accountable to the Creator of the universe. The efficiency of universities is no longer to be measured by the number of graduates produced, but by their quality and capacity to produce the knowledge required to reduce the widespread dependence and marginalization of the African countries and continent. To communicate effectively kingdom values and principles should be the standard measure.

Finally, periodic evaluation must be conducted. Christian universities should, on their own initiative, institute periodic evaluation both of the performance of the institution and of the teaching and research of their staff. There is also need for an evaluation and appraisal of university programmes on a continuing basis so as to ensure their relevance and responsiveness to changing national development efforts and strategies. Such an evaluation may save the institution from the pitfalls of decadence and immobility in a rapidly changing world. It will also keep the vision and mission of the institution in sight at all times.

Conclusion

If Africa is to overcome the present crisis and know peace and prosperity, African Christians must actively participate in the economic, political, and social development of their nations. Like the Jewish exiles in Babylon, they must work for the peace and prosperity of Africa (Kinoti and Kimuyu, 1997).

William Saint, a lead education specialist with the World Bank, (2005) argues that education is tightly linked to economic and social development. It is simultaneously a driver and a beneficiary of economic growth. Expansion generates

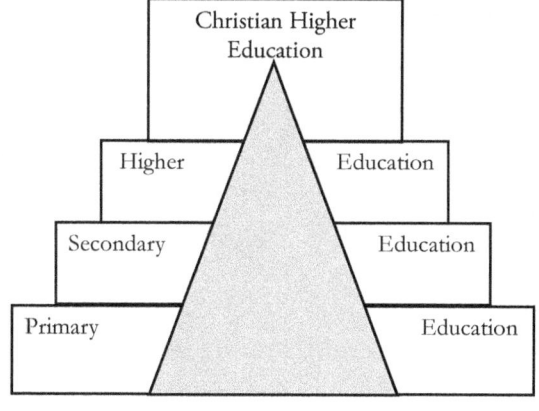

the resources to increase education provision; simultaneously economies thrive and basic education expands only when they are supported by an education system that takes significant numbers of students beyond the basic cycle including university completion.

References

Adeyemo, T. (Ed.). (2006). *Africa Bible commentary*. Nairobi: WordAlive Publishers.
Ajayi, A., Goma, L., & Johnson, A. (1996). *The African experience with higher education*. Accra: Association of African Universities.
Bediako, K. (1995). *Christianity in Africa: The renewal of a non-western religion*. Maryknoll, NY: Orbis Books.
Carpenter, J., & Sanneh, L. (2005). *The changing face of Christianity: Africa, the west and the world*. New York: Oxford University Press.
Daystar University. (2006). *Proposal for the degree of master of theology in African Christianity*. Nairobi.
Fowler, S. (1991). *A Christian voice among students and scholars*. Potchefstroom, South Africa: Institute for Reformational Studies.
Greene, A. (2003). *Reclaiming the future of Christian Education: A transforming vision*. Colorado Springs: Purposeful Design Publications.
Hulst, J. (2004). *Christian world view and scholarship*. Eltham, Australia: Amani.
Kinoti, G. (1997). *Hope for Africa and what the Christian can do*. Nairobi: AISRED.
Kinoti, G., & Kimuyu P. (Eds.). (1997). *Vision for a bright Africa*. Nairobi: AISRED.
Ledbetter, G. (2006). *Benefits of a Christian higher education: Education with a Biblical focus*. Retrieved August 30, 2006, from http://www.collegeview.com
Lont, J. (2004). The vital stake of the African church in Christian higher education's world view and scholarship. In J. B. Hulst (Ed.), *Christian world view and scholarship* (pp. 67-71). Eltham, Australia: Amani.

Mannoia, J. (1999). A vi*sion for Christian higher education.* Retrieved August 30, 2006, from http://www.greenville.edu

Mkena, T. (2004). Christian religious education in the 21st century: A shared Praxis. In J. B. Hulst (Ed.), *Christian world view and scholarship* (pp. 72-90). Eltham, Australia: Amani.

Ndoye, M. (Editorial). (2005). What kind of higher education for Africa? *ADEA Newsletter,* 17(3/4), 1-2.

Plantinga, C. Jr. (1998). Why Christian college education matters. *Calvin Seminary Forum,* 5(3), 6-7.

Public Universities Inspection Board. (2006). *Transformation of higher education and training in Kenya.* Nairobi.

Saint, W. (2005). Higher education and development *ADEA Newsletter,* 17(3/4), 3-4, 18.

van der Walt, B. J. (2002). The challenge of Christian higher education on the African continent in the twenty-first century. *Christian Higher Education,* 1(2-3), 195-227.

Venter, J. J. (2004). The role of philosophy in the Reformational Christian university. In J. B. Hulst (Ed.), *Christian world view and scholarship* (pp. 33-60). Eltham, Australia: Amani.

RESPONSE TO FAITH W. NGURU

Susan S. Hasseler

Dr. Nguru presents a comprehensive and thoughtful overview of both the history and the future of Christian higher education (CHE) in Africa. Based on her study of the history of higher education in post-Colonial Africa as well as her experience in higher education in Kenya, she presents a clear and comprehensive argument for why the time is right for the expansion of CHE on the continent. Many of the principles about CHE that Dr. Nguru shares apply to contexts outside of the African continent as well, including long-standing institutions of higher education in North America.

Higher education is situated in particular historical contexts
Dr. Nguru's analysis of the history of higher education in Kenya and in the sub-Saharan part of the continent reminds us that education is always situated in particular national and international contexts. In many places, both Christianity and higher education may have positive and negative historical associations. Christianity may be associated with oppression and colonization, with liberation and justice, or with both. Higher education may be associated with an elitist source of oppression or it may be viewed as a positive source of personal development and economic advancement. It is very important for those who are interested in promoting CHE to understand that the attitudes and policies of the current political and economic leaders in a particular setting have been shaped by history. A clear and deep understanding of the role(s) Christianity and higher education have played in a particular setting and the current perceptions of people in the community toward faith-based institutions of higher education could help educators avoid unnecessary conflicts and overcome potential barriers pro-actively rather than reactively. This pro-active response may shape the language we use as well as the policies we put into place to build trust with those who may have been negatively affected by religious or educational structures in the past.

Christian education involves taking risks
Dr. Nguru includes a particularly powerful section in her paper on the challenges of creating and maintaining Christian institutions of higher education that prepare students to think critically about and live transformationally in the world. Teaching students to ask hard questions and live in new and transformed ways in society can be risky business. Like many Christian colleges and universities in North America, it appears that students and their families in Africa may be choosing CHE to escape from the world or to develop increased personal piety without acknowledging our call as Christians to address systemic injustice and oppression in the world. This focus on personal piety alone can stand in the way of preparing students who can transform society in very real and practical ways. The integration of Biblical principles into professional programs allows institutions to support their constituents' interest in personal spiritual growth while also being true to our call to transform the world.

Broadening the focus of current Christian institutions of higher education to include professional programs will require a thorough knowledge of a particular setting as well as strong understanding of strategies for working through conflict in particular cultural contexts. A future goal for IAPCHE might be to provide opportunities to learn more about conflict resolution and organizational change strategies in order to facilitate this important transition in focus.

An additional issue facing those who hope to provide high-quality Christian professional programs is one of capacity. Partnerships between North American Christian institutions of higher education and Christian institutions of higher education on other continents may provide mutual benefits in this area. Models for effectively integrating Biblical principles into professional programs should be a specific focus in future IAPCHE events.

Making connections between CHE and P-12 education
Dr. Nguru also includes a timely and compelling look at the connections between Christian P-12 and higher education. She suggests that the growth of Christian P-12 schools is leading to an increased demand for CHE. It is very important for Christian institutions of higher education to foster relationships with Christian schools in their region in order to recruit students into higher education. Many Christian colleges and universities have specific partnership programs with primary and secondary schools that are designed to make students aware of their higher education options. The design and implementation of effective

college preparation and recruitment programs would be another good topic for IAPCHE to consider in future conferences or publications. The design and implementation of effective college preparation and recruitment programs would be another good topic for IAPCHE to consider in future conferences or publications.

Christian institutions of higher education can also support Christian P-12 schools by conducting research on effective teaching and curriculum development in particular school contexts. Faculty members in Schools of Education in Christian institutions of higher education need to be engaged in the ongoing study of culturally responsive teaching strategies that are effective in their particular context. In addition, they need to examine ways in which Christian schools can meet particular national standards and goals while integrating Christian perspectives into the curriculum in meaningful ways. This research needs to be shared with teachers and school leaders in ways that are accessible and applicable to practice. Again, IAPCHE can provide an excellent forum for Christian teacher educators to discuss their research on effective schooling practices and ways to share these practices with current and new teachers and school leaders.

Collaboration across multiple boundaries
The theme of collaboration is interwoven throughout Dr. Nguru's paper. She suggests that Christians must cross denominational boundaries as well as collaborating with public institutions and international partners. This call to collaboration is essential but it also presents multiple challenges. Denominational loyalties and particular interpretations of Biblical principles can be very strong. It often takes a crisis of significant magnitude to get Christians of different denominational backgrounds to work together. Dr. Nguru presents a strong case for the presence of an economic and social crisis in Africa that should motivate collaboration. There are some excellent models of cross-denominational models of collaboration on the continent already. In addition, there are models of collaboration between those in political and economic power and P-12 and higher educators that show the benefits to all those involved. The regional and international conferences hosted by IAPCHE provide excellent opportunities to share these collaborative models.

Dr. Nguru ends her paper with a wonderful diagram showing the expanding levels of influence that Christian education can have on society. However, one piece is missing from this model: collaboration among Christian institutions of higher education. A three dimensional model would be needed to show the intersection of institutions at the top level of the triangle with a powerful, multi-sided base that provides a firm foundation for the work of these individual institutions. I commend IAPCHE for providing the opportunity to build that firm foundation. In addition, I join Dr. Nguru in her powerful call for developing Christian institutions of higher education whose express mission is to transform the societies in which they are situated.

PRODUCTIVE PEDAGOGY AMONG ASIAN LEARNERS

LIZETTE F. KNIGHT

Introduction
This chapter defines productive pedagogy, its origin, and current research. Though focused on Asian learning styles, this chapter compares Asian learners with those from other parts of the world. Theories of learning are integrated as well, in order to see the motivational factors in the learning-teaching process of Asian academe. An "A2Z Teacher's Tips" is included as a section under the implications for productive pedagogy to assist Asian teachers as well as those who would like to teach in Asia.

Productive Pedagogies
The Productive Pedagogies project started from the Queensland School Reform Longitudinal Study and used the following definition of productive pedagogies:

> Productive Pedagogies are effective pedagogy, incorporating an array of teaching strategies that support classroom environments, and recognition of difference, and are implemented across all key learning and subject areas. Effective pedagogical practice promotes the wellbeing of students, teachers and the school community—it improves students' and teachers' confidence and contributes to their sense of purpose for being at school; it builds community confidence in the quality of learning and teaching in the school. (Queensland, 2002)

Current research related to productive pedagogies covers virtual schooling (Kapitzke & Pendergast, 2005), implementation (Hayes, Lingard & Mills, 2000), and success (Hinton, 2003). This also includes gender-related reflection and investigation (Keddie, 2006; Martino & Becket, 2004), teacher enhancement (Gore & Griffins, 2004), challenge of inclusion for all students (Allen, 2003), and the sociology of pedagogy (McFadden & Geoff, 2002). MacDonald argues that the processes of, and barriers to, curriculum change in this context can be explained by the tensions between modernism and postmodernism (MacDonald, 2003).

Research findings varied in their results and conclusions. Kapitzke and Pendergast (2005) said that "application of the Productive Pedagogies framework showed that the innovation held pedagogical potential that remained unrealized" (p. 1626). Martino and Becket (2004) concluded, "that teacher threshold knowledge about gender impact significantly on the execution or pedagogical practices and the implementation of curriculum in the HPE (Health and Physical Education) classroom" (p. 239). One asked questions related to the productiveness of particular pedagogies (Lewis, 2004). Gore and Griffins' (2004) research among student teachers revealed the need for "a more fundamental reorganization of teacher education to fully integrate Productive Pedagogy (PP), if the framework is to have a significant and lasting impact" (pp. 78-79). They further said that this requires a reevaluation of the goals and objectives of teachers in relation to their educational purposes to improve the quality of teacher effectiveness (Gore & Griffins, 2004).

Often research has examined the students' place in PP. McFadden and Geoff address the continuing challenge to encourage disengaged students toward educational success through social pedagogy (McFadden & Geoff, 2002). Lingard, Hayes, and Mills also argue that improving students' outcome involves both students and teachers engaged in the learning-teaching process (Lingard, Hayes & Mills, 2000). A recently conducted qualitative research revealed:

> But something has changed. Everywhere there is an increased excitement about learning. The curriculum has come alive. Student engagement is intense. Kids won't go out to lunch, don't want to go home in the afternoon. Teachers and students are talking, talking, talking. (Hinton, 2003, p. 4)

Productive pedagogy can happen, specifically, in the implementation in maximum teaching.

Maximum teaching
Productive pedagogy utilizes creative teaching and higher critical thinking in the academy. It utilizes diverse teaching methods in order to facilitate maximum learning possibilities (Rabin, Lehmann, Kedar, Hegar & Nechama, 1998) such as class projects where learners apply new concepts to important tasks for skill development (Share & Rogers, 1997). In addition, maximum teaching designs effective interdisciplinary activities for students (Barad & Landa, 1997) in which stronger students are motivated to use their intelligence to assist weaker students (Dwyer, 2002).

Acknowledging individual learning styles can allow learners to experience success for a better self-concept and sense of personal efficacy

(Newton & Smith, 1996). Once learners are motivated as they use their preferred learning styles, they can capitalize on this preference in difficult learning situations. However, educators need to be challenged to use the other domain for maximizing the use of the brain. The educator plays an important role in this aspect, as an authoritative teacher is needed "for students to be pushed toward maximum learning" (Vander Staay, 2004, p. 49). This means that students who are right-brainers have to venture using their left domain for creative thinking. Patricia O'Connel Killen says that teaching strategies are not sufficient, but are necessary for building the bridge from where the students are as composers of meaning to where they should be (Killen, 2002).

Maximum teaching uses varied teaching strategies so that all learners can be successful. The knowledge on how the brain learns provides a unique opportunity to reexamine training methods that will bring true understanding, empathy, tolerance, and respect for all learners (Dwyer, 2002). Realistically, traditional materials and methods can live side-by-side with the latest innovations to provide maximum learning, since maximum learning includes the full use of critical thinking in teaching (McLester, 2001). (The material in this section is handled in more detail in my paper *Maximum Learning through Balanced Critical Thinking and Creative Teaching*.)

Higher critical thinking
Phyllis Turner provides one definition of critical thinking in teaching. Based on Turner's appraisal, the following are significant attributes of critical thinking: analyticity, inference, interpretations, open-mindedness, intellectual reasoning, self-regulatory, synthesis, and truth seeking (Turner, 2005). Critical thinking is associated with creative thinking, problem solving, decision-making, diagnostic reasoning, and reflective thinking (Turner, 2005). It is characterized by authentic analysis and application. It requires a higher order of thinking that results in beliefs and behavior for contextualization.

Critical thinking is related to the left-brain characteristic of logic, analytical skills, objectivity, rationality, and an interest in facts and details (Flew, 2004). "An awareness of students' use of their own experiences and a consistent promotion of critical literacy skills throughout a child's, adolescent's, and adult's life strengthens awareness of the social, political, economic, and cultural implications of education" (Gruber & Boreen, 2003, p. 5). It is also the ability to reflect on one's personal and other individuals' ways of learning and teaching. Creative thinking is needed in order for learners to develop critical thinking for maximum learning. This can be done when creative teaching is implemented in the learning-teaching process.

Creative teaching
Creative teaching develops curriculum to create connections to the students' current experience for the purpose of helping them achieve maximum learning (Ritchart, 2004). Connection is important since "students best learn skills and concepts as tools to meet present demands rather than as facts to be memorized today in the hopes of application tomorrow" (Barad & Landa, 1997, p. 52). Relevant materials promote maximum learning and teaching.

Creativity is associated with such right-brain characteristics as intuition, subjectivity, emotion, and an interest in the "big picture" (Flew, 2004). Creative teaching utilizes "teaching strategies to provide opportunities for learners in all educational levels to expand their literacy skills" (Gruber & Boreen, 2003, p. 5). One creative teaching method is interactive reflection (McGuire & Inlow, 2005). Another is collaborative learning where students learn to develop ideas, explore their inner feelings, research, analyze, and learn how to work together on major projects (Hyde, 2005). Creative teaching involves sensitivity to what the learner needs, yet uses challenging teaching methods that may not be comfortable for some learners, along with high motivation from the teacher. The teacher as coach is essential to capitalizing on the learners' preferred learning styles. Creative teaching is a challenge, especially to left-brain educators not used to creative teaching. It is essential that teachers have a full understanding and mastery of techniques. Peer observation is one method in which creative teaching can be developed (Marshall, 2004).

Creative teaching allows learners to experience success, develop self-efficacy, and infuse excitement in learning; as a result, students' creativity is also cultivated (Ritchart, 2004). When a learner develops creative thinking, one can accept the challenge of using the other brain domain that was once inactive.

Individuals have unique learning styles and varied intelligences. Collectively, Asians have some distinct cultures and values in their learning and teaching. Part of productive pedagogy knows the cultural contexts.

Context of Asian teachers and learners
Educational changes have a tendency to support the interests of those who are in the majority in any given community (Nieto, 2002). It is

important to understand that the cultural context has an influence upon an individual's belief system. Through a survey, more than fourteen-hundred teachers from seven countries gave their beliefs about Mosston's Spectrum of Teaching Styles. The results revealed that the use of styles used by the teachers was significantly related to the teacher's belief system about the style used (Cothran et al., 2005).

Two interview studies compared student with teacher views of learning. The first study interviewed thirty Hong Kong teachers, while the second study interviewed thirty-two Hong Kong teachers. The results revealed that the students held a less sophisticated view of learning than did the Chinese teachers. Twenty-one of the thirty-two teachers interviewed in study two said that they developed lesson plans based upon the understanding of the differences between their students' views of learning and their own views. However, in the majority of the cases, the teacher just tried to adapt their teaching to their students' cognitive ability and level of motivation (Watkins, 2004).

Differences exist in Socratic or Western and Confucian or Asian educational philosophies.

> Socrates, a Western exemplar, valued private and public questioning of widely accepted knowledge and expected students to evaluate others' beliefs and to generate and express their own hypotheses. Confucius, an Eastern exemplar, valued effortful, respectful, and pragmatic acquisition of essential knowledge as well as behavioral reform. (Tweed & Lehman, 2002, p. 89)

The Socratic is the idea that "truth is not prescribed by authority" (Tweed & Lehman, 2002, p. 91). Confucianism continues to influence Asia, inspiring and providing intellectual and moral coherence to a large part of the world's population. It continues to affect the teaching and learning not only in the Chinese cultures of China, Taiwan, Singapore, and Malaysia, but in Korea, Vietnam, and Japan (Irwin, 1996).

Japanese society is education-minded to an extraordinary degree where success in formal education is considered largely synonymous with success in life. Today, a clear consensus exists that education is essential for both individual and social development and that it requires an active, sustained commitment of energy and resources of all levels of society (On, 1996).

Asian classrooms have been viewed as teacher-centered by both Western and Asian researchers. The students in these classrooms are highly successful in student achievement (Clarke, 2003). Through assimilation of student-centered teaching strategies into the traditional teacher-centered strategies, a unique teaching strategy consisting of both teacher's control and students' engagement in the process of learning emerges in the Chinese classrooms (Clarke, 2003). The Asian learner paradox is the

> apparent contradiction between the teaching methods/en-vironment in Asian schools (i.e. large classes, whole class teaching, examination-driven teaching, content rather than process-oriented, emphasis on memorization, etc.) and the fact that Asian students have regularly performed better than their Western counterparts in comparative studies. The paradox lies in the fact that the above characterization of Asian teaching describes features that much research shows are not conducive to effective mathematics learning. (Clarke, 2003, p. 15)

(The materials in this section are handled in more detail in Michael Scott Knight's findings on the topic "How Asians Learn.")

Learning theory among Asian learners

Biggs's theory discusses two kinds of mental processes in dealing with knowledge: simplistic and complex. Pupils who employ a more dualistic approach have a tendency to utilize a surface approach to learning, and students who are more relativistic and dedicated in regard to the Perry scales have a tendency to take a deep approach to learning (Zhang & Watkins, 2001).

Zhang and Watkins discovered that pupils who were recognized as dualists were inclined to generate work that was at the lower levels in Bloom's taxonomy, and those pupils who were recognized as relativists were inclined to generate work at the higher levels in Bloom's taxonomy (Zhang & Watkins, 2001). In addition, Korean, Chinese, and Japanese pupils are considered visual learners with Korean pupils ranking the highest (Zhenhui, 2005). Although Caucasian, Korean, and Chinese pupils demonstrated a negative preference for group learning, Vietnamese pupils demonstrated a major preference for group learning, and Filipino pupils demonstrated a minor preference for group learning, showing noteworthy ethnic group distinctions (Park, 2000).

The table below compares the four different learning styles in relation to five different ethnic groups: (1) Caucasian, (2) Korean, (3) Chinese, (4) Vietnamese, and (5) Filipino.

Table 1. Ethnic Group Preferences for Learning (Park, 1997)

Ethnic Group	Auditory	Visual	Kinesthetic	Tactile
	Mean	Mean	Mean	Mean
Caucasian	17.56	16.01	18.31	17.80
Korean	17.68	17.33	18.01	17.61
Chinese	18.05	17.88	18.47	17.44
Vietnamese	18.64	16.96	19.02	19.00
Filipino	17.97	17.68	18.80	17.73

Note: Preference means 18.00 and above = major learning style preference; 16.50 and above = minor learning style preference; 16.49 or less = negative learning style preference

Asian learning styles
Even though Chinese pupils perform better than Western pupils in mathematics and the sciences, they are not famous for their imagination and innovative thinking (Salili, 1996). Chinese learners have a tendency to adopt a concrete-sequential cognitive style (Kennedy, 2002). Chinese students reflect more upon the ideas that are being taught rather than being impetuous. They prefer a measured, precise, methodical approach and are not as content with forecasting (Kennedy, 2002). A Hong Kong report revealed that pupil-initiated sharing of learning strategies has been found to "promote the implementation of a deep approach to education and the use of high-level cognitive strategies" (Flowerdew, 1998, p. 325).

The pupils, in deciding which learning style to utilize, depended upon the teacher and how he or she presented ideas. If the ideas were presented with facts, students were led unreservedly to employ learning strategies that led to memorization, but when uncertainty was introduced by the professor's verbal communication, the student was encouraged to employ an element of questioning (Claxton, Atkinson, Osborn & Wallace, 1996).

Table 2. Student Preferred Learning Styles (Barron & Arcodia, 2002)

Ethnic Origin	Activist	Reflector	Theorist	Pragmatist
Japanese	47 Moderate	67 Moderate	62 Moderate	57 Low
Korean	47 Moderate	55 Low	52 Low	47 Low
Vietnamese	50 Moderate	73 Strong	52 Moderate	57 Low
Chinese	57 Strong	68 Moderate	59 Moderate	58 Low
Average CHC	50 Moderate	66 Moderate	59 Moderate	55 Low

The ways in which pupils are evaluated have a major effect on the way students approach their educational duties. Therefore, it is important that educators use evaluative procedures, which have a tendency in assisting a deep approach to education (Zhang & Watkins, 2001). Reading tactics and research methods are different between the West and Confucian traditions. In the West, reading is an individualized activity, requiring a type of disrespect toward the material and a research method that demands pupils to analyze and synthesize a critical answer to a certain situation. However, in the Confucian tradition, the goal of such reading was not to exhume an individual significance in the material, but to declaim and contrast the teachings acknowledged experts (Smith, 1999).

One study revealed significant differences in the perceptions of Hong Kong Chinese teachers and Western expatriate teachers as to what they believed to be beneficial teaching. Chinese teachers emphasized the significance of foundational information. They felt pupils needed to acquire a mastery of this as a beginning step in any field. The teacher was seen to be the authoritative source whose responsibility was to take pupils methodically through a set of objectives. Western expatriate teachers tended to perceive their job as the amplification and application of foundational information. Hong Kong Chinese teachers viewed themselves as having a pastoral function in leading and mentoring pupils outside the class. Western teachers seem to be less sympathetic than their Chinese colleagues, frequently describing pupils as indolent and not having the ability for deep thought. They were unable to connect the link between pupil behavior and the social structures of formal education and family life in Hong Kong (Pratt, Kelly & Wong, 1999).

Hong Kong pupils often ascribe their educational success to effort rather than to aptitude, and they are inclined to find ways in which they might develop their abilities; Western pupils have a tendency to assign past performance to things they cannot do anything about (Ho, Salili, Biggs & Hau, 1999).

Memorization and speaking in class
Asians believe that learning is reciting. If they recite it, then think it over; think it over, then recite it, then it will inherit some special meaning for them. If they recite it, but do not think it over, they still may not appreciate its meaning. If they think it over but do not recite it, even though they might understand it, their understanding will not be stable (On, 1996). This argument that memorization occurs in conjunction with efforts to reach understanding suggests that the assumption that these pupils were rote learning could be false. If learning involves understanding as well as memorizing, then it is neither rote learning nor a surface approach. The combined approach usually will result in high grades as the pupils can reach an understanding of foundational concepts, and thus are able to handle assignments requiring application or critical thinking ability. They are also likely to do well in tests, which require the pupils to demonstrate that they have understood a body of information as in table 3 below.

Table 3. Approach to Learning (Kember, 2000)

Approach	Intention	Strategy
Surface	Memorizing without understanding	Rote-learning
Intermediate 1	Primarily memorizing	Strategic attempt to reach limited understanding as an aid to memorization
Understanding and Memorizing	Understanding and Memorizing	Seeking comprehension then committing to memory Repetition and memorizing to reach understanding
Intermediate 2	Primarily Understanding	Strategic memorization for examination or task after understanding reached
Deep	Understanding	Seeking comprehension

The belief that pupils rely upon rote learning can be understood as a failure to realize that memorization could be related to an intention to seek understanding. Beliefs that students resist different forms of teaching other than traditional didactic ones probably started because the pupils were not given the time and encouragement to adapt from teaching styles they had not extensively experienced toward others to which they were accustomed (Kember, 2000).

Memorizing information or already well-known facts may be necessary to ensure success and is considered a deep approach (Ho, Salili, Biggs & Hau, 1999). One study surveyed twenty English teachers from China and Hong Kong. These educators believed that with each continuous reading of the material will come a new understanding (Marton, Ference, Alba & Kun, 1996). Another study compared German and Hong Kong Chinese learners' beliefs on the role of repetition in memorization and found that the Hong Kong Chinese learners were conscious of two options inherent in repetition: developing a deep impression on the cognition and creating new individual meaning. Furthermore, the stress on the attentive effort important in repetition is much more normal among Hong Kong Chinese pupils than among German pupils (Dahlin & Watkins, 2000). It has been suggested that pupils are not passive learners, but are more reflective. Chinese pupils value thoughtful questions, which they ask after much reflection, while less thoughtful questions may be scoffed at by other pupils (Crtazzi & Jin, 1996). It has been said, "Learning without thought or reflection is labor lost; thought without learning is perilous" (Leung, 2001, p. 39).

Confucian versus Socratic method of education
Teacher-dominated classrooms in Confucian-heritage cultures (CHC) are often seen as an environment not conducive to learning in Western countries. However, students from CHC countries have consistently performed well in international studies of mathematics achievement (Huang & Leung, 2005). It has had direct results on not only the Chinese cultures of China, Taiwan, Singapore, and Malaysia, but also in Korea, Vietnam, and Japan (Irwin, 1996).

Socrates, a Western exemplar, believed in private and public questioning of universal information and expected pupils to assess others' ideas and to produce and express their own hypotheses. Confucius, an Eastern exemplar, valued effortful, respectful, and practical acquirement of basic information as well as behavioral improvement (Greenholtz, 2003).

Confucian-oriented education involves effort-based conceptions of education, practical orientations to education, and acceptance of behavioral improvement as an educational goal. Socratic-oriented education involves obvious and private questioning, expression of personal ideas, and a desire for self-directed goals (Tweed & Lehman, 2002). It has been forecasted that Chinese pupils are more likely to focus on pragmatic outcomes of education than are Western pupils. Research has shown that culturally Chinese pupils are more likely than culturally Western pupils to consider education as a means to an end (Tweed & Lehman, 2002).

For Confucian learners, the expectation is for the teacher to guide them systematically through a clear set of objectives (Pratt, Kelly & Wong, 1999). In terms of behavioral improvement, pupils from individualistic cultures "tend to give more weight to norms than to attitudes as determinants of behavior" (Triandis, 1996).

The individualistic, Socratic, learner has learned to analyze critically and evaluate the hypotheses presented by the professor. In relation to attitudes of behavior, some believe in questioning the hypotheses of those in authority, and it has been stated that those who do not critically analyze the ideas of others have "irrational attitudes of submission to authority" (Tweed & Lehman, 2002, p. 95).

Western culture emphasizes independence and individualism, while Asia stresses integration and agreement (Leung, 2001). Asian countries with a CHC, such as China, Vietnam, Singapore, Korea, and Japan, share characteristics of a collectivist society. Researchers agree that this collectivist mentality strongly supports cooperation and that CHC's learners/workers best perform in groups (Nguyen, Terlouw & Pilot, 2005). Research has shown that "Asian students are exposed to strong family pressures toward high levels of achievement, attendance at prestigious universities, and that the Confucian recognition of education as a means to status and wealth develops a social approval orientation toward learning" (Pratt, Kelly & Wong, 1999, p. 247).

Table 4. Comparison of Asian and Australian Learning Styles (Ramburuth, 2001)

Asian	Australian
Rote learning is common.	Evaluative learning is preferred.
Non-critical reception of information	Critical thought is expected.
Students work hard to learn everything.	Students selectively learn the central concepts as well as detail.
Students are inclined to seek clarification.	Students are willing to seek assistance as part of the learning process.
Few initiatives are taken.	Independent learning and research are rewarded.
A willingness to accept one interpretation	Students are encouraged to apply general principles to specific situations and to test various interpretations.
Overall concepts are seen as important to understanding.	Analytical thinking is encouraged. Students are expected to support opinions with logical arguments.

Conclusion

With empirical research that shows how Asians learn and teach, research results of productive pedagogies, and maximum teaching, some tips are given below for teachers that can be derived for productive pedagogy among Asian Academia.

A2Z Tips for Productive Pedagogy

Amplify networking—Pedagogy productivity can occur through networking. Networking can be strengthened through an "involved and connected learning community" (Beck & Shelley, 2004, p. 98). This occurs when parents, teachers, students, and even community institutions join in the Christian learning and teaching processes. Utilize the relational virtue of Asia and its collectivistic nature.

Be creative like the Master teacher—Jesus was the Master teacher. He is creative. He used variety and diverse methods in his teaching. His classroom varied from the seashore to the middle of the roaring sea, the mountaintop, at the plains, and down the valley. He taught in public as well as in private. His school schedules were at day, at night, and even at noontime. He asked questions. He answered a question with a question. He loved his learners, prayed for them, and wept for them (Knight & Silbor, 2006).

Cultivate contextualized coaching—Significant national differences in teacher gender, amount of planning time, and duties outside class exist between different cultures. Within these differences, there are similarities in school organization, classroom organization, and curriculum content (Levitt, 2002). However, "Japanese, German, and United States teachers all appear to be working from a very similar cultural script" (LeTendre, Baker, Akiba, Goesling & Wiseman, 2001, p. 9).

Develop whole-brain pedagogy—Discipline is the foundation to whole-brain learning and teaching processes. Creative teaching methods will facilitate in meeting the needs of right-brain and left-brain students. Teachers ought to guard preferred teaching style, in order to plan consciously for different intelligences and learning styles of the students.

Enhance professionally—Teachers need to have a "high degree of self-awareness and recognition of skill limitations, sensitivity, and ability to respond to the needs of the learners, conceptual/theoretical understanding, program design and implementation skills, and research and evaluation skills" (Paige & Martin, 1996, p. 56).

Foster flexibility—There is a need for a "flexible and sustainable learning environment" (Beck & Shelley, 2004, p. 98). This is possible when communication is open, responses are fluid, and a desire is present to meet the ever-changing needs of participants and the community. Listen to the learners. Take time for talk on issues, and be prepared if adjustment is required.

Generate gentle guidance—Asia stresses integration and agreement because of their social orientation.

> Guiding without pulling makes the process of learning gentle; urging without suppressing makes the process of learning easy; and opening the way without leading the students to the place makes them think for themselves. Now if the process of learning is made gentle and easy and the students are encouraged to think for themselves, we may call the man a good teacher. (Lin, 1938, p. 247)

Hone students to quality questioning—In China, the thirteenth-century philosopher, Zhu Xi, believed that "if a student cannot raise any questions in his teaching the teacher should teach him. If a student raises many questions, however the teacher should help him" (Coortazzi, 1998, p. 47). Apply inventive questioning that can generate inquiring minds. Use group questioning and apply productive ways.

Increase a positive learning environment—In Japan's classrooms, "all students know and care about one another as people, know how to talk and listen to one another respectfully, and have the safety provided by strong, shared class norms of kindness, helpfulness, and putting our strength together" (Hatano & Kayoko, 1998, p. 92). Have an environment where learners are excited to come to their classroom—eager and ready to learn.

Justify "silence," but with limits—

> In the schools in Brunei, it is typical that only a few students ask questions in the classroom. This is due to the students' backgrounds and cultures. They expect to be quiet and respectful when confronting their elders, trained not to speak a lot or argue with them. Some teachers prefer silence in the classroom, not violating the classroom culture. (Coortazzi, 1998, p. 47)

Know your learners and yourself—Fowler (2006) wrote, "Knowledge of the basic assumptions of a people is indispensable to the interpretation of concrete behavior" (p. 405). Further, Mok and Morris said that self-knowledge is a basis of knowing students.(Palmer, 1998).

Liven up classroom interaction—A description of the Hong Kong mathematics classroom would be: "Although the teacher-centered characteristics persisted, the teacher essentially played an orchestrating role of linking and developing a sequence of classroom activities . . . liveliness was maintained via the teacher's effort, skilful mode of delivery, questioning, and receiving answers" (Mok & Morris, 2001, p. 466).

Maximize options creatively—The United States and Japanese teachers use different cultural scripts for running lessons. The apparent conflict is most often resolved by the fact that both United States and Japanese teachers draw on the same "whole-class, lecture-recitation, and seatwork lessons conducted by one teacher with a group of children isolated in a classroom," but they maximized their options in a different manner (Levitt, 2002, p. 21).

Nurture the less-dominant brain domain of learners—Asian learners need to be nurtured in evaluative learning, critical thinking, analytical assessments, independent study, and detailed orientations. Encourage students to vocalize their thought and even present arguments without losing respect for the teachers. More so, exhort students to explore various interpretations from general principles.

Observe physical setting—"A proficient and inviting curriculum-driven setting" (Beck & Shelley, 2004, p. 98) takes place when the physical setting supports and encourages development and change related to the needs of the community. Age-appropriate equipment is essential in classroom management. Furnish the right sizes of furniture. Check the safety and comfort of the learners.

Promote pupil participation—Greeno observed that "Methods of instruction are not only instruments for acquiring skills; they also are practices in which students learn to participate" (Greeno, 1997, p. 9). Group-work works wonders among Asians. When given ample time for preparation and practice, Asians can be active participants.

Query students to promote higher thinking—Next to lecture, questions, and discussions are the most used teaching method. That is why most teachers need to have questions and answers in their teaching sessions. The art of questioning can be learned by teachers to enhance the critical thinking of Asian learners.

Respect other cultures—In teaching cross-culturally and multi-culturally, it has been advocated that

> to be effective in another culture, people must be interested in other cultures, be sensitive enough to notice cultural differences, and then also be willing to modify their behavior as an indication of respect for the people of other cultures. (Fowler, 2006, p. 408)

Structure thoughts through storytelling—Two-thirds of the world consists of mostly concrete-relational thinkers (Cole, 2005), and they receive information best in the form of stories (Walsh, 2003), not in a literary Bible-teaching approach (Cole, 2005). Jesus himself used parabolic stories to teach audiences (Steffen, 1996), and approximately 75 percent of the Bible is in narrative form (Erickson, 1997). Thought should be structured through storytelling (Bradt, 1997) because it is found in learning styles around the world (Steffen, 2000).

Target transformational teaching—Asians are highly motivated learners because of their values, belief that success in education is related to success in life (On, 1996), and belief that education as the most reliable property and most important to one's life (Bae, 1991). However, Christian teachers need to refocus education from a success orientation to life's transformation. Start with one's life. Enter the classroom ready to teach to change lives through the Holy Spirit's prompting and power.

Update curriculum recurrently—Have "a cross-curriculum integration of research and development" (Beck & Shelley, 2004, p. 98). This takes place when the curriculum is updated on a regular basis through research studies and projects. Teachers and administrators alike need to keep current on their knowledge of the latest research findings.

Vitalize professional enhancements—It has been said, "Standards set the course and assessments provide the benchmarks, but it is teaching that must be improved to push us along the path to success" (Stigler & Hiebert, 1999, p. 2). Constant conscious efforts of the teachers' enhancement will aid students' successes.

Welcome assessments and evaluations—View evaluation as a friend not as a foe. This will identify your strengths and accomplishments as well as your weaknesses and failures. Teachers who desire excellence are not afraid of assessment. We who teach have greater accountability; therefore, teachers need to welcome these instruments as constructive challenges in our profession.

X-ray extremes that are counter-productive—Balance is the keyword to avoid extremes. Overwhelming lectures produce mental overload and eventually lead to boredom. Emphasis on exciting methodologies can hamper content delivery. Too strict or too lenient an approach will produce a counter-conducive environment. Have a balanced plan between materials and methods, concepts and conducts, and the use of preferred learning and expected results.

Yearn for productive pedagogy on Godly ways—Teaching is hard work. Nevertheless, God is with us, in us, for us, and working through us. Teachers need God to work in the "dailyness" of the task of teaching. Just remember that God provides strength (Philippians l. 1:6), wisdom (James 1:5), peace, joy, perseverance, character, hope (Romans 5:3-5), love, patience, kindness, gentleness, and self-control (Galatians 5:22-23), blessing, and prosperity (Psalm 128:2).

Zealously promote productive pedagogy for God's glory—Productive pedagogy calls educationalists to bestow their best. It calls academic practitioners to be concerned and committed, contextualized and current, and to be noble workers to be used by the Master toward students that come to their classrooms and lives. Keep the zeal of productive pedagogy.

References

Allan, J. (2003). Productive pedagogies and the challenge of inclusion. *British Journal of Special Education,* 30(4), 175-179.

Bae, C. K. (1991). Education top reason behind rapid growth: Schooling for economic takeoff. *Koreana,* 5(2), 56-68.

Barad, S. A., & Landa, A. (1997). Designing effective interdisciplinary anchors. *Educational Leadership,* 54(6), 52-56.

Barron, P., & Arcadia, C. (2002). Linking learning style preferences and ethnicity: International students studying hospitality and tourism management in Australia. *Journal of Hospitality, Leisure, Sport, and Tourism Education,* 1(2), 15-27.

Beck, B., & Shelley, J. (2004, October). Smart growth schools. *Urban Land,* 63(10), 98.

Bradt, K. M. (1997). *Story as a way of knowing.* Kansas City: Sheed & Ward.

Clarke, D. *Whole class patterns of participation and the distribution of responsibility for knowledge generation in the classroom.* Paper presented as part of the conference of the Learner's Perspective Study International Research Team—University of Melbourne, December 1-3, 2003. Available from http://extranet.edfac.unimelb.edu.au/DSME/lps/assets/2003conference/DavidEvents.pdf

Claxton, G., Atkinson, T., Osborn, M., & Wallace, M. (Eds.). (1996). *Liberating the learner.* London: Routledge.

Cole, H. (2005). Stories aren't just for kids anymore: A case for narrative teaching in missions. *Journal of Asian Mission,* 7(1), 23-38.

Coortazzi, M. (1998). Learning from Asian lessons: Cultural expectations and classroom talk. *Education 3-13,* 26(2), 42-49.

Cothran, D. J., Kulinna, P. H., Banville, D., Cho, E., Amade-Escot, C., MacPhail, A., Macdonald, D., Richard, J., Sarmento, P., & Kirk, D. (2005, June). A cross-cultural investigation of the use of teaching styles. *Research Quarterly for Exercise and Sport,* 76(2), 193- 201.

Crtazzi, M., & Jin, L. (1996). Cultures of learning: Language classrooms in China. In H. Coleman (Ed.), *Society and the language classroom* (pp. 169-206). Cambridge: Cambridge University Press.

Dahlin, B., & Watkins, D. (2000). The role of repetition in the processes of memorizing and understanding: A comparison of the views of German and Chinese secondary school students in Hong Kong. *British Journal of Educational Psychology,* 70(1), 65-84.

Dwyer, B. M. (2002). Training strategies for the twenty-first century: Using recent research on learning to enhance training. *Innovations in Education & Teaching International,* 39(4), 265-270.

Erickson, M. J. (1997). *The evangelical left: Encountering post conservative evangelical theology.* Grand Rapids, MI: Baker Book House.

Flew, T. (2004). Creativity, the 'new humanism' and cultural studies. *Ontinnum: Journal of Media & Cultural Studies,* 18(2), 161-178.

Flowerdew, J. (1998). A cultural perspective on group work. *English Language Teaching Journal,* 52(4), 323-329.

Fowler, S. M. (2006). Training across cultures: What intercultural trainers bring to diversity training. *International Journal of Intercultural*

Relations, 30(3), 401-411.

Gore, J. M., & Griffins, T. (2004). Towards better teaching: Productive pedagogy as a framework for teacher education. *Teaching & Teacher Education,* 20(4), 357, 375-387.

Greenholtz, J. (2003). Socratic teacher and Confucian learners: Examining the benefits and pitfalls of a year abroad. *Language and Intercultural Communication,* 3(2), 122-130.

Greeno, J. G. (1997). On claims that answer the wrong questions. *Educational Researcher,* 26(1), 5-17.

Gruber, S., & Boreen, J. (2003). Teaching critical thinking: Using experience to promote learning in middle school and college students. *Teachers & Teaching,* 9(1), 5-20.

Hatano, G., & Kayoko, I. (1998). Cultural contexts of schooling revisited: A review of the learning gap from a cultural psychology perspective. In S. G. Paris, H. M. Welman (Eds.), *Global prospects for education: Development, culture, and schooling* (pp. 79-104). Washington, D.C.: American Psychological Association.

Hayes, D., Lingard, B., & Mills, M. (2000). Productive pedagogies. *Education Links,* 60, 10-14, 399.

Hinton, L. (2003). Productive pedagogies: The link between new basics and philosophy in schools. *Primary & Middle Years Educator,* 1(1), 4, 7-13.

Ho, I., Salili, F., Biggs, J. B., & Hau, K. T. (1999). The relationship among casual attributions, learning strategies, and level of achievement: A Hong Kong case study. *Asia Pacific Journal of Education,* 19(1), 44-58.

Huang, R., & Leung, F. K. S. (2005). Deconstructing teacher-centeredness and student-centeredness dichotomy: A case study of a Shanghai mathematics lesson. *The Mathematics Educator,* 15(2), 35-41.

Hyde, A. (2005). Hyde Andrew. *Screen Education,* 37, 70.

Irwin, H. (1996). *Communicating with Asia.* St. Leonards: Allen & Unwin.

Kapitzke, C., & Pendergast, D. (2005). Virtual schooling service: Productive pedagogies or pedagogical possibilities? *Teachers College Record,* 107(8), 1626-1651.

Keddie, A. (2006). Pedagogies and critical reflection: Key understandings for transformative gender justice. *Gender and Education,* 18, 99-114.

Kember, D. (2000). Misconceptions about the learning approaches, motivation, and study practices of Asian students. *Higher Education,* 40(1), 99-121.

Kennedy, P. (2002). Learning cultures and learning styles: Myth-understandings about adult (Hong Kong) Chinese learners. *International Journal of Lifelong Education,* 21(5), 430-445.

Killen, P. O. (2002). Making thinking real enough to make it better: Using posters to develop skills for constructing disciplinary arguments. *Teaching Theology & Religion,* 5(4), 221-226.

Knight, L. F. *Maximum learning through balanced critical thinking and creative teaching.* Paper presented as part of the symposium of Asia Baptist Federation and Asia Baptist Graduate Theological Seminary, Bangkok, Thailand, January 5-7 2006, 3-7.

Knight, L. F., & Silbor, S. (2006). *A2Z creative teaching methods.* Makati City, Philippines: Church Strengthening Ministry.

LeTendre, G., Baker, D., Akiba, M., Goesling, B., & Wiseman, A. (2001). Teachers' work: Institutional isomorphism and cultural variation in the US, Germany, and Japan. *Educational Researcher,* 30(6), 3-15.

Leung, F. K. S. (2001). In search of an East Asian identity in mathematics education. *Educational Studies in Mathematics,* 47, 35-51.

Levitt, K., & Anderson, M. (2002). Teaching culture as national and transnational: A response to teachers' work. *Educational Researcher* 31(3), 19-21.

Lewis, D. H. (2004). How productive was my pedagogy. *Quadrant,* 48, 78-79.

Lin, Y. (1938). *The wisdom of Confucius.* New York: Random House.

MacDonald, D. (2003). Rich task implementation: Modernism meets postmodernism. *Discourse: Studies in the Cultural Politics of Education,* 24(2), 247-253.

Martino, W., & Beckett, L. (2004). Schooling the gendered body in health and physical education: Interrogating teachers' perspectives. *Sport, Education & Society,* 9(2), 239-251.

Marton, F., Dall'Alba, G., & Kun, T. L. (1996). Memorizing and understanding: The keys to the paradox? In D. A. Watkins, J. B. Biggs (Eds.), *The Chinese learner: Cultural, psychological, and contextual influences* (pp. 70-83). Hong Kong & Melbourne: CERC & ACER.

Marshall, B. (2004). Learning from the academy: From peer observation of teaching to peer enhancement of learning and teaching. *Journal of Adult Theological Education,* 1(2), 185-204.

McFadden, M., & Munns, G. (2002). Student engagement and the social relations of pedagogy. *British Journal of Sociology of Education,* 23(3), 357-366.

McGuire, A., & Inlow, L. (2005). Interactive reflection as a creative teaching strategy. *Conflict Resolution Quarterly,* 22(3), 365-379.

McLester, S. (2001). Convergent learning. *Technology & Learning,* 22(1), 30-31.

Mok, I. A. C., & Morris, P. (2001). The metamorphosis of the 'virtuoso': Pedagogic patterns in Hong Kong primary mathematics classrooms. *Teaching and Teacher Education: An International Journal of Research and Studies,* 17(4), 455-468.

Newton, F. B., & Smith, J. H. (1996). Principles and strategies for enhancing student learning. *New Directions for Student Services,* 75, 19-33

Nguyen, P., Terlouw, C., & Pilot, A. (2005). Cooperative learning vs. Confucian heritage culture's collectivism: Confrontation to reveal some cultural conflicts and mismatch. *Asia Europe Journal,* 3(3), 403-419.

Nieto, S. (2002). *Language, culture, and teaching: Critical perspectives for a new century.* Mahwah, NJ: Lawrence Erlbaum Associates.

On, L. W. (1996). On the cultural context for Chinese learners: Conceptions of learning in the Confucian tradition. In D. A. Watkins, J. B. Biggs (Eds.), *The Chinese learner: Cultural, psychological, and contextual influences* (pp. 25-42). Hong Kong & Melbourne: CERC & ACER.

Paige, R. M., & Martin, J. N.. (1996). Ethics in intercultural training. In D. Landis, S. Bhagat (Eds.), *Handbook of intercultural training* (pp. 35-60). Thousand Oaks, CA: Sage.

Palmer, P. J. (1998). *The courage to teach.* San Francisco: Jossey-Bass.

Park, C. C. (1997). Learning style preferences of Asian American (Chinese, Filipino, Korean, and Vietnamese) students in secondary schools. *Equity and Excellence in Education,* 30(2), 68-77.

Park, C. C. (2000). Learning style preferences of Southeast Asian students. *Urban Education,* 35(3), 245-268.

Pratt, D. D., Kelly, M., & Wong, W. S. S. (1999). Chinese conceptions of 'effective teaching' in Hong Kong: Towards culturally sensitive evaluation of teaching. *International Journal of Lifelong Education,* 18(4), 241-258.

Queensland (Department of Education and the Arts), (2002). *Productive pedagogies.* Retrieved September 18, 2006, from http://education.qld.gov.au/public_media/reports/curriculum-framework/productive-pedagogies/index.html

Rabin, B., Lehmann, S., Kedar, D., Hegar, A., & Nechama, D. (1998). Off-Site orientation program for medical social workers. *Social Work in Health Care, 27*(3), 43-55.

Ramburuth, P. (2001, May). *Cross cultural behavior in higher education: Perceptions versus practice.* Retrieved December 16, 2005, from http://ultibase.rmit.edu.au/Articles/mtway01/ramburuth1.pdf

Ritchart, R. (2004). Creative teaching in the shadow of the standard. *Independent School, 63*(2), 32-41.

Salili, F. (1996). Accepting personal responsibility for learning. In D. A. Watkins, J. B. Biggs (Eds.), *The Chinese learner: Cultural, psychological, and contextual influences* (pp. 85-105). Hong Kong & Melbourne: CERC & ACER.

Share, E., & Rogers, L. (1997). Get real. *Learning, 25*(4), 61-64.

Smith, D. (1999). Supervising NESB students from Confucian educational cultures. In Y. Ryan, O. Zuber-Skemit (Eds.), *Supervising postgraduates from non-English speaking backgrounds* (pp. 146-156). Buckingham: Open University Press.

Steffen, T. A. (2000). Reaching 'resistant' people through intentional narrative. *Missiology: An International Review, 28*(4), 471-486.

Steffen, T. A. (1996). *Reconnecting God's story to ministry: Cross-cultural storytelling at home and abroad.* La Habra, CA: Center for Organizational & Ministry Development.

Stigler, J. W., & Hiebert, J. (1999). *The teaching gap: Best ideas from the world's teachers for improving education in the classroom.* New York: The Free Press.

Triandis, H. C. (1996). The psychological measurement of cultural syndromes. *American Psychologist, 51*(4), 407-415.

Turner, P. (2005). Critical thinking in nursing education and practice as defined in the literature. *Nursing Education Perspectives, 26*(5), 272-277.

Tweed, R. G., & Lehman, D. R. (2002). Learning considered within a cultural context: Confucian and Socratic approaches. *American Psychologist, 57*(2), 89-99.

VanderStaay, S. (2004). Subvert. The subversives (but keep their inquiry). *English Journal, 94*(2), 49-54.

Walsh, J. (2003). *The art of storytelling: Easy steps to presenting an unforgettable story.* Chicago: Moody Publishers.

Watkins, D. (1996). Learning theories and approaches to research: A cross-cultural perspective. In D. A. Watkins, J. B. Biggs (Eds.), *The Chinese learner: Cultural, psychological, and contextual influences* (pp. 3-24). Hong Kong & Melbourne: CERC & ACER.

Zhang, L., & Watkins, D. (2001). Cognitive development and student approaches to learning: An investigation of Perry's theory with Chinese and U.S. university students. *Higher Education,* 41(3), 239-261.

Zhenhui, R. (2001) Matching teaching styles with learning styles in East Asian contexts. *Internet TESL Journal,* 1-9. Retrieved December 16, 2005, from http://iteslj.org/Techniques/Zhenhui-Teaching Styles.html

RESPONSE TO LIZETTE F. KNIGHT

Margaret Edgell

I am blessed by reading our colleague Lizette Knight's ideas on Productive Pedagogy (PP) among Asian learners. This paper seeks to foster student well-being in the primary and secondary settings through cutting-edge pedagogy. She describes for us her experience using PP, which is an experimental approach used in Australia. Its experimental nature is only partial, because it pulls together the most promising of several tried-and-true, validated pedagogies.

She chose PP because it is learner-centered. I find this highly appropriate. Recent literature on teaching and learning in higher education in the United States evidences a clear shift from teacher-oriented to learner-oriented pedagogies.

Improving pedagogy for Asian learners is very interesting from a United States standpoint. U. S. middle-school students achieve lower learning outcomes in math and science than Asian learners do. To explore the reasons behind this outcomes gap, my field of comparative studies contrasts Asian and U. S. pedagogies, and highlights differences, such as rote teaching, in Asian settings. This paper suggests that more critical thinking pedagogy goes on in Asian classrooms than is commonly perceived. However, the important differences may instead lie in learner motivation, cultural expectations, cultural homogeneity, and other factors outside of pedagogy. Because of my U. S. perspective, I find the discussion of the positive benefits of rote teaching one of the most interesting sections of this paper.

Our colleague introduces the reader to an impressive array of research concerning PP and related topics. She approaches educational well-being with a spirit of innovation and creativity. She includes elements of implementation appropriate for Christian schools. Because my interest is comparative education, the content that I found most interesting was in the comparative sections, not surprisingly.

I have three general critical comments. First, further develop your context-specific insights. This might be accomplished by further comparing Confucian with Socratic models of teaching and learning. You might also devote a whole section on the depth aspects of rote learning. Second, provide a stronger connection to the Track 2 question, "What can Christian higher education do to promote educational well-being?" Is the secondary school focus mainly college preparatory? How can colleges follow up on PP? I would also like to see a stronger connection to Christian education. Which elements of PP are congruent with Christian philosophy of education and practice? Are Christian schools experimenting with PP already? Third, I still need to be convinced regarding the validity of PP. PP appears to be a holistic and constructive view, incorporating important factors that have been tested and found valid, such as community, learning differences, and classroom environments. Perhaps breaking PP into its pieces and showing their time-tested validity will strengthen the case for PP. A related question is how to assess the relationship of inputs to outputs of PP.

Although Ms. Knight cites an impressive array of research, this paper does not provide a meta-analysis of the current research. A meta-analysis that reviews the relevant literature in a way that creates a new, synthesizing conceptual structure would more clearly assist with implementing PP in Asia. Yet some of the author's arguments seem to work against implementation. For example, if PP is right for Australian students, and Australian students are qualitatively different learners than Asian students, why would PP be right for Asian students? Is the answer that Asian students will follow the lead of their teachers into any learning style? Perhaps we should start with the Asian learner, and then see if PP is appropriate to him/her.

I am impressed by our colleague's passion for her students, her creative and experimental approach, and her knowledge of the literature. This combination of passion, creativity, and scholarship can only lead to positive outcomes for students' well-being.

RESPONSE TO LIZETTE F. KNIGHT

T. Stephen Tangaraj

Dr. Lizette F. Knight, you have selected a very relevant subject for your research paper. I congratulate you. Learners from different parts of Asia are compared along with learners from other parts of the world, highlighting Asian learning styles. Productive pedagogy (PP) promotes the well-being of students, teachers, and the school community. PP improves students' and teachers' confidence and contributes to their sense of purpose for being at school, and it builds community confidence in the quality of learning and teaching in the school. The well-being of students, teachers, and school has to be the main aim of the educational community throughout the world.

The basis for PP lies in the control of the left brain and the right brain of critical and creative teaching. At the school level, this is essential. Could you share with us your experience?

You have brought out the difference between Western and Eastern philosophies, Socrates and Confucius. It is interesting to note that Confucianism continues to influence Asian countries. Could you please cite a few examples? Our Indian children also mostly depend on memorization because from childhood they are trained to memorize "slogans" and "mantras," which they chant when worshiping their deity. Normally the Brahmins are the ones who follow this ritual and their children are outstanding in their academic performance.

It has been correctly assessed that the pupils who were recognized as dualists were inclined to generate work that was at the lower levels in Bloom's taxonomy, and those pupils who were recognized as relativists were inclined to generate work at the higher levels in Bloom's taxonomy. While Korean, Chinese, and Japanese pupils are considered visual learners, they also have a negative preference for jump learning. Is there any co-relation between this geographical location and their learning preference? Similarly, Chinese learners seen to be not imaginative and innovative in thinking seems to be controversial to the general belief.

Can you suggest a few models for the evaluative procedures assisting a deep approach to learning?

Ms. Knight presented the results of comparative studies. Although the Chinese teacher is seen as a source of authority with a pastoral function, the Western teacher is not able to connect the link between pupil behaviour and the social structures of formal education and family life in Hong Kong. Again, Ms. Knight cites research that Asians believe that learning is reciting. Is there any relation between the Chinese children's' learning habit and their religion? The learning styles and comparative studies of Asian and Australian students also contribute a lot to the value of this research paper. Citing the example of Jesus the "Master Teacher" adds weight to the conclusion.

PP calls educationalists to bestow their best. It calls academic practitioners to be concerned and committed, contextualized and current, and to be noble workers to be used by the Master toward students that come to their classrooms and lives. Keep the zeal of productive pedagogy! It gives me a great pleasure to respond to your paper.

THE TASK OF REDEEMING THE EDUCATIONAL PROCESS IN MEXICO

Darrel W. Hilbrands

I am grateful to God for allowing me the opportunity to write these lines to be able to participate in some way in the educational process of my adopted country. When we approached the task of providing an adequate preparation for the children of our children's home, we had to reflect seriously about several aspects of their lives. Many of them had never been in a school, they had many scars from a life that no one should live, they were socially out of place, emotionally unsure of themselves, and at times violent with little self-esteem. They were always the dunces, the rejected, the hurting. In addition, many were not formally registered; they did not exist legally. Many who had attended public schools showed little advancement for a variety of reasons.

I do not pretend to have great answers for our Latin American countries that suffer in a socio-political and historical situation prone to inequality, injustice, and economic oppression. Rather, I relate a specific story within a larger social milieu, and how with group of marginalized children the Lord of lords, the King of kings can reinitiate a process of recuperating the educational process of our children and the preparation of their teachers.

Our project
Because of the problems of these children, we started a primary school in February of 1994 that included several of the twelve children living in our home. More children arrived at different levels as well as more helpers to teach them. In September of that same year, we began with four groups with all of the home's children, around thirty. With the help of a special federal and state program directed at children who did not have the opportunity to study in the public schools, we could move the students at their own pace, many times this was a very accelerated pace. Many

devoured the official textbooks, taking and passing the corresponding exams so that a handful of them finished the requirements for the primary diploma that same school year.

Now we had another problem, should we send these students to the public junior high school, or should we start our own junior high? Due to the continuance of the problems already mentioned, we decided to begin a junior high school (grades 7-9) in September of 1995. The Lord was faithful to provide capable people for this task. I should mention that all of our teachers are volunteers, dedicating 6-24 hours a week to teaching. By this time, we had added a kindergarten whose primary task was to teach reading; in many cases, the children were 8, 10, or older.

The following school year our institution confronted a special challenge. Our property owner wanted the building for other uses. Suddenly we had to find another location. Providentially we did, but there were no classrooms. Therefore, we had to use bedrooms and an old van for classrooms. This "exile" lasted two months until we could find a more suitable situation. I mention this only to emphasize that the road has not been easy, but even without financial resources or an adequate place, we have been able to move ahead with this project.

After securing an adequate facility, we were able to dedicate ourselves more to the task of teaching. In September of 1998, we began a high school (grades 10-12). With the help of some people from out of the country, several of our children had the opportunity to study in Canada and the United States. Two received their high school diplomas outside of Mexico. Because of the needs of a growing school, over 80 students at that time, and with the option of using teachers without a teacher's certificate in this special program, we began to assign classes to these high school graduates. Although they did all they could, they lacked a more professional orientation.

During this time, we began a master's degree in Christian philosophy in an extension program offered by Juan Calvino Seminary in Mexico City. Through monthly visits by different teachers and this author, five local professional people finished their studies after two years. The program emphasized the sovereignty of the spheres as explained by the great Dutch philosopher Herman Dooyeweerd, and that as Christians we have the great responsibility to recuperate God's creation in all of its aspects.

As a result, we were interested in working with these new masters candidates. I had explained the problematic situation at the children's home. We felt that our best impact would be in the area of education. Four of us were career teachers and the other two had taught in their respective areas. At this same time, the Lord sovereignly put at our disposal John Van Dyk's book, *The Craft of Christian Teaching: A Classroom Journey* (that later we translated). This book emphasizes the ethical sphere, which includes teaching. We were tremendously impressed with our lack of understanding about the entire educational process, and how the humanist system had duped us. The book underlines the complete humanity of each child, that his or her role is as important as that of the teacher in a class that emphasizes community and one is responsible for his or her neighbor, how the teacher is the guide not a dictator or sergeant. We saw that many things had to change.

With this in mind, we started the process to found a civil association that would begin to change that mentality in teachers. The result was the establishment in 2004 of the Instituto Libre de México de Estudios Superiores, A.C. (ILMES) that has as its principal objective the training of Christian teachers. ILMES has as its mission the study and research of pedagogy. At this point, we only offer the bachelor's degree and special courses. ILMES promotes the rehabilitation of the Biblical office of teacher who should be directed by the Holy Spirit and the written Word of God. Therefore, the teachers should be believers and faithful Christians with aptitude and a calling to teach.

Christian teaching must start with a Biblical worldview in order to awaken the vocation and calling that God has for each human being and especially His chosen children. This way they can faithfully serve in the Kingdom of God as caretakers of their fellow beings and stewards of the creation. With these fundamentals and a small group of ten students, we began classes in August 2004. We have just started our third school year.

No institution develops in a social or historical vacuum. All owe a debt to socio-political and historical factors. Our situation is no different. First, the necessity of having a children's home reflects a dire social condition. In our case, we cooperate with state authorities in order to limit those entering the home to those cases of extreme urgency. The social agency in Mexico provides all of the juridical and social work support. They verify the cases and proceed according to the results of their investigations. In the majority of the cases that come to us, there is an extreme degree of abuse that usually cannot be resolved in a short period. As a result, the cases sent to us are usually of a longer period, generally or several years and in some cases indefinitely. This gives us enough time to dedicate time to the individual for his or her social, emotional, and spiritual development—in a word, their integral development. I might add that we have limited our cases to the State of Queretaro. If we wanted to extend the ministry of the home to other neighboring states, we could easily have ten times the quantity of children that we have. Part of our intention is to duplicate this effort in other cities, with one such home in Aguascalientes.

The social-historic milieu

Without beginning from the start of education in Mexico, I would prefer to start from the Mexican Revolution because of its modern significance, because of the establishment of many patterns that still influence private and public education, and most of all because of its development of the current social attitudes toward education. Obviously, this movement did not exist in an historic, socio-political vacuum either, but it provides a point of departure.

The Mexican Revolution, 1910-1917, was characterized by ideas of radical and violent change to the economic, political, and social structures of the society, with the goal of obtaining better life conditions. It sought social justice that implied an educational process and philosophy that had as a goal the production of new generations with the same ideas.

Since 1890, the state attempted to provide education to the masses of illiterates (almost 80 percent in the census of 1910) (Gómez Navas, 2004, p. 126). However, those attempts were frustrated for various reasons, principally because of the intransigence of the federal government that favored the oligarchy and for lack of social visionaries that could move this agenda. Mexico in the Porfirian Time (*el porfiriato*)[1] was infested with poverty, few patriotic workers, a lack of social fabric and cultural disharmony. "It only had order in its poverty; the homeland was a distant ray of brilliance; the society a practice ground; and knowledge was a luxury" (Valadés, 1941, cited in Matute, 2004, p. 188). In 1906, the Liberal Party of Mexico produced a manifesto that declared:

> In the primary school is the profound base of the greatness of a people, and you can say that the best institutions are of little value, and are in danger of disappearing, if at their side there does not exist many and well attended schools, in which citizens are trained so that in the future they can watch out for these institutions . . . The suppression of the clerical schools is a means that will produce for the country incalculable benefits. To suppress the clerical schools is to do away with the point of contention and division and the disputes between sons of Mexico; it is to concretize over the most solid

---

1 *El porfiriato* refers to the period of 1877-1911 when Porfirio Díaz governed Mexico. His legacy is still a contentious point among historians; some call him the vilest of all dictators while others praise him as the right man for his time.

base, for the near future, the complete brotherhood of the Mexican family. The clerical school that educates the children (in fanaticism, prejudices, and dogmas) is a great obstacle so that the democracy can reign serenely in our homeland . . . The lay[2] school, that lacks all of these vices, that is inspired by an elevated patriotism far from the petty religious acts that have as their motto the truth, is the only one that can make out of the Mexicans an illustrious, brotherly and strong people of tomorrow. (Gómez Navas, 2004, p. 121)

In addition to the profound anticlerical and anti-religious perspective, the *Manifesto* mandates instruction up to age 14, decent salaries for primary school teachers, and the teaching of basic skills in art, labor, and the military.

These ideas took form in the Constitution of 1917 and in the minds of the citizenry. The antagonism of the new rulers with the catholic clergy and the religious schools provoked not only rejection and contempt, but also laws that prohibited the teaching of whatever type of religion, although we can note that there was a certain compromise with the clerical schools. In the tradition of the Constitution of 1857 "religious teaching in public schools, whether federal, state or local" was strictly prohibited.[3] As any teacher knows, it is impossible to teach in a philosophical or spiritual vacuum. To imply such a possibility is to deny our nature as beings created in the image of God. To deny this liberty in the name of liberty is an irreconcilable contradiction. However, the decision of the First Commission of Constitutional Points on the Third Article (FC-CPTA), culminated December 11, 1916, established for the first time in the history of Mexican education, the lay principle, with an obligatory character for private teaching establishments of primary education. FC-CPTA describes "lay" teaching as:

> . . . the teaching removed from all religious belief, the teaching that transmits the truth and reveals error, inspired in a rigorous scientific criteria; FCCPTA does not find another word that expresses this idea better than "lay." This word has served, making certain that it is not its purpose to have a neutral meaning; the idea of laity shuts the lips of the teacher before all error clothed in whatever religious appearance . . . It is prohibited that religious enterprises, that ministers of churches or other persons who belong to a similar type of association, can establish or direct primary schools, nor teach personally in any school . . . The Catholic Church is the most cruel and tenacious enemy to our liberties, its doctrine has been and is to defend the interests of the

---

2 The term "lay" is the translation of *"laico."* The idea of the word in the Mexican sense has come to mean not religious, even neutral, rather than in the English sense of the word of not clerical. Trans. note.
3 Ley Reglamentaria de 14 de diciembre de 1874.

Church, before those of the homeland. (Gómez Navas, 2004, pp. 141-142)

The fact was that more than 90 percent of the Mexican population professed Roman Catholicism. Trying to uproot a great part of this belief with only one decree was more than just a misunderstanding, it was a lack of calculation; but it did not dissuade those of FCCPTA. In the end, the recommendation of FCCPTA was accepted, without so many bitter references, in the following terms:

> Teaching is free; but is to be lay, the teaching that is given in the official educational establishments, the same that is given in primary, secondary, and higher education in private establishments.
>
> Not one religious body, not a minister of a church, will be able to establish or direct a primary school.
>
> The private primary schools may only be established, submitting themselves to official oversight.[4]

In following years, the Third Article would be modified in order to conform to cultural realities, but the basic motives of its construction would leave its imprint on the national mentality. The same article established much more national coverage for primary education in order to imprint even more the mentality promoted by the revolutionary architects. Furthermore, the publication of official textbooks consolidated the diffusion of the liberal revolutionary mentality as the scientific rational truth against which there was no adequate response. With the establishment of the Secretariat of Public Education, the renowned professor, Secretary José Vasconcelos, carried this nationalism to even greater heights. He tried to convert indigenous peoples into full-fledged Mexicans, integrating the indigenous cultures with the Hispanic culture so that they could form a symbol of identity "by my race my spirit will speak."[5]

Nation building required an elaborate work plan for the rural school. This attempt was to interweave the educational action with the daily life of small towns, mainly towns of indigenous people and poor farmers. In the socialist tradition, the rural school does not consider the community as a series of individuals, but rather a group, a complete unity

---

4 See the discussion and quote in Gómez Navas, 2004, p. 147.
5 Matute, Á. La política educativa de José Vasconcelos. *HEPM*, pl 174. Vasconcelos was largely a Platonist, an idealist that book the educational process as an aesthetic process that culminated in the balanced formation of a citizen, for that reason a teacher should be an artist. His position differs from ours in that to us, the teacher, and the totality of the educational process is within the ethical sphere. The teacher is a guide for the development, capacitating, and vision of the student.

to which the school is integrated. The originators of the plan considered that the school was motivated from its interior, with elements of its own potential. The principles that governed it are of interest for our purposes. First, the school is a means where a child is instructed with what he sees and the working persons that surround him, therefore, there are no oral lessons, no disarticulated programs, no rigid schedules, or strict rules. Second, education is derived from a relationship of the child and a man with nature and the society by means of cooperative and practical work, and immediate positive feedback. Education is neither a simple monotonous script and readings nor the ideas made from fragmented lessons. Third, activities are used to explain the facts of natural and social phenomena instead of static programs that only the professors tend to understand. Fourth, punishments and rewards are proscribed in order to let the students be free and spontaneous, because human behaviors, such as virtue and truth, are not taught in theory, but rather by the personal use of liberty. Fifth, students should govern through committees that they themselves choose; that is to say, they do not play democracy because it is democracy itself (Mejía Zúñiga, 2004, p. 202). This "lay" tradition has persevered until the present in education. In large part, they are noble ideas that are very acceptable to most Christians, but the fact that they want to remove God from every consideration reflects their hollowness in many substantial ideas.

The Christian attempt to establish normal schools[6]

In spite of the humanist tidal wave against Christian education and teacher preparation, there have been several attempts to establish Christian Normal schools. In the mid 19th century, Malinda Rankin founded the Instituto Femenino de Rio Grande on the northern border. Rankin depended almost exclusively upon help from outside of the country to maintain the school. In 1877, this school had to close its doors. However, in 1879 it was again opened under the direction of Presbyterians from the United States of America. In 1888, it was moved to Saltillo, Coahuila with the name La Escuela Normal Presbiteriana de Saltillo. It offered courses for primary, high school, and higher education. In 1890, it had 24 students and 62 in 1896. Because of the Mexican Revolution, it was moved to Mexico City in 1916 where it was fused with the Escuela Normal Presbiteriana del Ciudad de México, founded in 1873.

---

6 The information in this section is in large part from the doctoral dissertation of Iglesias, J. M. Velázquez. (2004) *Perspectivas reformacionales de la educación*, México, D.F.: no pub. Seminario Teológico Juan Calvino. pp. 213-224.

The school in Mexico City had a history of difficulties, closing its doors on two occasions, but it was able to produce a number of teachers. From 1882 to 1907 more than 400 students attended classes with 77 graduates. In 1933, the government closed it definitively, because it competed with the newly formed government normal schools and ostensibly because of its Christian emphasis, not its "lay" emphasis.

Dr. José Velázquez numbers several reasons for the failure to establish Christian normal schools: the lack of adequate textbooks for Christian teaching, there only existed secular texts; the schools were generally directed by foreigners, usually Americans, thereby ignoring many aspects of cultural idiosyncrasies that caused misunderstandings with the nationals; a great part of the support came from the United States of America thereby causing a dependence upon foreign support which limited local initiative; the teaching in the local church did not emphasize the educational ministry as essential to the Christian community, therefore the members lacked motivation to initiate schools; included were non-Christian teachers in the schools, in some cases more than half were unbelievers. We might add that there was little emphasis regarding teaching Christianly among teachers, and the lack of political and social acumen on the part of the North American missionaries proved fatal to many schools with the advent of the Mexican Revolution. In 1914, President Woodrow Wilson ordered the evacuation of Americans from Mexico because of the fear of reprisals due to the invasion of American troops in Veracruz that same year. In 1914, a meeting was held in Cincinnati, Ohio between many of the most important denominations of the United States in which Mexico was divided into regional mission territories that corresponded to different denominations. The result was that if some missionaries had begun a work, let us say a school, they had to leave it in the hands of missionaries of another denomination to whom their region now belonged. Obviously many did not continue with the work of others. The Plan of Cincinnati of 1914 broke many contacts with those from United States therefore limiting resources for the continuance of these schools after the Revolution.

Dualist perspectives

All of these historic circumstances are the results of fundamental thoughts and philosophies. It is easy to understand why Mexico has had many problems, but we cannot begin to resolve them unless we understand their root causes. In our school, we make a concerted attempt to do so by examining the fundamental principle of any community, its religion.

Education has continued in Mexican life by claiming that religion is only a part of life. This dualist perspective has adversely affected the educational process as well as the social fabric of the country. First, it is due to the theology of the Roman Catholic Church, Thomism (the theology of Thomas Aquinas), and second, to humanism with its nature—liberty dialectic.

The Dutch philosopher Herman Dooyeweerd presents us with an excellent panorama of the social impact of Thomas Aquinas in his succinct book, *The Roots of Western Culture* (1998). Dooyeweerd begins by giving an analysis of the basic Greek motives, to a lesser degree those of the Romans, emphasizing the material/form dialectic of Aristotle.

> The Greeks believed that everything that came into existence came only through a divine activity of giving form to and unformed material that already existed. They conceived the divine formation only in terms of human cultural activity. The "rational God" was merely a "heavenly architect" that formed a given material according to a free design. He was not able to anticipate the blind autonomous activity of the principle material . . . The true center of the rational soul was theoretical thought, which was divine in character. The soul was the invisible "form" of human existence, and as a faculty of theoretical thought, was immortal. On the other hand, the material body, the "material" of a human being, was subject to the flow of life and to blind destiny. (1998, p. 115-116)

The strong dualist-pagan-Aristotelian base retained its influence with theologians of the Middle Ages, resulting in *scholasticism*. The scholastic searched for "a *synthesis* between Greek thought and the Christian religion" (Dooyeweerd, 1998, p. 118). As a result, they conceived the relation between the "soul" and "body" in philosophical Greek terminology. The soul became the immortal substance characterized by the ability to think theoretically and the body was only the material vehicle of the rational soul. This dualism still perturbs Christians by suggesting that sexuality itself is evil, education is only the transmission of knowledge, and religion is private and individual.

The joining of Greek thought with the fundamentals of Christianity lead in the Middle Ages to the formation of the basic motive known as "nature/grace." With the control of the temporal society by the Roman Church, this synthesis became deeply imbedded even in the thought of the Reformation. The scholastic maintained that God had given man a supernatural gift of grace. In the fall, man lost this gift, but retained uncorrupted his human nature directed by the light of reason. Therefore, human nature is only weakened by sin, not completely corrupted and can achieve grace, which comes from Christ, through the mediation of the institutional church.

As a result, Thomistic social development followed Aristotelian lines and his natural vision. For Thomas the "form" of Aristotle was the rational soul and his "material" the material body. Man's natural perfection consisted of the complete development of his rational nature with the innate natural law that motivated good and avoided evil. This concept is radically different from that of the Scripture that speaks of a total depravation of man, incapable of determining good by his own ability.[7]

According to the dualist perspective, man attains his salvation by participating in the Church, which is the basis for all of society. Furthermore, everything that man depends upon comes through the community. As a result, the Thomistic perspective speaks of a series of social associations that determine man's fulfillment, from the family to the state, which is the maximum communal expression because it has as its final goal the common good. This natural situation joins men so that they organize themselves in a unit for their mutual benefit. In other words, man, with his good intentions (reason), aspires toward God's perfection through the establishment of earthly institutions.

The basic motive of the Roman Catholic Church, nature/grace, requires that man not only needs his nature, vis-à-vis his reason, but above this he needs something supernatural, the grace that only the institutional church can supply. In other words, even the state requires a touch from the church in order to form a society that is unified. The error is that according to the Scripture, true unity only exists in the community of those who are born again, those circumcised of the heart.

> Just as the soul and man's radical spiritual unity do not lie in his temporal existence, neither do the radical spiritual unity and the true totality of the Christian life reside in the "visible church" which belongs to the temporal society. (Dooyeweerd, 1998, p. 134)

Roman Catholicism maintains that the family, the Christian school, social action, a book written on whatever theme, a political party, all should have the authorization of the church and that the state and the other spheres of life only are parts of one whole, they are not sovereign, and that this unifier is the Catholic Church (*kata*—according to; *holica*—the whole). For the same reason Thomas opposed the idea of Christian philosophy. To him, philosophy formed part of something bigger, theology. Philosophy was the result of rational man's thinking, the natural,

---

[7] Paul himself speaks very clearly in this regard (Romans 3:10-18 citing several passages of the Old Testament, Psalm 53:1-3; 5:9, Isaiah 59:7-8, etc.).

but it could not transcend to ultimate questions such as the existence of God and the ultimate consequences of being human, the "natural light of reason limited it."

Although this perspective had suffered many convincing attacks (such as William of Ockam in the 14th century and the great Reformation movement), it was able to survive because of the lack of sustainable proposals, because of its historic weight and in great measure because of the acquiescence of the reformers who developed their own scholasticism. Many evangelicals still manifest these inclinations.

The second dualistic perspective that has influenced our socio-historic and philosophical situation is the humanist dialectic of nature and liberty. This basic motive has been able to achieve more in questions of limiting the progress of a truly Christian education than has the motive of nature/grace. However, as we will see, its utility and sustainability have been greatly weakened to the degree that there is a general public outcry to do something to renovate the educational process. "Lay" education without religious reference, or without an ethical or moral base ("lay" morality is something relative that does not have definable parameters), is an unreality in whatever culture. The consequences of substituting the lie for the truth, immorality for morality, etc. provoke social chaos that cannot easily be resolved.

The decline of the nature/grace motive leaves two principle options. On one hand, one could follow the "natural" direction that little by little would lead to the complete liberty of man from the faith of the church, or, on the other hand, one could return to the Scriptural motive of creation, fall, and redemption through Jesus Christ. The first option led to the Renaissance, the second to the Reformation.

The Renaissance sought the autonomy of man, his liberation from whatever impediment to his complete realization. With the new emphasis in science, Renaissance man encountered tangible facts that he could use to prove the correct manner of thinking. The Copernican Revolution showed the inability of the church to dominate other spheres of life, and moved the humanist agenda when it showed that the world, in reality, was not the center of the universe. The church simply denied it.

The Renaissance was concerned with a new birth of man that would be exclusively *natural*. This rebirth had to occur without the nociceptive influences of Christianity. This rebirth came to project itself as an ideal of science, and hence of education, in which everything could be proven if there was sufficient experimentation, even the reason for the existence of man. The educational implications were profound. This new faith expounded that man could realize himself within this physical sphere, within his own experimentation. Therefore, modern man believed that he could achieve the highest expression of liberty through the domination of nature and therefore be able to dominate the "supernature." Proudly conscious of his autonomy and liberty, modern man took "nature" as a field of infinite possibilities in which he could show the sovereignty of the human personality through a complete dominance of natural phenomena. Faith in the absolute autonomy of the liberated personality could not tolerate a distinction between natural and supernatural truth.

Very quickly, a problem surfaced: man was trapped by his own nature. Man "declared that the natural scientific method could analyze and reconstruct reality as cause and effect completely predetermined without outside help" (Dooyeweerd, 1998, p. 176). If the nature of man was confined to scientific experiments, then man could not escape from this limitation and his liberation became a contradiction. This contradiction gave way to the humanist religion, the religion of the human personality. "Above this sensory ambit of 'nature' existed a 'supersensory' ambit of moral liberty that was not governed by the mechanical laws of nature, but by norms or rules of behavior that presupposed the autonomy of the human personality" (Dooyeweerd, 1998, pp. 178-179). This supersensory reality remains as a thing of faith. It is not the faith rooted in the true God as the Bible expresses, but rather a "reasonable faith" rooted in the same autonomous reason that is in complete agreement with the autonomy of the human personality. We see here that the classical ideal of humanism, of science, does not mesh with this new idea of the religion of personality. However, we should not underestimate this religion. Although it is not the intent here to analyze these problems, it is essential that we understand the intentionality on the part of the humanist in questions of education.

It is impossible to live (and teach) within a spiritual vacuum. Religion is always a part of teacher and school; we all teach some sort of religion. The question is what kind of religion? For those who doubt the implications of the humanist religion I cite a few of its proponents. Horace Mann, the father of the public school system in the United States, believed so strongly in the religiosity of his humanistic cause and its conflict with the cause of Christianity, that he wrote, "Those who are involved in the sacred cause of education have the right to see all parents as donators of hostages to our cause" (cited in Schultz, p. 110). C.F. Potter (1930), a signer of the original *Humanist Manifesto* in 1930 declared:

> Education is the most powerful ally of humanism, and each American public

school is a humanist school. What can Sunday Schools do that meet one hour a week and only teach a fraction of the children against the wave of a program of five days of humanism. (cited in Schultz, 1998, p. 110)

John Dunphy, from an award-winning essay in *The Humanist*, in 1983, says:

> I am convinced that the battle for the future of humanity has to be fought and won in the public schools by way of teachers who correctly perceive their role as proselytizers of a new faith: the religion of humanity that recognizes . . . the spark of divinity in each human being. These teachers have to preserver with the same dedication that the most dedicated fundamentalist preacher, because they are going to be another type of minister, using the classroom instead of a pulpit to communicate humanist values in whatever subject or level—preschool or in a great state university.
>
> The classroom has to be and is going to be the arena of conflict between the old and the new—the putrefactive cadaver of Christianity . . . and the new faith of humanism . . . Without doubt it will be a long, painful, and difficult struggle, full of anguish and many tears, but humanism will be triumphant. (p. 26)

Our mission

The Bible has much to say regarding teaching, instruction, training, and discipleship. We can define education in general, as Zacharías did at the Billy Graham Evangelistic Association 2000 conference, as "the process by which children, young people, and adults develop knowledge, abilities and character, especially through instruction, training, and formal study" (Schultz, 1998, p. 17). However, the danger of many educational efforts throughout history is the same that Eve confronted that terrible day when Satan lured her into error—he convinced her that knowledge in itself would better the person, and by extension, society.

We have seen through the historical and philosophical background of our context that there is a tremendous discrepancy between what we perceive to be the will of God in our educational practice and our reality. We see a continuing dualistic approach even among Christian educators and leaders. At a conference in a Mexico City seminary attended by educators, pastors, and pastoral candidates, I once argued that Christian education is a vital part of the Christian community. After six hours of discourse, interaction, fellowship, and exchange of ideas, the feedback that I received was in synthesis, "why make such a big deal about a new system when the system that we have is good enough."

Many educators believe that with better educational programs society can resolve all of her problems and God will not be necessary. Many times man sees in education a way to perfection, making it his own god. Christians should never forget that education, in whatever form, could never make anyone perfect. Only salvation in Christ can make the person perfect. We always have to recognize that education, no matter how good it is, can never transform one's life. It can never produce a moral person or a moral society. Horace Mann's statement sounds ridiculous: "If those taxpayers of the United States could provide an education for each child in the United States, very soon the effect of the system of public schools would empty all of the jails and prisons of the country" (Blanchard, 1971, pp. 88-89).

The Holy Spirit realizes the major moral impact in whatever life. This impact leads us to a greater understanding of principles found in the Word of God about the preparation of children and young people. As educators, we have to learn everyday about our own preparation, and that of future generations. The implications of office (prophet, king, and priest) ought to be explored, understood, and experienced throughout the school curriculum and through interaction with teachers. Through this, the student may find a more profound significance to his or her existence, based upon a worldview that promotes wisdom that comes from the Creator himself. His investigations will take reality as something integral with interdependence, without absolutizing any one aspect, integrating, and realizing the unity of the Creation of God, the Word of God, the redemption in Jesus Christ, and the vision that the Holy Spirit gives us. The teacher education student will realize his or her role as the image of God and how to see, respect, and lead students so that they too have their own understanding of their place in the Creation. He or she will learn how to demonstrate what is service and how to be a steward of the Creation, including neighbors. The development of this cultural mandate requires instruction at home, at church, and at school.

In our context, teacher education has the obligation not only to provide adequate academic preparation, but also to transmit the essence of the Gospel; the Christian life lived in community. The formation of Christian teachers without an understanding of this communal aspect is a contradiction. On the other hand, having this understanding of belonging to a group as a basic premise can be helpful in whatever circumstance. It gives a more profound dimension to the entire educational process that teachers are able to transmit to their students. Understanding our historical faults and strengths, identifying our individual and group philosophical biases, and projecting the integrated Christian worldview can do much to begin to redeem the educational process. As our mission becomes clearer so does our vision. As we begin to recognize the tremendous historical and philosophical factors that have so limited our self-realization, we begin to understand our true potential and place in God's kingdom. This in turn gives us not only the strength to confront the powerful spirits of this age, but also to actually go beyond conventional limits to make inroads into a society steeped in its own historical and philosophical morass.

Conclusion

In this brief essay, I have attempted to 1) explain our present situation and the background of our school of higher education; 2) give an historical and philosophical background as to the why of our situation; and 3) recognize the necessity of continuing with this effort against the tidal wave of opposition. During the composition of this paper, it has caused me several moments of reflection about the necessity of our work. When I examine our effort with that which occurs in a humanist system, I cannot conclude, in any way, that their system is better. To the contrary, I understand, without any doubt, that we have to continue. The Lord does not ask for less. He has placed in our hearts the imperative necessity of not only preparing these marginalized persons, but also giving them the best that we have.

I thank this forum for its interest in what interests me, for its enthusiasm that serves as a motivator, knowing that one is not alone. I hope that this type of interchange and expression can be helpful to many so that they might continue with the great commission that we have before us.

References

Blanchard, J. (1971, October). Can we live with public education? *Moody Monthly*, 88-89.

Dunphy, J. (1983, January/February). A religion for a new age. *The Humanist, 43,* 26.

Dooyeweerd, H. (1998). *Las raíces de la cultura occidental: Las opciones pagana, secular y cristiana*, trad. Adolfo García de la Sienra. Barcelona: CLIE. See especially the chapter "La gran síntesis". The English version of this book, *The Roots of Western Culture*, originally published by the Wedge Press in Toronto, 1979, was translated from the original Dutch *Vernieuwing en bezinning om het reformatorisch grondmotief,* Zutphen: J.B. van den Brink, 1959.

Gómez Navas, L. (2004). La revolución Mexicana y la educación popular. In F. Solana, R. C. Reyes, R. Bolaños (Eds.), *Historia de la educación pública en México (HEPM)* (pp. 116-156). México, D.F.: Fondo de Cultura Económica.

Matute, Á. (2004). La política educativa de José Vasconcelos. In F. Solana, R. C. Reyes, R. Bolaños (Eds.), *Historia de la educación pública en México (HEPM)* (pp. 166-182). México, D.F.: Fondo de Cultura Económica.

Mejía Zúñiga, R. (2004). La escuela que surge de la revolución. In F. Solana, R. C. Reyes, R. Bolaños (Eds.), *Historia de la educación pública en México (HEPM)* (pp. 183-233). México, D.F.: Fondo de Cultura Económica.

Schultz, G. (1998). *Kingdom education*. Nashville, TN: LifeWay Press.

Valadés, J. C. (1941). *El porfirismo (Historia de un régimen)*. México, D.F.: Porrúa.

RESPONSE TO DARREL W. HILBRANDS

Susheila Williams

It gives me great pleasure and satisfaction to respond to Dr. Hilbrands' paper "The Task of Redeeming the Educational Process in Mexico."

You emphasize that your institution is "need based." The children to whom you reached out were social outcasts, bearing the scars of the treatment meted out to them by society. Started in the year 1994 as a primary school, it is amazing to hear that you introduced the training of teachers in the year 2004. Besides that, you acquired 7½ acres of land for constructing dormitories, kitchen, and dining facilities. By employing teachers well-versed in the precepts of integrated life, you have added value to your institution.

Our institution parallels yours. Like yours, our college began in 1995 to combat the commercialization of higher education, a by-product of globalization. The last quarter of the twentieth century and the first five years in the twenty-first have witnessed far-reaching developments in Indian higher education. Higher education, elitist for centuries, has set itself on a march to become mass-based. The means of governments and public institutions to meet demand are so limited that partners have become inevitable. Governments find it necessary to permit, even invite and encourage, private providers, and parents have come to accept payment for services when public facilities are not available.

Our Coimbatore Diocese started the first college of Arts and Sciences with career-oriented courses that cover a body of knowledge, teach students how to learn, solve problems, appreciate values and ethics, and synthesize the old with the new, concentrating on holistic development. The Church of South India seeks to restore hope, happiness, belongingness, and concern for each other in the household of God. Its mission statement affirms its solidarity with broken communities. Christian missionaries pioneered education in India and encouraged social reformers like Raja Ram Mohan Roy to bring appropriate reforms, like the abolition of Sati and child marriage. The impact of education and the exposure to Christ's teaching spread by the early missionaries have transformed the lives of the social outcasts.

Like your institution, Dr. Van Dyke's visit to our college in 1999 and 2003 greatly influenced the teaching methods of our professors—"Teaching Christianly" changed the classroom atmosphere of the college.

As you have rightly commented, the ideals of rural schools are commendable, except that they do not have religious activities. It is interesting to note how Christian Normal Schools offered an alternative system of education, but was not successful. The explanation of humanism and humanist schools in Christian countries gives a sense of fear to Christians in a secular country such as ours. In our part of the country, openly witnessing and professing our faith is prohibited. However, we continue with our chapel service, prayer cells for students and staff members, retreats, and other spiritual activities. Our college has 47 percent Christian students and 95 percent Christian staff members. We keep our religious activities open for all the students; we never compel students of other faiths to participate. Our community development programmes and educational programmes reflect the character of Christ through action.

You give extensive details about the educational scenario in Mexico from 1898. It is strange to note that in a country with 90 percent Christians, schools belonging to the clergy were instructed to close down! The Liberal Manifest must have created a lot of upheaval among the Christian Community. To a certain extent, having only lay teaching in the schools is a practical idea. Churches can take care of religious studies. Our Christian students get a chance to do Bible Studies three hours a week. So far, there is no opposition to this from the students and parents.

Dr. Darrel, it was truly interesting to go through your paper regarding the problems faced by your institution. We agree that educational programmes cannot resolve all the problems of mankind. Rather, as Dr. Hulst said in his presentation on behalf of IAPCHE to administrators/representatives of eight church-related institutions of Christian higher education at Bishop Appasamy College on November 6, 2001:

> We, as Christians are called to the sanctification of our academic work . . . As we engage in this ongoing, Reformational academic activity, our point of departure must be the *creation order* and the recognition that, citing Al Wolters, "the Creator's sustaining and governing hand is not absent from the many ways in which human beings organise their living together."

This can be our guideline.

NEW WINESKINS: SUBVERTING THE "SACRED STORY" OF SCHOOLING

Doug Blomberg

The rapid expansion of Christian schools in the two-thirds world presents exciting opportunities. The very existence of a school that celebrates the Lordship of Christ is one more signpost to the Kingdom of God. It would be foolish on my part to generalize across the rich diversity of cultural contexts, each with its own unique challenges. However, there is one threat to authentic Christian schooling that I suspect is pervasive globally. The purpose of this paper is to elucidate this threat and to consider concrete ways in which Christian institutions of higher education can assist Christian day school educators in combating it.

My title of course alludes to Jesus' observation of what he takes to be common sense: do not pour new wine into old wineskins (Matthew 9:17). Christian schools recently starting out, indeed, putting down the first lineaments of a tradition, have a great opportunity to recognize and take critical distance from the cultural assumptions embedded in schooling structures in the West and to blaze alternative pathways to those that predominate there. And this despite, or perhaps because of, the pressures of globalization. The challenge is to develop structures that are rooted in a Biblical worldview and the indigenous culture.

We are accustomed to describing the proper work of schools in terms of "academics" and hence their goal as the pursuit of "academic excellence." I think it instructive that this term derives from the name of an ancient institution of higher learning, Plato's Academy. I believe we need to interrogate the assumptions built into this description, assumptions about the primacy of abstract, theoretical reasoning. Educationalists Connelly and Clandinin (1985) suggest that these assumptions constitute a "sacred story" in Western culture, a story that shapes not only how we think but also how we act. It is thus an ethical as well as an intellectual concern. This designation of "sacredness" is meant to shock, of course, not to commend, and it should be even more shocking to us, who are here because we have been called to embody the sacred story of the gospel.

Is this mere hyperbole on Connelly and Clandinin's part? Should we take them seriously? If we turn to the origins of this story in Greek philosophy, we find it nowhere better encapsulated than in Plato's Allegory of the Cave. Coming to know, for Plato, involves a "turning" from the "appearances" of everyday experience to face the reality that experience obscures. As Phillips and Soltis (1998) comment,

> In other places Plato spelled out more clearly what is involved here, and it is obvious that he valued the place of abstract reasoning; the person who had been trained to reason clearly (logically and mathematically) would be more likely to escape from the cave of ignorance and see the truth by using his mind. (p. 11)

Now, we are quite familiar with this notion of "turning": the Greek word is *metanoia*, a "change of mind," which we know from Scripture as "repentance." But whereas in Scripture this is turning *to* the concrete person of Jesus and accepting his proclamation that in him the Kingdom of God is coming (Mark 1:15), for Plato it is a turn in quite the other direction, away *from* the concrete and particular events of ordinary experience to the general and abstract world of eternal ideas. For Plato, the Counselor or Advocate (*parakletos*) that was to help with this transformation of the mind was none other than mathematics, as the most abstract of the disciplines. Only in this way could certainty be attained, by turning one's back on the ever-changing material world. Familiar as we are with "repentance" and the role of the Holy Spirit or "Paraclete" in leading us into the truth (John 14:26; 16:13), it does not require any stretch of the imagination to see the religious character of Plato's conception—nor, I might add, to consider the impact that Platonic and neo-Platonic notions have had on the way in which the gospel itself came to be interpreted.

Theorizing began to acquire its definitive shape among the pagan Greeks, but it is a gift of God to us nonetheless. While acknowledging the great value of theoretical knowledge embedded in the academic disciplines, however, we need to be wary of the claim that it is the *highest* value—or even a parallel, equivalent value—for this amounts to a religious claim, a claim of faith, as to where we are to put our trust. The attempt to synthesize the processes and products of the academic disciplines with the call to be disciplined by Christ—the "integration of learning and faith"—is inadequate, because we need instead radical reformation of the disciplines, so that we express discipleship not *alongside* the disciplines, as values added to the facts of the matter, but integrally within their reconstituted form. As Jesus' ironic response to the Pharisees who had set out to trap him implies—if we have ears to hear—there is one source of authority, not two, and we are to render everything unto God (Mark 12:13-17). Disciples of Jesus discipline their way of life by his teaching and example. Most important in discipleship is not theoretical knowledge but wisdom, judgment, discernment, that the right course of action will be chosen. No amount of knowledge *that* or knowing *how* will compensate for deficiency in respect to knowing *when* (Blomberg, 1998).

A large part of a college or university's task is preparing future professionals, and wise judgment is at the heart of what it means to be a competent professional. Certainly, a particular kind of judgment is required for solving theoretical problems, but this is of an attenuated form in comparison with that which is required in the much more complex context of daily life. Professionals make significant interventions in the multi-dimensional lives of others, sometimes in matters of life and death. A patient is more than "the kidney in bed 17A," and a student is more than a mind clinging precariously to a body. A "real-life" judgment requires attention to a range of norms or values that must be realized simultaneously, and nothing within a theoretical discipline or even a combination of disciplines can supply this holistic, multi-faceted perspective.

Such realization is not primarily an intellectual matter but rather addresses and is made by the whole person, whose feelings, values, and convictions are at work in any decision. Wisdom—which may be characterized as "the realization of value" (Maxwell, 1984/2007), in the two senses of realization, as discerning and actualizing, hearing and doing—begins with the fear of the Lord, with where we stand in relation to him, where we put our ultimate trust. It is a matter of the heart, of the character and integrity of the whole-bodied, historically situated person. Repentance means taking every thought captive to Christ, not turning to definitions and formulae. There is no realm of universal, neutral knowledge, because all knowing is always directed in either service of Christ or a substitute.

Professional judgment demands, as Donald Schön (1983; 1990) has so notably explored, reflection-*in*-action. For this reason, most professions require a period of internship before full certification is granted. Practice or experience transforms the novice into an expert over time. Most models of professional education adopt a "theory plus practice" model, with the internship added after the theoretical foundation, so-called, is laid. If we accept, however, that *experience* is foundational, and theory is an abstraction therefrom, would it not make sense to reverse this order, at least somewhat? John Elliot has concluded that:

> genuine theoretical statements about practice cannot be understood a priori. One does not first understand a theoretical principle about education and then apply it in an analysis of practice.... [T]heoretical knowledge contributes to the learning of a skill only after a certain level of practical knowledge has been acquired. (cit. Fullan, 1982, p. 270)

In addition, science educator Richard White (1998) observes:

> It is unfortunate for those new to teaching that judgment of what to include cannot be taught as principles; they have to acquire it from reflection on teaching sequences that went well and those that did not. That reflection becomes more productive as, through experience, they become familiar with the sorts of things students of a particular age might be expected to have done and to know. Until they acquire that familiarity, it is almost impossible for teachers to select well what to say from their own knowledge. (pp. 165-166)

Rather than privileging verbal and analytical abilities in the name of academic excellence—the articulation and memorization of theoretical statements or principles—schools at all levels should nurture the full complement of human qualities that the Scriptures promote as excellences, the most excellent virtue being that of love (Colossians 3:14, 1 Corinthians 13:13). For even though we have all knowledge, this is worthless if we are lacking in love (1 Corinthians 13:2).

What then is love? Though the parable of the Good Samaritan is a response to the question, "Who is my neighbor?" it cannot help but also be a response to the one it presumes, "What is love?" The expert knew that the commands to love God and neighbor were the essence of the law. In the parable the priest and the Levite pass by the battered victim, content in the conviction that it is sufficient to keep the first commandment through temple sacrifices and memorization of the law—but only the Samaritan in his actions honors the first command, by obeying the second. The two other travelers fail at both. When Jesus' interlocutor observes rightly that showing mercy is true neighborliness, true love, Jesus does not compliment his grasp of a definition, but commands him to *go* and *do* likewise. Truly grasping or understanding the law means being grasped by it, standing under it, keeping God's commandments not in the hearing but in the doing (cf. 1 John 2:3-6).

The interchange around the parable also illuminates that other great "philosophical" question of the New Testament, "What is truth?" Like the lawyer's question about who counts as neighbor, Pilate's question smacks of self-justification and evasion. Readers should remember that

Jesus had already given an answer. Whereas at the palace he says he has come to testify to the truth (John 18:37), earlier he had proclaimed, "I am the truth"—and that the truth is a way of going, a way that leads to life. Jesus' testimony is explicit: he himself is the truth, and he testifies of himself. And anyone who walks in his way will do what he has done—and even greater (John 14:6-12). His view of truth was the Hebrew one, of *emeth* or "faithfulness." Being true was to keep troth ("truth" and "troth" are etymologically linked)—to love God and one's neighbor. Truth is a quality of this person, and of all the persons who would walk in the way of life. Neither wisdom nor truth is so much a stable possession as a moment by moment process, a direction of going—"Jesus-wise," we might say (on analogy with "lengthwise" or "clockwise").

Some might say of the parable of the Good Samaritan, "It's all very well in theory, but it won't work in practice." This is a loose way of talking, and it is not the sense of "theory" that concerns us here. Admittedly, we often equate words, thoughts, and thinking with theory, but Plato and the Western tradition distinguish theorizing from ordinary thinking as a particular kind of thinking, one characterized by a focus on the abstracted properties of things rather than the concrete things themselves. The concern of theory—"real knowledge"—is not with this or that or the other particular horse, in all their individual variety, but with the concept or idea of horse, what constitutes "horse-ness" as an abstract, universal property. The parable of the Good Samaritan is not an abstract ethical treatise, but a concrete illustration or case study. It is understood fully not when the puzzle element is unlocked and the Samaritan is identified as the true neighbor, but when this realization moves into its second mode, of *actualization*. The teacher of the law who questions Jesus will only achieve full realization when he too stops to succor someone in need, when he demonstrates "the stuff, of which he is made," his character.

Observers as ancient as Aristotle were aware of what was at stake here:

> [O]pinion is divided about the subjects of education. People do not take the same view about what should be learned . . . either with a view to human excellence or a view to the best possible life; nor is it clear whether education should be directed mainly to the intellect or to moral character. (cit. Knight, 1980, p. v)

To put the issue most starkly, the Biblical perspective on knowing as a matter of character is antithetical to the Platonic view that it is a matter of intellect. We grasp true knowledge within, not beyond, the perplexities of experience, in the midst of change, not above it. The deepest significance of the creation account is that the world of experience is ordered, coherent, and meaningful. We meet God and his purposes historically, for God speaks to us with the voice of creation, not even primarily in its pristine state but more so in its humanly shaped complexity, for humans bear the image of God.

Though I am far from suggesting that all the blame should be laid at Plato's feet, for the tradition for which I have taken him as spokesman is a variegated one, we might heed Parker Palmer's injunction that, if we want to know a society's epistemology, we should look not to its leading philosophers but to the practice of its classrooms. In this respect, university educator Richard Bawden (1985) claims that:

> our entire formal education system has been grounded in belief of learning as the pervasive accumulation of preserved quanta of knowledge, generated from experience often long forgotten and certainly remote to the contemporary student. The model forges an awful reliance on both the aggregation of specialised and selective packages of second-hand information and on those who disseminate it to us in the name of teaching. (p. 44)

Bawden's critique applies directly to university education, but is by no means limited to it. Institutions of higher education, themselves with a legitimate orientation to theoretical investigation, can easily fall prey to the assumption that schooling at earlier levels should sort students according to their aptitude for theoretical pursuits. Thus, they traditionally exert a top-down influence on schools, demanding that they conform more and daily to the image of the Academy.

A Biblically informed approach should be oriented not towards theory (as knowledge in abstraction) but wisdom (loving understanding-in-action rooted in the fear of the Lord). This approach does not deny that Christian institutions should nurture their students in a Christian perspective on the disciplines, but rather reminds us that a way of *seeing* does not in itself issue in a way of *being*. The latter is engendered more by actions than thoughts, by ways of walking more than ways of talking, by organizational and communal structures that shape the habits of the heart. Thus, Christian institutions of higher education can be most helpful if they encourage pre-service and practicing teachers and administrators not only to question the assumptions built into the practice of schooling but also if they expose them to alternative models. We teach in the way that we were taught, and if universities proclaim by their practices that disciplinary structure represents the structure of the world, then teachers will learn and pass on this lesson. As Parker Palmer (1983, p. 10) says, "We cannot settle for pious prayer as a preface to conventional education. Instead, we must allow the power of love to transform the very knowledge we teach, the very methods we use to teach and learn it."

Jesus' approaches to discipling his followers may seem remote from the modern institution of schooling, which has its own distinctive demands, and Jesus was preparing his disciples not to practice one or another profession but to live their whole lives before the face of God. Yet while it is true that the professions have their own disciplines, if we are seeking to prepare *Christian* professionals, we will of course keep this whole life context in view. Central to professional work is the character of the practitioner; society depends upon her utmost integrity, and trusts and invests her with great authority and responsibility. Because professionals individually as well as collectively have so much control over their own actions and those of others, they should exhibit the qualities of love, patience, faithfulness, kindness, gentleness, goodness, self-control—yes, and joy and peace. Character formation, and not the transmission of information, is as much a responsibility of institutions of higher education, as it is of elementary and high schools. The ethics, skills, and knowledge of the practice ought to live through professionals as second nature. Such formation of character is possible only by "going and doing likewise."

Was it an accident that Jesus engaged in on-the-job training, leading his disciples through the country for a range of encounters, using opportunities as these arose in daily life as occasions for teaching? For three years, he immersed his disciples in his ministry, sending them out unsupervised on occasion to test their wings. He did not have an Academy like Plato, where people came to engage in dialogue and disputation, in the pursuit of clear and distinct ideas (if this anachronistic allusion to Descartes may be pardoned), but taught in response to problems posed by those he met. Where Plato was convinced that the disciplined pursuit of ideas was the necessary foundation for good practice, Jesus taught by having others follow in his footsteps, a way of living the truth.

I now turn to describe three pedagogies for higher education that a range of professional preparation programs has employed: problem-based learning, case studies and hypotheticals, and immersion programs (including mentoring).

Problem-based learning
I have long been an advocate of problem-posing pedagogy and curricula. (See e.g. Blomberg, 1980b; 1993; 1999.) I have suggested that such an approach has an ontic foundation: it is rooted in the kind of world in which we live, which is a *creation* that is *fallen*. This creation is entrusted

to us to ad*minister* (serve) as stewards, to open up the possibilities that God has structured into it. Unfolding creation toward what it can and ought to be is our calling, at the very heart of our image bearing. Discerning and actualizing these possibilities is the primal sense in which creation poses problems to us, and we pose problems to creation. But this is a fallen world, which adds a second dimension to what I am calling its "problematic" character. We live in a suffering world, and our task is to bring healing where there is brokenness, not merely to observe, describe and analyze, but to "show mercy" in our actions. This is further reason why the Creation Mandate cannot be assimilated to any mere notion of unbounded development. Development of what is—just going on as we have been, but with more of the same—will not suffice. There has to be continual correction and re-direction towards greater shalom or cosmic justice. Many Christian (and also non-Christian) institutions already incorporate "service learning" into their curricula, and the strategies I describe in this and the succeeding sections can each be adapted to this end, though likely with such projects playing a much more central role than they currently do, as addenda to the discipline-based curriculum.

The description "Problem-based learning" (PBL) directly indicates the order of priority in this approach: the problem comes first, as the initiator, and not at the stage of application of learning. That is, while problems are by no means foreign in schools or university teaching, they are used as means of assessing or practicing what students have studied beforehand in the classroom, and thus typify the theory into practice progression. Such problems are often more like puzzles, games to be solved within the matrix of a theoretical framework. They are not problems for students in any existential sense. They are tests of whether pre-specified learning outcomes have been attained.

In PBL, messy, ill-structured problems—the kind we meet in daily life—generate learning objectives and processes and provide the criteria by which the quality of learning will be assessed. We know a problem has been resolved when we can responsibly move on to something else, which may not immediately be another problem, but simply a well-earned rest!

PBL is a ready site for cooperative learning, with groups of students bringing their varied expertise to bear and researching different aspects of the problem, further differentiating their expertise as they do so. This team approach mirrors the situation in many work environments—hough sadly, not that of school teaching. It is thus especially in respect to the latter profession that experiences in higher education could help engender a more collaborative culture in schools, and also encourage teachers, by their having lived through the experience themselves, to employ cooperative learning strategies in their own classrooms. Though cooperative approaches are not mandatory for PBL, their employment affords a welcome respite from the individualistic and competitive regimes that are so characteristic of higher education, and so antithetical to the Biblical teaching about the body of Christ and the centrality of community.

Case studies and hypotheticals

Harvard Business School has been employing *case studies* almost since it commenced, early last century. This is their description of the pedagogy:

> Typically, an HBS case is a detailed account of a real-life business situation, describing the dilemma of the "protagonist"—a real person with a real job who is confronted with a real problem. Faculty and their research assistants spend weeks at the company that is the subject of the case, detailing the background of the situation, the immediate problem or decision, and the perspectives of the managers involved. The resulting case presents the story exactly as the protagonist saw it, including ambiguous evidence, shifting variables, imperfect knowledge, no obvious right answers, and a ticking clock that impatiently demands action. (http://www.hbs.edu/case/hbs-case.html)

MBA students typically grapple with over fourteen cases per week; they study each case for a couple of hours on their own and then test their thinking before class in small study groups. First-year sections of about ninety students meet for about four hours a day throughout the year. Class usually begins with a "cold call," "a provocative question the professor poses to one specific student to open the case" and stimulate the class' thinking. Over the year, each student is cold-called at least once. The class then engages in "eighty minutes of analysis, argument, insight, and passionate persuasion." The professor will often be the author of the case under discussion, and the actual case protagonist might participate in the class in person or through a video link to answer questions and explain how things finally turned out. Classes rarely end with a tidy solution to the dilemma, but hopefully foster a deeper appreciation of the complex factors involved, a clearer understanding of how to employ relevant techniques to analyze and evaluate the problem, and further insights into dealing with the uncertainties of the business world (http://www.hbs.edu/case/case-work.html).[1]

---

[1] Judith Shulman (1992) has edited a helpful text on the use of case methods in teacher education.

A variation on the case study, the "*hypothetical*" is a common pedagogical device in faculties of law in the United States. Hypotheticals are distinguished, as the name suggests, by teaching that proceeds by the posing of a series of "what if" questions, counterfactuals introduced progressively in discussion after a legal dispute has been outlined. My direct experience of the hypothetical is as a series of television programs for the Australian Broadcasting Commission hosted by barrister Geoffrey Robertson. No doubt what helped to make it compelling viewing were the prominent public figures who appeared on the show and placed in roles that often mirrored those in their actual careers. The candor of their responses to various ethical dilemmas was often astonishing, and the use of hypotheticals in law schools, teacher education, and elsewhere has the same potential to generate discussion that penetrates the more technical concerns of a profession to these underlying normative concerns and quandaries.

Immersion programs and mentorship
The two pedagogies I have described are "immersive," but they are in most cases simulations (including medical students' collaborative diagnosis of a real patient, which does not leave them with the ultimate decision-making responsibility, for obvious reasons). Full immersion programs place students in the actual situations in which they are preparing to practice professionally, in a situation of cognitive apprenticeship under the guidance of a mentor.

University of Melbourne "Course B"[2]
Two of the most exciting teachers with whom I have been privileged to work are graduates of the "Course B" Diploma of Education begun at the University of Melbourne in the mid-seventies (Dow, 1979). This was a pre-service program for graduates in other disciplines who were aspiring high school teachers, and it involved a substantial and continual experience in schools. This required close working relationships with schools, representatives of which had a significant advisory role in the course. Teachers benefited directly from this engagement as mentors, and were able to use student teachers to reduce the size of classes and work with individual students. The findings of Michael Fullan (1991) support this approach: collaborative ventures between schools, system offices, and colleges of teacher education are the most effective means of bringing about change in schools.

---

2 This section draws on material previously published in Blomberg (1995).

For the course designers, becoming a teacher is an intensely personal matter: teachers' beliefs about the meaning of their experience are crucial. They have to establish a basis for their actions in terms of what makes good teaching possible, which requires not only subject-matter expertise, but pedagogical content-knowledge as well. Students thus need to reflect on the nature and the teachability of their subjects. Where they had been used to answering other people's questions, they had now to learn to ask their own questions. However, many of them had "a very shadowy and arid idea of the nature of their subject . . . . as staff, we could do little about it unless we saw what happened when these students were teaching" (Dow, 1979, p. 11).

The course framework included two morning or afternoon Methods seminars and two days spent in a school, and rather than spending a block here and a block there, this was the same school throughout the year. On Friday mornings, students returned to university for Curriculum Studies, a problem-centered course. The compartments were not neat and tidy; Curriculum Studies and Methods were tied closely to each other and to students' teaching, "to what different students are looking for because of the particular problems they are experiencing in their schools, and to what each of those schools and its supervisors are like" (Dow, 1979, p. 13).

Gwyneth Dow's evaluation of the course, drawing extensively on student diaries, provides significant evidence of the program's success. Her conclusion is worth quoting:

> There seems little doubt that the mismatch between teacher training and the school system must be met by more school-based courses which bring the two together and help to invigorate both . . . . Thus, the distinction between pre-service and in-service education tends to be blurred . . . . The future for rejuvenated teacher education and for a "self-renewing" educational system would seem to lie in strengthening and extending school-based approaches to pre-service and in-service teacher education. (Dow, 1979, p. 246)

Sadly, Course B did not survive for long. In later years, the University of Melbourne introduced what might be regarded as a compromise program. It extended the one-year end-on Graduate Diploma of Education to two years, with the second year given over to student placement in a school under the guidance of a mentor. I say this was a compromise, in that it continues the theory into practice sequence, at the same time as it gives equal weighting to these two components.

Cooperative education

Course B is a variant of what today is termed "cooperative education" (in distinction from "cooperative *learning*"), in which periods of academic study alternate with curriculum-related work experience. It is now more widely recognized that personal engagement in the working environment is essential for developing some kinds of understanding. However, the predominant epistemological model is probably still one of *application* of classroom knowledge to real-life situations in business and industry, although it would seem inevitable that the flow would be in the other direction as well.

Professional practice schools

Professional practice (or development) schools are restructured schools with teacher education roles that are also conceived as sites of ongoing research by teachers themselves. The Regional Collaborative Professional Development Schools in Washington provide one appropriate model (Sagor, Curley, Manning, Piland & Taylor, 1994). These schools incorporate pre-service instruction, taught collaboratively by university and school staff; student teacher field experience; new teacher induction; visiting appointments of staff from other school districts; and research conducted by practitioners and university faculty on issues of practice. Immersed in the school context, novices and older teachers, in company with teacher educators, critically address educational problems. Primary, secondary, and tertiary educators blend pre-service and in-service professional development, establishing linkages across the levels of schooling to the benefit of all concerned.

Collaborative action research: the PEEL Project

The ethos of PEEL is encapsulated in its full title, "Project to Enhance Effective Learning" (Baird & Mitchell, 1993; Baird & Northfield, 1992). That the emphasis is on *learning* rather than teaching is key, and is even more significant given that the original context was *secondary* schooling, where transmission of subject matter is more often the norm. Commencing in 1985 at Laverton High School in suburban Melbourne, the project is still going strong, with uptake not only elsewhere in Australia but in other countries as well. What is significant in the present context is that it was designated a "*collaborative* action research project" not mainly because it involved groups of teachers working together (as advocated by Kemmis and McTaggart (1988) in their version of action research) but because it involved cooperation between teachers and university academics *as equal partners*. That is to say, it was not a "top-down" venture in which professors or graduate students invited themselves into schools in order to conduct research projects, but one in which they were invited to join a teacher-initiated project. These teachers and academics

> shared concerns about the prevalence of passive, unreflective, dependent student learning, even in apparently successful lessons. They set out to research classroom approaches that would stimulate and support student learning that was more informed, purposeful, intellectually active, and independent. The project was unfunded and not a result of any system or institution-level initiative. PEEL teachers agree to meet on a regular basis, in their own time, to share and analyse experiences, ideas, and new practices. (http://www.peelweb.org/index.cfm?resource=about)

Conclusion

My thesis has been that institutions of higher education need to change their practices if the practices of schools are to change, so that they better reflect the primacy of experiential knowing as this typifies a Biblical wisdom perspective, rather than continue to uphold the rival "sacred story" of *theory into practice*. The ways in which teachers are taught will be one of the most significant influences on the ways in which teachers teach. This is most significant in teacher education faculties of course, where professional teachers are prepared: teaching is not only the process of such faculties, it is also the product. But in other faculties as well, many graduates will themselves go on to be teachers, either returning to universities as full-time or associate faculty, or mentoring their junior colleagues informally (but quite crucially) on the job.

Though I have asserted the need for inner Biblical reformation of the disciplines, I have focused instead on the institutional structure of teaching and learning themselves. My longstanding concern has been with the relative futility of pouring new wine into old wineskins, of entrapping Christian education (which is education for discipleship) within the theory into practice framework (education for the disciplines).

It may seem paradoxical, if not contradictory, to draw my examples from the secular world. I said at the outset, that we have much to learn from Plato and the theoretical tradition he helped to initiate (though I might also be chided for not celebrating this more). That we can learn from the secular world is an important conviction of Reformational Christian scholarship, for all people are made in God's image and live in his world, sustained by the power of God's Word and his grace shed abroad. The Lord God is sovereign over all human activity, including the activity of those who do not acknowledge him. In addition, we must remember that the antithesis cuts not between two communities, but through every human heart: we, too, often go astray, and by no means unfailingly think and act faithfully. If it is indeed the case that the commitment to theory as delivering the key to life is a religious one, this is not to imply that our institutions of higher education need to abandon theorizing, which would be to abandon a significant part of their proper character. It is rather to relativize theorizing, especially in respect to their teaching function, which is the other, perhaps yet the major, role of the undergraduate college or university.

References

Baird, J. R., & Mitchell, I. J. (Eds.). (1993). *Improving the quality of teaching and learning: an Australian case study - the PEEL project* (2nd ed.). Melbourne: Monash University.

Baird, J. R., & Northfield, J. R. (Eds.). (1992). *Learning from the PEEL experience*. Melbourne: Monash University.

Bawden, R. (1985). Problem-based learning: An Australian perspective. In D. Boud (Ed.), *Problem-based learning in education for the professions* (pp. 43-57). Sydney: Higher Education Research and Development Society of Australasia.

Blomberg, D. G. (1999). A problem-posing pedagogy: Paths of pleasantness and peace. *Journal of Education & Christian Belief,* 3(2), 97-113.

Blomberg, D. G. (1980). Curriculum guidelines for the Christian school. In J. Mechielsen (Ed.), *No icing on the cake: Christian foundations for education in Australasia* (pp. 111-122). Melbourne: Brookes-Hall.

Blomberg, D. G. (1993). Teacher as researcher, curriculum as hypothesis: Implications for the education of educators. In P. DeBoer (Ed.), *Educating Christian teachers for responsive discipleship* (pp. 63-84). Lanham, MD: University Press of America.

Blomberg, D. G. (1995). Teachers as articulate artisans. In D. C. Elliott (Ed.), *Nurturing reflective Christians to teach* (pp. 99-118). Lanham, MD: University Press of America.

Blomberg, D. G. (1998). The practice of wisdom: Knowing when. *Journal of Education & Christian Belief,* 2(1), 7-26.

Dow, G. (1979). *Learning to teach: Teaching to learn*. London: Routledge.

Fullan, M. G. (1982). *The meaning of educational change*. Toronto, ON: OISE Press.

http://www.hbs.edu/case/case-work.html retrieved September 16, 2006.
http://www.hbs.edu/case/hbs-case.html retrieved September 16, 2006.
Kemmis, S., & McTaggart, R. (Eds.). (1988). *The action research planner.* (3rd ed.). Burwood: Deakin University.
Knight, G. R. (1980). *Philosophy and education: An introduction in Christian perspective* (2nd ed.). Berrien Springs, MI: Andrews University Press.
Maxwell, N. (1984/2007). *From knowledge to wisdom: A revolution in the aims and methods of science.* Oxford: Blackwell.
Palmer, P. J. (1983). *To know as we are known: A spirituality of education.* San Francisco: HarperCollins.
http://www.peelweb.org/index.cfm?resource=about retrieved September 16, 2006.
Sagor, R. D., Curley, T., Manning, J., Piland, J., & Taylor, T. (1994). *The professional development school: A fundamentally new approach to teacher and program development.* Paper presented at the Association for Supervision and Curriculum Development Conference, Chicago.
Schön, D. A. (1983a). *Educating the reflective practitioner: Toward a new design for teaching and learning in the professions.* San Francisco/Oxford: Jossey-Bass.
Schön, D. A. (1983b). *The reflective practitioner: How professionals think in action.* New York: Basic Books.
Shulman, J. H. (Ed.). (1992). *Case methods in teacher education.* New York/London: Teachers College Press.
White, R. T. (1988). *Learning science.* Oxford, UK/Cambridge, MA: Blackwell.

RESPONSE TO DOUG BLOMBERG

David MacPherson

In responding to the paper, I ask two basic questions: First, is the threat identified in the paper the *one threat* to *authentic Christian schooling?* Is the traditional model necessarily *old wine*? Second, can we adopt new teaching practices in the context of limited resources (human and economic) and external pressures? Is the *new wine* available and applicable in the two-thirds world?

A consideration of the legitimacy of the basic thesis
I begin by stressing that I largely share the author's convictions regarding what constitutes *authentic Christian schooling*—a process of discipleship where Christian character formation and cultivation of wisdom are the key goals. That said do we presume all our pupils are "disciples?" Presumably, a necessary condition for being discipled is being a disciple. While we may legitimately consider children from the covenant community "disciples," what of pupils whose parents make no credible Christian profession? For many Christian schools in the two-thirds world the majority of the pupils do not proceed from Christian homes. As Blomberg rightly asserts "wisdom . . . begins with the fear of the Lord, with where we stand in relation to him, where we put our ultimate trust. It is a matter of the heart . . .," I agree, but how do you develop or even cultivate wisdom in those who lack the prime ingredient—fear of the Lord? I do not pretend to have the answer but I simply raise the question for consideration.

Blomberg's paper suggests that the key issue in ensuring *authentic Christian schooling* is the methodological one i.e. the introduction of the "practice-theory" approach in place of the "theory-practice" approach. I am not convinced this is the case.

We can identify three models for Christian schools, recognizing the danger of generalizations and caricatures that necessarily accompany reducing the alternatives to three. First, the Prayer Sandwich Model. By this, I refer to schools that demonstrate Christian identity through the presence of Christian staff and worship but where the academic curriculum does not differ in any meaningful way from the curriculum in secular institutions. In other words prayer to start the day and prayer to conclude the day but the academic burger in the middle is not distinctly Christian—hence the sandwich! Second, the "Christian" curriculum Model. In this model there are the Christian elements mentioned above (staff and worship) but it also includes an explicit attempt, however modest, to *nurture their students in a Christian perspective on the disciplines* while retaining the basic "theory-practice" model with respect to the methodology of teaching. Third, holistic Christian schooling model involves the Christian elements of a. and b. above (staff and worship, Christian perspective on the disciplines) but also includes the adoption of a methodology of teaching biased toward the "practice-theory" approach. This involves a careful introduction of the pedagogies described in Blomberg's paper (problem based learning, case studies and hypotheticals, immersion, and mentorship) and others to replace or at least supplement pedagogies based on the *primacy of abstract, theoretical reasoning.*

All things being equal I do not hesitate to opt for the third model, but having said that I am also convinced that all three models are capable of providing *authentic Christian schooling.* The key issue is the Christian character—let us talk about Christ-likeness—of the staff. Even in the prayer sandwich model Christ-likeness in the staff will ensure meaningful discipleship—modeling by example to the pupils the fruit of the Spirit. In the context of the two-thirds world, it may not be possible to staff a Christian school with teachers who have had exposure to and experience of "practice-theory" approaches but it is realistic to aspire to identify Christian teachers who will model Jesus and reflect the love of Jesus to their pupils.

In summary, I wonder whether the "risk" identified by Blomberg is the primary risk faced by Christian schools in the two-thirds world and consequently also question whether Christian schools in the two-thirds world need to discard the old model and begin with a new model that focuses on experiential learning. I suspect that in this case we can still go with the old wine without fear of bursting the new wineskins.

That said I heartily support the contention that Christian schools must recognize the dangers of abstract theoretical approaches and the need for more experiential approaches. I guess the crux of the matter is whether this issue would be number one on the agenda or maybe down at number three.

Assuming that we accept the basic thesis—be it unreservedly or guardedly—there remains the real issue of applicability. Four factors prevent the current substitution of the theoretical model with the experiential model. First, in the two-thirds world, or perhaps more accurately and modestly in Peru, all teachers have been trained in 'theory-practice' approaches. An individual school must—at least in the short to medium term—accept that reality and seek those who are able to apply that academic approach most effectively. Second, Blomberg rightly considers that Christian institutions of higher education must take on the challenge of assisting day school educators in the task of introducing experiential approaches to day schools. What happens when there are no such institutions? In the whole of Peru, there is one teacher training college that qualifies as Christian. The challenge then is to support coherent initiatives that seek to fill this vacuum. Third, many schools lack teaching material based on experimental approaches. Ideally, these would not be translations of English materials but original and contextually appropriate materials. Finally, Blomberg rightly identifies the *top down influence* on schools to *conform to the image of the Academy*. I suggest this is more pronounced in Peru where university entrance is a function of the capacity to regurgitate accumulated knowledge across the disciplines. This is accentuated by the *horizontal* influence of parents who in opting for a Christian school which is necessarily (in the Peruvian context) also a private school aspire to a university education for their children and will often judge and choose a school as a function of the schools capacity to prepare their child for university entrance.

Conclusion
I share Blomberg's conviction that in the context of *the rapid expansion of Christian schools in the two-thirds world* the *challenge is to develop structures that are rooted in a Biblical worldview and the indigenous culture*. That said I think such an affirmation would have to be qualified or developed in the following three ways. First, structures, though important, are not necessarily the key issue. Second, while sharing a Biblical worldview it may be possible to arrive at quite different structures depending on context. Third, even if we theoretically have arrived at a conclusion regarding the most appropriate and Biblically rooted structure, we may find that the application of that structure involves a process that could take a significant period of time—but then a mature wine is worth the wait!

RESPONSE TO DOUG BLOMBERG

Samson Makhado

It is an honour and privilege to participate in this debate. In fact, the debate is overdue, as Western overemphasis on theoretical knowledge has seriously devalued concrete, oral, and other forms of knowledge. Blomberg is trying to move our thinking out of well-packed boxes. I am impressed by the way he captured his whole critique using Jesus' statement, "do not pour new wine into old wineskins" (Matthew 9:17), as his driving force.

The politicians and missionaries who came to Africa focused more on the advancement of Western culture than using the Bible to reform host cultures. They did not realise that African cultures had their own system of education and way of thinking. Van der Walt regards the dominant pronoun of the Western culture as "I"; South Africa has created schools that reflect a Western ethic and value system on this base. However, the dominant pronoun of the African cultural value system is "we" (van der Walt, 1997, pp. 28-32). These pronouns demonstrate the difference between African and Western worldviews. The two worldviews differ in their anthologies (understanding of reality), their anthropology (view of man or view of society), their epistemology (theories of knowing), and axiology (norms and values). One outstanding difference between the two cultures is that Africa emphasises human community and the West emphasises the individual (van der Walt, 1997, p. 28).

Blomberg's holistic approach combines educating for justice with wisdom. If the original advocates of Christian education had understood this holistic way of thinking, the so-called "Christian education" in the East and in Africa would have been appropriately fertilised in those cultures. Unfortunately, these advocates advanced their own Western cultures in "Christian" education at the expense of Asian and African cultures.

Blomberg's approach is supported by his fellow Australian, Fowler, who also strikes a balance between Western and African patterns of thought. Fowler mentions three characteristics of traditional African education that should not be neglected. First, it can provide a much broader perspective on values. It teaches not only survival values, as in Western education, but also "trans-survival" values (Fowler, 1965). Second, traditional African education teaches how to live as an effective member of the community, fulfilling social obligations, and developing personal relations that promote healthy communal life. Third, traditional African education emphasises learning by involvement in the practical affairs of daily life, not withdrawal from daily affairs to the segregated environment of the classroom (Fowler, 1965, pp. 145-147).

Throughout Africa, education systems are built on the philosophy of "I." It is only important that *I* get to my goal; it does not matter whether anyone else reaches his or hers. In a multicultural system, if we do not use cooperation and relationship, tension and conflict remain the norm of that particular class. Schools that work for all children must be grounded in a system that values cooperation and relationship.

A Biblically informed approach should be oriented not towards theory (as knowledge in abstraction), but wisdom (loving understanding-in-action rooted in the fear of the Lord). This is not to deny that Christian institutions should nurture their students in a Christian perspective on the disciplines, including the theoretical background, but rather a reminder that a way of *seeing* does not in itself result in a way of *being*. The latter is engendered more by actions than thoughts, by walking more than talking, by organizational and communal structures that shape the habits of the heart. Thus, Christian institutions of higher education would be most helpful if they encouraged pre-service and in-service teachers and administrators not only to question the assumptions built into the practice of education but also to expose them to alternative models. We generally teach in the way that we were taught, and if universities proclaim by their practices that disciplinary structure represents the structure of the world, this is the lesson that teachers will learn and pass on. As Parker Palmer (1983, p. 10) says, "We cannot settle for pious prayer as a preface to conventional education. Instead, we must allow the power of love to transform the very knowledge we teach, the very methods we use to teach and learn it."

If the purpose of Christian education is to take action in the world that helps bring about human flourishing, then we cannot remain indifferent to the plight of those around us. Christian universities and colleges must take Blomberg's criticism seriously, especially the suggestion that he made towards the conclusion: "We need to see the tears of God behind the wounds of the world and meet a wounded God behind the injustice that exists around the globe."

Modernity managed to marginalise the church and its alliances (Christian schools) by making them irrelevant. Post-modernity could easily marginalise the church and its alliances by trying to make the truth relative. Thank God post-modernity has cleared the square for us; no one owns the public mind; no one is claiming to do it right. The time is now for the Christian story to go back to centre-stage and bring healing to the broken world.

Christians can interpret and bring real meaning to truth and reconciliation. We who are forgiven understand the real meaning of forgiveness. This should be at the centre of our curriculum. The curriculum should become our means of bringing healing to the many children coming from dysfunctional families. In my country, divorce is growing at an alarming rate, HIV/AIDS is increasing the number of single parents, and the number of child-headed families is now over two million.

Blomberg's thinking creates an opportunity for Christian education to go back to the public square. This opportunity can be used, misused, or completely missed. If we do not use it, other religions are ready to use it and shape our young ones for their own purposes and gains. Now is the time to change. It is the time to learn from each other's stories. We need a paradigm shift in our leadership. We need collegial leadership for meaning, for problem solving, for shared responsibility, that serves educational purposes, that demands a great deal from everyone, and yet is tender enough to encourage the broken-hearted. This means that among other things leaders will also be counsellors, mentors, nurturers, and guides. They will need to be able to shape the community for a common vision.

This helps us to understand that we are engaged in a generational war, sometimes in the thick of it. In most instances, we do not understand how we got here or where the lines are drawn. We wonder where it will lead. As I said before, we are living in a world of moral relativism and post-modernism. Reality is no longer what it used to be; "truth" is twisted.

What worries me most is the fear and insecurity among Christian teachers and parents. As a result, the relationship between Christian schools, which provide salt and light, and the society, which provides the curriculum content, seems to be in a shaky, unstable condition. A Christian school should be a place where all stakeholders experience and seek *shalom*. Seeking *shalom* involves a concern for justice. A *shalom*-seeking classroom ought to embrace a pedagogy of tactfulness and trust, a curriculum of justice and harmony, a discipline of discipleship, and an ethos of celebrating God's majesty.

In conclusion
Blomberg gave good suggestions on the direction we need to take. If these suggestions are embraced, we will have teachers who can be the agents of Christian education in the global societies.

I want to thank Blomberg for stimulating the debate. My prayer is that this will enable us to use new wineskins. We must honestly evaluate to what degree our Christian education and schools are Christian.

Shalom! I thank you!

References

Fowler, S. A. (1996). *Christian voice among students and scholars.* Potchefstroom, South Africa: Potchefstroom University for Higher Education.

Palmer, P. (1983/1993). *To know as we are known: Education as a spiritual journey.* San Francisco, CA: HarperCollins.

van der Walt, B. J. (1997). *Afrocentric or Eurocentric? Our task in multicultural South Africa.* Potchefstroom, South Africa: Institute for Reformational Studies.

van der Walt, B. J. (2001). *Transformed by the renewing of your mind.* Potchefstroom, South Africa: Institute for Reformational Studies.

van der Walt, B. J. (2002). *The liberating message: A Christian worldview for Africa.* Potchefstroom, South Africa: Institute for Religious Studies.

van der Walt, B. J. (2003). *Understanding and rebuilding Africa: From desperation to expectation for tomorrow.* Potchefstroom, South Africa: The Institute for Contemporary Christianity in Africa.

van der Walt, B. J., & Swinepoxes, R. (1995). *Confessing Christ in doing politics: Essays on Christian political thought and action.* Potchefstroom, South Africa: Institute for Religious Studies.

EQUIPPING CHRISTIAN STUDENTS TO CONNECT KINGDOM CITIZENSHIP TO ISSUES IN TODAY'S SOCIETIES

Henk Jochemsen & Johan Hegeman

Introduction

Christian higher education tries to help students to grow in wisdom and knowledge as persons, to develop their talents and abilities to become equipped to contribute as Christians, that is, as Kingdom citizens, to society in its various relationships and practices.

Of course, this very general statement indicates a direction for educational work but that as such does not suggest how it should or could be achieved. This paper tries to formulate an answer to that question. How can Christian education help students to become able and willing to get involved as Christians in the issues our societies face?

In dealing with this question, we will differentiate it into two sub-questions:

First: how can we help them to understand the issues properly from a Christian perspective?
Second: how can we equip them to get involved as Christian professionals in a faithful way?

The study and reflection on these questions fall under the discipline of ethics understood in a broad sense as the (scientific) study of responsible living in the light of God's norms for reality. Hence, in answering these questions we will use concepts and theories from the discipline of ethics.

Understanding the issues

It is, of course, impossible to deal with the content of the various issues that are pressing our societies now—issues like the HIV/Aids epidemic in a number of relatively poor countries, globalisation, the constant flow of immigrants/refugees into the European countries with concomitant cultural and religious tensions, the issue of the organisation of a just health care system, medical ethical issues pertaining to the dignity of human beings, etc.

We are concerned here with helping students to be involved properly, based on a sensible analysis and understanding of the situation. By "the situation," we do not primarily mean the policy level on a national or international scope. We are primarily thinking of the large variety of practices in which professionals work in governmental institutions, in economic enterprises, in helping and caring organisations, in the mass media, as professors in educational institutions, in all kinds of NGO's, and of course, also in politics. The students who graduate from our institutions most often get jobs in such practices.

We have not chosen the word "practice" by accident. It is a key concept in answering this first question. Before explaining this concept and its significance for our topic, we want to point out a presupposition with respect to the structure of reality.

In our view—based on our understanding of the Bible and Christian philosophical thinking—reality is normatively structured and human life and social entities have a *telos*, a built-in purpose because they rest in God's creative and redemptive purpose and providence. Social structures somehow reflect the created normativity of human social life. This normativity manifests itself in the flourishing of human communities where it is observed, and in the frustrations and problems that result where that normativity is violated.

The concept of practice as we will use it is based on this understanding of reality. It does not just refer to the factual situation of professional work, but implies that for that particular context a diversity of norms and values applies. This does not mean that in our view this normativity is obvious; it is not. Because human existence is frail, mortal, and susceptible to evil, this normativity is often elusive. It needs to be (re-)discovered and (re-)elaborated by human beings and given shape in their everyday lives. Hence, our understanding of social reality must be based on a painstaking analysis of the situation and the normativity entailed in it, undertaken in the light of all the empirical evidence available. This process of learning how to interpret the validity of ethical norms in a particular situation is a journey of discovery, not one of mere construction. In this journey, we need the light of the Word of God and the guidance of the Holy Spirit.

With this attitude of modesty and dependency, we will now undertake an analysis of the normative structure of professional practice. This sounds quite abstract—and in a sense, it is—but we hope that with examples it will become clear.

A normative analysis of professional practices
In our view, a fruitful start for a normative analysis of professional practices is MacIntyre's definition of a practice. This well-known definition runs:

> By a "practice" I am going to mean any coherent and complex form of socially established cooperative human activity through which goods internal to that form of activity are realized in the course of trying to achieve those standards of excellence which are appropriate to, and partially definitive of, that form of activity, with the result that human powers to achieve excellence, and human conceptions of the ends and goods involved, are systematically extended. (MacIntyre, 1981/1983, p. 187)

In our analysis, we will elaborate this definition with the aid of Reformational philosophical thinking. An important insight of this philosophy is the distinction between structure and direction (Wolters, 1988, pp. 95-122). Analogous to this distinction we distinguish between the constitutive side and regulative side of professional practices.

We begin our analysis of a professional practice with a description of the constitutive side of normative (professional) practices. Our analysis is normative in a double sense. In the first place, it is normative in the sense that it tries to elucidate the normativity embodied in the different practices as they are actually realised. Let us explain. In human communities, ideals, motives, and beliefs always are operative of good and bad, of what is a good life and what is not, of what ought and ought not to be done. By their ways of life, people always respond to the challenges life in this world presents to them. By doing so, they give expression to such ideals, motives and beliefs. These ideals, motives, and beliefs function mostly in the form of unwritten, sometimes even unspoken codes of conduct and customs, convictions about what is decent and indecent. It is this tacit moral knowledge that forms the fabric of human community. This also holds for professional practices. In the way professionals behave, they respond to normativity they encounter in reality, whether this is made explicit or not. Our analysis tries to elucidate this normativity in its structure, not in its content that will be different for different practices and contexts.

In the second place, our analysis is normative in the sense that it is also a representation of the formal normative structure of practices that, in our view, are prescriptive for those practices.

Constitutive side of normative practices
The constitutive side of professional practices will be described by elaborating the main elements of MacIntyre's definition.

Socially established human activity
First of all a practice is a form of *socially established human activity*. This entails that the practice exists before the individual practitioner enters the practice. For instance, the practice of medicine has developed by a long historical process and is the result of many decisions and processes that embody normative choices. This is also true for newer practices such as accounting, business management, and education. The individual practitioner is initiated into the practice by learning a certain way of doing things. The practice shapes the behaviour of individual practitioners before they can begin to reshape the practice.

This characteristic of practices also implies that relationships between people involved in a practice are not just voluntary relationships between two free rational agents on the basis of mutual consent and interests, as liberalism would have us believe. Each practitioner is subject to an historical, conditioned, and coherent form of socially established human activity.

Telos
Secondly, a practice has a certain *finality*, a reason, a core value for which the practice exists. Probably the Aristotelian term *telos* suits best here. MacIntyre speaks of internal goods at this point, but the exact meaning of this term appears to be unclear.[1] The activities making up a practice are directed at the realisation of this finality, this *telos* of that actual practice. It is important to distinguish this finality from goals that individual practitioners may have. Goals set by individual or collective actors in, for

---

1 This is pointed out by David Miller, 'Virtues, practices and justice', in J. Horton, S. Mendus (eds.), *After MacIntyre*, Cambridge 1994: Polity Press (Blackwell), 247-251. He argues that the internal good of medicine according to MacIntyre would be the good of being an excellent doctor. If this means 'being an exemplar of those standards of excellence which have evolved in the medical community', it should be noted that the two may diverge. In a medical community, sometimes the one with the highest technical ability is considered the exemplar of the standards of excellence whereas that person may not be the best healder of the sick. So the concept of the internal good can become too 'internal' and lose its power to characterise the reason for the existence of a practice in society. The concept of *telos* is defined in this way and therefore serves better in describing the normative structure of a social practice.

example, the medical practice, do not necessarily contribute to the realisation of the *telos* of medical practice simply because one is a practitioner. A physician may want to be an entrepreneur and make money, but trying to realize that goal does not necessarily serve the optimal realisation of medicine or of the enterprise. The *telos* of a practice belongs to the very nature of the practice and is not founded in the intention of the practitioner or the client/patient/user.

Standards of excellence
The third essential element of a practice is that human activities in a practice are seen as *rule-guided behaviour* in which the "rules of the play" are understood as the standards of excellence for that practice. These standards or rules constitute the practice, at the same time define excellent practice, and provide criteria to evaluate the activities of individual practitioners. In this context, the concept of "rule" does not so much refer to rules in the sense of "knowing that," which implies the ability to formulate explicitly the applied rules. Rather, it includes knowing rules in the sense of "knowing how," in which the rules are embodied in professional conduct consisting in the ability to act according to a rule and to assess the correctness of this application even without making the rule explicit.[2] One can easily see that performing a practice, for example playing the violin, practicing medicine, or managing a company, cannot be learned just by instruction about the practice even if this instruction involves a demonstration before the novice's eyes. Actually engaging in the rule-governed "forms of activity" of that practice is indispensable. When one carefully observes the rules of the practice by carrying out those forms of activity, the *telos* of the practice is being realized. A practitioner who is able to practice in accordance with the rules and in compliance with the *telos* is a competent practitioner. In other words, competence reflects the ability to act according to the (usually implicit) rules of that particular practice.

Qualifying constitutive rules

An important question that arises from this description of practices is: How do we find the constitutive rules of a practice? To answer this question we draw on Dooyeweerdian philosophy. As a social entity, the

---

2 From this description it will be clear that we use the word rule here in a broader sense than a strict directive for action that has the structure of "If a, then do b." Our use of the word comprises directives for action but also norms at a higher level of abstraction. Roughly stated, we mean context-dependent norms and directives that can be derived from context-independent normative principles, like beneficence.

practice functions in all the modal aspects described in Dooyeweerdian philosophy. This means that all the meaning-kernels of the modal aspects can be understood as normative principles for the performance of the practice. From these principles, the constitutive rules can be derived. By making the principle operative in a specific context, we realise the principle becomes concrete in the form of rules that prescribe a certain behaviour. Of immediate importance for most professional practices are principles entailing the scientific (logical) and technical (formative, historical), the psychic, the lingual, the social, the economic, the juridical, the esthetical and the ethical aspects. However, it is important to point out that the normative principles related to all these aspects do not function in the same way in all practices. One of these will function as the qualifying principle of a certain practice, which in our model can be identified with the *telos* of that practice. For example, we can take the practice of nursing and ask what the qualifying principle of that practice is. We will answer that the principle of care, which we hold to be the normative principle of the ethical aspect,[3] is the *telos* of all caring practices, and therefore qualifies the practice of nursing. This means that the other normative principles should be observed under the guidance of the qualifying principle. Extrinsic motivations such as becoming a famous nurse are subservient to the *telos* or qualifying principle of care. Other examples are the practice of a musician that is aesthetically qualified, the practice of an entrepreneur that is economically qualified (Verkerk & Zijlstra, 2003), and the practice of education that is qualified by the formative aspect (Hegeman, 2006).

Founding and conditioning constitutive rules

Among the other modal aspects, we can distinguish between the founding aspect and the conditioning aspects. The founding and conditioning constitutive rules can be derived from their respective normative principles. The *founding* constitutive rules are those rules that *prescribe* the activities that give a particular practice its characteristic content. As far as we can tell, for all professional practices in society the founding aspect is the historical, formative aspect. It is the aspect of reality that refers to (intentional) human actions by which human beings and communities give shape to their lives and circumstances. We have argued this in more

---

3 Puolimatka defines the core value of the ethical aspect as "a normative attitude which regards the well-being of others as intrinsically valuable". T. Puolimatka, *Moral realism and justification*. Dissertation. Helsinki 1989: Suomalainen Tiedeakatemia, 144. We use the word 'care', which can also be understood as the combination of benevolence and beneficence, to refer to this attitude.

detail for the caring practices, for which the formative aspect can also be understood as the technical aspect in which technical must be understood in a broad sense, hence also comprising social and organisational techniques, etc. For the state of the art of methods and techniques in a practice reflects a moment in their historical development, but at the same time refers in particular to the formative power manifest in the possibilities to intervene technically or methodically.

The other aspects, like the psychic, the social, the economic, and the juridical, are conditioning aspects from which the conditioning constitutive rules are derived. These rules formulate conditions that should be observed in performing a practice, but they neither define the "technicalities" of the practice nor its finality. They are simply conditions that are fulfilled in a competent performance of the practice.[4] An adequate, competent performance of a practice requires the simultaneous realisation of all the constitutive rules thereby resulting in an integral normativity. Compliance with the founding and conditioning rules should be guided by the normative principle of the qualifying aspect of that specific practice. In an assessment of the way in which a certain practitioner performs his practice, those constitutive rules function as norms.

Rules and virtues

Competent performance of a practice requires the observation of the principles and rules of the practice and thus realizes its finality, its *telos*. As we saw, the rules governing behaviour mostly have an implicit, tacit character. This means that rules can be followed even without a conscious decision of the practitioner at each moment that they are applied. Here we can establish a link to the way in which MacIntyre sees the role of virtues in the performance of practices. Practitioners need to have certain virtues in order to perform a practice competently or, to use our terminology, to observe the constitutive principles and rules competently. In our view, virtues can be considered as the embodiments of the normative principles in stable normative attitudes of the practitioner. Hence, we agree with MacIntyre that indeed virtues are essential for a competent performance of practices.

So far, we have gained a clear insight into the architecture of a practice. We can say that the structure of a practice, its constitutive side, corresponds to the Dooyeweerdian view of reality. However, our analysis

---

4 This is elaborated to some extent for the (founding) technical rules and the (conditioning) economic rules in: J. Hoogland, H. Jochemsen, 'Professional autonomy and the normative structure of medical practice', *Theoretical Medicine and Bioethics* 21 (2000), 457-475.

is not yet complete for we have only dealt with the structural side of practices.

Regulative side
To understand a practice fully we have to consider not only the structural side but also its regulative side. What we mean by the regulative side can be described in the following observations.

    a. The constitutive side of a practice as described above embodies the normative constitutive principles and rules that (should) guide the performance of the practice and provide the norms required to assess that performance. However, any performance and assessment involves a specific interpretation of the rules (cf. the interpretation of a piece of music in a particular performance). Such an interpretation departs from a wider interpretative framework concerning the meaning of that practice for human life and for society and, hence, on the direction performances of that practice should have. In addition, one's understanding of the virtues required to perform practices competently depends on a wider view of the telos of human life (MacIntyre, 1981/1983, pp. 185-187).

    b. Therefore, the regulative side of practices pertains to motivations and beliefs about human life in the world, about our past and future and reason for existence, and about the role and meaning of the practice for human life and society. These fundamental attitudes, beliefs and motivations reflect the worldview and, if they are religious, the religious beliefs of the people involved.

    c. Any performance of a practice is regulated by those worldview beliefs and religious beliefs. There is no "neutral" performance of a practice, even though the secular liberal understanding of society tends to claim a neutral point of view that should govern the public discourse. Particularly in our pluralist society, the beliefs and ideas that regulate the performance of practices should be open to debate. Christian professionals will draw on their Christian beliefs and motives when dealing with issues in their professional work.

    d. These beliefs pertaining to the regulative side also form the reference points for a critical assessment of existing ways of performing practices by practitioners and of innovation and improvement of practices. This is a very important point. Without this explicitly critical function of the regulative side—an integral part of a full description of a practice—the concept of normative practices easily takes on a conservative and self-referential character. The fact that a certain community of practitioners accepts certain standards of excellence does not mean that those standards are the best ones possible. In the light of other regulative ideas, they may need revision.

From practice to performance
In summary, we see the regulative side of social practices as essential for a fully normative understanding of the reality of practices and the behaviour of practitioners. Hence, relating the performance of practices to one's religious beliefs is fully justified. This always is done, whether implicitly or explicitly. If Christians do not do so consciously, they run the risk of adopting the predominant regulating views concerning their practice. Clearly, this is an important point when thinking about helping students to relate their faith to their (professional) involvement in social issues.

Before elaborating this, we want to point out a few consequences of our model of professional practices.

1) Based on the presented model, we hold that the professional quality of a professional does not primarily reside in his or her specialized knowledge and (technical) skills but in the competent realisation of the *telos* of the practice. So, it is evidenced in adequate, beneficial caring, in respectful exemplary teaching, in fruitful sustainable agriculture, etc. In the technology-driven Western culture, this is not as self-evident as it should be; technical effectiveness and economic efficiency often dominate the intrinsic value of the *telos* of practices. For example, when caring, educational, or even agricultural institutions are organised and run based on maximizing (financial) profit, the practices comprised in these institutions will become distorted. Personally, we think that the predominance of the perspective of economics and competition—in other words, the idolatry of Mammon—is one of the main issues underlying a number of other problems.

2) Another implication is that the managers of those institutions must have a good grasp of the normativity of the practices that are performed within the organisational and juridical framework of their institution. Their own management practice

should account for that.

3) Our model of practices implies that practices do not exist to fulfil the subjective desires of clients/patients/employees/ users. This, however, does not mean that the opinion and experience of these people should not be taken into account. The integral ethical responsibility not only applies to professionals but certainly also to the users. Respect for and participation of non-professional participants in practices forms a vital element of our model, because the professional ought to observe the psychological, social and juridical rules of the practice as well as demonstrate the corresponding virtues of empathy, openness and respect for freedom of choice (among others). In the final analysis, professional practices exist primarily to render help, care or a service to people who need them. In fact, the virtues of helpfulness and readiness are indispensable for all professional practices.

4) The virtues holding for the professional can be understood as the embodiment of normative principles in the professional. Hence, competent performance requires certain virtues in the professional. It follows that professional education striving for excellence requires the cultivation of virtues as care, respectfulness, justice, integrity, courage, truthfulness, and confidentiality.

5) This model of professional practices also provides a useful starting point for the ethical evaluation of professional performance from different normative ethical perspectives. (Remember we understand ethics in the broad sense of responsible behavior.) The idea that the principles and rules of a practice are to be followed by competent performance provides an opening for deontological reflection. In addition, the notion of the *telos*, the finality of the practice, implies that also the teleological and consequentialist approaches must contribute to the ethical analysis and assessment of moral conduct in practices. By combining the different perspectives in what we call a responsibility ethics, we want to refer to our understanding of the human being as *homo respondens* (Geertsema, 1979) and stress the integrality of the individual's responsibility (Jochemsen & Glas, 1997, pp. 174-218).[5]

---

5 See also H. Jochemsen. (2003). Christian medical ethics and current ethical trends, in L.C. Steyn (red.), *Health care: What hope?* Voorthuizen: HCF-Nederland, pp. 49-71.

Moral formation

This notion of integral responsibility brings us to the second main question of this paper: How can we equip students to become involved as Christian professionals in a faithful way?

We now see that this question can be reformulated as: How can we realise the moral formation of professionals. Because, taking into account what we have seen so far, moral formation entails the following:
- understanding the intrinsic normativity of the practice in which one is involved,
- knowing how to relate one's faith to and make it fruitful for competent professional practice, and
- knowing how to develop the virtues required for competent performance of professional practice that expresses kingdom citizenship.

Students who acquire these competences have learned how to relate their kingdom citizenship to the challenges we face as Christians in our societies.

We will now consider three sources for moral formation and relate them to the three competences just mentioned (though not in the sense that each source would be related to one of the competences).

Three sources for moral formation

We find a helpful starting point in a dissertation by Van Ek on the wisdom literature in the Bible, especially the books of Job, Proverbs, and Ecclesiastes.[6] Van Ek distinguishes three main elements in this growth in practical wisdom and responsibility: tradition, experience, and revelation. We will explain these sources below as underpinning any moral formation. We will also relate this to our ethics of responsibility. (See point 5 above.)

Tradition

In the wisdom training of the young Israelite, tradition certainly played an important role. (See Job 15:17-19.) The transferral of the wisdom of former generations upon the newer generation even today constitutes education. Formation here certainly includes the transfer of knowledge as such. As we know, professions entail a body of knowledge that should be transmitted to the new generations of upcoming professionals. In spite

---

6 G. van Ek. (1997). Mens en maatschappij tussen chaos en kosmos. Een onderzoek naar de fundamenten voor sociale kritiek in de wijsheidsliteratuur in het oude Nabije Oosten en met name in oud Israel. Proefschrift Utrecht. pp. 118-124.

of the emphasis of the so-called new learning (competence learning) on personal and experiential knowledge, in our view we cannot do without a body of positive knowledge that the student should gain, given its truth-value.

In the context of moral formation, we may differentiate two traditions. First, we recognize the tradition of Christianity and a Christian worldview. (This pertains to the regulative side of our model of professional practices.) Over the ages, we find a codification of much deliberation on ethics concerning education and formation and the importance of Christian principles guiding these processes. In moral formation, this entails a good knowledge and insight into this Christian tradition and worldview.

A second tradition is the tradition of the profession at stake. Professions have a tradition, which demonstrates how people in the course of history have interpreted the normativity intrinsic in their practice (we refer here to the constitutive side of practices). For instance, medicine and nursing have long traditions of expressing Christian values and virtues that may help us to understand the *telos* of those practices. In addition, education, politics, and agriculture, to mention just a few others, have a respectable and insightful tradition.

Normative insights in these traditions sometimes have crystallised in professional codes of conduct or ethical codes or the like. This means that the ethical perspective central in this contribution to moral formation is duty ethics (deontology). In this perspective, the morally good is the (professional) duty, as defined by the codes, guidelines, and principles that should guide professional action. For moral formation, this implies that those codes and principles should be taught and that their practical relevance should be explained.

We have differentiated so far two traditions, which may or may not be congruent in their ethics. Obviously, the two traditions should be mined for moral formation but may well contradict one another. This means that the codes, rules, and principles prevalent in the predominant practices in a country or geographical area should be evaluated in the light of the Christian tradition and that (potential) conflicts should be pointed out, argued and discussed. These conflicts, however, must not lead to moral and spiritual dissonance within the professional, so that a lack of veracity becomes part of one's professional profile.

Experience
The second source of moral formation is that of experience. In the epis-

temological process that follows experience, Van Ek differentiates four phases, as reflected in Proverbs 24:30-34; "I looked upon it, I set my heart upon it, I considered it well, I received instruction."[7]

The admonition begins with the use of the senses: observing fully. In newer educational models, we see this strongly emphasized as experiential learning. In the context of moral formation, it also involves the observation of best examples and practices, understanding why good role models are good. The third and the fourth step of the admonition, "I considered it well, I received instruction," involve an understanding of what is being done and experienced and a resulting willingness to accept the proper practical moral action directives for behaviour. From a Biblical perspective, we can speak of the right intention of the heart. This of course concerns the student's spirituality, about which we will say more later. Putting this Biblical standard into the language of today's educational insights, we can say that learning, not in the least modern competence learning, is a process of which the learner her- or himself is the subject within a certain context. Epistemologically, learning must be done by the learner, even though it is not done by the learner alone; it is always contextual, within a certain social practice. Very much so, learning how to behave in a morally and spiritually responsible way entails competences that can only be learned in practice (See I Timothy 4:7b.), by having clear aims and honest assessments of failures.

Competences are capacities that enable the competent person to solve certain problems and realise the values pursued in a specific context. Hence, the ethical perspective related to this source of moral formation is foremost the goal ethics (teleology and consequentialism), as used in educational training, in particular internships.

Revelation

The third source we draw on as people growing in wisdom is, according to Van Ek, special revelation. This may be understood as an extraordinary revealing of truth, a special message from God. This may take place through the revelation of God's Word, but also by an inspiration or vision. In addition, we may come to recognize that certain happenings, such as illnesses, may contain a special message from God. (See Job 33: 14-22.)

Transferring this to our situation, we believe that through special revelation we encounter God speaking and his will through his Word and Spirit. We must acknowledge that in our own practice of moral for-

---

[7] See also the analogy of the ant in Proverbs 6: 6-11.

mation, our use of traditions and our own experiences are insufficient without revelation. We hold that a full-fledged practice of Christian care cannot be practiced and thereby taught without its practitioners having a personal relationship with God's Word and without the help and guidance of his Spirit in their lives. This needs some explaining and we will focus on the personal profile involved.

We should acknowledge that when we seek a professional identity which is influenced by our faith in Jesus Christ, our being "in Christ" must influence our assessment of ourselves. With this profile, placing an overriding emphasis on professional-technical competencies no longer needs to be the sole criterion of professionalism. When we trust that Christ helps us to form our profile, we can be set free from unholy struggles for power and status or a sublimation of our own fears, knowing that our professional skills may bear witness to such longings. Then our professional techniques may be exorcised of possibly false pretences of "salvation" and become serviceable for care that is focused on the advancement of the "good life," as far as that is possible in this broken and vastly derailed world.

It will be obvious that we have crossed the conceptual limits between morality and spirituality. Our definition of spirituality in a generic sense is the functioning of religion and/or worldview in a person's life. This definition allows us to study spirituality as a dimension of human functioning even apart from any specific religion or worldview or ideology. This is not mere dualism, but more a recognition and respect for the existence of spirituality in all people. From a Christian perspective, we talk about the Christian religion and a related worldview and strive towards unity and not duality between faith, morality, and practice. On the other hand, we recognize that spiritualities and dualities differ and that a certain religious functionality can be found holding for us all. In this sense, spirituality in professional practice is not a "plus" or the hobby of spiritual gurus. As we have seen, any realisation of a professional practice will take place under the guidance of regulative beliefs that pertain to the spirituality of the professional.

Drawing from the three sources mentioned above, we hold that students in their moral formation should integrate their morality and spirituality in order to excel in the performance of their practice. How do these three sources flow together in the performance of the professional? We will deal with this question in the last part of this paper by discussing one aspect of the didactics.

Deep reflection as a central activity

In this section, we cannot cover all aspects of the process of moral formation. For the sake of time (and space), we will focus on one crucial element concerning how learners in professional training can achieve unity in their morality, spirituality and professional practice. As we know, supervision and reflection exercises during professional training are aimed at helping students gain a proper sense of their moral identity to help them become better professionals.

Next to many other valuable didactics, we think organised and structured reflection is a central educational tool to further the integration of (moral and spiritual) knowledge with experience and one's own spirituality in one's professional (or broader: occupational) practice. Based on some research, it is our impression that much formal reflective activity does not involve spirituality and morality. Reflection in educational practice is often limited to professionals who embody professional "know-how," but in daily practice, this knowledge is often used without reflection. (For example, the way we use language: we do not think of the rules of grammar, even if we know them.) As a consequence, a great deal of professional activity encounters the danger of adapting uncritically to customs which may very well be disclosed in supervision and reflection, thereby making apprentices more aware of a need to adjust customs or change them. Reflection often is limited to learning ways of doing things which may be suitable for maintaining oneself within a hostile environment but which are not good, or at least not optimal, for one's being a Christian. This is much like avoiding spelling errors without learning the grammar involved. Certainly, we acknowledge that reflecting on a "best practice" is potentially quite beneficial for good professional practice, but this does not mean that merely learning how to adjust oneself to the practice, as such, ought to be our highest standard. We may have to work towards change.

Reflection exercises are meant to help professionals become aware of what they have been doing, share that with colleagues, receive feedback, and reflect on it together. The purpose is to evaluate particular actions in the light of what should be considered best practice (encompassing "evidence-based" practice). It will be clear that such reflection and evaluation will always, consciously or unconsciously, take place in the light of professional knowledge, experience and the basic convictions (the spirituality) of the participants on what constitutes a best practice. As such, that is good.

At the same time, we have discovered in our Christian professional training that reflection sessions often concentrate on the social and psychological aspects of the cases that are being discussed. There is ample discussion about the relations between those involved, the feelings that play a role, and the attitudes that have been or should have been demonstrated. Empirical research carried out among nursing and social work students at our schools and at one other secular nursing school in the Netherlands demonstrates that in these supervised discussions the deeper (spiritual) aspects of the moral questions and quandaries are often not addressed. This means we are failing to teach Christian students to become professionally aware of the proper way to integrate their morality and spirituality with their professional conduct.

That is why we propose a form of reflection that digs deeper than the ordinary reflective practice, a form that we call "deep reflection." In this type of reflection, two layers or loops can be distinguished. The first loop is the common reflection as presented above.

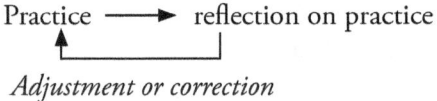

Adjustment or correction

Figure 1: Common supervision/ reflection in professional education

In this reflection model, the basic values and beliefs that function as standards are presupposed and accepted silently or adapted to as normative. Single loop reflection evaluates practice in the light of those shared, commonly accepted beliefs. This reflection does not require the supervisors/participants to draw upon their personal motivations and beliefs. However, if one wants to go deeper and explore the integration of those beliefs with one's professional practice, then those personal spiritual beliefs need to be expressed and discussed with respect to their implications for one's practice. This does not mean that one has to be prepared to give up one's beliefs. However, one should be able to explain them and to relate them to one's practice. This second type of reflection practice involves a second layer, or loop, and is shown in figure 2:

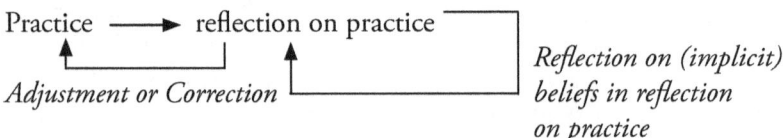

Figure 2: The two loops of deep reflection

The type of reflection in figure 2 is called *deep reflection*. A principled reflection assumes the first type of reflection, as it takes place in interactions between instructors and students or between professionals. Deep reflection calls for reflection on the normative beliefs and stances that often are taken for granted during the first loop of reflection. Deep reflection is a type of meta-reflection on one's own reflection, because the exercise of it calls for competency in delving into the sources that one needs for moral formation. In Christian education and reflection, these are at least the three sources mentioned above.

In conclusion
In higher education, young people are educated and trained to equip themselves for functions and tasks in society. This also applies to Christian higher education. A central question in Christian higher education is how we can educate and equip our students in such a way that they are able to connect their kingdom citizenship to the issues they will face as Christian professionals or graduates. This requires in the first place a proper understanding of the issues and the specific contribution different professions can make to deal with it. This, we have argued, requires insight into the normative structure of the practice in which one is involved. An important element of this normative structure is the understanding that practices are always developed under the guidance of regulative beliefs and ideals with respect to human beings and the world. To be faithful to their faith, or rather to Christ, Christians cannot escape the attempt to relate their faith to their profession. If they do not do this explicitly and conscientiously, their professional performance will be guided by other regulative beliefs.

In trying to relate the Christian faith to professional work, the professional can draw upon three sources: upon traditions, upon experience, and upon revelation. These three sources allow learners to aim for integrity in their profile of themselves as professionals. We have pointed out that an important educational tool for making these sources fruitful for competent Christian practicing is a special form of reflection called deep reflection. Deep reflection is not limited to what customarily is considered proper behaviour and actions but very much deals with the explicit or implicit motives and reasons—in short, on the spirituality—of the students. It certainly requires a supervisor who knows how to address the spiritual and moral aspects of life and of professional practice. That means professional trainers ought to be able to address the problem of a lack of unity between morality and spirituality in the professional lives of students. This, in turn, requires a philosophy of education in professional training that makes the heart and soul of the learner its highest priority.

References

Geertsema, H. G. (1979). *Geloof voor het leven.* Amsterdam: Buijten en Schipperheijn.
Hegeman, J. H. (2006). Stewardship and integral learning. In B. de Muynck & H. van der Walt (Eds.), *The call to know the world*, (p. 58). Amsterdam: Buijten & Schipperheijn.
Jochemsen, H., & Glas, G. (1997). *Verantwoord medisch handelen.* Amsterdam: Buijten en Schipperheijn.
MacIntyre, A. (1981/1983). *After virtue. A study in moral theory.* London: Duckworth.
Verkerk, M. J., & Zijlstra, A. (2003). Philosophical analysis of industrial organisations. *Philosophia Reformata,* 68, 101-122.
Wolters, A. M. (1988). *Schepping zonder grens.* Amsterdam: Buijten & Schipperheijn.

RESPONSE TO HENK JOCHEMSEN & JOHAN HEGEMAN

Sergio Saavedra Belmonte

Translated from Spanish by Alicia Hines

Introduction
I am honored by the invitation to comment on Dr. Henk Jochemsen's essay. This is the first time that I have participated in an event like this and as the date drew near, with Jochemsen's work in my hands, I had a growing fear that this might be the last time.

I am not exaggerating when I say that, as a teacher, I feel academically limited for the task that has been entrusted to me. Jochemsen's work has been developed in a field that is not my specialty, the normative ethic, and little has been circulated in my language on the topic of the philosophical perspectives of the scholars Hermann Dooyeweerd and Alisdair MacIntyre.

I ask you to keep this in mind if you feel my comments are like the clumsiness of a bull in a china shop. I say this because, as a good Latino, I am worried that the commentary that I am going to make, which expresses more criticism than appreciation, might ruin Jochemsen's friendship even before I meet him.

Work evaluation
The work is divided into three bodies of argumentation: a) the presentation of a theoretical (and abstract) model of *practice*, based on the field of normative ethics, and influenced by MacIntyre's neo-Aristotelian ideas, b) arguments on the moral formation of the students, according to Van Ek, and c) a didactic methodological application of the proposal, something that Jochemsen calls "profound reflection as central activity" in the classroom. I see positive and questionable aspects of Jochemsen's arguments.

The positive aspects: the construction of a "practice architecture" or "social practices model" based on what he designates "a normative analysis of professional practices" from a philosophical Dooyeweerdian focus and the ethic of MacIntyre's virtue.

The questionable aspects: From my point of view, he does not really answer the principal question that motivates the essay. It seems to me that he makes a large ethical and metaphysical detour, one which takes us to a conceptual edifice—somewhat sophisticated—about the professional practice, but which distances us from the path that would make us confront the critical problems that face our societies along with our students.

Foundation for my evaluative judgment

The question that this essay attempts to answer is: How can Christian education help students to want and to be able to get involved—as Christians—in issues that face our societies? The author points out that in order to answer this question, one has to answer two other questions first; in my opinion, this is where he begins to detour from the main issue.

The first question: To understand the practices

The first of Jochemsen's two questions is: How can we help students understand the issues properly from a Christian perspective? He is right when he says that students "must get properly involved, on the basis of a sensible analysis and understanding of the situation."

Nevertheless, the instrument of analysis that he uses does not seem exactly Christian to me. When he starts his analysis of the "critical issues" in our societies, they are reduced to the neutral concept of "social practices" understood based on MacIntyre's normative ethic. This first reduction presents the problem of ignoring the profound evil and sinfulness that is offensive to God and gives rise to these critical issues or social problems that MacIntyre practically ignores.

Although MacIntyre has contributed an academic base to the Christian ethical perspective, by reinstating the centrality of the *telos* or intrinsic finality of the practices, he remains quiet on the basic problem of sin; but without considering sin, we can hardly sustain a distinctly Christian ethical argument. The Bible, on the other hand, from the very beginning, reveals the appearance of the evil in human beings—which includes Satan and his lies—and with this, all of the moral bankruptcy of that which is and will be hopelessly ruined: *his animosity against God.*

From Jochemsen's analytical perspective, the problem arises from the violation of the underlying rules of the mentioned practices, because of an incorrect understanding of the presumably "good" intrinsic end that these practices would have.

As he points out, the social structures reflect the orderliness created by God. If this orderliness is violated, there are frustrations and problems. Therefore, the proposed solution is that each person should recognize the normative structure of the practice, regarding both its constitution (the structure of the practice) and its regulation (the direction of the practice).

But the apostle Paul warns that the problem of sin lies precisely in *knowing how to do the good, but not being able to do it* (paraphrased synthesis of Romans 7:7-25). An interior force of rebellion, beyond reason and will, drives a person, like a prisoner violating every kind of orderliness.

On the other hand, the "Christian perspective" from which the issues need to be understood is actually the Dooyeweerdian philosophical concept of reality.

Jochemsen is very clear when he explains his understanding of reality. "The reality is structured normatively and social entities have a *telos*, a built-in purpose, because they rest in God's creative and redemptive purpose and providence." I do not agree that this concept is necessarily Biblical, but rather exclusively philosophical-Christian. I would like this concept of reality—to which the students would also have to convert—to help me comprehend a social entity as old as the military. Was it a human creation or God's creation? Would the American military or the Iraqi military have behaved more according to the *telos* of God? How do we analyze, from this perspective, what happened in the Vietnam War, in which the American military was defeated by an unconventional military with tactics of war very different from those of the West?

I am not trying to minimize the importance of Dooyeweerd's thoughts, but simply to point out that he takes us on a philosophical detour, which draws us away from the central problem that we now have. Dooyeweerd's Cosmonomic Philosophy is a closed system that redefines the concepts and gives them new meanings that can only be understood if one agrees with the premises of this thinker. In fact, this approach does more than help students; it seems like it would make the understanding of the issues that the students must face more complicated instead of helping them. It demands that they make a double conversion: to Christ in the first place, and to the mentioned thinkers in the second place.

The second question: Moral formation

The second question in which Jochemsen strays from the central question is: "How can we equip them so that they can get involved as Christian professionals in a faithful way?" At the same time, in the second half of his essay, he reformulates this second question to sound like this: "How do we understand moral formation?"

The answer will demand, according to Jochemsen, the achievement on the part of university students of three educational competences:

a) To comprehend the intrinsic normativeness of social practices;
b) To know how to relate personal faith to make it fruitful for competent professional practice;
c) To know how to develop the virtues required for competent performance of professional practice that express kingdom citizenship.

As I said before, this continued reinterpretation of the original question has kept us from a direct, Biblical, Christ-centered orientation for finding the answer. In the end, we are on philosophical ground with indirect answers that may appeal too much to reason as a guide and solution.

In reference to the first of these required "educational competences," according to Jochemsen, to accomplish an adequate moral formation, I have shown superficially that the attempt to understand the intrinsic orderliness of the social practices may be accessible for someone who can master Dooyeweerd's and MacIntyre's theoretical framework, but not for a common 18-20 year old student, whose commitment to Christ does not necessarily bring him to understand reality like these philosophers.

Even if we were among intellectuals who were familiar with these theoretical perspectives, I have the impression that we would debate a great deal before reaching an agreement about the concrete definition of the *telos* or the intrinsic normativeness of a single social practice.

Jochemsen is correct about the second necessary educational competence for moral formation. He comments:

> We must recognize that in our own practice of moral formation, and our use of traditions and our own experience are insufficient without revelation. [Then:] . . . our being "in Christ" must influence our assessment of ourselves . . . set free from unholy struggles for power and status or a sublimation of our own fears . . . then, our professional techniques may be exorcized of possibly false pretences of "salvation" and become serviceable for care that focuses on the advancement of the "good life," as far as that is possible in this broken and vastly derailed world.

Truthfully, our Christian universities must make an effort to provide a professional "identity" based on the fundamental identity of being a "child" of God. In Luke 2:41-52 we see how this identity, when it is well established, carries the child to confront the established erroneous practices. In this concrete example, it was Joseph's responsibility to present Jesus, who was 12 years old, before the religious authorities to be legally accepted in the Jewish community. However, according to the Bible story, this does not seem to be Jesus' parents' intention in this particular trip to Jerusalem. Therefore, although it seems Jesus was challenging the authority of his human parents; in reality, he was correcting the practice that they did not carry out. This correction of his parents' practice evidently seems motivated by the unquestionable certainty that Jesus had as God's Son.

The third required competence, according to Jochemsen, in order to consolidate a moral formation, leads us to ask: "What are the necessary virtues of the citizen of the Kingdom?" From the first lines of the essay, beginning with the initial question, this is the theme that should have received primary consideration, but up to this point, we have seen that Jochemsen is not going to say much about this. Like they commonly say, "We were left with the headlines," since there is no mention of the concrete virtues that allow a professional to face the difficult problems with which we struggle, except for some reference to the ones that are known traditionally as liberal virtues: honesty, responsibility, etc.

For example, would Jochemsen include among these so-called virtues the ability to lead non-conformist social movements? Would it be considered a virtuous action for a kingdom citizen to provoke and confront an illegally established authority?

I would have liked Jochemsen's paper to go farther, to touch the sore spot a little more. I must confess that my style is different from the author's and maybe that is why I ended up with unsatisfied expectations after analyzing his answer to the initial question.

I do not want to minimize the value of Dr. Jochemsen's work. I am sure that inside the Dooyeweerdian community this essay would have provoked a much richer and more detailed analysis of the thesis that he proposes. Unfortunately, as I said before, I do not belong to this tradition and all I have is second-hand knowledge of this philosopher. This limitation of my own formation has made me ask the obvious: Is the question answered?

Attempt to contribute to the answer

It would be irresponsible on my part if I did not offer my own perspective on the question after critiquing the document. Personally I prefer to seek direct answers from the Bible that I can then clarify with scholars' contributions (Christian or not). In this way, I would like us to consider some orientations that are given to us in Luke 3:1-20. The question that we are trying to answer is: "How can Christian education help students to want to and to be able to get involved, as Christians, in the issues that our societies face?" In direct reference to the question, this passage shows us the cases of two different types of professions whose current practices were seriously in question under the Jewish community's ethic of the time: tax collectors and soldiers, probably Herodians.

Let us imagine for a moment that the tax collectors in the story were not full-fledged professionals but rather students learning that profession. Imagine that in the middle of their career, they have a vocational crisis because of having heard the controversial "Dr." John the Baptist, who was famous for confronting current hot topics, touching the "sore spot" from his public platform near the Jordan River.

These students studying "tax collecting" probably chose this questionable profession because of its hefty salary. They chose it even though it would practically turn them into traitors of their country since they would be working for the Romans or for King Herod and would economically exploit an already poor and oppressed nation. The ethically controversial situation could be defined in this way: Is it fair to collect taxes from a poor nation in order to enlarge the glory of a pagan and idolatrous empire?

These students, unlike their classmates, who did not ask the uncomfortable ethical questions, were disturbed by "Dr." John the Baptist's exhortations about leaving their unfruitful religiosity and living according to the justice of the kingdom of God. What should they do? How do they face this political-economical injustice from this profession as citizens of kingdom of God?

This seems to me to be the main concern of our theme. We can find some keys to the answer in the Bible itself:

a) It is evident, as in the case of the tax collectors, which professional practices are the result of specific historical, cultural, and socio-political contexts—there are no universally-valid professional practices.

b) It is evident that the normativeness of these practices, and with them, their purpose (*telos*), is defined by the people who have political and economic power. In our example, the Romans demanded that they collect a certain amount, but they looked the other way and militarily protected all the abuses that the tax collectors committed to benefit themselves. It results in a very forced proposition that the transcendent normativeness of this professional practice had been designed and proposed by God.

c) Regarding the system for collecting taxes for the benefit of the kings, an extremely old custom; it is evident that God had explicitly warned his people that it was a burden they could have avoided if they had been faithful to him (1 Samuel 8:14-18). At least, one cannot argue, with a Biblical basis, that it has been a professional practice normed by the Word of God.

d) God, knowing that this is a heavy burden, continues to provoke the popular uprising and in this way keeps his promise of justice against King Rehoboam (1 Kings 12:1-24). Therefore, one cannot say that God is breaking his established normativeness. There is simply no such thing. The human being defines the technical and deontological methods of a professional practice and God respects them (and uses them).

e) Nevertheless, turning back to Luke, God's advice through the mouth of the prophet is not that this person should abandon tax collecting because it is inherently bad. Nor does it seek an understanding of its internal normativeness or of its deontology. As can be seen in many places in the Biblical story, God contextualizes himself, he descends to the exact place where human sin has fallen, and he redeems it. In this case, he resends the students to keep studying tax collecting and to transform the professional practice in the process.

f) Of what does the transformation consist? Doing it in a way that reflects that their conversion from the cult of Mammon to the living, sustaining God.

g) Therefore, to synthesize the answer to our question, it seems like the best way to prepare our academic institutions' students for confronting and getting involved in the most critical issues that afflict our societies, in their chosen professions, is to urge them to switch from worshipping Mammon to worshipping the almighty God. We must not forget that the love of money is the root of all evil (1 Timothy 6:10).

h) This answer has profound implications for the content of our academic studies and the orientation of our universities' research and outreach functions. "John the Baptist's Desert University" will produce professionals prepared to face and denounce the unjust and structurally-globalized mechanisms of wealth accumulation and a generation of poverty, along with all the evil that this creates. They will also learn how to create production chains and alternative subsistence that favors those who are traditionally excluded from the benefits of the great academic and scientific explosion of the 19th and 20th centuries.

Conclusion

In summary, my argument is that Jochemsen does not respond fully to the question and what he offers us as an answer is a theoretic construction, interesting to a certain intellectual community, but sophisticated and impracticable for the typical student.

We might get closer to the answer if we directly indicate the "origin of all evil" and target the sore spot head on: the conversion of our students and scholars, along with our curriculum, research, and extension projects, from Mammon to the living, all-sufficient God.

Dr. Jochemsen does not ignore this conversion. At one point, he says, "Personally I think that the predominance of the economic perspective and of competition, in other words, the idolatry to Mammon, is one of the principal issues that underlie a great number of problems." It seems that he does not articulate this conviction consistently in his work and he replaces it with a theoretical approach that weakens the impact of his proposal.

The conversion from Mammon to God in our institutions is not only carried out on an ethical level. It would also bring strung socioeconomic, political, and cultural consequences by, freeing the tremendous power of knowledge concentrated in Christian academic institutions in order to "make the blind see" (knowledge made available to those that have been traditionally excluded) (John 9:39).

However, the assignment that comes from this conversion does not end there. It also implies "to make those that see blind," i.e. to seek to make the human and spiritual mechanisms of evil and injustice evident. (John 9:39) This, without a doubt, will involve carrying a cross since it presumes to confront the established powers, human and spiritual, that define professional practice in terms convenient to their own interests and who would not be willing to contract any of our graduates that had this transforming seed as part of their professional identity.

However, in the light of the project of God's kingdom and justice of which we are part, do we have another choice?

References

Berger, P. (1999). *El dosel sagrado. Elementos para una teoría sociológica de la religión* (3rd ed.). Barcelona: Editorial Kairos.
Berger, P., & Luckmann, T. (1968). *La construcción social de la realidad. Un tratado sobre la sociología del conocimiento.* Buenos Aires: Amorrortu editores.
Bosch, D. J. (2000). *Misión en transformación. Cambios de paradigma en la teología de la misión.* Grand Rapids, MI: Libros Desafío.
Gonzales, J. L. (2001). *Mapas para la historia futura de la iglesia.* Buenos Aires: Kairos ediciones.
Mangalwadi, V. (1996). *Truth and social reform* (3rd ed.). New Delhi: Nivedit Good Books Distributors.
Naugle, D. K. (2002). *Worldview: The history of a concept.* Grand Rapids, MI: Eerdmans.
New Bible of Jerusalem. Revised and augmented. Bilbao: Descle De Brouwer.
Nishioka, Y. B. (1997). *Rice and bread: Metaphorical construction of reality: towards a new approach to world view.* Dissertation presented to the Faculty of the School of World Mission and Institute of Church Growth. Fuller Theological Seminary. May, 1997.
Oakes, E. T. (1996, August-September). The achievement of Alasdair MacIntyre. *First Things,* 65, 22-26.
Padilla, C. R. (1988). *Ciencias sociales y compromiso cristiano.* BT2 31:247-251.
Padilla, C. R. (2002). *Economía humana y economía del Reino de Dios.* Buenos Aires: Kairos Ediciones.
Padilla, C. R. (1984). Hacia una hermenautica contextual. *Encuentro y Diálogo,* 1, 1-23.
Padilla, C. R. (1986). *Mision Integral. Ensayos sobre el Reino y la iglesia.* Buenos Aires: Nueva Creacion y Eerdemans Publishing.

THE PARENTAL ROLE IN ESTABLISHING CHRISTIAN VALUES AS THE STARTING POINT OF KINGDOM CITIZENSHIP IN AN AFRICAN (SOUTH AFRICAN) CONTEXT

Tom Larney & George A. Lotter

Introduction
The way in which moral and ethical values are transmitted within a family and family relationships can be viewed from different sides. Within a Christian community, the light of Scripture will evidently shine upon the education and faith development of children. The transmission of values has a vertical and horizontal dimension, and therefore Christian parents, to whom the vertical dimension is important, will take seriously the foundational responsibility to confirm faith in the lives of their children.

From a Christian perspective, it is clear that parents cannot create faith in their children, but that the parents' life and witness can strengthen their children's faith. These parents will realize that transmission of values is because human beings are created in the image of God and portray what God is like: hence, the focus on an ethical and moral lifestyle with the full knowledge that people's lives should be in accordance with the intention and will of the Creator. When, however, the transmission of moral and ethical values is done from a humanistic consideration, the horizontal dimension will be accentuated.

Method
This paper focuses on the views of some philosophical schools regarding the transmission of values as well as the anthropological stance from different traditions. The context within which the transmission of moral,

ethical, and religious values from parents to children takes place will be discussed and a specific focus on an African situation will be given, ending with recommendations regarding how parents could establish Christian values with their children as the starting point of kingdom citizenship. In the first part of the paper, values and the transmission thereof will be discussed in a general sense as explained by philosophical schools and social and psychological theories. The latter part will concentrate on religion-focused values.

Parents' roles in the moral and ethical development of the child
There is a relationship between the role of the family, the values connected to religion, and the importance of the transmission thereof as described in the literature.[1] These sources discuss at great length the specific ways in which moral values are formed in childhood.

Moral and ethical values will be understood as guidelines for responsible and acceptable decisions regarding yourself, your place in society and the world, and behaviour that can be taken with integrity towards yourself and other people. Religious values imply that behaviour will be directed by the knowledge that your life is subservient to a higher power. For believers this means the application of Scriptural guidelines and the acknowledgement of the transcendental. These values will definitely contribute to the religious development of a child and a religiously orientated behaviour.

The role of parents, be it in cooperation with other groups or under the influence of other factors, is unmistakably important in the transmission of values in a general but also in a specifically religious sense. Certain philosophical points of departure, which developed along with psychological approaches regarding this issue, lead to intense reflection on the transmission of values to children.

Grusec (1997, pp. 3-4) indicates that different philosophical traditions sparked lively reflection and discussion regarding the moral development of people and especially the ways in which these values were transmitted from one generation to the other. Especially philosophical reflection within the Western tradition created the intellectual space, which influenced modern theories regarding the transmission of values. Grusec distinguishes three perspectives regarding the transmission of moral values.

For a long time, the view that human beings were inherently cor-

---

1 See for instance the views of Walker, Hennig and Krettenauer (2000); White (2000); White and Matawie (2004); Knafo and Schwartz (2003).

rupted dominated Judean-Christian theology. Grusec (1997, p. 3) shows how the roots of this view can be traced to diverse individuals like Hobbes, the Puritans and John Wesley. Grusec also indicates that less extreme forms of this view can be traced back to modern psychoanalysis, which believes that a young child is dominated by the id that has instinctive desires, which call for instant gratification (Grusec, 1997, p. 4).

Completely opposite to the position of inherent corruption, stands the view that young children are inherently good and virtuous (Grusec, 1997, p. 4). This view originated with Jean-Jacques Rousseau, who believed that society should be held responsible for the moral degeneration of the individual. In the 20th century, Jean Piaget and his followers further developed this view. The claim that children are inherently good and virtuous leads to the approach that children should be better understood and less disciplined. Children should therefore be allowed to negotiate with their parents as they grow up (Grusec, 1997, p. 4).

The third position on the moral status of children is somewhere in between the previous two viewpoints: they are neither evil, nor good. Children are seen as a tabula rasa (clean slate) on which moral values can and should be written (Grusec, 1997, p. 4). This in particular represents the view of the 17th century English philosopher, John Locke. Even today, the perspective that a child is a tabula rasa is found among the behaviourist approach, which sees the child as the product of a diverse array of learning experiences.

Parents have some kind of a role to play in all the different models discussed previously. However, Walker (1999, p. 261) shows that parents have often been sidetracked. He ascribes this development to the dominant role of psychology and more especially the development during the past century of a specific scientific approach, that of the structuralism. Apart from this, two other approaches that afforded parents a larger role in value formation and transmission also call for attention.

The structuralist approach mostly dominated research and development in the field of value formation and transmission. Windmiller (1980, p. 2) explains that this approach had its origin in the Kantian view that the individual is a self-organizing entity who develops on the basis of his or her own actions while structuring his or her own experiences. Jean Piaget, one of the most important exponents of the structuralist view, researched the moral development of young children and adolescents and distinguished between different developmental phases with this age group. This research was done in the thirties. Kohlberg continued the work of Piaget regarding the stadia of moral development (Windmiller,

1980, p. 2). Structuralists contend that the cognitive development of a child determines the moral development, while cultural influences and decisions about right and wrong are denied (Windmiller, 1980, p. 3). This is probably why structuralists devalue the importance of parents in the moral development of children. Walker (1999, p. 261) argues on the other hand that peer groups are very important because the interaction between equals will lead to spontaneous growth in moral insight.

The view that people "learn" within the social context and are trained by society, may be seen as the direct result of the opinion that a human being is a tabula rasa (discussed before). This approach had its origin in the empiricism of John Locke and the behaviourism of John Watson (Windmiller, 1980, p. 4) who assert that learning is being brought about by inter alia the family, the social class one lives in as well as inherited cultural traditions where individuals gain experience of life. In the USA and in South Africa, school programs were thus developed that were supposed to create moral values and positive citizenship. The school not only had to do formal training but also had to teach the children social responsibility (Windmiller, 1980, p. 4). The danger is that society at large may prove better equipped to do this. According to the sociologist Emile Durkheim, the family was too limited a societal structure to do this job efficiently (cf. Bouas, 1993, p. 181; Turner, 2005, p. 701) and he suggested that parents relinquish this task to the school.

The proponents of this viewpoint (that human beings learn socially) also see rules as socially and culturally determined and something that should be transmitted (or even forced) onto the individual, while on the other hand the structuralists will see rules as self-generated by the individual and something universal.

Sigmund Freud is generally seen as the founder of psychoanalysis and the first researcher who made a formal analysis of discipline and the internalizing of values (Grusec, 1997, p. 6). According to the psychoanalytical approach, the parents' enforcing of values onto children inevitably leads to feelings of resentment and hostility, but children will suppress the negative feelings out of fear of punishment. This will of necessity result in people having irrational impulses, which are determined by social rules or taboos (Windmiller, 1980, p. 5).

Still, according to Windmiller, (1980, p. 6) this view is an important development in the research on values for two reasons. First, psychoanalysis is the only theory concerning moral development where influences, which form the personality of the child, also have a mechanism that limits the human being morally and maintains his or her personality.

Second, psychoanalysis overlaps with the Biblical principle of original sin.

It was indicated earlier that the different approaches discussed had varying foci on the role of parents. It is crucial to give special attention to it especially where the roles of parents are important in the research regarding faith and faith development within children.

In the earlier discussion, it was clear that the structuralist view accorded the least important role in the development of moral values in children to parents, whereas the influence of peer groups is rated high. Piaget for instance held the position that the child plays an important role in moral formation and stressed that a child going about it in an interactive way creates his or her own intellectual and spiritual structures (Windmiller, 1980, p. 14). However, Piaget did not completely downplay the influence of parents but indicated that they have some influence until the peer group takes over. Kohlberg, following Piaget, attributed less influence to the parents and did not deem the parents as crucial in the moral forming of children (Windmiller, 1980, p. 18). Walker (1999, p. 261) is of the opinion that this is due to Kohlberg's high regard for the kibbutz system.

According to this viewpoint, humans learn and are formed within the community where they are placed. Of the three positions mentioned before, this one accords parents the most "normal" position in the child's development of moral values. The presupposition here is that children from a young age onward learn from parents by way of modeling and copying. Values became part of a child and are internalized in a positive or negative way (Windmiller, 1980, p. 22) and can be divided into (1) the direct modeling role of parents; (2) a system of rewards and punishment; and (3) the general impact of parents on children.

Freud is the founder of this school and an important principle is that of the superego (the conscience) where the child accepts his/her parents' value system due to the love towards the parents or out of fear that the love of the parents may be lost when not heeding or accepting their values (Windmiller, 1980, p. 25). This suggests that the final origin of all values, morally and otherwise, lies in the relationship of children and parents (Windmiller, 1980, p. 26).

From what was discussed previously, it is clear that determinants other than the family (for instance society and peer groups) also play an important role in the formation and transmission of values. Still the importance of parents and the family cannot be negated and different factors influencing the important role of the family will be discussed.

Although different studies focus on the close relationship between family closeness (cohesion) and the effective transmission of values, White (2000, p. 78) indicated that there is a correlation between cohesion and more advanced moral judgment. This may be due to family boundaries so that when these boundaries are more "closed," the parents have a bigger influence on the forming of values. Where there is more openness, the family's influence decreases.

For her research, White (2000, p. 87) used a sample of 500 families in Australia and found support for this hypothesis. In those adolescents who experienced their families as a strong binding force and where there is warmth, more credit is given to the important role of parents in the forming of moral values.

As with family cohesion, the ability of families to be flexible in their authority structure, negotiating style and relationships all affect the way values are confirmed and followed by children (White, 2000, p. 79). In families where there is flexibility and sensitivity toward change, there is a greater opportunity to express one's own ideas and the possibility to experience other views or learn from diverse viewpoints. In more rigid families, there are fewer opportunities to experience different opinions (White, 2000, p. 87).

Positive communication skills like empathy, the ability to listen and supportive reaction toward someone else are at stake here (White, 2000, p. 79). If something is valuable for the parents and it is visible to the child, it becomes an important determinant for parents and children on which to agree.

Ongoing, open discussion regarding issues of importance is conducive to agreement and rapport between parents and children, but children are less prone to accept parents' values where this is done in a negative way. Kuczynski, Marshall and Schell (1997) show that a two-way approach is imperative for understanding and measuring families (Kuczynski et al., 1997, p. 23) and that parents will be more successful with such an approach than a one-way method of communication. Steyn (1996, p. 146) argues that two-way communication works better in the South African context. Jennings, Stoker, and Bowers (1999, p. 13) have shown that in the political arena (of the USA) parents had more influence on the values of their children where this approach has been followed.

The transmission of religious values: The role of parents
In the previous divisions, specific attention was paid to the transmission of values to children from the viewpoint of various philosophical and

scientific approaches, as well as to the role of parents in this process. The next part will deal with the position of parents in the formation and transmission of religious values.

Boyatzis and Janicki (2003, p. 252) state that many factors form the religious side of a child. As the English saying goes: "it takes a village" to socialize a child. This is especially relevant to the South African and African context where there is a dominant social and family structure. The relevance of this will be discussed again in the recommendations at the end of the paper.

Bjarnason (1998, p. 741) shows that within the variety of concepts with relation to the positive influence of religion in the life of the individual and society, two aspects are of importance. It is clear, in the first place, that religious communities play an important role in the individual's integration into society, while, secondly, emphasis is placed on the way in which religious convictions are constitutive of and give sense to the individual's life and worldview.

Bjarnason uses Durkheim's concepts to create a model of social integration by way of support and religious transmission by showing that common involvement and identity provide people with a sense of belonging and purpose, which is to their benefit (Bjarnason, 1998, p. 743). The results of such a communal religious experience are: (1) The creation of an external reality which can be observed objectively and provide stability to the individual; (2) Communal religious experience that act as a constraint that the individual experiences as an obligation toward the demands of society (Bjarnason, 1998, p. 752).

It was shown previously that there is an array of contributing factors in the transmission of values to children. Two aspects regarding the relative influence and importance of parents will therefore be discussed.

Quite a number of studies have been done on the important role of mothers in the religious formation of children. In their research on the nature and influence of religious-determined communication between parents and children, Boyatzis en Janicki (2003, pp. 263, 265) found that mothers were primarily responsible for filling in the daily reports needed for the research, while Francis & Gibson (1993, p. 250) and Dudley & Dudley (1986, p. 13) likewise concluded that mothers' religious practice and religious-based values were better indicators of children's faith development than that of the fathers involved.

In addition to the importance of family, peers, and society at large, other societal structures are important in the transmission of values in children.

Kelley and De Graaf (1997, pp. 654-655) bring to attention the importance of national influences and even dare to state that this sometimes has a bigger role than that of families. This influence is strengthened by friends, colleagues, and potential marriage partners. In an African context, this can also be very important in close-knit societies where there is one culture or long-standing struggles with other groups (Rwanda is a good example of this). Where there are stronger religious commitments in a country, this influence is more far-reaching than in a secular country (Kelley & De Graaf, 1997, p. 655).

The acceptance of friends (in and out of the school) is also a contributing factor in the transmission of values. Regnerus et al. (2004) addresses this issue and shows that if friends do not attend church often, it has an influence on other youths in the church (p. 34). In the same vein, a correlation has been drawn concerning the general level of religiosity in a school and the religious inclination of children in the school (Regnerus et al., 2004, p. 35). If the parents are above-average religious, they will encourage their children to befriend other children of like-minded values. Cornwall (1988, p. 227) conducted the same kind of research and found that peer-groups have a considerable influence on the religious development of children.

The way in which religion has been conveyed to children is as relevant as the fact of religious activity. Cornwall distinguished in her research (1988, pp. 227-228) three contributing processes whereby parents may establish and maintain the religious development of their children.

The family context in significant ways is the foundation on which a child's life and worldview is built. The firmer that foundation based on faith in God, the more secure a child will feel regarding his or her faith. In this regard, narration and discussion are very important in conveying religious values to children. In narrating to the child, difficult religious concepts can be taught in a comprehensible manner.

Not only should children be aware of and comprehend the world around them, but they should also become involved in organised religious life. This will include an awareness of what such involvement will entail and what responsibilities it will bring about. Religious involvement comes not only from the worldview someone holds, but also from the example that has been set by parents and significant others. Martinson and Martinson (1998, p. 69) found that the way that parents justified their behaviour is a mechanism through which children develop character.

It has been indicated before that the way parents channel their own religious preferences influences their children as well. The way religious groups go about maintaining the involvement of the people, is also well known because it is crucial for the survival and strength of the group (Cornwall, 1988, p. 228). Group cohesion and the strengthening of the group are necessary as one of the ways in which the formation and development of faith in children are fostered.

In discussing the role of religion in the formation of values, it is also imperative to address the reason behind it (the why question). Here the motivation comes into play and this will include why certain factors are detrimental and others are advantageous to religious development.

Hoge et al. (1982, pp. 576-578) found that five distinct influences can be identified. In the first place, the younger the parents, the more effective the transmission of value to children. Secondly, when parents agree on religious matters, it works positively towards the transmission of values. This also holds for the case where parents agree on parental style and supportive ways in the family to enhance the intrinsic religious devotion (Giesbrecht, 1995, p. 236). When, however, there are conflicts about their educational philosophy, the results are negative (Spilka et al., 1985, p. 84). Thirdly, when parents' own religious involvement are high (in other words, when they are religiously active), the transmission of values can be done successfully—especially in the case of girls (Hoge et al., 1982, p. 557).

Fourthly, religious socialization within the family is important. The seriousness of parents' religious socializing and the pressure they are prepared to place on their children play a significant role in children's own religious socializing. Also, the extent to which parents communicate with their children about religion has a significant impact on girls but not boys (Hoge et al., 1982, p. 577). Martinson and Martinson (1998, p. 68) stress the creation of a positive emotional climate within the family as conducive to the transmission of values.

Finally, the child's relationship with his or her parents can have a large effect on the transmission of values. Dickie et al. (1997, p. 31) found that when children see and experience their parents as caring, the same characteristics are ingrained as the image of God which these children have. This conclusion is confirmed by Bjarnason (1998, p. 750) when he shows that parental support has a positive effect on the experience of God in their lives.

Although much of the research above in mostly from an European and Western perspective, the principles deduced from it are also applicable to Africa and the African context, since the transmission of values is a common human practice and the way God ordained it to be. In the following part, the application of these principles in an African context will be discussed briefly.

Transmission of values in an African context (with special reference to South Africa)

The authors are both from South Africa and are thus in a position to know more about the context of South Africa, but the situation is very much the same in many African countries to the north of South Africa. A lot had been written about the differences between Euro-centrism and Afro-centrism (cf. van der Walt, 2006, p. 1) and it is abundantly clear that there are vast differences between these two cultures and approaches to life. Some of those differences will be discussed below. One issue that remains unchanged, is the fact that values (of whatever kind) are transmitted by parents (in whatever form of parenthood) to children and have a life-long influence on them and the consequent way in which they themselves bring up their children.

Since the African culture is a much more social than an individualistic one, transmission of values are mostly done in the society, through the churches, and through other groupings. Parents in Africa will more easily get involved with other parents' children than would be the case in Western societies.

In some, often more remote, parts of the continent, paternal domination is still strong, making the father the most important person to convey values to children, although the mother would often be closer to the children in many ways. Even among westernized Africans, the more dominant role of the man in relationships and society is still a strong factor to be kept in mind.

The urbanization in Africa has had a negative effect on the transmission of values and many conservative values have all but disappeared in new societies where people have lost their identities; new values are being transmitted, which would often be materialism and others associated with Western societies, values which are foreign to the typical African context. In many cases where single people went to look for jobs in and around cities in order to survive or improve their livelihood, the bond to extended families has been broken. This leads to a "disconnected" situation where the family and clan have little remaining influence on the individual.

Due to diseases like HIV/AIDS wiping out large numbers of adults, children often become caretakers to other children, which means that there is no proper transmission of values from an adult to children. This leads to more misery due to a lack of proper training and guidance for children.

Often in "children households" as mentioned above, the only value that exists is that of survival. The tragic reality is that there is little expectation that this will change around, because of the prevalence of HIV/AIDS being on the increase (Gill, 2006, p. 74).

Poverty is a huge problem in Africa and in Southern Africa and this also undermines value transmission, because crime is often the only mode of survival; hence the only values that children experience and pick up from parents, are that to steal someone else's possessions is "normal" and should be done in order to survive.

A cancer that threatens all African countries (South Africa included) is the growing problem of corruption, which has at its root a value crisis. Since the first fully democratic election of 1994 in South Africa, corruption has increased tremendously and is unfortunately transmitted by parents to their children. The extended human rights culture has opened possibilities for more criminal behaviour and the possibility for more crime without the resulting punishment, which was the case in the pre-1994 situation. Cases are known where dishonest businesspersons and their sons both were involved in fraudulent schemes.

As a conclusion to this part, one can state that this transmission of values in Africa (and more specific South Africa)—although a universal practice—has a definite and distinguishing feature: the greater involvement of a bigger societal structure than with the western kind of culture and life style. Transmission of values is not only done within the smaller family unit, but in the extended family, clan, and bigger social groupings.

Of course, the question remains in what ways the spread of Christian values and education, and specifically Christian higher education (CHE), can contribute, not only in Africa and in South Africa, but also across the world, towards solving the values crisis, which has the potential of engulfing and paralyzing whole communities. Two initial observations must be made: it is only through the grace of God that any attempts by man can hope to bear fruit. Secondly, no amount of education can ever be a quick fix solution. Nonetheless, Christians in Africa, and their brothers and sisters elsewhere, face an undoubted calling to continue to pray for and work towards the establishment of viable institutions of CHE on this continent, thus to ensure that ever increasing numbers of men and women are available and equipped to spread the gospel in all fields of human endeavour, to inculcate Christian values and so to stem the tide of moral degeneration.

Conclusion

Whatever philosophical viewpoint or scientific theory one subscribes to, there can be little doubt that parents will always play a pivotal role in the transfer of values to their children. In the case of Christian parents this role is no mere coincidence or passive responsibility, but a calling from God Himself. As such it is not only the task of parents to answer to this call; it is incumbent on society, and specifically on Christian society to devote resources towards assisting parents and towards creating conditions in which they are better able to fulfill their responsibility. Such responsibility and devotion are, in the final instance, ones towards God's Kingdom and towards the citizenship of his children in that Kingdom.

References

Bjarnason, T. (1998). Parents, religion, and perceived social coherence: A Durkheimian framework of adolescent anomie. *Journal for the Scientific Study of Religion, 37*(4), 742-754.

Bouas, M. J. (1993). The three R's of moral education: Emile Durkheim revisited. *The Educational Forum, 57*(2), 180-185.

Boyatzis, C. J., & Janicki, D. L. (2003). Parent-child communication about religion: Survey and diary data on unilateral transmission and bi-directional reciprocity styles. *Review of Religious Research, 44*(3), 252-270.

Cornwall, M. (1988). The influence of three agents of religious socialization: Family, church, and peers. In D. L. Thomas (Ed.), *The religion and family connection: Social science perspectives* (pp. 207-231). Provo, UT: BYU Religious Studies Center.

Dickie, J. R., Eshleman, A. K., Merasco, D. M., Shepard, A., Vander Wilt, M., & Johnson, M. (1997). Parent-child relationships and children's images of God. *Journal for the Scientific Study of Religion, 36*(1), 25-43.

Dudley, R. L., & Dudley, M. G. (1986). Transmission of religious values from parents to adolescents. Review *of Religious Research, 28*(1), 3-15.

Francis, L. J., & Gibson, H. M. (1993). Parental influence and adolescent religiosity: A study of church attendance and attitude toward Christianity among adolescents 11 to 12 and 15 to 16 years old. *The International Journal for the Psychology of Religion, 3*(4), 241-253.

Giesbrecht, N. (1995). Parenting style and adolescent religious commitment. *Journal of Psychology and Christianity,* 14(3), 228-238.

Gill, P. (2006). *Body count: How they turned AIDS into a catastrophe.* Johannesburg: Jonathan Ball.

Grusec, J. E. (1997). A history of research on parenting strategies and children's internalization of values. In J. E. Grusec & L. Kuczynski (Eds.), *Parenting and children's internalization of values* (pp. 3-22). New York: Wiley.

Hayes, B. C., & Pittelkow, Y. (1993). Religious belief, transmission, and the family: An Australian study. *Journal of Marriage and the Family,* 55(3), 755-766.

Heyns, L. M., & Pieterse, H. J. C. (1998a). *A primer in practical theology.* Pretoria: Gnosis.

Heyns, L. M., & Pieterse, H. J. C. (1998b). *Eerste treë in die praktiese teologie.* Pretoria: Gnosis.

Hoge, D. R., Petrillo, G. H., & Smith, E. I. (1982). Transmission of religious and social values from parents to teenage children. *Journal of Marriage and the Family,* 44(3), 569-580.

Jennings, M. K., Stoker, L., & Bowers, J. (1999). *Politics across generations: Family transmission re-examined.* Institute of Governmental Studies: Working Paper 2001-15. Retrieved June 18, 2004, from www.igs.berkeley.edu/publications/working papers

Kelley, J., & De Graaf, N. D. (1997). National context, parental socialization, and religious belief: Results from 15 nations. *American Sociological Review,* 62(4), 639-659.

Knafo, A., & Schwartz, S. H. (2003). Parenting and adolescents' accuracy in perceiving parental values. *Child Development,* 74(2), 595-611.

Kuczynski, L., Marshall, S., & Schell, K. (1997). Value socialization in a bidirectional context. In J. E. Grusec & L. Kuczynski (Eds.), *Parenting and children's internalization of values* (pp. 23-50). New York: Wiley.

Martinson, R., & Martinson, S. A. (1998). Work of families: Roles of families. In H. Anderson, D. Browning, I. S. Evison & M. S. Van Leeuwen, *The family handbook* (pp. 63-70). Louisville, KY.: Westminster John Knox.

Okagaki, L., & Bevis, C. (1999). Transmission of religious values: relations between parents' and daughters' beliefs. *The Journal of Genetic Psychology,* 160(3), 303-318.

Regnerus, M. D., Smith, C., & Smith, B. (2004). Social context in the development of adolescent religiosity. *Applied Developmental Sci-*

ence, 8(1), 27-38.

Spilka, B., Hood, R. W., & Gorsuch, R. L. (1985). *The psychology of religion: An empirical approach.* Englewood Cliffs, NJ: Prentice-Hall.

Steyn, A. F. (1996). Values that support quality marital and family life. *South African Journal of Sociology,* 27(4), 143-147.

Tamayo, A., & Desjardins, L. (1976). Belief systems and conceptual images of parents and God. *The Journal of Psychology,* 92, 131-140.

Turner, S. P. (2005). Durkheim, Emile. In K. Kempf-Leonard (Editor-in-chief), *Encyclopedia of social measurement, volume 1* (pp. 699-704). Amsterdam: Elsevier.

van der Walt, B. J. (2006). *When African and Western cultures meet: from confrontation to appreciation.* Potchefstroom, South Africa: The Institute for Contemporary Christianity in Africa.

Walker, L. J. (1999). The family context for moral development. *Journal of Moral Education,* 28(3), 261-264.

Walker, L. J., Hennig, K. H., & Krettenauer, T. (2000). Parent and peer contexts for children's moral reasoning development. *Child Development,* 71(4), 1033-1048.

White, F. A. (2000). Relationship of family socialization processes to adolescent moral thought. *The Journal of Social Psychology,* 140(1), 75-91.

White, F. A., & Matawie, K. M. (2004). Parental morality and family processes as predictors of adolescent morality. *Journal of Child and Family Studies,* 13(2), 219-233.

Windmiller, M. (1980). Introduction. In M. Windmiller & N. Lambert, E. Turiel, *Moral development and socialization* (pp. 1-33). Boston, MA: Allyn & Bacon.

RESPONSE TO TOM LARNEY & GEORGE A. LOTTER

Perry L. Glanzer

From the start, Larney and Lotter's paper contains a tension. It appears they are uncertain about whether to engage in a modern or postmodern paper. The title of the paper is "The parental role in establishing Christian values as the starting point of kingdom citizenship in an African (South African) context." They indicate they will be focusing on a particular subject within a particular context from a particular Christian perspective. However, the first sentence of the abstract states, "the primary focus of this paper is to describe the characteristics and nature of the process of transmitting moral, ethical, and religious values from parents to children." In this case, the focus is a much more general subject addressed to a less particular and universal audience.

In my reading of the paper, I believe they actually ended up favoring the latter approach. Using general social science research they provide a helpful outline of the different views of the basic nature of human beings, the ways that a person develops morally and the role of parents in the different models. They also detail some important aspects of the role of parents in the transmission of values, their importance concerning other structures, and what could contribute to religious and moral development in a family context. The few particular references to the Christian tradition and the South African context do not seem to be integrated into the overall paper as a whole. Take out those sections and the paper could be given to any group in any context.

I believe, for a number of reasons, the paper would have been more helpful to this audience if the authors had given greater attention to the subject of their title. First, I do not believe it is helpful for Christians to talk in vague universalistic terms about transmitting values, a language that is foreign to the Christian narrative. Instead, we should talk about developing good humans who bear the triune God's image or making disciples of Christ who teach others about the Kingdom of God. When we talk about making disciples of Christ who bear the image of the triune God, what it means to engage in moral development becomes clearer. We do not want kids with Christian values, we desire saints. In other words, we understand what it means to be a good person, not according to some form of cognitive moral development similar to Kohlberg, but according to Christ.

Second, general discussions about values transmission fail to capture important dimensions of moral education. The best way to think about this task is like other practices such as sports or crafts. For instance, if we want to help a child become a good basketball player, we do not transmit basketball values. We motivate, teach, train, and coach them. We tell them stories about what it is like to play in an Olympic, World or NBA championship. Of course, we also teach them the rules. We help them practice the virtues/skills of dribbling, shooting and passing. We want them to understand that the true end of basketball is not entertaining the crowd (although like the Harlem Globetrotters, basketball can be used for such ends), but it is scoring the most points. We help find them great coaches and role models who can give them wisdom.

If we aim to form a good person, we do the same. We do not merely transmit Christian values through academic courses in Christian ethics. We engage in moral formation that not only teaches the good but also helps them love, pursue, and act out the good. Like Israel, we must teach our children the rules of the game of life and the stories that help us understand the character of the God who revealed those rules to us. We must also do whatever we can to help our children understand the purpose of this game (glorifying and loving the triune God), the unique realization that they cannot achieve that end but through the grace of God, and the role virtues/fruits of the spirit such as love, humility and gentleness play in relation to this end, and hold before them good models (e.g., the saints and Christ) who give them knowledge and wisdom. They must also practice spiritual disciplines taught us by these coaches and imbibe the wisdom of past coaches (e.g., the wisdom literature).

Third, although I find the outline of the different approaches and how they understand the role of parents helpful, I think it would be of greater benefit to the Christian community and the larger community if they critiqued these different views in light of a more explicit theological perspective. Instead of providing this critique, the authors are content to set a Judeo-Christian perspective alongside other perspectives. They then proceed by simply saying, "The importance of parents and the family cannot be negated and different factors influencing the important role of the family will be discussed."

In contrast, I think an explicit attention to theological context with regard to the role of the parents would also be helpful. We must acknowledge that parents can both help and hinder a child's moral development. In other words, according to the Christian story of creation, fall, and redemption, all of the social institutions that may help form character (e.g., parents, extended families, political entities, neighbors, etc.) can also hinder its formation or deform one's understanding and practice of it. Instead, the paper discusses the "determinants of effective value transmission" outside of a theological context. The reliance on this general social science research implies that we can discover universal rules for how to transmit any set of values as long as one follows these social scientific processes. The actual substance of the values transmitted is not given explicit attention.

Fourth, because the authors choose to examine this issue from a more general perspective, they do not emphasize or highlight the important and unique role of the church or other Christian institutions in this process (although they do mention briefly the importance of religious institutions). Instead, they focus on the role of parents, the role of other social structures, national influences, and school and peer-group pressure. If they were to discuss kingdom citizenship, the role of the Church, the concrete embodiment of God's kingdom on earth, should have been part of that discussion.

Fifth, because the authors seek to speak in a more universalistic way instead of from within the Christian metanarrative, the paper insufficiently addresses the all-important role that political metanarratives have played in influencing what they call values transmission but what I would call moral formation. In some countries these political metanarratives involve overtly nationalistic approaches that more subtly push a vision of goodness informed by the liberal democratic metanarrative. Lawrence Kohlberg's work is a good example of how the ideals of a secular liberal democrat will influence the overall story of moral development. The end of moral development looks much like an ideal secular liberal democrat.

Overall, although I believe it is helpful to consider various theories of how we translate our moral cultures and the role parents play in such transmission in general, I believe the title of the paper would have been a better guide for exploration. Christians need an analysis of moral education that is more akin to what John Milbank has done with social theory. They need an analysis that speaks and analyzes different views from a particular Christian perspective with the narratives and ends of the Church in mind and then sets forth a plan for how to know, love and do the good (as defined within the Christian tradition).

RESPONSE TO TOM LARNEY & GEORGE A. LOTTER

Stan L. Lequire

Introduction
This paper is a good overview of many views and theories of child development and psychology. I found it a helpful review of this important field of study. Furthermore, the list of challenges within the African context is concise and a good outline. Each of the factors that the authors mention is vital to understanding the context of values transmission in the African context: animism, urbanization, culture, gender, human health, etc.

What follows are a few critiques of the content and structure of the article.

Cultural critiques
This paper seems weighted toward Western perspectives on this topic. To a large degree, Western academics and theoreticians own the largest voice in the article. At times, the authors indicate an awareness of this dynamic. For example, they do identify "individualism" as a tendency in the research upon which they base their paper. Indeed, hyper-individualism is a hallmark of Western cultures and quite foreign in most African cultures. A more global or contextual perspective could strengthen this paper. Such perspectives may be under-valued in academia and/or these cultural perspectives may remain to be adequately researched. Nonetheless, it is vital to make every effort to include these voices as well. This is particularly important because parental roles and families in the West seem to be in as great a crisis as those in Africa. A case could be made that years of Western research and theory have not particularly strengthened Western families. Although the West can certainly lend its voice to topics such as parental roles and kingdom citizenship, it must be asked if the West continues to provide credible and authentic leadership in establishing Christian values for the kingdom.

Methodological critiques

It is the section of the paper, "Transmission of values in an African context," which is so vital and which needs much more attention. What might kingdom citizenship look like in an African context? It must be a captivating and dynamic reality. How can Christian parents move their children toward citizenship in this kingdom practically and effectively?

One specific encouragement for the authors would be to avoid any appearance of negative evaluations of African culture. For example, the authors describe corruption as "a cancer which threatens all African countries." While it is true that corruption is evil and must be addressed, corruption of different kinds also exists in the West. A case can also be made that the hyper-materialism of the West is equally cancerous, if not more destructive to kingdom children. As a second example, it is stated "poverty undermines value transmission." I risk playing word games and ignoring the grinding dehumanization of poverty. However, I believe it is important to point out that wealthy countries cannot be assumed to have an advantage in the domain of values. Furthermore, a case could be made that wealth may also undermine value transmission and that, at times, the poor may actually have very healthy values.

Conceptual or theoretical critiques

I believe it would be helpful for the authors to define what they mean by "Christian values." This phrase appears in the title of the paper, but appears to be assumed rather than delineated. What are these "values?" How will parents know that they are passing on healthy, Christian values? In addition, pertinent to points made above, can we be sure that Western values are not being assumed *de facto* to be Christian values? At one point, the authors mention the disappearance of "conservative values" due to urbanization. While urbanization is certainly a challenge that must be addressed, what are these "conservative values" and are they good because they are conservative? Since kingdom citizenship transcends both conservative and liberal, clarity would strengthen the important points the authors wish to make.

Another topic, which needs clarification, is the horizontal and vertical dimensions, which are mentioned early on in the paper. I will assume that vertical is synonymous with spiritual and that horizontal is synonymous with all other dimensions—social, emotional, etc. Such a framework could yield difficulties in applying what the authors are attempting to say. First, a horizontal/vertical differentiation could encourage a tendency to spiritualize an outlook on the world and on parenting.

A vital, Biblical worldview must carefully affirm the goodness of creation in all its dimensions—be that horizontal or not. Furthermore, all areas of human culture are the purview of the believer, not just the vertical as might be implied by the authors. For example, the authors state, "When, however, the transmitting of moral and ethical values are done from a humanistic consideration, the horizontal dimension will of course be accentuated." Christian parents, and not just humanist parents, must accentuate the horizontal under the lordship of the All-mighty who rules over "all things," and not just the vertical. Secondly, surely other cultures will also demonstrate interest in the "vertical." One could just as easily insert "Muslim" as the first word in the following sentence taken from the article: "Christian parents, to whom the vertical dimension is important, will take seriously the foundational responsibility to confirm faith in the lives of their children." Surely, Muslim parents are also concerned about the "vertical" and strive to confirm faith in the lives of their children. They may even be more zealous about this than Christian parents may.

Conclusion

This paper whets my appetite for the parental role in kingdom citizenship in Africa. This topic is vital and deserves attention and research. Certainly, thought and practice in the West have not guaranteed healthy families. We all look to the Christian community in Africa to provide fresh perspectives and new leadership in raising children for the kingdom.

IMPACT OF CHRISTIAN HIGHER EDUCATION IN BRINGING SOCIAL CHANGE IN THE LIFE OF DALITS IN SOUTH INDIA

J. Emmanuel Janagan

Preface
"To obey God's will: love God with all we are and our fellow humans as ourselves." (Matthew 22: 37-40)

Dalits in India have been socio-economically oppressed, culturally subjugated, and politically marginalized for centuries. They have now begun to articulate their identity, asserting not only equality for themselves but also struggling to bring about revolutionary changes in the social order based on equality and liberty. Dalit identity conveys their aspirations and quest for a new social order. This is essentially a political agenda. For that, they launch struggles on various issues and participate in electoral politics. Their path is arduous and long-drawn.

The word "Dalit" is a controversial one. Many scholars define the word in different ways. The word "Dalit" is used for the ill-treated and humiliated castes. Who is a Dalit? A Dalit is one who is culturally, socially, economically, and politically suppressed and exploited. Dalits have different names in different parts of our country. They are called as Holaya, Panchama, Chandala, Samagarer, Chammal, Adikarnataka, Adidiravida, and Adijambuva. Dalits are not a homogeneous group; they have a number of divisions among them. It is probable that these internal divisions prevented them from effectively voicing their problems.

The Dalits are land-less labourers living in a cluster of huts or slums. Their poor economy and illiteracy have forced them to believe in superstitious customs. Untouchability is the age-old practice, which is inhuman in the name of religion. To add fuel to the fire many Dalit men are addicted to intoxicants. Their villages are usually far away from towns and sources of recreation available to urban people are denied to them.

Therefore, naturally after a day's work, a Dalit goes in for recreation in liquor, and comes home drunk and quarrels with and beats his wife and children. The poor woman somehow has to get along with physical and mental torture at the hands of her drunken husband. The sad thing about it is most of the liquor shops are near the Dalits settlements.

Present Dalit realities
Most of the Dalits are coolies on daily wages, but what they get is very low compared to their counterparts. In towns, 80 percent of women do menial jobs, work in fields, and work in industries. Though their workload is the same as that of men, women are paid less than men. Yet, they have no option. During the lean periods, they have to find some work, any menial work to earn something. Even the women, who work in such industries as handloom, power loom, fire works, tailoring centres and tea estates, do not enjoy security. Their job is not permanent. The problems they meet with are generally, no holidays, or holidays without any wages, no medical aid, heavy workload, no physical protection.

There are four occupations that the majority of Dalits in India pursue. Many work as coolies under a contractor in building construction. Others work as housemaids, cleaning the house and vessels, cooking, baby sitting, and looking after old people or cattle. Still others work as agricultural labourers in the tea estates.

Regardless of their particular work, Dalits face many similar problems. Their work is impermanent, heavy, and subject to constant review in order to get the next day's work. These jobs are without housing, convenient transportation, or schooling for children. Often the work is hazardous, and women are in danger of rape. Dalits are the objects of insult and often unjustly accused of theft. Wages are often low, inconstant, or even recalled in case their products are not sold.

Whenever the high caste male has anything against his low caste men, his first target is the low caste woman. Beating and stripping them and making them walk down the street, and gang-raping of women are some of the usual punishments given to low caste people. No action could be taken against the so-called high caste master simply because he was exercising his birthright.

When the downtrodden, under-privileged women started wearing upper cloth, the high caste women were asked to take off their jackets just to make the difference. So many of the women of the masters' houses are still without their jackets.

The Indian context is characterized by the pervasiveness of the caste system. It is a unique Hindu, Indian social institution that does not manifest itself outside India (except in the neighbouring countries where the caste-minded Hindus have migrated). Though it cannot be seen, it provides the atmosphere in which Indians live in terms of language, religion, economic status; the primary or controlling identity comes from caste. Of the different caste groups now, there is crystallization of two groups: caste people, and out-caste people or Jait people and Adi people. Nearly every one of six *lakh* villages in India is geographically divided into two parts, confirming this division. Now there is growing hostility between Dalits and Non-Dalits, which is assuming the character of organized assaults. Dalits experience death, and the wider society experiences decay.

In India, Dalits work hard for long hours yet remain poor. They are poor and are making others rich. Dalits do every kind of menial job. They take upon themselves the task of keeping others and their environment clean, and in this process, they supposedly become an unclean and untouchable people. Dalits serve the world that persecutes them for exhibiting values of love and tolerance, instead of hatred and retaliation. Dalits are the victims of organized violence, and they shed their blood and sacrifice their life in order to humanize the society that is reduced to inhumanity, due to caste system.

In India, women are an oppressed majority and the Dalit woman is the most oppressed of all. Dr. Ambedkar has pictured Indian society as a number of pots arranged one above the other, a common scene in village homes. On the top is the Brahmin male, followed by Brahmin female, below them are the *Kshatriya* male and female. At bottom are the Dalit male and Dalit female. The concern for humanity in the Indian context should start from concern for Dalit women where humanity is most disgraced.

Dalit's culture is matriarchal; some of its features have already been mentioned above. In spite of the Aryan cultural invasion, the mother goddesses could not be annihilated. Features of the goddesses in the Dalit religions symbolize popular resistance to the control of women's power in the Brahminical religious tradition. There is now a resurgence of mother goddess cults among the Dalits.

> The religious myths of Brahmins may tell the story of woman's destructive power and how it was constrained by men through control of women's sexuality. But the religion of the common people tells the story of women's continuing power and their resistance to male control. (Zelliot, 1991, p. 189)

We have to keenly notice the violence against the Dalits. Modern world has become a hotbed of hatred, violence, and terrorism. Civilization has not made many people different from brutal animals. The politically powerful divide the downtrodden for their benefit and encourage them to kick and kill. One such form is the senseless killings of innocent Dalits. Anyone who has a gun and who has lost the sense of balance takes it into their head that the gun must be used against anyone, unmindful of whether the latter is a Dalit or any other low caste. Currently, the hands of hatred and violence are toward the poor people, especially the Dalits people.

The life-style of Christian Dalits changes their relationship to nature and neighbour in diverse ways: serving, sharing, giving, caring producing, and enriching. When the Dalits become Christians, they are socially, economically, and politically empowered. Socially they are treated as members of an equal caste by the high caste. In the villages, Christian Dalits are also treated with high dignity, as equal to the higher community. They are allowed to use public places like roads and public wells. Economically, Christian Dalits are allowed to own land and have been included in most of the profitable forms of employment. Politically they gain power. Psychologically, they are allowed to live next to a higher status family with comfort and dignity.

Society changes as well when Dalits are treated better
When a Dalit becomes a Christian, one can witness many changes in the culture, and the increased literacy rate plays a very important role. These changes provide a new perspective on office, authority, power, and responsibility. They encourage real democracy and counteract every form of totalitarianism. When shared by the society as a whole, these changes can be seen in the social structure of family, marriage, and celebrations in the occupational structure and the level of education. Changes are also evident in life-style, social participation, and economic conditions.

Impact of Christian higher education (CHE) on Dalits
Proverbs 22:6 reads, "Train children in the right way, and when old, they will not stray." Solomon says that this is the way God has woven the moral fabric of the universe. He states that when the affairs of everyday life reflect God's presence the child will never escape that teaching as long as he lives. The fear of the Lord will be passed on, and the next generation will say that God's presence is real. His power is valid and His character faithful. Christian Dalits were provided with value-based education, which has brought lot of cultural changes in the families of Dalits. Education has become an eye-opening tool to realize their living

condition and to understand better habits, customs, traditions, folkways, and mores.

There are many ways in which CHE has great social importance as a social institution especially in the modern, complex industrialized societies. First, it can complete the socialization process. The main social objective of Christian education is to complete the socialization process. The family gets the child, but the modern family tends to leave much undone in the socialization process. The school and other institutions have come into being in place of the family to complete the socialization process. Now the people feel that it is "the school's business to train the whole child even to the extent of teaching him honesty, fair play, consideration for others and a sense of right and wrong" (Massey, 1999, p. 97). The school devotes much of its time and energy to the matter by emphasizing co-operation, good citizenship, doing one's duty, and upholding the laws. Directly through textbooks, and indirectly through the celebration of patriotic programmes, sentiments are further instilled, the nation's past is glorified, its legendary heroes respected, and its military ventures justified.

Second, CHE can transmit the cultural heritage. All societies maintain themselves by the exploitation of a culture. Culture here refers to a set of beliefs and skills, art, literature, philosophy, and music that are not carried through the mechanism of heredity. Culture must be learned. This social heritage (culture) must be transmitted through social organizations. CHE has this function of cultural transmission in all societies. It is only at the upper levels of the college that any serious attempt has been or now is made to deal with this area.

Third, CHE can assist in the formation of a social personality. Individuals must have personalities shaped or fashioned in ways that fit into the culture and its value base. Christian education everywhere in India has the function of the formation of social personalities. Christian education helps in transmitting culture through proper moulding of social personalities; in this way, it contributes to the integration of society. It helps men to adapt themselves to their environment, to survive, and to reproduce themselves with Christian values and principles.

Fourth, CHE can cause a reformation of attitudes. Christian education aims at the reformation of attitudes wrongly developed by the students already. For various reasons the students may have absorbed a host of attitudes, beliefs, loyalties and prejudices, jealousy and hatred. These are to be reformed. It is the function of Christian education to see that unfounded beliefs, illogical prejudices, and unreasoned loyalties are removed from the students mind. Though the institution has its own limitations in this regard, it is expected to continue its efforts in reforming the attitudes of the students.

Fifth, CHE can prepare Dalits for occupational placement. In this way it will also serve a practical purpose in the life of Dalits. It should help the adolescent Dalit earn his livelihood. Education has come to be today nothing more than the instrument of livelihood. It should enable the student to make out his livelihood. Education must prepare the student for a future occupational position. The youth should be enabled to play a productive role in society. Accordingly, great emphasis has been placed on professional courses.

Sixth, CHE can confer status on Dalits. Conferring status is one of the most important functions of education. The amount of education is correlated with class position. This is true in U.S.A, U.S.S.R., Japan, Germany, and some other societies. Education is related to one's position in society in two ways. First, an evaluation of one's status is partially decided by what kind of education he has received. Second, many of the other important criteria of class position such as occupation, income and style of life, are partially the results of the type and amount of education one has had. Men who finish college, for example, earn two and a half times as much as those who have only a grammar school education.

Seventh, education encourages the spirit of competition. Education instils co-operative values through civic and patriotic exhortation or advice. Yet the institution's main emphasis is upon personal competition. For each subject studied the student is compared with his companions by percentage marks or rankings. The lecturer admires and praises those who do well and frowns upon those who fail to do well. The institution's ranking system serves to prepare for a later ranking system. Those who are emotionally disappointed by a low ranking in college are thereby prepared to accept limited achievement in the larger world outside the college.

Eighth, economy and education are closely related. For example, the number of engineers produced by education limits the number and productive capacity of engineering firms. In a planned economy—normally planned years in advance—a definite number of doctors, engineers, teachers, technicians' scientists, etc are produced to meet the social and economic needs of the society. Christian education institutions also provide values and orientations specific to certain occupations. For example, social work students socialize and are educated in a particular way in college. This may help them become good social work practitioners. Educational institutions also provide other values and orientations relevant to the functioning of industrial society.

Finally, CHE changes the personal and social values of Dalits. These changes are evident in such areas as politics, personal values, and sociality.

Education fosters participant democracy. Participant democracy in any large and complex society depends on literacy, allowing full participation of the people in the democratic processes. Literacy is a product of education. The educational system has thus economic as well as political significance. Education imparts personal values. The curriculum of a college, its "extra-curricular" activities, and the informal relationships among students and teachers communicate social skills and values. Through various activities, a college imparts values such as co-operation or team spirit, obedience, and fair play. This is also done through curriculum.

Education acts as an integrative force in society by communicating values that unite different sections of society. The family may fail to provide the student essential knowledge of the social skills and values of the wider society. The educational institutions can help the child learn to interact with people of different social backgrounds.

CHE and social change
The role of CHE as an agent or instrument of social change in the life of Dalits is visible, and social development takes place in the living conditions of Dalits. Social change may take place when a person needs change, when the existing social system or network of social institutions fail to meet the existing human needs, or when new materials suggest better ways of meeting human needs—social changes do not take place automatically or by themselves.

As MacIver says, social change takes place as a response to many types of changes that take place in the social and non-social environment. Education can initiate social changes by bringing out a change in outlook and attitude. It can bring about a change in the pattern of social relationships and thereby cause social changes.

Christian educational institutions and teachers were engaged in transmitting the way of life to the students. Education was more a means of social control than transmitting a way of life to the students. Traditional education was meant to provide an unchanged knowledge of all that is, knowledge about science, technology and other type of specialized knowledge. Education was associated with religion. It has however become secular today. It is an independent institution now. Education today has been chiefly instrumental in preparing the way for the development of science and technology. Education has brought about phenomenal changes in every aspect of man's life. Francis J. Brown remarks that education is a process, which brings about changes in the behaviour of society. The process enables every individual to participate effectively in the activities of society, and to make positive contributions to the progress of society.

In the social sphere, the influence of Christian higher educational institutions has comprehended much of social life in South India since it has improved the Dalit's family, marriage, caste system, modes of dress, and life in general. Mainly, the Christian influence on Indian families is evident in the breakdown of the joint family, growth of progressively smaller families, reduction in male dominance within the family, growth in independence of women and general instability of the family institution as such. As a result of contact with Christians, Dalit members of Indian society came to look down upon child marriage and to encourage late marriages. The basis of marriage changed from ritual to love, and even the methods of marriage ceremonies underwent considerable modification. On the one hand, the relationship itself took on a temporary nature though at the same time monogamy was encouraged. Caste is no longer regarded as an important factor in marriage. On the other hand, many people felt encouraged to remain bachelors or spinsters, for such a state is no longer considered completely abnormal.

As a result of Christian influence and teaching, a new awakening began to spread among the Dalit women of India, and the westernized education that they received made them self reliant and effective competitors of men in all fields. Apart from this, many of our Dalit women took over the western mode of dress.

CHE has limited the caste system. One of the major advantages of Christian influence has been the reduction in the practice of Untouchability, and this was achieved by the untouchable castes, which converted to Christianity so that they could be equal to the higher castes. This helped remove the superstition from Indian belief so that there is no longer a general repulsive feeling of Untouchability.

Christianity's influence can be seen in every sphere of Dalit life in India, change in the dietary habits, use of furniture, improvement in the standard of living, dress, interest in hairstyles, use of cosmetics, mode of greeting, and a hundred other forms. Many of these changes can be seen in Dalits living in India who were suppressed and under bondage of slavery for many hundreds of years, but in the present time these changes are the result of CHE. One immediate effect of CHE was that many Hindus changed their religion, but then the more intelligent among the Hindus felt impelled to modify their religion. Besides, Christians initiated numerous movements aiming at social and religious reform within the country, the more important groups being the Brahma *samaj*, Prarthana *samaj*, Ramakrishna mission, and Theosophical society. It was left to the Arya *samaj* to protect Hindu religion.

Christian education, social stratification and social mobility
Social stratification, which is necessitated by the phenomenon of social differentiation, refers to "a process of placing people in different strata or layers" (Bhushan, 2004, p. 135). It is a ubiquitous phenomenon of human society. All the existing societies are stratified. The essence of social stratification is social inequality, which manifests in various forms. It may involve the differential allocation of income, status, privileges, and opportunities. A stratified society represents a ladder of hierarchy in which its population is distributed. People who occupy the higher place in this hierarchy or ladder enjoy higher status opportunities, and privileges, and the people who occupy a lower position have limited access to the same.

Social mobility refers to the movement of an individual or group from one social position or status to that of another. People who occupy different places in the hierarchy may often change their places depending upon the opportunities made available to them.

Based on this movement of people from stratum to stratum, one can discern two systems of social stratification. The open society or the fluid system of stratification has greater scope for movement up and down the hierarchy. The western society, with its class system of stratification, is very often cited as a typical illustration of this. The closed society or the rigid system of stratification is the second one in which the boundaries of various strata are very rigid and movement between the strata is extremely difficult, if not impossible. The Indian caste is very often mentioned here as the typical example of this. It may, however, be noted that as to broad type they are not found in pure form in any society of the world. Existing societies, however, lean towards one or the other.

The correlates of social stratification and mobility vary from society to society depending upon the level their socio-economic and technological development. In general, education, occupation, income, and wealth have been found to be the main correlates of social stratification and mobility in urban industrial societies.

In technologically advanced countries, education has become the most important criterion of social stratification. In such societies, occupation is the determinant of income. Educational levels of individuals determine recruitment to various occupations in these societies. In technologically advanced countries, normally the occupational and educational levels define the status gradation.

> Briefly, in view of the close relationship between education and occupation, and to the extent that occupation is an important, if not the only avenue for income and social status, education acquires significance as a determinant of social placement and social stratification. (Jain & Bhatnagar, 1997, p. 249)

It is noticeable that in the industrial societies the most prestigious jobs tend to be not only those that yield the highest incomes but also the ones that require the most education. The more education people have, the more likely they are to obtain good jobs and to enjoy high income.

There is a complex relationship between Christian educational institutions and social stratification Christian educational institutions act as a generator of upward mobility. The reciprocal relationship between education and social stratification affects education primarily. This effect is greater than the effect of education on stratification.

In many societies the educational facilities for higher-level occupations and professions like medicine, engineering, management etc, are limited. However, the number of aspirants to make use of such facilities is very high. Because the cost of higher education is very high and several constraints govern admission to such courses of education, only a select section of a society can manage to enter such courses. This section is normally the privileged section of society. Such a system of higher education, with all its constraints, is often defended on meritocratic grounds. Thus, general educational institutions are forced to function as an agency of "status retention." However Christian higher educational institutions help students pursue higher studies by sponsoring Dalit students, providing fee concession and in some cases, first generation Dalit students are provided free education.

Social stratification affects lower levels of education especially in the rural areas. Generally, students belonging to the lower stratum drop out of school; even when education is provided free and additional incentives are given, the situation does not seem to improve much. It is true that education can change the system of stratification. Special programs, including drop-out children evening schools started by the Christian institutions have played a very important role in drastically reducing the drop-out rate, encouraging Dalit students to continue higher studies.

In urban industrial society, Christian educational institutions promote upward social mobility. In such societies, occupation is the principle channel of social mobility. Occupations that promote social mobility require certain educational qualifications. In this context, education acquires significance as a promoter of upward of social mobility.

> The functions of educational system are to provide people with the qualification and aspirations to meet society's occupational needs. Built into the system is the assumption that people will or should want to be upwardly mobile. Underlying such reasoning is, then, the belief that social mobility is a desirable characteristic of the society and that the education system exists to promote and facilitate it. (Jain & Bhatnagar, 1997, p. 249)

Education is not tied to economic mobility but rather social mobility. In developed nations, people want to attain higher levels of education to equip them to obtain jobs that are more prestigious. What is observed is that people want to receive extra years of education even if it is not necessary for some of the jobs or occupations they seek. There is evidence that educational achievement has no consistent relationship to later job performance and productivity. What is significant, however, is that the lack of education restricts the social mobility of those people who for one reason or another have been unable to obtain them.

Christian educational institutions can serve as a solvent of inequalities, especially in societies where the traditional systems of stratification do not permit large-scale social mobility. Here the introduction of formal education (as was done by the British in India) gave an opportunity for people who were hitherto confined to lower or intermediary statuses in the traditional system of stratification to attain a higher status. Thus, education has the potential to radically alter the previous system of stratification and has often been hailed as a solvent of inequalities.

There are a number of factors that impede social mobility, referred to here as constraints on mobility. These constraints may be internal or external. The internal constraints are values, aspirations, and personality patterns of the individuals. The external constraint is the opportunity structure of a society.

System of beliefs and values
The major constraint in upward mobility is the prevailing system of beliefs and values. Lower socio-economic groups place less emphasis upon college education as necessary for advancement, and are less likely to desire college education for their children. This holds true in the Indian situation.

Further, opportunities for education to the lower classes are very limited, particularly in the rural areas. Thus, the prevalent value system governs their aspiration and actions. Hence, they may lag behind the upper classes in this regard. At this time, Christian higher educational institutions have been the first to accommodate Dalit students.

Upward mobility is also restricted by family influences. In a study made by Stephenson it was found that occupational plans and aspirations are positively associated with the prestige ranking of the father's occupation. If the family itself lacks initiative, it is reflected in the child's desire for not moving out of the family bonds. The child develops a tendency to take up a job, which the parent wants him to take up in his hierarchy. The child also does not show much interest in education because the parents are least concerned about it. This influence is very much visible in joint families.

Individual personality structures may also contribute to immobility. It has been found in a number of studies that achievement, motivation, intelligence, aspiration, and values are related with mobility. One study found that intelligence quotient tests rely on solid school performance in the early years of an individual's life. As the person grows older, his family and friends shape him. Here the desire to go college is taken as an aspect of mobility. One who performs well is expected to go college and thus is mobile in an upward direction.

The upper status boys learn that good performance in school is necessary, and they are expected to do well enough in secondary school to be admitted to college. On the other hand, a boy from a lower status home is taught that college is either not meant for him or at best a matter of indifference to his parents. The boy's friends are not interested in college or in high school. Consequently, even a bright boy among them gets discouraged.

The desire to achieve is clearly related to upward mobility. It seems that youth from the upper strata of society may not need strong personal motivation for mobility because such youth get good advice; they live in environments where "looking up" is encouraged and where they are provided with career counselling. This is not the case with lower class youth. They have to learn a great deal to make these decisions.

The problems faced by Christian Dalits is a living, existing reality and has a direct relationship with the overall approach of the missionaries which was later carried on by the Christian higher educational institutions in India. Religious concepts such as individual salvation, personal holiness, equal human dignity, and basic rights adopted by the Christian educational institutions transformed the Dalits. The total "upliftment" of the Dalits has more impact on present Dalit movements. Christian Dalits enjoy the fundamental rights given to their counterparts in other religions under the constitution of India.

Conclusion

The role of CHE has brought changes in the life of Christian Dalits, and their living and working conditions have improved the family status. Value-based Christian education has brought light in the darkness of Dalit lives. We have to look on Dalits as a sacred trust that the Lord has committed into our hands. What shall it profit me indeed, even though I gain a career, wealth, or fame if I should neglect Dalits? But don't lose hope for Dalits. Continue to commit them into the loving arms of our heavenly Father, for He is able to work, reach, and touch where even the best human parents have failed.

References

Ahmad, I. (1978). *Caste and social stratification among Muslims in India.* New Delhi: Sage.
Al-Biruni, D. (1988). *India by Qeyamuddin Ahmed.* New Delhi: Rawat Publishers.
Bhushan, V. (2004). *Introduction to sociology.* New Delhi: Sage.
Cole, S. (1968). *The sociological method.* New Delhi: Kitas Mahal Publishers.
Dal., S. V. (1988). Dalit. In Sir M. Williams (Ed.), *A Sanskrit-English dictionary* (p.493). New Delhi: McGraw-Hill.
Dalit Panthers. (1973). Dalit Panthers Manifesto. In J. R. Barbara (Ed.), *Untouchable! Voices of the Dalit liberation movement* (pp. 141-147). London: Zed Books.
Galanter, M. (1984). *Competing equalities in law and the backward classes in media.* New Delhi: Pearson.
Ghurye, G. S. (1979). *Caste and race in India.* Bombay: Ashish Publishers.
Grewal, J. S. (1979). *Guru Nanak in history.* Chandigarh: Sage.
Gupta, S. K. (1985). *The schedule castes in modern Indian politics.* New Delhi: Sage.
Hutton, J. H. (1946). *Caste in India.* New Delhi: Cambridge University Press.
Isaacs, H. R. (1965/1978). *India's ex-untouchables.* Bombay: Everest Publishers.

Jain, P. C., Jain, S., & Bhatnagar, S. (1997). *Schedule caste women*. New Delhi: Rawat Publications.

MacIver, R. M., & Page, C. H. (1971). *Society: An introductory analysis*. New Delhi: Sage.

Massey, J. (1999). *Dalits in India*. New Delhi: Rawat Publishers.

Norman, B. W. (1961). The content of cultural continuity in India. *Journal of Asian studies,* 20(4), 17.

Watson, F. (1998). *A concise history of India*. Southampton: New Delhi: Cambridge University Press.

Zelliot, E. (1991). *Dalit essays on Ambedkar movement*. New Delhi: Sage.

RESPONSE TO J. EMMANUEL JANAGAN

Samuel P. Ango

My response to this paper is made from my background as a Nigerian Christian who comes from northern Nigeria. Like the Dalits of India, Christians in the northern parts of Nigeria experience socio-economic marginalization because northern Nigeria is predominantly Islamic. Christians are discriminated against in education, politics, and economic opportunities. And like the Dalits of India, the northern Nigerian Christians are increasingly becoming politically active.

Again, like the Dalits, the heterogeneity of faith expression among the Christians in northern Nigeria sometimes hinders their coming together to present a united political front. However, Christians in general in Nigeria, and even in northern Nigeria in particular, are not as poor, or as ostracized (untouchable) as the Dalits of India are reported to be. But, as with the Dalits, alcoholism is high among Nigerian Christians, especially among the low-income earners.

Christians in northern Nigeria find it difficult to get jobs, as compared to their Muslim counterparts, but their conditions are somewhat better than those of the Indian Dalits. Christian girls in northern Nigeria may be forced to marry Muslims against their Christian parents' wish, but the Christians seem to have better recourse to legal protection in Nigeria than the Dalits have in India.

In terms of housing, there are areas of northern Nigeria where Christians cannot own houses or build churches or schools. But they are usually given other designated areas for such purposes. The discrimination is traumatizing, but it is nowhere as severe as it is for the Indian Dalits. Again, religious upheavals are common in northern Nigeria, during which Christians are slaughtered, their homes, businesses and churches destroyed. They provide services as teachers, artisans, and businessmen, but they may be attacked with impunity. However, there is supposed to be official provision for their security. The discrimination is not officially recognized, as it seems to be for the Dalits in India.

Most societies in Nigeria, unlike in India, are patriarchal. The killing of the innocent under flimsy excuses is however common to both societies.

For Nigerians in general, like for the Dalits, education provides brighter opportunities. But in northern Nigeria, if a Muslim becomes a Christian, it can lead to threats of, or actual loss of economic, educational, and social status for the convert. Christians are even enticed sometimes to abandon the faith and become Muslims to enhance their economic chances.

Most higher education in the era after independence (1960) in Nigeria was provided by the government. But in the past ten years, many churches have established universities, which aim to inculcate Christian values in students, along with general education. Also, the education provided is expected to be of better quality than that provided in government institutions because the institutions are better equipped and staffed and are less prone to interruptions by union strikes and students' restiveness than the government-owned institutions. However, Christian universities are more expensive than most Christians can afford. So the effect of Christian higher education (CHE) may be more limited among Nigerian Christians than among Indian Dalits. Though western education was initially provided by Christian missionaries, along with its influences on culture and economy, today in Nigeria most education is provided by the government, and is not controlled by Christian norms and values. But it has brought about a lot of changes in the lot of the rural population, with greater liberties and mobility for women. Superstitions and unhygienic practices have been stopped. This is not limited to Christians. However, Christians in Nigeria are quicker to embrace western education and values than their Muslim counterparts, and where there is no discrimination; they tend to experience more rapid economic, social, and political mobility.

The connection between education and job placement is generally the same in Nigeria as noted by Janagan for India and other places. However, sponsorship for higher education that is available for the Dalits is not available for the average Nigerian Christian, especially in the north. Only high-income earners can afford higher Christian education, except for seminary education, which is less expensive.

There was a time when Christian education in general, or education provided by Christian schools, was the greatest factor for upward mobility, for Christians and non-Christians alike, in Nigeria. Many Christian individuals and groups are establishing schools now to provide better quality education.

But for a majority of Christians in Nigeria, such schools are unaffordable. They have to make do with the poorer education provided by public schools.

What CHE has done for the Dalits in India gives much cause for joy about what the word of God can do in the lives of a downtrodden people. Such uplifting should be a principal activity of the church in any part of the world where people are oppressed.

RESPONSE TO J. EMMANUEL JANAGAN

John Hiemstra

"Therefore, I urge you, brothers and sisters, in view of God's mercy, to offer your bodies as living sacrifices, holy and pleasing to God—this is your spiritual act of worship. Do not conform any longer to the pattern of this world, but be transformed by the renewing of your mind. Then you will be able to test and approve what God's will is—his good, pleasing and perfect will." (Romans 12:1-3)

Thank you, Professor Janagan, for your informative and insightful paper. I am encouraged to hear you conclude that Christian belief has indeed had a transforming impact on the lives of Dalits in India. As an outsider to India and the Dalits' experiences, I offer a few questions as a sympathetic Christian outsider who wishes to learn more about an important justice issue.

The thrust of your paper, as I understand it, is that Christianity has contributed to a liberating movement away from an oppressive caste structure towards a more open and participatory social system. You outline the negative social, economic, and other consequences that this strict hierarchical caste system has had on the Dalits, ranging from making them "untouchable," to overt oppression, lack of mobility, lack of land tenure, labour problems, poor work conditions, and a variety of other social atrocities. Your paper argues that a turn to Christianity, as well as the influence of institutions of Christian higher education (CHE), has "brought light in the life of poor Dalits by which a wholesome transformation is taking place." You show how these influences are beginning to produce new behaviours, institutional arrangements, and an overall "new social order" that together are improving their social, economic, political, and cultural circumstances. It is amazing to see the breadth of the changes that are occurring, including altered family patterns, marriage practices, roles of women, transformation of caste system, and other life changes (diet, dress, hairstyle, cosmetics, social mores, etc).

On types of oppressive hierarchy

You speak convincingly of the dangers of oppressive social hierarchies, and of the liberating effects of Christian faith and CHE on the life of Dalits, especially in terms of social, economic, and political mobility. Clearly, major improvements are evident in their lives, as you describe them. But eventually, I wonder, is there not also a danger of slipping into new types of hierarchies, perhaps hierarchies of class, profession, or income that result from Western thinking? Both planned economies and market economies have produced income and professional hierarchies that take on new forms of exclusion, and then new problems of social stratification and lack of social mobility re-appear in these social structures. Are there resources within the Christian worldview that not only help us escape oppressive hierarchies, but also help us to develop distinctively Christian views of society and politics? In view of the Dalits' unique situation and context, can these Christians avoid both the social stratification and lack of social mobility evident in the caste system and also prevent the adoption of distorted western systems of stratification? In sum, what type of social structures should Christians develop and build when their hearts are turned to Jesus Christ—especially in light of St. Paul's words: "for from him and through him and to him are all things?" (Romans 11:36, Colossians 1).

On multiple Christian influences

A couple of questions to explore the types of Christian influence that brought about this change in the lives of Dalits. You note that *education* overcomes "social stratification" and identify, for example, the number of years one is educated as a factor that produces this result. Is it possible to distinguish the contributions of *education* per se in changing the lives of Dalits, from the specific contributions of *Christian education* in bringing about these changes? You further note a variety of things that Christian institutions have done to help Dalits, e.g. changing attitudes to schooling, financial sponsorship, and helping prevent children from dropping out. Is it possible, or helpful, to sort out the general effects of *Christian values* in helping Dalits overcome oppression and social hierarchy, and the effects of *distinctively Christian education* in achieving this end? For example, you note that CHE taught Christian principles that helped improve the situation of Dalits. You listed "individual salvation," "personal holiness," equal human dignity, basic rights, and show they "transformed Dalits." Again, are these *general Christian values* that were taught in many contexts after conversion, or are they specifically related to the distinctive role of higher education? Are these practices unique to Christian educational institutions, or are they general Christian values which one would expect to see practised, regardless of whether there was higher education or not? I agree strongly that *Christian values* can have the effect you note, but is it also possible to identify what is exactly the "value added" contribution of distinctively CHE, which other non-Christian institutions of higher education would not be expected to produce?

In light of the above, can you further discuss *which distinctive Christian approaches to higher education* helped produce these results? The various Christian traditions have developed a variety of approaches to CHE, many represented at this conference.[1] Other Christian institutions of higher learning will be interested to learn from the institutions that helped the Dalits, what specific Christian educational approaches, practices, theories, and emphases were involved in improving the Dalits' lives.

To summarise the above, we need to unpack which of the following elements influenced the Dalits lives: general increase in the level of education, Christians enabling Dalits to access more education, introduction of Christian values and beliefs, Christian values being passed on through CHE, exposure to distinctively Christian approaches to higher learning, or a combination of these.

On comparative religious influences
You argue that the caste system in India—a strict hierarchical society—is a "unique Hindu, Indian social institution." Would it be correct, in your opinion, to argue that Hinduism *caused* the development of this feature of Indian society? I would be interested to hear your analysis of which elements within Hinduism might have contributed to the formation of the caste system. Perhaps this exercise may be helpful in identifying *what* specifically within Christianity, and CHE, has been countering the specific cause(s) of the caste system, and thereby producing these positive changes for the Dalits.

A related question would be to ask whether there have been things about "becoming Christian" and the impact of CHE that might have had negative impacts on the Dalits. For example, you mention that families suffer more from "general instability." Has the way Christianity was

---

1 See for example, Nicholas Wolterstorff, *Educating for Shalom: Essays on Christian Higher Education*, edited by Clarence W. Joldersma and Gloria Goris Stronks, Eerdmans, 2004 and Joel Carpenter, "New Evangelical Universities: Cogs in a World System, or Players in a New Game?" to appear in Ogbu Kalu Ed., *Interpreting Contemporary Christianity: Global Processes and Local Identities*, Eerdmans/Curson Press.

brought (by missionaries and others) and the way Christianity has been passed on by CHE, also had some negative impacts? Or conversely, are there also positive contributions of Hinduism to social life?

On Christian political action
A final question is rooted in my vocation as a Christian political scientist. I am curious to learn more about what you refer to as "essentially a political agenda." How has politics become part of this transformation process in the life of Dalits? Did the Gospel influence the types of political actions involved in this transformation, an influence that would allow you to conclude that Christian political action helped CHE to transform Dalit oppression and social hierarchy? Given your findings in this paper, what are your thoughts on how Christians should think about the state's role in doing justice within, and to, a religiously plural society?

Thanks again for sharing your insights and research on this important topic in the life of Christ's worldwide church.

WAYS THAT THE PEDAGOGY AND PHILOSOPHY OF SERVICE-LEARNING CAN BE USEFUL IN TEACHING STUDENTS IN INTERNATIONAL CONTEXTS

Jeffrey P. Bouman & Lauren Colyn

Introduction
Institutions of Christian higher education (CHE) pursue multiple simultaneous goals spanning student learning, fiscal responsibility and viability, Christian discipleship and mentoring, and the development student skills. Because of the nature, size and complexity of colleges and universities, these goals are often carried out without full and open communication, and therefore with less than ideal intra-institutional collaboration. Here we examine two rapidly developing programs at Calvin College with an eye toward improvement through collaboration.

Study-abroad options for Calvin students have developed and flourished over the past decade, parallel to a concomitant rise in academically-based service-learning in metropolitan Grand Rapids. On the surface, one might observe that due to the geographic foci of each of these programs—the one international, the other domestic, and even local—a certain institutional distance would be understandable. Yet upon further examination, the fact that these two relatively new and growing pedagogical opportunities have shared little mutual benefit is somewhat surprising.

Currently, in many of Calvin College's eight semester-long international study programs, students, faculty, and their families are regularly involved in acts of service and social justice while living and studying abroad. When they occur, these acts are conducted through no formal connection to Calvin's extensive program of service-learning, which offers theoretical models and substantial research and literature that might support these efforts. The present research attempts to address the ramifications of including formal service-learning components within international contexts via Calvin's existing study abroad semester programs. Where implemented, these efforts would connect the college's existing commitment to the pedagogy of service-learning to its well-structured and popular international study programs.

Appreciating the value of a link between study abroad and service-learning is not possible without a fuller understanding of the underlying goals of both international study and service-learning. The places where these two programs intersect include their efforts to introduce students to people, locations, cultures, and languages different from their own in order to create learning environments that will foster: the cognitive dissonance necessary for deep learning; opportunities for the observation, practice of, and reflection on the virtue of hospitality; an understanding of reciprocity in learning; and experiences outside of one's comfort zone in order to overcome natural tendencies toward provincialism. Service-learning is traditionally linked to these goals in domestic settings, while study-abroad programs approach them outside the students' country of origin.

A variety of inherent challenges may inhibit the successful linking of these disparate programs. These challenges center on individual, institutional, and cultural resources. In order to implement a successful study-abroad program, institutions must dedicate significant resources simply to the traditional elements of the learning environment: living and learning. Effective, academically-based, service-learning programs that link students with learning opportunities that contribute meaningful and effective service also require significant effort in initiating and sustaining human relationships. Adding this second requirement to the task list of a faculty member already stretched and living in a temporary context will sometimes be ultimately prohibitive.

And yet, because of the potential value for the realization of core missions, the effort to weave justice and mercy together in a context in which service-learning is achieved within an international academic curricula seems worth investigating. There are many tensions in CHE, and the goal of this research is two-fold: first, to provide suggestions for improving Calvin College's academic program in both study abroad and service-learning; and second, to generalize these suggestions to the larger CHE community. In this paper, we will lay out our findings to date. We have examined Calvin's mission, its off-campus offerings, service-learning program, and curriculum requirements—all in the context of a larger review of the relevant literature. We also conducted a survey of the Calvin faculty who have led off-campus semesters since 1996, and visited two international programs with service-learning components.

Calvin College in context—two programs
The vision of the college
Calvin College's mission statement, in brief, sets forth three primary goals: to engage in vigorous liberal arts education that promotes lifelong Christian service; to produce substantial and challenging art and scholarship; and to perform all our tasks as a caring and diverse educational community. The college mission strongly emphasizes "lifelong Christian service" as well as working in a "caring and diverse educational community." From an awareness of the growing importance of context and pedagogy in fulfilling the goals Calvin sets forth in its mission we examined service-learning's potential in Calvin College's international programs.

Off-campus programs

Calvin College has drawn national attention for its percentage of students studying off-campus. Two hundred eighty Calvin students participated in an off-campus semester program in 2006, while an additional 489 students participated in a month-long off-campus Interim program during January. The college sponsors eight international off-campus semesters in seven different countries. Students can choose from fall semesters in China, France, Ghana, Honduras, and Hungary or spring semesters in Britain, Honduras, and Spain. The Calvin faculty who lead these semesters plan cultural excursions in the host countries and teach some of the classes offered during the semesters. Host organizations and local faculty teach the other required and elective courses. All programs are connected with some local host country university. Students live with host families while studying in Honduras, Spain, and France, as these programs are language focused. However, in Britain, China, Ghana, and Hungary students live in the college residence-hall settings. Below is a listing and brief description of the international semester offerings for Calvin College students.

- **Britain**—Students study and live at Oak Hill College, a Christian seminary, in the Southgate section of London. Two courses are taught by the program director, with elective options at the host college. There are also opportunities for internships. Generally about 20 students study in Britain each spring semester, and the faculty director changes each time the semester is offered.
- **China**—Living and studying at Capital Normal University al-

lows students to interact with Chinese and foreign students. Three courses on China are taught by the program director with the opportunity to take other classes at the university. Students also take a 5-credit language course with a Chinese instructor and tutor. The semester also includes several cultural excursions. Until 2006, this semester program has averaged 17 students and was directed by Kurt Selles, a Christian Reformed missionary with permanent residence in China.

- **France**—This semester is for students studying French at the advanced level. Located in Grenoble at the University of Grenoble's Centre Universitaire d'Etudes Francaises, students live with French families and study French with other foreign students from around the world. The program director is always one of several faculty members from the French department who teaches two courses while other classes are taken at the university. This is a larger program with about 25 students each semester.
- **Ghana**—Located in the capital city of Accra, students study at the University of Ghana, Legon. Students live in the International Student Hostel on campus but have host families that include them in outings and family activities. The program director teaches two courses and students take other classes, including a one-credit language course, at the Institute for African Studies with Ghanaian professors. This semester is generally focused on development and in recent years the program has grown to average 17 students. The program director is drawn from a number of diverse departments at Calvin, and typically changes each fall.
- **Honduras - Development**—Students study in the capital city, Tegucigalpa at La Universidad Pedagógica Nacional and live with host families for the semester. The program director, Kurt Ver Beek, has permanent residency in Honduras and teaches all of the classes which focus on development issues. A multi-faceted service-learning component was incorporated into class requirements for the first time in 2006. A Spanish language course is also required.
- **Honduras - Spanish**—Similar to the development semester, students study in the capital city, Tegucigalpa at La Universidad Pedagógica Nacional and live with host families for the semester. This program requires a summer session on Honduran language and culture for the first week and a half. All classes are taught in Spanish, as the focus of the program is language studies. However, a

poverty and development course is also integral to this program. The program director for the fall Spanish semester is typically a member of the college Spanish department, and rotates between a few members of the department.

- **Hungary**—Students live in a student residence in Budapest, the capital of Hungary. The program director, a member of the Calvin faculty from a rotating slate of departments, teaches the two required courses. Students also take a two-credit language course and have the option to take their other electives at one of many universities in Budapest. The ability and opportunity for travel throughout Europe is integral to this semester program.
- **Spain**—This semester has both a core and an advanced program for students, both of which require participation through Calvin's January term and the spring semester. The core program is intended for students to fulfill the language requirement at Calvin. The advanced program is to develop Spanish language skills through immersion in Spanish culture. Regardless of the program, all students are located in the city of Denia and live with host families. The semester in Spain is one of the largest at Calvin, with well over 25 students each spring semester.

Service-Learning Center
Since 1964, Calvin College's Service-Learning Center (S-LC) has been facilitating civic engagement, volunteering, and service-learning for Calvin students in the Grand Rapids metropolitan area. Begun by students at the grass-roots level as a way to put into practice the Reformed vision of renewal where Christ transforms culture, the program quickly grew and became institutionalized in the early 1970s. In the early 1990s as the pedagogy of service-learning grew in popularity as a result of the work of Campus Compact, a national organization encouraging colleges and universities to engage their students in actual social issues, work of the S-LC grew to include a plethora of departments and courses incorporating service into the learning goals and syllabi of faculty members.

Having recently celebrated four decades of partnership with dozens of local agencies, schools, churches and other non-profit entities, the S-LC employs a staff of three full-time professionals, and 15 students who work to connect students, faculty, staff and community partners through student-initiated and academically-based service-learning. In 2005, *US News and World Report* began ranking colleges' efforts in service-learning, and Calvin was mentioned on a list of 19 colleges and universities nationally as a top program in service-learning in both 2005 and 2006.

Student participants are presented with myriad opportunities to become engaged with local issues and service opportunities through the work of the S-LC. Strong efforts are made by the S-LC staff to provide sufficient training and orientation to students and faculty to enable them to see the community as a set of assets, to enter and exit existing communities appropriately, and to approach community relationships with the concept of reciprocity in mind, rather than that of helper.

Cross-Cultural Engagement
In 2000, Calvin kicked off its first full revision of its Core Curriculum requirements since the late 1960s. In the new set of requirements, the college seeks to provide students learning opportunities in the areas of Knowledge, Skills, and Virtues. One important addition is a requirement for all students to fulfill a Cross-Cultural Engagement option, either in an international setting, or in an intentional set of relational experiences with a person or group from a distinctly different culture locally.

Calvin's international off-campus programs offer students the opportunity to meet their core curriculum requirement in Cross-Cultural Engagement (CCE). The topics and content of these courses vary, but are required to include an introduction to the culture *via* readings, films, or other materials, 20 hours of face-to-face personal engagement with persons of a culture significantly different than the student's own culture, and a careful, specific reflection component. The goal of the CCE credit is for students to

> gain skills in cross-cultural communication, to understand how the world might look from the standpoint of another community of interpretation and experience, to learn how to discern and, where appropriate, adapt to the cultural expectations of the other, to learn how to distinguish between the enduring principles of human morality and their situation-specific adaptations, and to witness other cultural embodiments of faith, and thus to reflect on the substance and definition of one's own faith by comparison.

One idea that has been presented in our research has been to match this course requirement with a service-learning component. The course would provide a relatively easy existing requirement with which to integrate service-learning as it already has a time/hour requirement and it shares the cultural learning commitment from a faith perspective. However, the resources to carry it out would require much more than the designing of a CCE course.

Literature review
The available literature on International Service-Learning provides insight into how difficult it is to define; it emerges as pedagogy, philosophy, *and* practice. More and more work is being done on the issues of preparation, collaboration, partnerships, language barriers, cultural barriers, effects, etc. of service-learning in international contexts. Richard Kiely (2004) notes that little research has been done on long-term effects of international service-learning (see also Hartman & Rola, 2000). There also remains to be found a working solution to the question on how to integrate service-learning into Christ-focused, rigorously academic international study programs for undergraduates.

Challenges to international service-learning
Well-documented abuses of the service-learning model provide us with at least three major reasons not to participate in international service-learning: paternalism, cost, and risk. Many fear that international service-learning is more or less set along a global North-South divide, providing a pedagogical justification for wealthy North American and European students to travel the world to briefly touch others' misery for their own educational purposes. In this model, north exploits south in a position of paternalistic *noblesse oblige* (Grusky, 2000). In addition, there are high costs of travel, making the enterprise increasingly elitist. And liability risks are high, both in safety as well as in healthy partnership relationships, according to the work of Simonelli (2000). Finally, the work of Richard Kiely (2004) raises ethical questions about the transformational effects of international service-learning experiences on students' emotional and moral foundations.

In the context of these threats, educators must have strong philosophical and pedagogical support for implementing programs as resource-demanding as international service-learning. One strong impetus for such programs is that of broadening students' views of the larger world. Those students who want to understand economic, social, and environmental issues must be aware of the interdependent nature of our world. David Hartmen and Gail Rola make the case in their research that

> the United States . . . can no longer produce college graduates who respond to world events with ethnocentric biases, insufficient information, and a general lack of interest in world events. Undergraduates now must possess language and cross-cultural communication skills, as well as be culturally sensitive. (2000, p. 17)

Students from all countries will do well to consider the world from a variety of cultural and national perspectives, but particularly students from countries with an inordinate balance of power where myopic views of the world are more likely to lead to unnecessary and inappropriate uses of power.

In addition, a renewed focus in higher education on value development—selflessness, participation, cooperation, interest, and initiative—encourages international service-learning (Berry & Chisholm, 1999; Hartman & Rola, 2000). The interconnectedness of the university with communities, nations, and the world, the need for active responses, and responding to the needs of modern society highlights the need for renewed attention to core values. Because the undergraduate experience involves a transitional period—from child to adult, from home to independence in the world—colleges need to assist students developing these values. Cross-cultural pedagogical experiences help them make connections and links between classroom teaching and real community applications (Porter, 2003; Porter & Rapoport, 2001).

Benefits and costs
Short-term changes from international service-learning are all positive (Hartman & Rola, 2000). The result of the study by Myers-Lipton (1994) demonstrates that service-learning increases students' international understanding by increasing their global concern, cultural respect, civic responsibility and by decreasing their racial prejudice. Students also make perceptional shifts regarding membership, connection, responsibility ("as a means to social transformation rather than as a sign of obedience") and purpose (Porter & Rapoport, 2001). Well-rounded students emerge who see themselves as learners rather than experts in a community while gaining contacts and valuable skills (Frank & Lee, 2005). A quantitative study *International Cross-Cultural Service/Learning: Impact on Student Development* done by Richard Pyle (1981) found that four of thirteen variables—autonomy, interdependence, mature life-style plans, and total/sum score—were statistically significant for positive student development.

However, little is known on the long-term impact of international service-learning. Richard Kiely's (2004) research found that "long-term impact . . . on [students'] ability to change their lifestyle habits, resist cultural norms, and engage in social action is often ambiguous and problematic" (p. 5). Kiely describes a "chameleon complex" where students often struggle internally with decisions to conform or resist conflicting cultural norms, rituals, and practices. Based on the chameleon complex, Kiely finds that the tough process of worldview transformation is necessary, but not enough, for a change in lifestyle and long-term action. In fact, in his 2005 article *Transformative International Service-Learning*, Kiely writes that transformational learning comes through a six-step process: crossing borders, experiencing some type or level of dissonance, personalizing experiences, processing these experiences—reflection, connecting to host country and culture, and gaining an global consciousness. Grusky claims that "it is not so much a 'life-enriching' but rather a 'complacency-shattering' or 'soul-searching' experience that international service-learning is trying to accomplish" (2000, p. 866).

Other points of caution in the service-learning transaction involve the difficulty in knowing whether service-learning efforts are helping or hindering local communities. Faculty and community planners must be careful to forge partnerships that reflect community needs and incorporate a cross-section of community leaders so that factionalism can be avoided (Simonelli, 2000). It is difficult, sometimes impossible, to build trust in such short periods, especially if there are vying interests.

Mission statement
Support for an international service-learning program must come from the mission of the involved schools, departments, and organizations. (Alon, 2004; Berry & Chisholm, 1999; Ward, 2003) Guevara and Ylvisaker (2003) recognize that in order to implement international service-learning into a program there must be institutional as well as faculty support and initiative, student interest and ability, and a mission statement that supports service-learning and international studies.

Preparation
This is arguably one of the most important aspects in the success or failure of any service-learning program, including international programs (Eyler & Giles, 1999; Frank & Lee, 2005; Jones & Esposito, 2006). Pre-trip courses, seminars, and discussions are often used to help students in their ability to recognize what they will experience in the upcoming international program. Jones and Esposito (2006) suggest that requiring some of the reading prior to departing helps keep students from feeling overwhelmed during the service period. Schools that have found this important include Grand Valley State University, Indiana University and Elon University (Guevara & Ylvisaker, 2003; Jones & Esposito, 2006; Riner & Becklenberg, 2001). Although they note its importance, Guevara and Ylvisaker have found that pre-trip efforts can only partly prepare

students, as the element of surprise in international service-learning is what most encourages the learning process in students.

Reflection

Active reflection is extremely important for long-term transformational learning and student re-integration into life at home (Kiely, 2005; 2004; Stachowski & Visconti, 1998). Reflection is important for self- and group-assessment as well as for creating an outlet in times of uncertainty (Frank & Lee, 2005). Post-trip strategies are necessary for translating student's new values and global consciousness into meaningful action (Kiely, 2004). Guided reflection can be encouraged by requiring students to set learning goals prior to their departure (Jones & Esposito, 2006). However, the effect of post-trip reflection on student ability to take initiative in domestic/local service-learning is limited. Because there is "often a disconnect between what students want to do and the actions they actually take", Kiely (2004, p. 16) suggests post-program courses connecting students to a network of program alumni. Affective learning gained through personal contact with locals in international service-learning stimulates reflection that can lead to social change (Kiely, 2005).

Reflective learning during community service-learning programs must not ignore global or cross-cultural components lest it sell itself short (Frank & Lee, 2005). Instead, service-learning should be coupled with reflective studies of national and global culture as well as history.

Collaboration and mutuality

In-country collaboration and reciprocity is extremely important. "Success . . . attest[s] to the momentum that can be generated when a cycle of reciprocity is ethically and continually renewed." (Porter & Monard, 2001, p. 7) There are different ways to set up collaborative international service-learning programs. Each has strengths and weaknesses. Faculty-led programs, which Guevara and Ylvisaker (2003, p. 83) call the "home" model; depend greatly on a collaborative relationship between the faculty leaders and the host country's partnering organizations. These faculty-led programs can build on already-established partners or can establish new linkages. Creating partners with NGOs increases flexibility and directness while setting a common level of shared interests and the ability to meet the needs of both the students and the NGO clients. Limitations in the "home" model include less peer-to-peer contact for students, limited formal classroom-setting learning, and limited access to English-speaking translators and instructors.

Using connections with pre-existing university programs in international host countries can also develop international service-learning programs. In this "host" model, the in-country university facilitates the service-learning. It is important for host and home institutions to maintain contact between faculties to ensure continued shared vision, interests, support, and resources (Guevara & Ylvisaker, 2003; Kiely & Nielsen, 2003; Simonelli, 2000). Both "home" and "host" models require faculty to reach out and collaborate with non-faculty members of the host institution and community (Ward, 2003).

It is important to consider balance in evaluating service benefits. Riner and Becklenberg (2001) give three principles regarding how program design affects potential outcomes:

> those being served control the services provided, those being served become better able to serve and be served by their own actions, and those who serve are also learners and have significant control over what is expected to be learned. (p. 235)

So, whereas the work must be of value to the host community (Guevara, 82), it must also be acknowledged that because multiple groups and people are involved there will invariably be vying goals and interests (Grusky, 2000). There are ways to minimize these differences. For example, according to Porter and Monard (2001) it is important to work within the mindset of the host country by finding terms and ideas already inherent to the culture. Pre-trip classes and discussions also increase understanding while downplaying differences (Frank & Lee, 2005; Grusky, 2000).

Service at the cost of learning
Spending time serving in the field invariably takes time away from classroom studies. It does not have to come at the cost of learning; rather each can complement the other. "Curricular needs often precede the integration of service-learning opportunities into existing courses, but sometimes service can lead to the development of new courses, offering a more organic integration of theory and experience in our curricula" (Ward, 2003, p. 27). Several sources suggest pre-trip classes/readings for preparation, structured group discussions prior to departure, and scheduled time for daily reflection (Frank & Lee, 2005; Jones & Esposito, 2006; Kiely, 2004).

Replicability
Many scholars recognize that international programs are not universally replicable. In their book *How to Serve and Learn Abroad Effectively,* Berry

and Chisholm (1992) write that successful programs do not come about by replicating what other universities are doing. Instead, international service-learning initiatives must consider the home and host universities' missions and histories, the host country's national system of education, the field study requirements of the students, and the historical and social culture/community being entered (Berry & Chisholm, 1992; Mendel-Reyes & Weinstein, 1996). Setting up each international service-learning program requires hard work and many active facilitators to provide benefits to local partners and students (Mendel-Reyes & Weinstein, 1996).

Surveys
During the summer of 2006, as part of a McGregor Research Fellowship coordinated internally at Calvin College, an on-line survey was developed and distributed to all faculty members at Calvin who have led international, semester-long programs since 1996. The survey was used to gather faculty feedback on what was being done in terms of service-learning in the semesters they had directed and how they viewed the potential for developing service-learning in certain countries in terms of the resources (time, energy, etc.), culture, interest, student and faculty availability. Faculty was also given the chance to indicate what would be necessary to make international service-learning work, or why they did not think it would work. The survey was made up of ten 6-point Likert-scale questions, multiple choice questions, short answers, and essays. Twenty-one of twenty-nine surveys were returned. General impressions from the surveys confirm that faculty is not of one mind on whether the risks match the rewards of international service-learning—many felt already stretched to the breaking point with administrative and teaching details. In addition, context and contacts clearly mattered to them in terms of their confidence regarding whether or not they thought such an effort might succeed and add to their teaching efforts.

Case studies
We were able to carry out two case studies in 2006 with the support of an internal Calvin College Faculty Grant. In April, Jeff Bouman, Director of Calvin's Service-Learning Center, traveled to Tegucigalpa, Honduras to see how the Director of the Calvin Honduras Development semester had begun to incorporate service-learning into his program. Jeff was able to interview students, community partners and recipients on their experience and understanding of service-learning. Because this program was directed by a faculty couple with eighteen years of living in Tegucigalpa,

and numerous local contacts, the program of both urban and rural service-learning was an unqualified success. Students reported a great deal of increased learning as a result of their placements.

In July, we were also able to see how service-learning is implemented in an international context by visiting the New Horizons Foundation in Lupeni, Romania. New Horizons is a non-government organization with seven years of program experience delivering adventure education programs, service-learning opportunities, and civic engagement club development throughout Romania. We met with the New Horizons Foundation director and founder. These interviews and conversations, as well as our observations of the *Viata* adventure education program and the *Impact* clubs, provided us with examples of successful ways in which service-learning and adventure education can be used internationally for building social capital. A holistic program that addresses the local context and history of a host area can provide deep and meaningful opportunities for college student learning. As in the Honduras case, the presence of a host faculty member with years of living experience will likely make the difference regarding program viability.

Conclusions

In international contexts where colleges and universities have established strong local partnerships through a long-term presence, and where faculty members have significant living experience, the pedagogy of service-learning can be a meaningful method for teaching students. Well-developed partnerships offer an opportunity for Christian colleges and universities to discuss the part of faith communities in missions, development, and relief activities. A cross-cultural partnership based on our equality before God enables Christian colleges and universities to conduct an ongoing dialogue regarding an emerging pedagogical opportunity. In international study semesters where faculty are less permanent and arrangements are more temporary, service-learning partnerships will require much more work, and preliminary feedback indicates that it is likely too high a cost to pay in most cases to be effective. Additional research, as well as practical experience will be required to explore strategies to overcome those obstacles in the area of international service-learning.

References

Alon, I. (2004). Service-learning and international business education. *Academic Exchange Quarterly*, 8(1), 23.

Berry, H., & Chisholm, L. (1992). *How to serve and learn abroad effectively: Students tell students.* New York: International Partnership for Service-Learning.

Berry, H., & Chisholm, L. (1999). *Service-learning in higher education around the world: An initial look.* New York: International Partnership for Service-Learning.

Eyler, J., & Giles, D. (1999). *Where's the learning in service-learning?* San Francisco: Jossey-Bass.

Frank, R., & Lee, J. (2005). Service-learning in Mongolia. *Academic Exchange Quarterly,* 9(1), 145-149.

Grusky, S. (2000). International service-learning: A critical guide from an impassioned advocate. *American Behavioral Scientist,* 43(5), 858-867.

Guevara, J., & Ylvisaker, R. (2003). Home and host models of collaboration for service-learning: Grand Valley State University programs in El Salvador and South Africa. In L. Healy, Y. Asamoah & M. Hokenstad (Eds.), *Models of international collaboration in social work education* (pp. 81-90). Alexandria, VA: Council on Social Work Education.

Hartman, D., & Rola, G. (2000). Going global with service-learning. *Metropolitan Universities,* 11(1), 15-23.

Jones, K., & Esposito, J. (2006). Service-learning abroad and global citizenship. *Academic Exchange Quarterly,* 10(1), 85-90.

Kiely, R. (2004). A chameleon with a complex: Searching for transformation in international service-learning. *Michigan Journal of Community Service-Learning,* 10(2), 5-20.

Kiely, R. (2005). Transformative international service-learning. *Academic Exchange Quarterly,* 9(1), 275-281.

Mendel-Reyes, M., & Weinstein, J. (1996). Community service-learning as democratic education in South Africa and the United States. *Michigan Journal of Community Service-Learning,* 3(1), 103-112.

Myers-Lipton, S. J. (1994). *Effects of service-learning on college students' attitudes toward civic responsibility, international understanding, and racial prejudice.* Unpublished doctoral dissertation, University of Colorado.

Porter, M. (2003). Forging L.I.N.C.S. among educators: The role of international service-learning in fostering a community of practice. *Teacher Education Quarterly,* 30(4), 51-67.

Porter, M., & Monard, K. (2001). Ayni in the global village: Building relationships of reciprocity through international service-learning.

Michigan Journal of Community Service-Learning, 8(1), 5-17.

Porter, M., & Rapoport, L. (2001). Enhancing students' sensibilities of membership, connection, responsibility, and purpose. *Academic Exchange Quarterly, 5*(2), 12.

Pyle, R. (1981). International cross-cultural service/learning: Impact on student development. *Journal of College Student Personnel, 22*(6), 509-514.

Riner, M., & Becklenberg, A. (2001). Partnering with a sister city organization for an international service-learning experience. *Journal of Transcultural Nursing, 12*(3), 234-240.

Simonelli, J. (2000). Service-learning abroad: Liability and logistics. *Metropolitan Universities, 11*(1), 35-44.

Stachowski, L., & Visconti, V. (1998). Service-learning in overseas nations: U.S. student teachers give, grow, and gain outside the classroom. *Journal of Teacher Education, 49*(3), 212-219.

Ward, J. (2003). Serving the mission: A study-abroad and service-learning case study. *ADFL Bulletin, 34*(3), 25-29.

RESPONSE TO JEFFREY P. BOUMAN & LAUREN COLYN

Ken Bussema

I would like to thank Dr. Bouman for his helpful paper identifying the often-parallel paths that experience-based study-abroad programs and intentionally designed service-learning courses and projects have usually followed. Sharing common goals, especially those of reflective processing to facilitate deep learning and an awareness and desire to respond practically and constructively to community needs, service-learning initiatives, and culture crossing off-campus programs would certainly benefit from a more deliberate integration. Analyzing this "gap" between two powerful learning strategies and offering potential strategies for adopting service-learning pedagogy in study-abroad settings, Dr. Bouman provides us with some very serviceable insights.

I found it particularly helpful to think about this gap in terms of the differences between international service-learning (pedagogy, philosophy, and practice) and volunteering abroad. In my experience directing both service-learning and study-abroad programs, culture crossing programs often emphasize the philosophy and practical importance of "service" as a valuable tool for understanding another cultural setting, demonstrating global citizenship and good will as well as for developing cross-cultural communication skills, but seldom utilize the pedagogical strengths of a service-learning instructional model. Students in faraway places as well as those closer to home often report that some of their most memorable experiences occurred when they were participating in some sort of community service. Study-abroad students boast that they have become more able to see life through the eyes of another through engaging in a variety of activities, side-by-side with locals. This engagement offered through providing direct volunteer service offers opportunities for conversations, observation of actual living conditions, recognition of practical actions, which make a difference, and relationship building. These gains are generally unattainable for those who only travel through another culture, seldom seeing beyond the window on the bus. Through volunteer service activities, students quickly discover that they, although privileged educationally and economically, often have more to learn about life than those they came to serve. These are powerful learning opportunities and when combined with careful and skilled processing and reflection, students' lives are often changed. However, in the majority of study-abroad settings, course work, and "academic" accomplishments are primarily conceptualized in more traditional course projects, papers, and exams. The educational yield from service projects or volunteering is generally described in terms of attitudinal shifts, consciousness raising, and instilled motivation to alter life style practices—all invaluable and often unreachable in the traditional classroom. Yet, as valuable as these shifts in what students care about can be, does acquiring a heart for service generate an eye for justice? Will worldviews be informed, challenged, and changed through acts of compassion and opportunities to work shoulder-to-shoulder with those in need? Put another way, will building a new front porch or fixing a leaky roof bring about deeper cultural understanding? Don't get me wrong here, I am not devaluing the importance of direct involvement in lives and living circumstances of others, but rather I'm asking whether merely providing service, doing good works is the best learning experience we can offer. Great memories, useful community contributions, greater sensitivity to the needs of others and excellent group bonding are valuable outcomes, but are these worthy of academic credit?

In contrast, service-learning programs begin with an intentional pedagogical design, which recognizes the importance of the personal and interpersonal dimensions of acting together to meet important needs but also focuses on higher order cognitive goals. Service-learning as a pedagogical strategy begins with articulating particular learning outcomes related to a specific discipline, cognitive skill or theoretical framework and then relating these to the activity, processing, and consequences of the service activity. The learning "yield" emerges out of the preparing for, guiding, and evaluating the service activities. The service-learning model requires considerable effort to specify which concepts, skills, and information, etc. can be gained, strengthened, and deepened through performing specific tasks in community. Once learning objectives are identified, activities in the community can be evaluated for their potential to provide real-time testing, practice, and problem solving. Reflecting on the adequacy of preparations, expectations, encountered successes and failures, and discovery of new problems or solutions can then facilitate new and deeper understandings. These reflective activities throughout the service project, with increasing integrative and analytical focal points, along with careful assessment of what has been learned, mastered, and discovered as still to be learned are where the 'real learning' takes place. Service-learning as a pedagogical strategy requires conceptualizing the entire study-abroad experience in terms of an experiential learning framework uniting theory, thought, and practice (e.g. Kolb). I believe that the demands of developing and implementing a comprehensive learning approach is probably the major reason that most study-abroad programs operate at the practical level of doing 'service' projects which are only loosely connected to the goals of the program. It is fairly easy to schedule service weeks, days, or afternoons; however, to build curricular goals around a service-learning pedagogy is much more demanding.

We have been looking at the potential and challenges of incorporating a service-learning model within a study-abroad context primarily from the student/professor perspective. An additional set of challenges and concerns emerges when we stop to consider the "recipients" of the service—the community where the activity takes place. Are these communities really served? Have they participated in the selection, direction, and implementation of the projects? Are we guilty of exploiting their poverty, living conditions, social or emotional challenges for educational and attitudinal gains for already greatly advantaged American college students? Will community members experience the "help" as patronizing or heaven sent? Do they tire of being needy, so others can feel good about being helpful? Do they want to share their lives, stories hardships etc. with a new group each semester? These are difficult questions, whether service-learning is employed at home or abroad, but necessary to face. It seems to me that these challenges stem in part from our notions of service, which as much as we like to think a win-win activity, allude to positions of superiority and advantage. I think we need a new way of conceptualizing real world actions that address important human needs, injustices, and suffering. Actions/service we are called to perform together as fellow image-bearers, learning from, and instructing each other as we labor together to build His kingdom.

RESPONSE TO JEFFREY P. BOUMAN & LAUREN COLYN

Premalatha Dinakarlal

Christian educationists of today are challenged to experiment with new pedagogy, as learning cannot be confined to classrooms. In the modern global village, students yearn for new experiences and wish to widen their spectrum of knowledge, and hence they are to be exposed to new methods of learning. Christian institutions of higher learning are called upon to come out of the traditional stereotyped teaching-learning process and experiment with innovative methodologies.

Jeffrey Bouman's paper is in fact an empirical study that discusses the study-abroad and service-learning programmes of Calvin College. Bouman tries to present in this paper how these two programmes are interconnected and have almost identical ends, and how they intersect. This paper analyses in detail how Calvin College organizes the programmes, and gives an objective evaluation of their success. Bouman agrees to the fact that study abroad may not be affordable to many as travel involves big money. The non-affordability makes the programmes smack of elitism. Further, in service-learning programmes, learning gets primary importance, and service is only secondary. This self-criticism is indeed the strength of the paper and it is this openness, which helps one to evaluate Bouman's paper in a highly objective manner.

Bouman proceeds to make an impartial assessment of the impact of study-abroad and service-learning programmes of Calvin. His paper evaluates the off-campus semester course and also the month-long off-campus interim course. The paper in fact takes us on a tour to eight international off-campus programmes in seven countries, namely China, France, Ghana, Honduras, Hungary, Britain, and Spain. The students who participate have a cultural excursion and also take elective courses. The Service Learning centre of Calvin College has been enabling students in volunteering and service-learning since early 1970s. The paper shows how the pedagogy of service-learning has grown in popularity. It also analyses the curriculum requirement in cross-cultural engagement.

Bouman's paper is a learned research paper as it analyses the views of different educationists who have expressed their views through their research papers. His paper in this respect is exhaustive. Bearing all these views in mind, Bouman analyses whether service learning is done at the cost of classroom learning, and also accepts that the same type of programmes cannot be implemented in all parts of the world. He draws conclusions and learns lessons through surveys conducted by Calvin College and through two case studies conducted by him. After making an in-depth analysis, he comes to the conclusion that "the pedagogy of service-learning can be a meaningful method for teaching students in a context of service and partnership." Bouman says that these programmes can be linked to our faith concerns as "well-developed partnerships in this vein offer an opportunity for Christian colleges and universities to become involved in a mainstream dialogue with new insights relative to parallel activity on the part of faith communities in missions, development, and relief activities."

Any good research paper should make a reader ask questions beyond the purview of the discussions made in the paper. It should encourage one to ask questions and think of its applicability in different contexts. If this is the sign of a good paper, one can say that Bouman's paper is such a one. Some of the questions that one tends to raise are—can these programmes be just elitist, or can even the financially less privileged participate in this? Can all Christian higher educational institutions emulate Calvin College, and design study abroad and service-learning programmes? How can these programmes contribute to the intellectual and spiritual growth of the students? Do these programmes help students to develop their personality, and make them better human beings? Does service get pushed to the background, and learning get priority thereby making the programme self-centred and narrow in its outlook? Do these programmes enrich the experience of students and make them worthy citizens? Of course, such questions help us to further the inquiry made by Bouman in his paper. The paper also makes us ask some very practical questions about the practicality of implementing these programmes in different situations. One tends to ask whether all Christian educational institutions of higher learning think of designing and implementing such programmes. Instead of students from the West coming to the East, can there be a flow of students in the opposite direction as well? Can Christian institutions come together and think of strategies to have these programmes without excluding the less fortunate Christian educational institution of the developing countries? Can the affluent institutions of the West have tie-ups with Christian institutions of the other parts of the world so that an effective exchange programme can be effected and facilitate better mobility of students and effective exchange of ideas? Above all, two very important pertinent questions that come before us are what best can be done in an international conference like this, and what should be the role of IAPCHE?

Bouman's paper "Ways that the Pedagogy and Philosophy of Service-Learning can be Useful in Teaching Students in International Contexts" is a well thought out discussion that is suitable for an international convention like Congreso International 2006, and I am sure that this paper will encourage the participating institutions and individuals to plan strategies to introduce study-abroad programmes, twinning programmes, exchange programmes and service-learning programmes involving Christian institutions of higher learning throughout the world. It will also make IAPCHE think of strategies to bring its member institutions and individual members together to plan effective study-abroad and service-learning programmes. The responsibility of IAPCHE is to find member institutions with financial, infrastructural, and academic competency, which can undertake such innovative activities.

METAPHOR AND EMBODIMENT: NEW PERSPECTIVES ON COGNITION AND MEANING

M. Elaine Botha

Every legal system and every moral code is based on a set of assumptions about what people are, have, or do. And, I might add, significant changes in law or morality are preceded by a reordering of how such metaphors are employed.

Our language habits are at the core of how we imagine the world. Metaphor provides access to a discipline's assumptions about the way the world is structured. (Postman, 1996, p. 176)

Introduction
The demise of the objectivist paradigm of knowledge, new embodiment theories of metaphor and empirical research concerning metaphor comprehension in a wide variety of disciplines, have brought about changes in the understanding of the nature of knowledge, reference, truth, meaning, reality, and the relationship of language to the world. These theories have also provided new incentives to articulate views of embodiment that can do justice to both the multiplicity of meanings generated and discovered through metaphor and the multi-vocality and multi-facetedness of the possible worlds to which metaphors refer. As the result of these and other developments, so called non-epistemic factors such as socio-cultural, religious, metaphysical, and ideological, formerly regarded as epistemically out of bounds in the realm of science, are now seen as constitutive of conceptual meaning, cognition and conceptual changes in both ordinary experience and theoretical endeavours. The Postman quote at the beginning of this article points to the pivotal role that the analysis of metaphor can play in a transcendental critique.

Discussions of metaphor inevitably lead to a labyrinthine trail of often-unresolved issues in a vast interdisciplinary terrain. The discussions of these issues display similar characteristics to the phenomenon they are trying to grasp: wide-ranging, multivocal, and hard to pin down. The complex discussions fan out over a wide-ranging area from traditional rhetoric and literature studies to cognitive linguistics, cognitive psychology, cognitive science, religion, and theology. A highly theoretical vocabulary has developed which addresses issues starting from the conventional, ordinary language distinctions between literal and metaphorical language and meaning to detailed empirical analyses of meaning transfer, cross-domain mapping, conceptual blending, knowledge acquisition, and ontological issues. Even though many of these discussions constitute unique discourses with their own technical vocabulary they have common themes which include the relationship between objectivism and relativism, the mind-body polarity, alternative views concerning cognition, reference and language, meaning, interpretation, reality, and truth. Theories about the pivotal role of metaphor in these domains abound, as do diverse accounts of how metaphorical mappings and analogical meaning transfer take place on the level of perception, concept formation, conceptual integration, language, communication, cognitive processes in general and scientific cognition specifically. All of these accounts address first, the mediating, hermeneutical, and semiotic function of metaphor and second the way metaphorical meaning is generated, conditioned, and constrained.

Many have attempted to give an account of the nature of analogical information processing within metaphors and metaphorical meaning transformation across diverse contextual and semantic domains. Hesse (1988a, pp. 317-340), Rothbart (1988, pp. 377-399), Johnson (1987), Lakoff and Johnson (1999), Kittay (1987), MacCormac (1985), Kövecses (2002; 2005) et al. have recently provided us with theories which have supplemented, modified, accommodated, and clarified existing accounts of analogical understanding, and the mechanisms of meaning shift which take place when concepts are "displaced" (Schön, 1963) through changes in theory. Overall, these accounts are related to and dependent upon general metaphor theories of which so many are in circulation that various classifications have already been made. Significant new avenues of exploration are the so-called embodiment-, domain-, and mental space theories. Lakoff, Johnson, and Rohrer et al.'s introduction of embodiment and image schemata as the basis of cognition accommodates factors previously regarded as "subjective" or "non-epistemic" in the act (interaction or enactment) of cognition. Their recognition of diverse but related domains of experience present in the embodied cognitive act also opens up new avenues for the exploration of the constitutive role of religious convictions within scientific cognition.

Argument
The main line of the argument is as follows. First, the double language thesis, with its rigid delineation of literal and metaphorical language, needs to be replaced by the thesis that metaphorical and literal meaning is relative and contextually determined and that all language (both literal and metaphorical) is categorical. Second, contrary to traditional views of metaphor, which ascribe emotional, aesthetic or deviant roles to metaphors, metaphors actually do refer to and depict reality and therefore do have cognitive import. Third, embodiment theories of metaphor which allow for the recognition of the role of non-epistemic factors in theorizing, open avenues for the serious consideration of the presence and role of fiduciary factors in scientific cognition. Fourth, the implementation of metaphorical hermeneutics will show that metaphor and its underlying analogical structure are significant keys to the understanding of the metaphorical stratification of reality and the analogical nature of scientific cognition. Fifth, in order to show how religious beliefs function constitutively in theories, a revised notion of "religious beliefs" is required. Finally, the analysis of the role of root-metaphors and the presence and function of fiduciary moments interacting between semantic fields of metaphors are indicators of the control beliefs at work in theories.

Metaphor: A dubious legacy?
The classical view of metaphor is that of Aristotle who distinguished between "proper" and "improper" naming derived from the theory of natural kinds and essences (Hesse, 1983, pp. 29-30). A metaphor is a word borrowed from an alien context; its use is therefore deviant. This view gave rise to what Johnson (1981) calls a "triad of half truths": that metaphoric transfer is located at the level of words, that metaphor is understood as deviance from literal usage and that it is based on the similarities between things. A definition of metaphor is: understanding, describing, interpreting some unfamiliar situation, event, act or thing in terms of a more familiar situation, event, act or thing. More simply; a metaphor interprets one thing in terms of another. Different theories attempt to provide an account of the nature of the transfer of meaning that takes place in metaphors. Reductionist theories (comparison and substitution theories) ultimately reduce metaphorical meaning to literal meaning. This view of metaphor and literal language became part and parcel of the "objectivist view of meaning" described by Johnson. "Rationality is 'disembodied' in the sense that it consists of pure abstract logical relations and operations which are independent of subjective processes

and sensorimotor experiences in the bodily organism" (1989, p. 110).

Scientific language would therefore predominantly be literal and objective.

One of the first challenges to the dominant positivist view of language was I.A. Richard's (1936) *The Philosophy of Rhetoric*. He challenged the dominant tradition on three counts. First, metaphor is not only a matter of language, but also an omnipresent principle of thought. Second, metaphor is not only deviance from ordinary speech, it actually permeates all discourse. Third, the way metaphors work are that two thoughts of different things are "active together" and supported by a single word or phrase whose meaning is resultant of their interaction. Because scholars have missed the first two points, they have taken metaphor to be a cosmetic or rhetorical device or stylistic ornament. Max Black's (1962; 1977; 1979) essays on metaphor further developed the basic tenets of Richard's position. Simultaneously with the demise of the objectivist paradigm of knowledge the research of Lakoff, Johnson, Turner et al. (1981; 1988; 1989) proposed the existence of "conceptual metaphors" and anchored metaphorical meaning in embodiment.

New views of metaphor
All these developments gave rise to some new insights into the nature and functioning of metaphors, which are listed briefly:
- Metaphor is ubiquitous, pervasive, polyvalent, and expresses an understanding of one thing in terms of another. Metaphors are incongruous, if taken literally. The distinction between literal and metaphorical is not an absolute distinction, but a relative one and moreover it is contextually determined
- Metaphors come to expression in thought: thinking about something "as if . . ." it is something else. They come to expression in language: concepts, words, sentences, texts. They express our deepest religious insights: Myths, worldviews, religious systems, root-metaphors (Pepper, 1942; 1970), and world hypotheses. They permeate Biblical language: God is a shepherd, judge, father, redeemer; the church is the body of Christ. Metaphors are experiential, present in all dimensions of life such as art and literature, prose and poetry, religion, myth, and worldviews and in thought, language, and cognition. Metaphors form the bases of many philosophical systems and theories in both the social and the natural sciences and often form basis of models in science (machine, system, organism, circulation). We cannot make

meaningful statements without the use of metaphor; metaphorical meaning is unique and cannot be substituted with literal meaning. Metaphors convey meaning and have cognitive weight (is true, actually refers to and depicts reality). Metaphors are not merely a comparison of the characteristics of two things being compared but always create new, imaginative meaning which cannot be reduced to the semantic fields of the two poles of the metaphor. Not all metaphors have two poles. Creative and imaginative metaphors reveal not-yet-discovered realities.
- Metaphors are based on analogies (similarities and differences) which in turn presuppose the existence of kinds, categories and classifications—the same categorizations that "literal" language is based on.

These new embodiment theories of metaphor and empirical research concerning metaphor comprehension, in a wide variety of disciplines, have brought about changes in the understanding of the nature of knowledge, reference, truth, meaning, reality, and the relationship of language to the world. These theories have also provided new incentives to articulate views of embodiment that can do justice to both the multiplicity of meanings generated and discovered through metaphor and the multi-vocality and multi-facetedness of the possible worlds to which metaphors refer. As the result of these and other developments, so called non-epistemic factors such as socio-cultural, religious, metaphysical, and ideological, formerly regarded as epistemically "out of bounds" in the realm of science, are now seen as constitutive of conceptual meaning, cognition, and conceptual changes in both ordinary experience and theoretical endeavours.

The body of our knowledge and the knowledge of our body
Traditional understandings of the double language thesis (the distinction between "literal" and "metaphorical" language) with its moorings in the objectivist paradigm of cognition and the representational-computational view of mind are being challenged and redirected by the introduction of these new notions of embodiment. This has forced scholars to revise theories of metaphor to accommodate the questions raised by embodiment theorists from both empirical and philosophical angles. Weighty evidence in recent empirical research in cognitive semantics and cognitive linguistics demonstrate that metaphors are more than mere lingual phenomena and are based in "experiential gestalts" expressing embodied human understanding and empathetic interaction. This has led to pos-

tulating different positions concerning the nature of embodiment, truth, cognition, and reference. Lakoff and Johnson (1980; 1999) and Johnson (1991) and others have proposed the notion of "conceptual metaphor." Sweetser (1990) and Brandt (2000) in turn have worked in "domain theory" and Fauconnier (1994) has proposed the theory of "mental spaces."

I build critically on these insights by introducing a new angle on current discussions concerning conceptual metaphor and its basis in human embodiment. Can the multiplicity of possible meanings, which metaphors generate, be grounded in the human mind, the body or in the nature of the world? The most fertile and productive line of argument localizes metaphor in the embodied inter-acting human being, creating, discovering and opening up new meanings in this process. A view of embodiment is presented which grounds conceptual metaphors and the wide spectrum of possible meanings and possible worlds, which they convey in the ineradicably relational nature of human embodiment. This includes at least the following four levels: The relationship of the whole human being to herself, to others, to the environment, culture, and history and to that which is regarded as ultimate, god, spiritual, God, etc.

This project follows an interdisciplinary approach, drawing from recent developments in a diversity of academic fields. It also attempts to reformulate and refocus the traditional discussions of the relationship of science and religion in light of new understandings of both metaphor and embodiment. The project explores the significance and impact of these embodiment theories of metaphor on some traditional formulations of the relationship between science and religion and introduces a methodology based on the distinction of a number of universal domains of meaning discernable in human embodied experience, cognition, and reality.

Faith constitutive of theorizing
Arguments, which claim that faith intrinsically influences scientific theorizing, often neglect to show how this is true. Proponents of this position often argue that it might be possible to demonstrate this claim in the social sciences and humanities, but that it is impossible in the realm of natural science. It is also often argued that such influence might be demonstrated in historical periods when both culture and science were strongly influenced by religion, such as medieval times and the seventeenth century, but that the demonstration of the claim is impossible in highly secularized periods when the influence of religion is not as apparent. I propose that religious convictions actually do influence both social and natural

sciences and that religious factors are at work in scientific theorizing even in apparently secular settings. In order to demonstrate this, a redefinition of the term "religious" is argued for, the classical double language thesis (the traditional distinction between "literal and metaphorical" language) is critically assessed and a methodology of metaphorical hermeneutics is introduced. I work with a reformulation of the notion of religious beliefs as proposed by Clouser (1991, chapter 2; 2005). The significance of this reformulation is that religious beliefs are not necessarily related to gods/ God, worship, liturgy, moral and ethical practices, but to that which is regarded as divine and therefore non-dependent. This notion of "religious" provides a significant basis for distinguishing between the deeply religious function of root-metaphors on the one hand and the subsidiary, tacit (Polanyi, 1974), fiduciary role of some controlling (analogical) beliefs in science on the other hand. The methodology shows metaphor and its underlying analogical structure to be a significant key to the understanding of the "metaphorical" nature of both reality and cognition. It acknowledges the embodied nature of human understanding, proposes the distinction of a number of universal domains of meaning, and facilitates the understanding of the mediating function of metaphor between deeply held metaphysical beliefs and theorizing. This shows that the restriction of metaphorical meaning to primarily a linguistic notion is inadequate and requires deepening and expansion.

The still controversial claims that "all language is metaphorical" and that metaphors have cognitive content, forms the basis for the argument that metaphorical and analogical language mediates between religiously determined views of reality and the actual theories based on such metaphors. The groundbreaking work of Kuhn with its recognition of the role of paradigms, metaphors and analogies in science, has been appropriated by some scholars in defense of claims that one's worldview, and more specifically theoretical view of reality, is the vehicle, which conveys religious assumptions into theoretical work. Although I doubt whether Kuhn's views actually substantiate the latter claim, I believe there is merit in pursuing his proposals in order to trace the constitutive role of metaphor and analogy in theorizing. But more is required in order to show that religious convictions are constitutive of theorizing. Both pre-theoretical and theoretical worldviews are often deeply rooted in root-metaphors of a religious nature, which permeate theories in constitutive and decisive ways.

The changes in the understanding of the nature of language and specifically metaphorical language have also had significant consequences for the interpretation of religious language and more specifically religious metaphors and the way one views the influence or presence of religious convictions in scientific theorizing. Moreover, in some of the primary literature on metaphor the issue of "spirituality" surfaces and is appealed to as a basis for embodied metaphorical meaning. These proposals need serious and critical attention and the consequences of the arguments presented for the notions of scientific realism and spirituality require further exploration.

Metaphorical meaning: An infinite regress?
Arguing against the double language thesis and for the thesis that "all language is metaphorical" poses a number of problems, the most significant being the question whether the lack of a literal base does not give rise to the spectre of an infinite regress of meaning. It also implicitly harbours the question concerning the relationships between analogy and metaphor. I show that metaphor needs to be distinguished from proper analogy and that literality is as much a problem as metaphoricity because literality is as much dependent upon classification and categorization of reality as is metaphorical language (Hesse, 1983, p. 40). Having said this, the classical problems related to metaphoricity and literality are not resolved, but moved to a different level. In this work, I argue for the recognition of the contextual qualification of the distinction between literal and metaphorical language and literal and metaphorical meaning is relative and does not necessarily require a two-tier view of cognition or reality. I maintain that the possibility of stable meaning and communication is guaranteed through a new understanding of proper analogy.

Perhaps the most significant findings with respect to metaphor have been that both literal and metaphorical language ultimately related to that which is regarded as the acceptable, conventional classification or categorization of the pre-conceptual and experiential structures of reality at a specific historical point in time. Metaphor brings about the expansion and changes in such classifications and categorizations of reality. This holds for conceptual displacements in everyday language, meaning shifts in theoretical language and certainly also in changes of understanding concerning the nature of God and His revelation.

The literal-metaphorical distinction needs to be replaced by a distinction between non-analogical and analogical meaning of domains and concepts. The non-analogical meaning is the original, primary, "home base" or domain meaning that is characterized by a unique meaning nucleus. This is the way in which one of the multiplicities of original, irreducible semantic domains of reality presents itself. The intriguing characteristic of non-analogical domains is the fact that they harbour the full gamut of potential references to the wide spectrum of meaning of our multi-ordinally (Korzybski, 1933) structured world. When concepts are formed the meaning of these non-analogical concepts are expressed in a vast array of analogical moments which relate this original, non-analogical primary, primitive, univocal meaning to other semantic domains. Once a concept from such an original source domain is utilized in any other domain, it acquires a qualification, which indicates its analogical use. The history of the differentiation of scientific disciplines rests on the process of exploring and opening up these analogical elements of original, irreducible domains of reality (Stafleu, 1978; 1979).

The fiduciary dimension and "control beliefs"

The fiduciary, also called certitudinal or confessional, dimension of reality constitutes one such non-analogical or original semantic domain characterized by the nucleus of "trust." All entities in reality (facts, things, events, acts, and relationships) passively or actively participate or function in this domain; so do theories and models. In any theory attempting to understand reality, there are always a number of assumptions or presuppositions which are accepted on face value and which act in a fiduciary manner, without being questioned. In the conceptual frameworks of such theories concepts are utilized which acquire a meaning from some original domain, e.g. force as a physical phenomenon. When the meaning of the term is unpacked, it becomes clear that it is imbued with a specific conceptual connotation. A good illustration is Hesse's (1988, p. 120) comparison between the difference in meaning of the concept "negative charge" in 19th century atomism and electromagnetic theory. The difference in emphasis on a specific analogical moment in each one of these two theories plays a significant role in the differences of meaning of the concepts utilized in the respective theories. Ultimately, the decisive fiduciary role played by such an analogical moment ought to be taken into account when attempting to understand the basic difference between these two theories.

Amongst these analogical moments that are present in theoretical language, there is often a decisive, regulating, and controlling analogy constitutive of the metaphorically constituted theory terms. The controlling analogy within a theory or model based on a metaphor often functions as the fiduciary component of a theory. These reflections first highlight our assumption that a fiduciary component is a significant domain of embodied human existence, cognition, and theorizing. Therefore, it is constitutive of all acts of knowing that are obviously always embodied. These distinctions warrant the introduction of a clear demarcation between metaphor and analogy.

Metaphors and analogies
Metaphors are usually used in specific references and refer to entities. Metaphors can be replaced by other metaphors. Yet, there are some metaphors which refer to some deeper ontological coherence of the diversity of reality and are therefore of a different kind. They cannot easily be replaced by other metaphors. Such metaphors are original, primitive, or non-analogical. Hart (1984, p. 156) calls these metaphors, which express analogical relationships between aspects or facets of reality, modal. Modal in this sense should be differentiated from notions of "modality" used elsewhere in philosophy, logic, and metaphor theory. Modal refers to aspects or facets of reality or to diverse ways in which reality functions. These proper analogies, ontological metaphors or unavoidable analogical structures play a significant role in the process of uncovering the unavoidable analogical moments that are pregnant expressions of the coherence and interrelatedness of original and irreducible domains in reality. This becomes apparent in the way metaphorical modeling functions in theorizing. Metaphors mediate access to these ontic analogies through the process of analogical concept formation. These concepts are closely related to the basic metaphor or root-metaphor operating in a discipline or theoretical perspective.

Metaphorical language and cognition reflects the intrinsically "metaphorical" nature of the embodied human experiential and conceptual system and also correlates with the metaphorical stratification of reality. The methodology of metaphorical hermeneutics shows that metaphor and its underlying analogical structure are significant keys to the understanding of the metaphorical nature of reality and cognition. The changes in the understanding of the nature of language and specifically metaphorical language also have significant consequences for the interpretation of religious language.

For the Christian scholar all of this raises a number of questions: How does the metaphorical nature of religious and Biblical language relate to the metaphorical nature of everyday and theoretical language and how do they both in turn relate to growing insights into the metaphorical/analogical structure of the world we live in? In which ways does Biblical metaphorical language and religious language in general distinguish itself from metaphorical language used elsewhere in a diversity of fields? Does Scripture harbour central or root metaphors or a hierarchy of such metaphors that regulate the itineraries of meaning (Ricoeur, 1980) of the full story line of Scripture and therefore dictate the reading and interpretation of the diverse texts that constitutes it? Which candidates are the most likely and most Biblically responsible root construals of the central reality of Christianity?

Biblical language and religious language is intrinsically certitudinal and confessional in nature and relates to the concrete, experiential relationship of the community of faith. One dimension of the life of the community of faith is scholarly and academic activities. When seeking justice-in-shalom in this dimension of life, the scholar is called to work out the claims of her religious allegiance in the area of theorizing. It requires at least an exploration of the relationship of theoretical and other root-metaphors to the overall itinerary of meaning in the overarching Biblical story.

Embodiment and the grammar of creation (Steiner, 2001): Real certitudinal anchors

Earlier I argued that the methodology of metaphorical hermeneutics assumes an analogical structure to the world, human experience, and cognition. In the final instance, the central question raised in the title of my essay deals with tracing the consequences of this ontology, for the realism debate and the debate concerning the role of religious convictions in science. The recognition of original and irreducible analogical domains of reality approximated by metaphorical language and models holds promise for the resolution of the interminable double-language thesis debate. This approach claims that metaphorical thought, images, language, and models are able to access this structure of the world and that they mediate discovery and the opening up of the complex interrelated spheres of meaning of reality. This structure constitutes the "moorings" of metaphorical meaning and reference. It is a realist position—but a qualified realism. Such a claim will no doubt be disputed by many involved in the realism vs. anti-realism debates, mainly because in the philosophical discussions realism is defined in diverse ways. (Delaney, 1985) Whether a realist understanding of theoretical knowledge and the cognitive role of metaphor qualifies as a foundationalist approach is open to discussion. This is an important issue, but not one that I shall address here.

Post-modernism questions any essentialist or foundationalist claims of knowledge and suspends the possibility of accessing reality outside of the interplay of texts and writing. The double-language view in which literal and metaphorical language is differentiated and juxtaposed often seeks the grounding or mooring of the meaning of the metaphorical concepts in some bedrock of literal meaning. Pan-metaphoricism on the other hand, argues that which is expressed can only be expressed metaphorically or is only accessible via metaphor. In general, these positions do not necessarily address the grounding or mooring of metaphors, nor do they necessarily have explicit positions on the cognitive status of metaphorical devices. Whether these metaphors have cognitive import, actually refer to states of affairs in reality, and are constrained by the structure for reality, remains the contentious issue. The critical background issue in this debate is what Bernstein (1983) calls the "Cartesian anxiety" (pp. 18-19) which he identifies as the root or basis of the subjectivism-objectivism debate. He says:

> The primary reason why the agon between objectivists and relativists has become so intense today is the growing apprehension that there may be nothing—not God, reason, philosophy, science, or poetry—that answers to and satisfies our longing for ultimate constraints, for a stable and reliable rock upon which we can secure our thought and action.

Foundationalism and its critics have developed a wide arsenal of responses to this quest—responses that each have a different answer to the question of the mooring or anchoring of metaphorical meaning. Answers range from reductionist positions that anchor metaphorical meaning in literal language to positions that seek the moorings of metaphorical meaning in social conventions and constructivist positions. Anti-realist positions often anchor meaning in some dimension of the subjective world, whereas realists argue that there is an objective and independent world out there, which can be accessed. The realism espoused in this work argues for the real existence of conditions or structures for human existence, experience, and reality. These structures do not only condition cognition but also condition the empirical existence of all entities and dimensions of reality.

Realism in everyday use of metaphor and scientific realism associated with the implementation of theory constitutive metaphors in scientific theorizing have points of contact but are also vastly different. The difference in the cognitive import of metaphor is related to the widely divergent contexts in which they function. What is common to both everyday usage of metaphors and its use in science is the fact that it rests on human embodiment in the senses discussed earlier. Even more fundamental is the fact that human relational embodiment in turn is anchored in the "deeper grammar" of reality.

Both Bernstein (1983) and Slingerland (2004) grapple with the nature of this stable and reliable foundation or common core of human existence. Slingerland comes to the conclusion that there is a position between Enlightenment realism and post-modern anti-realism (2004, pp. 1-31) and argues for an ". . . embodied realism in which the commonalities of human bodily experience can serve as a basis for cross-cultural commensurability . . ." (2004, p. 1). When demonstrating the commonalities between Confucian and Western theories of morality Slingerland (2004, p. 16) states that "both these theoretical conceptions grow out of and make use of a deeper metaphysical grammar that has its roots in common human embodied experience." He also calls this a common core. The crux of his argument is that these commonalities "are not reflections of some a priori order existing independently of humans, but arise out of the interaction of human bodies with a fairly stable physical world over the course of both evolutionary and personal time . . ." (2004, p. 17). Against the anti-realists, Slingerland argues that there are structures of cognition common to all human beings regardless of their culture, language or a particular theory (2004, p. 17). Slingerland therefore chooses for embodied realism, a choice that I am willing to share but with a number of caveats.

The first caveat pertains to the requirement of a view of the creation order, which acknowledges the reality of the basis of metaphorical meaning in human embodiment, but also recognizes the structural traits of all of non-human reality. The creation order exists both as condition for human and non-human reality (in that sense it is "independent") but also takes shape in and through human and non-human response to these conditions. In the chapter dealing with the grounding of metaphorical meaning, the role of embodiment and the structures for creation that condition the existence of human embodiment is dealt with. There is one important strand of this argument that still needs to be teased out. I argued that Lakoff and Johnson's suggestion of "embodied realism" is a more acceptable and responsible realistic view than the rationalistic realism, which hales from the Enlightenment. Yet, embodied realism as espoused by Lakoff and Johnson and their school of thought does not fully consider two dimensions. The first is that human embodiment is conditioned and structured by even deeper layers of reality, as grammar would structure a language. Hart (1984, pp. 82-83) articulates a position that considers "the thesis that the existing empirical world has an irreducible correlate in the order of the world." Further, both individuality or particularity and universality are "real," are mutually irreducible and correlative. This means that "natural kinds, social order, norms for behaviour and laws are all real" (Hart, 1984, p. 82) as are the particular phenomena in reality that we designate as natural kinds, etc. Used in this sense the term "realism" acquires a different meaning to the standard meaning found in most literature on the subject.

With respect to realism in science, theories based on metaphorical models, and tested and corroborated in confrontation with empirical reality, provide a realistic approximation of reality. This choice is made over and against the position of instrumentalism, which argues that metaphors are merely heuristic devices utilized for purposes of discovery. This position remains critical of anti-realism even though Hesse's contributions to the discussions concerning "modified realism" have shaped my own understanding of the matter in many ways. However, Hesse holds to an anti-realist or moderate realist position, mainly because of her rejection of the existence of universals, natural kinds, and essences. I agree with her that the maintenance of a realist stance requires a rejection of the traditional (or absolute) theory of universals. Her network theory of meaning based on her appropriation of Wittgenstein's family resemblance notion is closer to a modified view of natural kinds and universals that I too find acceptable, but I do believe realism and scientific realism requires some construal or reformulation of a theory of universals and natural kinds in order to escape the potentially relativistic consequences which an anti-realist position entails. Such a theory of universals requires the recognition that the underlying classificatory system on which metaphorical reference is based represents more than conventional, sociologically determined semantic reality. It requires a positive recognition of the presence and knowability of God's presence in and through His creation order.

God's presence . . . .?
George Steiner (1989, p. 3) states that

> . . . any coherent understanding of what language is and how language performs . . . any coherent account of the capacity of human speech to communicate meaning and feeling is, in the final analysis, underwritten by the assumption of God's presence.

The wager on the meaning of meaning "is a wager on transcendence" (1989, pp. 4, 214). Steiner's "...conjecture is that 'God' is, not because our grammar is outworn; but that grammar lives and generates worlds because there is a wager on God" (Steiner, 1989, p. 4). And this wager is ". . . on the informing presence in the semantic markers which generates . . ." all kinds of works of art. He says, "They are re-enactments, reincarnations via spiritual and technical means of that which human questioning, solitude, inventiveness, apprehension of time and of death can intuit of the fiat of creation, out of which, inexplicably, have come the self and the world into which we are cast" (Steiner, 1989, p. 215). Elsewhere Steiner (2001) speaks of the "grammar of creation."

One could argue that "knowing God" and "knowing His order for His creation" are two different matters and that even if one were to concede the knowability of God through His presence in His creation, the order for creation still remains way beyond our theoretical grasp and can only be approximated. That being the case, I believe realism defined as the recognition of the existence of a creation order, which we approximate inter alia with metaphorical models, is still a position preferable to anti-realism. A realist position constitutes a bulwark against relativism. In the inextricable correlation between the fiat or grammar of creation and our human articulation of this grammar via metaphor and analogy the mooring of metaphorical meaning becomes apparent.

References

Beardsley, M. (1967). Metaphor. In P. Edwards (Ed.), *The encyclopedia of philosophy* (pp. 284-289). New York: Macmillan.
Bernstein, R. (1983). *Beyond objectivism and relativism: Science, hermeneutics and praxis*. Philadelphia: University of Pennsylvania Press.
Black, M. (1962). *Models and metaphors: Studies in language and philosophy*. Ithaca: Cornell University Press.
Black, M. (1977). More about metaphor. *Dialectica,* 31(3-4), 431-457.
Black, M. (1979). More about metaphor. In A. Ortony (Ed.), *Metaphor and thought* (pp. 19-43). Cambridge: Cambridge University Press.
Boyd, R. (1979). Metaphor and theory change: What is 'metaphor' a metaphor for? In A. Ortony (Ed.), *Metaphor and thought* (pp. 356-408). Cambridge: Cambridge University Press.
Brandt, P. (2000). The architecture of semantic domains: A grounding hypothesis in cognitive semiotics. *Revista Portuguesa de Humanidades,* 4(1 & 2), 11-51.
Burrell, D. (1973). *Analogy and philosophical language*. New Haven: Yale University Press.
Clouser, R. (1991). *The myth of religious neutrality: An essay on the hidden role of religious belief in theories*. Notre Dame, IN: University of Notre Dame Press.

Clouser, R. (2005). *The myth of religious neutrality: An essay on the hidden role of religious belief in theories.* (Rev. ed.) Notre Dame, IN: University of Notre Dame Press.

Delaney, C. (1984). Presidential address: Beyond realism and anti-realism. *Proceedings of the American Catholic Philosophical Association,* 59.

Fauconnier, G. (1994). *Mental spaces: Aspects of meaning construction in natural language.* Cambridge: Cambridge University Press.

Hart, H. (1984). *Understanding our world: An integral ontology.* Lanham: University Press of America.

Hesse, M. (1985-86). Texts without types and lumps without laws. *New Literary History,* 17, 31-48.

Hesse, M. (1983). The cognitive claims of metaphor. In J. van Noppen (Ed.), *Metaphor and religion* (pp. 27-45). Brussel: Vrije Universiteit Brussel.

Hesse, M. (1988). Theories, family resemblances and analogy. In D. Helman (Ed.), *Analogical reasoning: perspectives of artificial intelligence, cognitive science, and philosophy* (pp. 317-340). Dordrecht, the Netherlands: Kluwer Academic Publishers.

Hesse, M. (1987). Unfamiliar noises II: Tropical talk: The myth of the literal. *Proceedings of the Aristotelian Society for the Systematic Study of Philosophy Supplementary,* 61, 297-311.

Johnson, M. (1989). Image-schematic bases of meaning. *Semiotic Inquiry,* 9(1-3), 109-118.

Johnson, M. (1991). Knowing through body. *Philosophical Psychology,* 4(1), 3-18.

Johnson, M. (Ed.). (1981). *Philosophical perspectives on metaphor.* Minneapolis: University of Minnesota Press.

Johnson, M. (1987). *The body in the mind: The bodily basis of meaning, imagination, and reason.* Chicago: University of Chicago Press.

Kittay, E. (1987). *Metaphor: Its cognitive force and linguistic structure.* Oxford: Clarendon Press.

Korzybski, A. (1933). *Science and sanity: An introduction to non-Aristotelian systems and general semantics.* Lancaster, PA: The Science Press.

Kövecses, Z. (2002). *Metaphor: A practical introduction.* New York: Oxford University Press.

Kövecses, Z. (2005). *Metaphor in culture: Universality and variation.* Cambridge: Cambridge University Press.

Kuhn, T. (2000). *The road since structure: Philosophical essays, 1970-1993, with an autobiographical interview*. Chicago: University of Chicago Press.

Lakoff, G., & Johnson, M. (1988). Cognitive semantics. In E. Umberto, M. Santambrogio & P. Violi, *Meaning and mental representation* (pp. 119-154). Bloomington: Indiana University Press.

Lakoff, G., & Johnson, M. (1981a). Conceptual metaphor in everyday language. In M. Johnson (Ed.), *Philosophical perspectives on metaphor* (pp. 286-328). Minneapolis: University of Minnesota Press.

Lakoff, G., & Johnson, M. (1980). *Metaphors we live by*. Chicago: University of Chicago Press.

Lakoff, G., & Johnson, M. (1999). *Philosophy in the flesh: The embodied mind and its challenge to western thought*. New York: Basic Books.

Lakoff, G., & Johnson, M. (1981b). The metaphorical structure of the human conceptual system. In D. Norman (Ed.), *Perspectives on cognitive science* (pp. 193-206). Norwood, NJ: Ablex.

Lakoff, G., & Turner, M. (1989). *More than cool reason: A field guide to poetic metaphor*. Chicago: University of Chicago Press.

MacCormac, E. (1985). *A cognitive theory of metaphor*. Cambridge: MIT Press.

Pepper, S. (1942). *World hypotheses: A study in evidence*. Berkeley: University of California Press.

Pepper, S. (1970). *World hypotheses: A study in evidence* (6th ed.). Berkeley: University of California Press.

Polanyi, M. (1974). *Personal knowledge: Towards a post-critical philosophy*. Chicago: University of Chicago Press.

Postman, N. (1996). *The end of education: Redefining the value of school*. New York: Vintage Books.

Richards, I. (1936). *The philosophy of rhetoric*. New York: Oxford University Press.

Ricoeur, P. (1980). The Bible and the imagination. In H. Betz (Ed.), *The Bible as a document of the university* (pp. 49-75). Chico, CA: Scholars Press.

Rohrer, T. (2005). Embodiment and experientialism. In D. Geerarts & H. Cuyckens (Eds.), *The handbook of cognitive linguistics* (pp. 49-91). Oxford: Oxford University Press.

Rohrer, T. (2001). Pragmatism, ideology and embodiment: William James and the philosophical foundations of cognitive linguistics. In R. Dirven, B. Hawkins & E. Sandikcioglu (Eds.), *Language and ideology, Vol. 1: Theoretical and cognitive approaches* (pp. 49-82).

Amsterdam/Philadelphia: John Benjamins.

Rorty, R. (1985/1986). Texts and lumps (of matter). *New Literary History,* 17, 31-48.

Rorty, R. (1987). Unfamiliar noises: Hesse and Davidson on metaphor. *Proceedings of the Aristotelian Society for the Systematic Study of Philosophy Supplementary,* 61, 283-311.

Rothbart, D. (1988). Analogical information processing within scientific metaphors. In D. Helman (Ed.), *Analogical reasoning: Perspectives of artificial intelligence, cognitive science, and philosophy* (pp. 377-399). Dordrecht, the Netherlands: Kluwer Academic Publishers.

Scheffler, I. (1979). *Beyond the letter: A philosophical inquiry into ambiguity, agueness and metaphor in language.* London: Routledge.

Schön, D. (1963a). *Displacement of concepts.* London: Tavistock.

Schön, D. (1963b). *Invention and the evolution of ideas.* London: Tavistock.

Slingerland, E. (2004). Conceptual metaphor theory as methodology for comparative religion. *Journal of the American Academy of Religion,* 74(1), 1-31.

Stafleu, M. (1979). The isolation of a field of science. *Philosophia Reformata,* 44(1), 15-27.

Stafleu, M. (1978). The mathematical and technical opening up of a field of science. *Philosophia Reformata,* 43(1), 18-37.

Steiner, G. (2001). *Grammar of creation.* London: Faber & Faber.

Steiner, G. (1989). *Real presences.* Chicago: University of Chicago Press.

Sweetser, E. (1990). *From etymology to pragmatics: Metaphorical and cultural aspects of semantic structure.* Cambridge: Cambridge University Press.

CHRISTIAN HIGHER EDUCATION AS A WORLDWIDE MOVEMENT

Joel Carpenter

What a delight it has been this week to engage in a rich conversation about our common vocation, about being transformed by the renewing of our minds. It is humbling to be asked to gather the thoughts of this talented and thoughtful group. This visit also has been my first to Nicaragua, and I do hope to come back and see more of this beautiful country.

I am reminded of a humorous story of another Yankee who spoke to a Christian gathering in Nicaragua. Perhaps you heard that the American evangelist, Jimmy Swaggart, had a stadium campaign in Managua some thirty years ago. Mr. Swaggart came with his staff, and they organized an event for the city's football stadium. So there he was, stalking back and forth across the stage, preaching in that Jimmy Swaggart way, but with a talented Nicaraguan pastor on the stage with him, providing a simultaneous translation of the sermon. Swaggart preached on, and the local pastor stayed right with him. Swaggart got fired up, and the local pastor stayed right with him. On it went, preacher and translating preacher, and then, at the end, a Gospel invitation. The people in the stadium seemed to be touched by the message, and many came forward. Swaggart's staff leader talked to some of the audience afterward, and asked them what they thought. One pastor from a rural area told him, "Oh, the preacher was on fire for the Lord, and God really blessed his efforts. But there is one thing I don't understand. Who was that rude Yankee who kept interrupting him?"

It is humbling to be asked to gather the thoughts of this talented and thoughtful group. The conversation has been deep and dynamic this week, and I am very reluctant to interrupt it. It seems almost rude. Yet perhaps I can do us a service by collecting our thoughts on what has transpired here. No doubt, my efforts will be improved in the translation.

I am not an old-time veteran of the IAPCHE organization, so I am grateful for John Hulst's reflections on some turning points in the movement's history. Given this perspective, the picture comes clearer as to what this conference is accomplishing. More than any earlier IAPCHE meeting, this one is turning the tables. I see four main transforming dynamics at work here this week:

- First, whereas IAPCHE's early organization and thought patterns were emanating from the global North, this meeting has reflected the rise of Christian intellectual and educational impulses from the global South and East.
- Second, IAPCHE had its origins among Dutch neo-Calvinists who were building an overarching Christian worldview, "from above," as it were, from the realms of abstract theory. By contrast, this meeting has featured contextual thought–"from below"–responding to the concrete and the local.
- Third, although much of the early IAPCHE impulse was for Northerners to "teach what we have learned to the nations," this meeting has featured teachers from Africa, Asia, and Latin America, so that we from the North come as learners.
- And fourth, this meeting has taken a more holistic and evangelical view of Christian higher education's (CHE) work, not as a companion to the missionary work of the church, but as integral to it.

So these four trends are at work among us this week, and we will go away pondering them, wondering what to make of them, and what they tell us about the road ahead.

A new educational impulse

When IAPCHE held its last international meeting at Dordt College in the summer of 2000, I came expecting to see the familiar group of Dutch and Dutch-American philosophers and the same neo-Calvinist ideas and rhetoric that had permeated its prior meetings and publications. What I saw instead were delegates from 30 nations, representing the powerful and protean world Christian impulses that have been unleashed in our time. I remember saying to John Hulst at one point: "My friend, you have a tiger by the tail." What I did not say but I wondered, was whether this new wine could be held in the old wineskins. What we are seeing here is that by God's grace, IAPCHE is being transformed as an institution. With vigorous regional bodies and increasing institutional and individual membership, IAPCHE has grown and flexed to meet the challenge of representing a worldwide Christian movement for higher education. But what of this worldwide movement? Most of us have been intently focused on local needs and national contexts, and it may come as something of a revelation that there are kindred initiatives such as ours, dozens and dozens of them, all over the world.

Coming out of the 2000 IAPCHE meeting, I received an invitation to write and speak for a conference on the Currents in World Christianity, sponsored by Cambridge University and hosted by the University of Pretoria, in South Africa. After Dordt, I knew what the topic needed to be, the rise of new Christian universities worldwide. I did not know very much about the topic, but I started to learn. Scarcely a month has gone by since then without a conversation with someone who felt called to found a new Christian university.

This is a movement with amazing scope, all told. When I presented my paper at the conference in South Africa, I said that my quick search turned up 41 new Christian universities worldwide. Almost immediately, members of the audience started telling me of ones I had missed. Professor Nguru informs us that there are more than 100 new, privately established universities across Africa, and no doubt, many of these have a Christian mission. Moreover, the situation is every bit as dynamic in East Asia, South Asia, and Latin America. Worldwide, two new Christian universities or theological schools are starting every month!

So what is going on? Two great forces of our time are prompting and shaping this worldwide educational impulse. One of these is globalization, which means a major increase in the volume and rapidity of international exchanges of goods, services, money, people, information, ideas, and artistry. These exchanges are leading to greater interdependence and mutual awareness across greater distances than ever before (Carpenter, 2003a; Carpenter, 2003b). In a globalizing economic and cultural milieu, there is a growing need for more highly educated "knowledge workers," a growing awareness worldwide that higher education can boost personal and communal advancement, and a growing demand for higher education which many governments cannot meet. Across the world, therefore, governments have begun to charter independently organized universities. Sharp debates arise about this trend (Guillén, 2001), but the point is that the rapid growth of new Christian universities is riding the wave of this larger trend (Albrow, 1997; Lewis, 1998; Robertson, 1992).

But why are so many Christian groups worldwide now investing huge amounts of time, talent, and treasure in Christian universities? Are these moves merely responses to social and economic forces? No, there are religious dynamics at work here as well. We are in the midst of one of the greatest periods of religious change in the history of the world,

Christianity's dramatic growth in Africa and Asia, and its transformation in Latin America. And at this moment, as has happened repeatedly in the past, movements for Christian evangelization and renewal are now making a transition from a nascent, protean, "awakening" phase into a consolidating or "institutionalizing" phase.

Today's developments resemble episodes in the history of Christianity in the United States during the 1830s, 1840s and 1850s, where in the aftermath of the Second Great Awakening, rapidly growing evangelical movements began to found new missionary, benevolent and reform societies, and dozens of secondary schools and colleges. These "uncommon schools," as historian Timothy Smith called them, aimed to equip Christian leaders for the ongoing mission of revivalism, social reform, and building new Christian societies on the frontier (Smith, 1978). Now we are hearing distinct echoes of this impulse in the founding of new Christian universities. Hear, for example, the Rev. Dr. Kingsley Larbi, who was the founding head of Central University College in Accra, Ghana. In the Undergraduate Catalogue, he said that the college's mission is to advance

> the great commission of our Lord Jesus Christ in its multifaceted dimensions: sharing in God's concern for reconciliation and justice throughout human society and for the liberation of man; evangelism and social action, without fear or favour, denouncing evil and injustice wherever they exist; being part of Christian duty and necessary expressions of Christian doctrines of God and man's love for one's neighbour and obedience to Jesus Christ; to exhibit His Kingdom ethics and to spread its justice and righteousness in the world.

More concretely, according to Larbi, Central University College aimed to help solve "the crisis of leadership [that] is the greatest threat to an African renaissance" (Larbi, 2001). Not all of the new Christian universities are quite so vivid or pointed in their statement of mission, but common to nearly all are the linked aims of serving the church and serving society. Again, I hear echoes of the past.

So, in sum, the rise of Christianity in the global South and East has in many places reached a critical mass, and with these movements' new salience comes a stronger sense of collective responsibility. The Spirit has been moving, millions have been saved, signs and wonders have followed, but Jesus has not come back yet. Faced with a "now what?" sort of mission question, with the opportunity offered by widespread privatization of higher education, and with fresh and urgent needs prompted by economic change, many Christian movements are responding with two replies: 1) train up our children "in the way they should go," and 2) "teach the nation."

I hope that this conference has been for many of you an opportunity to reflect on this great educational movement in our time. The labors in your corner of God's world correspond to those of others near and far. We need to rejoice together and give God the glory; "great things He hath done." I was deeply moved by the stories of new Christian universities in Mexico and in India, rising out of Gospel initiatives to make God's love and care known to the poorest and most vulnerable. I wept tears of joy as I read Brother Janagan's account of how CHE is fuelling social change among Dalits in South India. Next to the reading chair in my study is a text of Isaac Watt's famous hymn, "Jesus Shall Reign," and my eyes fell on verse six:

> Blessings abound where'er he reigns:
> The prisoner leaps to lose his chains,
> The weary find eternal rest,
> And all the sons of want are blest.

Whether our universities serve most directly the children of want or those who are more privileged, we serve a faith whose average adherents in the world today are the plain and poor. It should be central to our mission; we have heard repeatedly this week, to engage in the struggle for God's *shalom*, bringing release to the captives, sight to the blind and good news to the poor (cf. Wolterstorff, 2004).

Contextual education to the fore

This "*shalomic*" impulse appears to me to be one of the main drivers of a second theme emerging from the conference, the drive for educational relevance, for contextually responsive education, and for corresponding approaches to teaching and learning. We are finding out at Calvin College as we engage in academically based service learning that students take more care to do their work well when they see real-life people, issues, and results at stake (Heffner & DeVries Beversluis, 2002).

> Conference papers also discussed contextual education from the standpoint of learning a practice. Whether one is preparing to be a teacher, a lawyer, a physician, a researcher, a pastor, or an accountant, each of these fields brings one into a practice, which employs knowledge, skills, outlook, and habits of mind and heart appropriate to that realm of endeavor. Education needs to be about forming whole persons in the professions, we have been reminded. Internships, problems-based learning in the classroom, professorial role modeling, and Christian integrity in campus life more generally are necessary to

the education of caring and competent Christians for professional service.

Contextual education means little if it does not directly address the most pressing issues arising from the particular context, insists Professor Rajuili in his compelling paper. Higher education in Africa has decontextualized a whole generation of students, he argues, and it needs to attend more closely to African problems and issues. It must take advantage of African ways of knowing and communicating as well, he adds, suggesting that professors might consider allowing students to enact what they are learning with music and choreography as well as in oral and written presentations. Contextualizing the humanities requires an appreciative and analytical eye for local culture, argues Professor Alcántara Mejía. We need to counteract the colonial impulse to elevate the Western cultural inheritance over others.

A contextual education for Mexico and South India, we learn from Professors Hilbrands and Janagan, must mean material improvement for the graduates and their families, and empowerment for them to be reformers of society as well. Professor Rajuili adds that the curriculum must address the age's most compelling problems. He recommends, for example, that every student in Africa have a course specifically on HIV/AIDS.

Others, notably Professors Alcántara and Nguru, caution that in the name of relevance, "job training" approaches to higher education are crowding out humanistic studies in philosophy, literature, and history. These fields can help teach students how to make a life as well as a living, to be critical of the status quo, and to be wise and discerning as well as proficient. Theology, sadly, was excluded by secular learning long ago. We are agreed, however, that the old, Greek-derived rationalism, which valued abstract reasoning over engaging the concrete and particular, is a deficient perspective in itself. We need a more Biblical approach, one that calls for "wisdom" (I Kings 3:9). We need not disparage abstract reason and logic, but we should relativize them. They are fellow citizens, interacting with the other contributors to create a higher education. They are not the kings.

Even so, neither the current job market nor the most recent social problem should dictate terms to CHE. Professor Alcántara is right to raise the alarm that the worldwide demand for "knowledge workers" in certain narrowly articulated fields is crowding out the realms of inquiry that have taught critical thinking, wise discernment, and big-picture perspective. The modern era suffers from incessant pressure to reduce learning to acquiring information and competencies, something that the poet,

T.S. Eliot (1934), saw seventy years ago when he wrote:
> Where is the life we have lost in living?
> Where is the wisdom we have lost in knowledge?
> Where is the knowledge we have lost in information?

CHE therefore has some very broad aims: serving God and humanity, and practicing citizenship in the kingdom of God. Contextual approaches to CHE need to keep these broad contexts in mind, and not focus merely on workforce competency. Even in the United States, the pressure to narrow education's purposes is relentless (Lt. Governor's Commission, 2004). I can only imagine the pressures that more recently founded universities feel from national ministries of education to follow these current trends toward hyper-specialization. We need to stand by each other in our determination to structure programs that honor Christ's lordship over all of creation and all of the realms of thought and action.

Wisdom from the South and East
This conference, in fact, has shown that we need to become even broader in our outlook. We need a Christian worldview that casts its vision more to the South and to the East. The Scottish mission historian, Andrew Walls, predicted thirty years ago that the agenda for Christian thought and action would be set increasingly by the rising Christian movements from the global South and East (Walls, 1976). Very few people, outside the realm of "mission studies," paid Walls any heed but today the signs of this change are everywhere. If I may preach to the North Atlantic delegates a bit, it is time for us to take heed. The rest of you may want to listen in, because it is time for you to step up to take the lead.

Inevitably, the great questions and issues for Christian thought come from the front lines of the Christian mission in the world; the places where the preponderance of the world's Christians struggle with their most pressing concerns. So where might those places be? In 1900, 80 percent of the world's Christians lived in Europe and North America. A century later, nearly 70 percent of the world's Christians now live in Africa, Asia, and Latin America. Christian adherence and vitality are waning in the North, and they are rising in the South and East. In Great Britain, for example, only about 1 million of the 26 million members of the Church of England attend on Sundays. In Nigeria, there are now 18 million Anglicans, and their churches are packed on Sunday. Half of the world's Anglicans now live in Africa (Allen, 2003; Barrett & Johnson, 2006; Bowder, 2004; Gledhill, 2003; Knippers, 2003).

We northerners have heard about the rise of southern and eastern Christianity, but we still tend to think that Christianity elsewhere derives from our older brands. But as it takes root in the global South and East, Christianity is being transformed. Never before has the world seen the faith of the Cross expressed in so many languages and cultural forms. Increasingly these facts contradict the assumption that Christianity is a European faith. African Christian scholars, for example, see Christianity as an African religion, not an import. That is the main point of the Ghanaian theologian Kwame Bediako's stirring and provocative book, *Christianity in Africa: The Renewal of a Non-Western Religion* (1995). Yale historian Lamin Sanneh, a Christian from the Gambia, has an eloquent little book, *Whose Religion Is Christianity? The Gospel beyond the West* (2003), which portrays a stunning contrast between today's post-Christian West and non-Western Christianity.

So Christianity is becoming predominantly non-Western. What ought that fact to imply to us? It ought to say, among other things, that what happens in Africa, Asia, and Latin America will have a growing influence on what Christianity will be like worldwide. Conversely, what happens in Europe and in North America will matter less. Tite Tiénou (2003), the West African theologian who now heads Trinity Evangelical Divinity School near Chicago, insists that "the future of Christianity no longer depends on developments in the North" (p. 91). Andrew Walls (2001) concludes that "it is Africans and Asians and Latin Americans who will be the representative Christians, those who represent the Christian norm, the Christian mainstream, of the twenty-first and twenty-second centuries" (p. 47). The rising Christianity of the south and east is no longer distant or exotic. It is in fact starting to change the whole church, even up in the North.

Time does not permit me to point out all the ways in which Christianity worldwide is being changed by the rise of southern and eastern Christianity, but let me suggest a few of them, briefly. First, one worldwide Christian fellowship after another now has a leader from the global South. The head of the World Council of Churches is Samuel Kobia, a Kenyan Methodist. The executive director of the World Alliance of Reformed Churches is Setri Nyomi, a Ghanaian Presbyterian. The general secretary of the Lutheran World Federation is Ishmael Noko, from Zimbabwe.

Second, the most compelling public leaders and thinkers for the Christian church are beginning to come from the global South and East. If you asked who is the leading Christian public theologian or intellectual

50 years ago, people might say Karl Barth, a Swiss theologian. Today, it is Desmond Tutu, a South African.

Third, Christians from Africa, Asia and Latin America are enlivening Christian witness and fellowship in the global North. The largest congregation in London is headed by a Nigerian Pentecostal. The same is true in Kiev. In the United States, the Catholic Church is being transformed, once again, by immigrants. Three thousand U.S. Catholic parishes now have Spanish-language masses each week. There are three thousand African Christian congregations in Great Britain. Twelve hundred Chinese evangelical congregations now grace the U.S. and Canada. In Grand Rapids, in addition to the burgeoning Latino presence in Catholic and evangelical churches, we have Korean, Cambodian, Syrian, Kenyan, Sudanese and Ethiopian congregations. Religious demographers tell us that the main reason why Christianity continues to grow in the U.S. is immigration (Warner, 2004).

It is not difficult to predict, then, that in our North Atlantic world, Christians will take their cues more and more from the parts of the world where Christianity is on the rise, where the churches are becoming movers and shapers in society rather than declining, and where critical and compelling, life-and-death struggles abound. My friends, this is where the main stage for Christianity is today, where the average Christians live and give witness. We from the North stand on the far reaches of a global religious network whose heartlands are to the South and East.

So the time has come for North Americans and Europeans to learn from Christian brothers and sisters from the South and East. That is not easy for us to do. We tend to think of Christianity to the south and east of us being quite fragile, and still dependent on us for help. So we send our missionaries, relief and development workers, and our short-term service teams. We send our money. We Americans send our parachurch superstars to preach the purpose-driven life. My friends here in the South, I don't want to romanticize African, Asian and Latin American Christian movements and traditions, which you would readily agree, have their own problems and issues. But you have much to teach us northerners. In this conference, I see your perspectives coming to the fore.

Time does not permit a lengthy exposition of all these perspectives, but let me cite one example, the exchange between Professor Ganzevoort from the Netherlands and Professor Gaiya from Nigeria over how one might teach about religion in a plural world. In Professor Ganzevoort's paper, Europe appears as the contemporary paradigm, and he outlines its situation. Religious and spiritual dynamics still exist in Europe, he finds, but in protean and eclectic individual perspectives, because religion has been radically de-institutionalized. Professor Ganzevoort argues, therefore, that the new situation of religious pluralism demands a new teaching approach in religion. Neither theologically orthodox indoctrination nor detached liberal neutrality of belief meet today's needs. Rather, he says, we need a dialogic approach, which assumes that we all have evolving and open religious identities. This approach invites all to come and learn from each other, and be changed thereby.

His respondent, Professor Musa Gaiya from Nigeria, reminds us that most of today's Christians encounter Islam in a radically different context from that of Europe. In Nigeria, for example, the religious situation is not merely plural but polarized; not individualistic but communal, not relativistic but dogmatic, with robust religious institutions that are organized to make converts. In this and many other contexts, such as Indonesia or Egypt or the Indian subcontinent, religious pluralism has been a basic fact for centuries. Europeans, by contrast, who have lived for centuries with the idea of Christendom, are perplexed and dismayed about a 3-5 percent Muslim minority in their midst! Christians elsewhere in the world say, in effect, "We have something to offer by way of engaging in Christian-Muslim dialogue. Come and learn something from us." They would agree with Europeans that a dialogical approach is the best way to relate to one's religious neighbors, even when there are firm and clear lines and identities and each is seeking the other's conversion.

It would be easy to respond in a relativistic way, with the Europeans saying, "your way works for you, but we have to do something different here." That is a step back from the long-standing assumption that Europe is the paradigm, the way of the future for all of humanity. It now seems that Europe is the anomaly. As people from the rest of the world continue to migrate to Europe, Europeans may want to get ready to be the ones who are doing most of the changing, not the newcomers.

Education as Gospel work
As Christian thought from the global South and East comes to the fore in IAPCHE, we are seeing yet another turning point in its history and mission. IAPCHE is becoming more evangelical. For some of the old-timers in IAPCHE, this development takes some digesting. As you all know, IAPCHE has its roots in that remarkable nineteenth-century revival of Calvinism in the Netherlands that went everywhere the Dutch Reformed immigrants and missionaries went. As Reformed confessional Protestants, the founders of this organization have been rather reluctant

to wear the evangelical label. Their neo-Calvinist movement has made common cause with evangelicals in some matters, but in others, it presents a conservative Protestant "third way" that seeks to avoid the weaknesses it perceives in both liberal and evangelical approaches to Christian witness.

For those who are new to IAPCHE, it may be helpful to see what the basics of its neo-Calvinist thought have been. That movement's greatest leader was the redoubtable Abraham Kuyper (1837-1920), a born-again convert from liberal Christianity who led a revival and re-application of confessional Christianity in the Netherlands in the late nineteenth and early twentieth centuries. Kuyper also led a Christian democratic political party, edited a newspaper or two, founded a Christian university, championed the working classes, supported labor unions formed on a Christian basis, wrote both theological and devotional books, and served one brief term as prime minister of the Netherlands.

Kuyper's pioneering work in neo-Calvinist thought can be summed up in four ideas that are still relevant for Christians today.

First, Kuyper developed a value-laden, commitment-driven theory of knowledge. As a rebel against Enlightenment rationalism, Kuyper insisted that one's knowledge of the world is inevitably colored and shaped by one's prior commitments concerning the nature of reality. Knowing is never value-free; science cannot be completely objective. Scientific naturalism thus has no claim to a privileged position over against other worldviews, including religious ones.

Second, Kuyper developed a Christian approach to the modern world's growing plurality and diversity that has been called "principled pluralism." Kuyper reasoned that people quite naturally formed communities of the like-minded that shared a singular view of reality, a distinctive life pattern, and a sociopolitical agenda. A just society would respect this social, intellectual, and religious plurality and encourage diverse communities to negotiate the common good. Christians should affirm political arrangements that honor plural beliefs, while not sacrificing their particular worldviews and religious commitments. They could still put their commitments to work in the public arena by joining the common struggle for justice for all.

Third, Kuyper believed that God created human beings to be the stewards of the creation. This he called the "cultural mandate." Being faithful to God entailed giving witness to God's whole-earth plan of redemption. Personal piety that fled the world and its cares was sub-Christian, he thought. So Kuyper's neo-Calvinist movement called for Christian engagement in every realm of nature and culture. Christ is Lord over all of creation, so serving him entails a world-engaging faith.

Fourth, Kuyper helped serious Christians practice a world-engaging faith while remaining critical of the world. He taught "common grace," essentially a robust doctrine of creation and divine providence, stating that God providentially sustains the creation and humanity, allowing much that is good and worthy to persist, even in a fallen world. At the same time, Kuyper insisted, the effects of the fall are radical, and the spirit of the age carries "the antithesis," rebellion against God, at its heart. Christians need to be careful discerners of the lines of God's continuing love and care, on one hand, and on the other, the demonic spirit of despoiling and rebellion, both of which run through all of culture.

In sum, Kuyper laid out some critical intellectual tools and modes of operation for vitally engaged Christianity in our times. He criticized and provided a sturdy alternative to three other Christian approaches of his day, which are with us still: liberalism's too-easy baptism of culture, fundamentalism's crusade to identify God with country, and pietism's flight to sectarian enclaves. Communities of faith and values could play public roles, yet not feel compelled to choose between dominating, accommodating, or withdrawing (Bratt, 1997; Mouw, 1999).

Kuyper has taken his lumps, and deservedly so, in recent years. His ideas of sphere sovereignty and cultural pluralism were used by the racist theologians and philosophers who invented the ideology of *apartheid*. And in the era of high imperialism a century ago, he was a believer in the racial and cultural superiority of Europeans (cf. Botman, 1996; Kuyper, 1996). Yet I hope we can retain the great value that his main ideas hold.

At the same time, I have long thought that Kuyperians make too much of sphere sovereignty. It seems almost more a concession to the chopped-up nature of life in the modern West than a universally appropriate prescription for how Christians ought to live. It is useful, sometimes, to be able to say to the modern state, as Kuyper did, that there are limits to its interests. On the other hand, sphere sovereignty can be used to segregate activities in ways that seem rather arbitrary and certainly are not rooted in the Biblical narrative.

So I applaud some of our Southern conference presenters' attempts to define CHE's domain broadly, even if they make some of our Kuyperian colleagues nervous. For lack of a better way of describing this tension, I would call it an evangelical outlook rubbing against a neo-Calvinist outlook. As something of an evangelical and Reformed hybrid, I favor this cross-fertilization.

In this conference, to cite some examples, points of tension have come out between the Kuyperian predilections for what its adherents call "principial thinking," moving from abstract theory and norms to application that is more concrete. Our evangelical colleagues, by contrast, seem to prefer more concrete, contextually responsive, and directly Biblical approaches. I think in particular of the exchanges between Professors Helleman and Rajuili over whether CHE ought to "lead students to accept Jesus as Lord and Savior of their lives," or the exchange between Professors Jochemsen and Saavedra over the roles of Bible and theory in teaching a Christian approach to the professions.

We are in fact looking at two very different ways of reading, interpreting and applying the Bible to contemporary life. We northerners practice the more rationalistic, categorizing, individualistic, and overall, "distancing" approaches to Scripture that shape post-Enlightenment northern Christianity, while our southern colleagues approach it more "immediately," from the more holistic, undifferentiated, communal world of southern Christianity (cf. Jenkins, 2006). Those here who are Africans, Asians, and Latin Americans are more willing to see life whole, and to see the Christian life and mission—evangelism, service, and discipleship—all inseparably linked and blending over into each other. Which tasks belong to the churches, and which belong to Christian-founded schools and service agencies? What is the relative value of building models and theories, versus going straight to the Biblical narrative? North and South may answer these questions quite differently. The answer, I suspect, is "Don't be too eager to separate them." For those of you from the South, that perspective comes naturally. For those of us from the North, that will take a major reorientation.

In general, terms, I would counsel that the South and East get a respectful hearing in making their case and that they receive some deference in any consensus we might hope to form. They represent the new Christian heartland, and those of us who struggle on the faith's thin northern margins are perhaps falsely confident of our own answers. Indeed, for us in the North, Southern and Eastern Christianity have the potential to rock our world. The Scottish historian, Andrew Walls (2002) observes that northern Christians have

> long grown used to the idea that they were guardians of a 'standard' Christianity; . . . [but now] they find themselves in the presence of new expressions of Christianity, and new Christian lifestyles that have developed . . . under the conditions of African, Indian, Chinese, Korean, and Latin American life . . . . (p. 79)

There are two temptations to avoid in responding to southern Christianity, Walls (2002) observes.

> One lies in an instinctive desire to protect our own version of Christian faith, or even to seek to establish it as the standard, normative one. The other, and perhaps the more seductive in the present condition of Western Christianity, is the postmodern option: to decide that each of the expressions and versions is equally valid and authentic, and that we are therefore each at a liberty to enjoy our own in isolation from all the others. (p. 79)

Neither approach, Walls, insists, is the gospel way. As the Epistle to the Ephesians points out, we make up the Body of Christ only when we are brought together, for

> each of the culture-specific segments [is] necessary to the body but . . . incomplete in itself. Only in Christ does completion, fullness, dwell. And Christ's completion, as we have seen, comes from all humanity, from the translation of the life of Jesus into the lifeways of all the world's cultures and subcultures through history. None of us can reach Christ's completeness on our own. We need each other's vision to correct, enlarge, and focus our own; only together are we complete in Christ. (2002, p. 79)

The implications of incorporating Northern, Southern and Eastern Christianity are immense. They range across matters of personal piety and worldview, communal worship and witness, mission aims and outlook, and all the realms of theology. For those of us who are called to CHE, this great new religious fact of our time changes everything. Every field of inquiry, every learned profession, must factor in this seismic shift in placement, practice, and priorities. There will be plenty of reorienting work for the scholars of IAPCHE to do.

But at every turn of the pilgrim's road, Christ gives us the gospel invitation, "Come, and follow me." That is our call, my friends, whether it is heard in church or in college. That is our labor of love, as Nelly García put it, the missionary work that we have taken up. May God grant us the strength, wit, and grace we need to stay the course.

References

Albrow, M. (1997). *The global age*. Palo Alto, CA: Stanford University Press.
Allen, C. (2003, August 10). Episcopal church plays Russian roulette on the gay issue. *Los Angeles Times*, p. M-1.
Barrett, D. B., & Johnson, T. M. (2006). Missionmetrics 2006: Goals, resources, doctrines of the 350 Christian world communions. *Inter-*

national Bulletin of Missionary Research, 30, 27-29.

Botman, R. (1996). 'Dutch' and reformed and 'black' and reformed in South Africa: A tale of two traditions on the move to unity and responsibility. In R. A. Wells (Ed.), *Keeping faith: Embracing the tensions in Christian higher education* (pp. 85-105). Grand Rapids, MI: Eerdmans.

Bowder, B. (2004, January 16). Worship numbers fall again. *Church Times*. Retrieved from the Church Times database.

Bratt, J. D. (1997). What can the Reformed tradition contribute to Christian higher education? In R. T. Hughes, W. B. Adrian (Eds.), *Models for Christian higher education: Strategies for success in the twenty-first century* (pp. 125-140). Grand Rapids, MI: Eerdmans.

Carpenter, J. (2003a). New evangelical universities: Cogs in a world system of players in a new game? Part 1. *The International Journal of Frontier Missions,* 20(2), 55-65.

Carpenter, J. (2003b). New evangelical universities: Cogs in a world system of players in a new game? Part 2. *The International Journal of Frontier Missions,* 20(3), 95-102.

Eliot, T. S. (1934). *The Rock.* London: Faber & Faber.

Final report of the Lt. Governor's commission on higher education and economic growth. (2004, December). A recent report and policy recommendations regarding higher education in the State of Michigan, U.S.A. Lansing, MI.

Gledhill, R. (2003, July 26). Archbishop thanks Africa for lessons on faith. *The Times*, p. 20.

Guillén, M. F. (2001). Is globalization civilizing, destructive or feeble? A critique of five key debates in the social science literature. *Annual Review of Sociology,* 27, 235-260.

Heffner, G. G., & DeVries Beversluis, C. (Eds.). (2002). *Commitment and connection: Service-Learning and Christian higher education.* Lanham, MD.: University Press of America.

Jenkins, P. (2006). *The new faces of Christianity: Believing the Bible in the global South.* New York: Oxford University Press.

Knippers, D. (2003, August 25). The Anglican mainstream: It's not where Americans might think. *Weekly Standard*, (8)47. Retrieved from www.weeklystandard.com

Larbi, E. K. (2001). *The challenges of leadership* speech delivered by the Vice Chancellor on the third matriculation ceremony of Central University College, January 13, 2001, retrieved at www.centraluniversity.org

Lewis, D. M. (1998). Globalization: The problem of definition and future areas of historical inquiry. In M. Hutchinson, O. Kalu (Eds.), *A global faith: Essays on evangelicalism and globalization* (pp 26-46). Sydney: Centre for the Study of Australian Christianity.

Mouw, R. J. (1999, January 4/January 11). The Protestant theology of Abraham Kuyper. *The Weekly Standard*, (4)16, pp. 28-31. Retrieved from www.weeklystandard.com

Robertson, R. (1992). *Globalization: Social theory and global culture*. London: Sage.

Smith, T. L. (1978). *Uncommon schools: Christian colleges and social idealism in Midwestern America, 1820-1950*. Bloomington, IN: Indiana Historical Society.

Tiénou, T. (2003). Christian scholarship and the changing center of world Christianity. In S. M. Felch (Ed.), *Christian scholarship . . . for what?* (pp. 87-97). Grand Rapids, MI: Calvin College.

Walls, A. F. (2001). Christian scholarship in Africa in the twenty-first century. *Journal of African Christian Thought*, 4, 47.

Walls, A. F. (2002) The Ephesian moment. In A. F. Walls, *The cross-cultural process in Christian history* (pp. 72-81). Maryknoll, NY: Orbis Books.

Walls, A. F. (1976). Towards understanding Africa's place in Christian history. In J. S. Pobee (Ed.), *Religion in a pluralistic society* (pp. 180-189). Leiden: Brill.

Warner, R. S. (2004). Coming to America: Immigrants and the faith they bring. *Christian Century*, 10, 20-23.

Wolterstorff. T. N. (2004). *Educating for shalom: Essays on Christian higher education* (C. W. Joldersma, G. G. Stronks, Eds.). Grand Rapids, MI: Eerdmans.

IAPCHE: WHERE WE ARE TODAY

Nick Lantinga & Anne Maatman

In his banquet address, John Hulst presented an excellent overview of IAPCHE's activities during the past 30 years. Today, Anne Maatman and I want to give you an overview of recent activities. Our presentation will review IAPCHE efforts since Conference 2000. We will review the goals achieved thus far under our Long Range Plan (LRP) dated 2003-2013. (See Appendix A.) We undertake this review recognizing that we stand on the shoulders of giants.

The following objectives in the LRP dated 2000-2010 were accomplished by 2003:
- established procedures governing our board elections with regional representation,
- recruited regional advisors to the Secretariat,
- accepted Dordt College's offer to provide a central office,
- assisted the ICS (Toronto) in the development of the Faith and Learning Network, and
- developed a financial plan (membership structure).

Organization: 3 objectives

> **LRP Objective 1:** "enhance the identity and functionality of IAPCHE's 5 regions"

We begin by noting the Regional Development Initiative (RDI), led by our North American regional advisor John Vanderstelt in 2003-2004. This effort reviewed the various capacities of our regions and recommended ways to better work with and develop regional expressions. In June 2004, the IAPCHE board adopted this work as "Moving Forward Together: The Regional Development Initiative." (See Appendix B.)

"Moving Forward Together" contained four key recommendations. First, each region should establish regional councils with a recommended membership of three to seven members, two of whom would serve as IAPCHE board members. Second, regional councils will be familiar with

IAPCHE programs, maintain regular contact with IAPCHE and their own members, develop conferences and other programs as needed, and encourage networking throughout the region. Third, regional councils should develop, encourage and maintain membership, prepare budgets, and generate long-range plans. Fourth, regional councils should work within IAPCHE's membership structures and promote fiscal accountability. IAPCHE commits $1,000 annually for operational expenses. Councils may request additional funds for regional programs.

African Region
"Moving Forward Together" provided the basis for further cooperation between IAPCHE and the Centre for the Promotion of Christian Higher Education in Africa (CPCHEA). Indeed, as of October 2006, CPCHEA will serve as IAPCHE's official regional expression in Africa. Rev. Isaac Mutua of Kenya serves as its director. In March 2005, CPCHEA organized a conference in Nairobi with the theme: *Making a Difference in Today's Africa: Penetrating Every Corner of Society with the Liberating Light of the Gospel*. CPCHEA also hosts an extensive website and an online journal, *The African Journal of Transformational Scholarship*.

Asia/Oceania Region
The RDI formed the basis for the recently established Asia/Oceania regional council, formed after two IAPCHE sponsored conferences in the region: one in Los Baños, the Philippines (2002) and another in Chennai, India (2005). Currently Professor J. Dinakarlal serves as the director of this regional organization. We are delighted to announce the appearance of the published Chennai proceedings at this conference: *Christian Higher Education in Asia/Oceania: Moving Towards a New Vision*.

European Region
Although there is no formal European council, our board members, Peter Blokhuis and Alexei Bodrov, along with regional advisor Natalia Pecherskaya, have provided significant leadership over the last several years. One of our first regional conferences was held in Hungary in 1993. Since then we have held conferences in St. Petersburg, Russia (1999), Budapest, Hungary (2002), and in Moscow, Russia (2005). Proceedings of these conferences include: *Higher Education in XXI Century Russian Culture: A Christian Perspective* (1999) in Russian and English, *God's Word for the Academy in Contemporary Culture(s)* (2002), and *Christian Responsibility in Civil Society: East and West* (2005) which we are pleased to introduce at CI06.

Latin American Region

The RDI recognized the regional work of AIPESC, our Latin American expression. Sid Rooy has served as the catalyst in many AIPESC efforts, connecting scholars, schools, and publishers throughout Latin America. Spanish proceedings from all of the Latin American regional conferences include *Educando Como Cristiana en el Siglo XXI* (1999), *Presencia Cristiana en el Mundo Academico* (2000), and *Los Retos del Conocimiento: La Educación Cristiana en un Mundo Globalizado* (2002).

Rooy also sparked the creation of ABPEC, the Brazilian expression of IAPCHE. IAPCHE board member Alexandre Brasil Fonseca has provided leadership to ABPEC. In 2004, ABPEC conducted its first conference in Sao Paulo with the theme: *Higher Education and Social Inequality: Towards a Pedagogy for Justice*. We are pleased to jointly announce the publication of this volume at CI06, with articles in both Spanish and Portuguese.

North American Region

In North America, where there is considerable ferment and growing interest among Christian colleges and universities, IAPCHE has been pleased to work within several networks, most notably the Council for Christian Colleges and Universities (CCCU) and the Association of Reformed Institutions of Higher Education (ARIHE).

The CCCU has grown to include 105 institutions in North America and 74 international affiliates from 23 countries. IAPCHE participated in the CCCU's recent International Forum and we continue to consult on ways to support Christian institutions of higher learning around the world.

All but one of the ARIHE members maintain institutional membership in IAPCHE. Both John Hulst and Nick Lantinga have had the privilege of participating in their biannual meetings. The chair of ARIHE, Carl Zylstra, is facilitating the institutional conversations segments at CI06.

LRP Objective 2: "insure adequate funding"

In order to provide for the association's financial security, we have promoted our association to individual scholars, reviewed our institutional dues, and sought funding support from granting agencies and church denominations.

We promoted our association to individual scholars with brochures (in both Spanish and English) and with advertisements in *Christian*

Scholar's Review and *Christian Higher Education*. This conference was also announced in the *Chronicle for Higher Education*. We have also promoted IAPCHE at a Baylor conference on faith and learning in March 2004 and with a booth at the CCCU International Forum in early 2006.

In 2003, Anne Maatman completed a review of dues paid by various institutional members around the world. She reviewed dues in light of enrollments and economic conditions, placing our institutional members in the following grid:

Economic Classification/ Number of Students	1st year or portion thereof	Small < 500 students	Medium 500-1500 students	Large 1500-3000 students	Very Large > 3000 students
HIGH - 100 percent	$500	$1000	$2000	$3000	
UMC - 75 percent	$375	$750	$1500	$2250	$3750
LMC - 50 percent	$250	$500	$1000	$1500	$2500
LIC - 25 percent	$125	$250	$500	$750	$1250

High=high-income class, UMC=upper-middle income class, LMC=lower-middle income class, and LIC=low-income class. We used the table "Classification of economies by region and income, 2007" from the *World Bank Development Report, 2006*. (New York, Oxford University Press, 2006, p.287), which divides country economies among income groups according to 2005 GNI per capita, calculated using the World Bank Atlas method.

We sought funding by writing two major grants, one to the U.S. Department of Education, which included IAPCHE as a resource agency, and another to a private foundation for CASC resources. We also wrote many lengthy introductory letters to other granting agencies, such as the Mustard Seed Foundation, but with no effect. A consulting firm for non-profit associations, and a telephone seminar in which Lantinga participated both indicated that the single most important factor in the success of appeal to granting agencies is first-person familiarity. Without this level of familiarity, and without further expert opinion on the writing of grants, we are reluctant to devote further resources to this effort.

We have begun to appeal directly to churches for support. By placing

IAPCHE on its list of approved causes, the Christian Reformed Church of North America has permitted us to appeal directly to many congregations. We currently receive support from five congregations and continue to seek to broaden this base with presentations at regional church meetings.

LRP Objective 3: "insure appropriate staffing"

Currently, Lantinga serves as the executive director at 40 percent time and Maatman serves as the director of operations at 80 percent time. John Hulst continues to provide excellent advice as the Executive Secretary Emeritus. In 2003, we hired Marlene Veenstra as a part-time office assistant. We also rely on many other contract workers, such as Evelyn Hielema in copyediting and Dordt students for general office work. We have been blessed with volunteers who have assisted us in many tasks while preparing for this conference.

Program: 8 objectives

LRP Objective 1-3: Conferences

With CI06, we have now scheduled and held our next conference for *institutional* and *individual* members—although we have missed our five-year target by one year. We continue to strategize, particularly here, on a conference in 2009 or 2010. We have conducted the following regional conferences:

- 2000: Quito, Ecuador, hosted by SEMISUD
- 2002: Barranquilla, Colombia, hosted *by Corporacion Universitaria Reformada*
- 2002: Budapest, Hungary, hosted by Károli Gáspár Reformed University
- 2002: Los Baños, the Philippines, hosted by Buklod Buyayang Kristiyano Inc.
- 2004: Sao Paulo, Brazil, hosted by Baptist Seminary of San Pablo
- 2005: Chennai, India, hosted by CSI Bishop Appasamy College of Arts and Sciences and St. Christopher's Training College
- 2005: Nairobi, Kenya, hosted by Nairobi Evangelical Graduate School of Theology
- 2005: Moscow, Russia, hosted by St. Andrew's Biblical Theological Institute

At several of these conferences, we encouraged education-specific conferences. At our Moscow conference, we expanded the theme to include health care and business. The Research Expo (REx) at CI06 extends this even further without impeding the many discipline-specific Christian associations at work, particularly in the United States.

LRP Objectives 4-6: Publication/communication

We continue to publish our website weekly with ongoing updates and new information. An online directory was added with the capability to search by name, institution, country, region, and/or research area. We have increased the number of *Contact* newsletters to four each year. We now offer this publication primarily online along with our "Academic Insert." We supplement the newsletter with occasional e-mail announcements.

Currently the following conference proceedings are distributed to new members and available for purchase:

- *Christian Responsibility in Civil Society: East and West* (2005 Regional Conference: Moscow—273 pages)
- *Educação e Justiça na América Latina* (2004 Regional Conference: Sao Paulo—171 pages), in Spanish and Portuguese
- *Christian Higher Education in Asia/Oceania: Moving Towards a New Vision* (2005 Regional Conference: Chennai—128 pages)
- Manila Leadership Conference papers are posted on the IAPCHE website.
- *Los Retos del Conocimiento: La Educación Cristiana en un Mundo Globalizado* (2002 Regional Conference: Colombia—194 pages), in Spanish
- *God's Word for the Academy in Contemporary Culture(s)* (2002 Regional Conference: Hungary—259 pages)
- *Challenges for Christian Higher Education in the 21st Century* (2000 International Conference: USA—215 pages)
- *Educando Como Cristiana en el Siglo XXI* (1999 Regional Conference: Costa Rica—236 pages), in Spanish
- *Christian Worldview and Scholarship* (1999 Regional Conference: Nigeria—203 pages)

- *Higher Education in XXI Century Russian Culture: A Christian Perspective* (1999 Regional Conference: Russia—279 pages), in English and Russian
- *The Challenge of Marxist and Neo-Marxist Ideologies for Christian Scholarship* (1981 International Conference: USA—280 pages)

> **LRP Objective 7:** "Encourage institutions of higher education to assist in the training of Christian teachers in elementary and secondary schools around the world."

We have pursued this objective primarily through two efforts with the support and assistance of John Van Dyk. First, we have devoted full track discussions to this topic at five regional conferences (Budapest, Los Baños, Sao Paulo, Chennai, and Moscow) and at CI06. These tracks have served to connect current teacher training efforts with those actively involved in Christian teaching within their regions.

We have also fulfilled this objective by convening with Dordt College's Center for Educational Services education consultations from 2001 through 2006. These consultations encourage interagency and multi-institutional collaborations in meeting the needs of developing Christian schools. We have seen a steady growth in participation each year, culminating this year when representatives attended CI06 from every region. Reports from all these conferences are on the website, and include descriptions of the work going on around the world at many different levels.

> **LRP Objective 8:** "Continue to administer the CASC program"

Since Conference 2000, we have worked to refine the proposal first made at Conference 2000. In this effort, Harry Fernhout was particularly helpful. We recruited a steering committee with regional representation; designed promotional material; recruited, reviewed, and improved courses so that there are now ten courses offered, two of them in distance mode. Five more distance education courses have been submitted to the steering committee for approval. However, because we have no students enrolled, we are actively seeking your input in the CASC 101 sessions at CI06. We strongly encourage at least one member of every institution represented here to attend one section of CASC 101, conducted by two members of the steering committee, Doug Blomberg and Tom Soerens. Let us know how best to tailor this program to fit the needs in your culture.

Projects: 2 objectives

LRP Objective 1: "Develop criteria for determining what projects IAPCHE should undertake"

This item remains to be completed.

LRP Objective 2: "Continue to assist ICS in the development and implementation of a Faith and Learning Network."

We continue to support the Faith and Learning Network (FLN). The FLN brings together the knowledge of scholars who are exploring a Christian worldview in their academic work and includes:

- Bibliographic database and special library collection, bringing Christian resources together in one physical and virtual location. Currently over 4200 citations are included.
- A knowledge base of scholars whose work is included in the bibliography (still in development).

In most cases, the material found in the database can be found in the ICS library, which will provide all material to IAPCHE members at significantly reduced rates. Books, for example, are delivered anywhere in the world at no charge! (Of course, you must pay to have them returned.) Modest fees are charged to IAPCHE members for chapters and articles to be sent as photocopies or facsimiles. The online location of the FLN is http://web2.icscanada.edu/library/fln.shtml

Membership: 4 objectives

LRP Objective 1: "Increase individual memberships from 275 to 550 by 2005"

LRP Objective 2: "Increase institutional memberships from 31 to 62 by 2010:
LRP Objective 3: "Increase affiliate memberships from 5 to 25 by 2013"
LRP Objective 4: "Increase associate memberships from 12 to 50 by 2013"

IAPCHE Membership Report showing change from December 2001 until the present

Member Type	December 2001	2003 mid year	November 2006
Individual	345	434	643
Institution	36	39	53
Affiliate	9	10	19
Associate	11	21	26
Consulting	4	5	5

In May 2005, we met the objective for individuals with 570 members. IAPCHE's individual members hail from 63 different countries. Currently we have 53 Institutional members from twenty different countries. We are making steady progress toward the goal of 62 members. We have nineteen affiliate members currently. Clearly, more work needs to be done here in order to expand the network of those who can receive and offer support to our members. Currently we have 26 associate members, just over halfway to our goal of 50. Note: the associate member category was redefined to include donors (annual contribution of $200-999) and supporters (annual contribution of $1000 or more). While this change broadened our support base, it has not significantly increased the monies received.

Conclusion
We challenge you delegates to take this information, along with the reports from the track discussions, to your regional strategy sessions. There you can discuss and prepare practical proposals for future IAPCHE activities at both the international and regional levels.

Appendix A

Long Range Plan 2003-2013

The purpose of IAPCHE, an organization of individuals and institutions, is to serve Jesus as Lord, by fostering worldwide the developments of integral Christian higher education through networking and related academic activity.

Organization

1. Objective 1: Enhance the identity and functionality of the five IAPCHE regions: Africa, Asia/Oceania, Europe, Latin America, North America
    - 1.1 Consider the relationships between the secretariat and IAPCHE's regional expressions
        - 1.1.1 Consider subdividing Asia/Oceania
        - 1.1.2 Develop a set of principles, which would guide and clarify the relationship between regional expressions and the secretariat with reference to the proposals developed within each region.
        - 1.1.3 Support regional associations, such as AIPESC and CPCHEA, as they develop committees to conduct conferences and publish proceedings.
        - 1.1.4 Consider extending IAPCHE membership to individual members in all organized regional expressions
    - 1.2 Set policy for selection of regional coordinators
    - 1.3 Continue to work with ARIHE as one regional organization which promotes CHE in North America
2. Objective 2: BUDGET-insure adequate funding.
    - 2.1 Continue to aggressively promote IAPCHE's mission to individual Christian scholars
    - 2.2 Continue to recruit additional associate members
    - 2.3 Review institutional and individual dues to reflect growth in membership, publications, and programs.
    - 2.4 Seek funding for CASC program through granting agencies.
    - 2.5 Recommend to denominations and/or churches related to institutional members to provide financial support for IAPCHE's kingdom service.
3. Objective 3: PERSONNEL—insure appropriate staffing.
    - 3.1 Hire one additional staff member to handle new mem-

berships, mailings, etc. in light of added responsibilities.
- 3.2 Appoint John Hulst as a senior advisor.
- 3.3 Extend schedule for future staffing of the secretariat.

Programs

4 Objective 1: Schedule and hold an international conference for institutional members every five years.
- 4.1 Develop a model, with policies and procedures, for conducting such conferences.
- 4.2 Consider in the model such items as scheduling, selecting a location, defining purpose, budgeting, etc. Important input should come from administrative officers of our institutional members.
- 4.3 We encourage, where possible, that institutional conferences be held conjointly with individual conferences.

5 Objective 2: Schedule and hold an international academic conference for individual members every five years.
- 5.1 Develop a model, with policies and procedures, for conducting such conferences.
- 5.2 Consider in the model such things as scheduling, selecting a location, defining purpose, budgeting, etc.
- 5.3 Encourage discipline-specific opportunities to advance academic discussions and networking.

6 Objective 3: Encourage regions to hold regional conferences periodically.
- 6.1 Involve regional representatives in developing guidelines for conducting such conferences.
- 6.2 Develop the guidelines.
- 6.3 Encourage discipline-specific opportunities to advance academic discussions and networking.

7 Objective 4: Continue to publish a membership directory in online format, distributing in hardcopy only when so requested.

8 Objective 5: Communicate regularly with membership
- 8.1 Work toward publishing Contact quarterly, in electronic and print format
  - 8.1.1 Work with regional advisors in preparing material for publication
- 8.2 Provide multilingual editions of publications when feasible

8.2.1 Share this responsibility with the regional committees
8.3 Facilitate ongoing electronic communication
8.3.1 Distribute Timeline electronically as an update between issues of Contact.
9 Objective 6: Continue to publish conference proceedings and consider ways to make scholarly papers available to a broader public
9.1 Develop policies for the publication of conference proceedings
9.2 Develop policies for the publication of other scholarly papers
10 Objective 7: Encourage institutions of higher education to assist in the training of Christian teachers in elementary and secondary schools around the world
10.1 Collaborate with Center for Educational Services (Dordt College) to encourage consultations among agencies similarly concerned
10.2 Encourage regional conference discussions on the relationship between CHE and primary and secondary Christian education
10.3 Encourage the development of teacher training through networking with IAPCHE member education departments and related educational service organizations
11 Objective 8: Continue to administer the CASC program.
11.1 Seek outside funding through granting organizations

Projects We will consider various projects (one-time services).
12 Objective 1: Develop criteria for determining what projects IAPCHE should undertake (see objective 4 in Conf. 2000 long range plan)
13 Objective 2: Continue to assist ICS in the development and implementation of a Faith and Learning Network.

Membership
14 Objective 1: Increase individual memberships from 275 to 550 (2005)
14.1 Review dues schedule with sensitivity to varying individual resources.
14.2 Encourage institutional members to increase individual membership within their institutions.

14.3 Consider student membership proposal.
15 Objective 2: Increase institutional memberships from 31 to 62 (by 2010)
16 Objective 3: Increase affiliates 5 to 25
17 Objective 4: Increase associates 12 to 50

Appendix B

The purpose of IAPCHE, an organization of individuals and institutions, is to serve Jesus as Lord by fostering, worldwide, the development of integral Christian higher education through networking and related academic activity.

Moving Forward Together
REGIONAL DEVELOPMENT INITIATIVE
Adopted by IAPCHE Board, June 16, 2004

Anticipating continued development of Christian higher education throughout the world, and recognizing the need for all Christians to work together, the IAPCHE board adopts the recommendations of the Regional Development Committee (RDC). Herein we focus on the relationships among and between IAPCHE's five regions and its Secretariat.

The work of the RDC began with an in-depth consultation with our five advisors regarding the condition of Christian higher education in each region. We then took into account other reports, analyses, and opinions in drafting our recommendations. Even with this information, we do not seek to resolve all questions and issues related with regionalization. Instead, we seek the limited goal of directing emerging cooperative efforts in IAPCHE's various regions within a globally international context. Our proposal seeks to build on the principles of accountability, stewardship, flexibility, and mutual assistance. Above all, we hope that our efforts will further contribute to our Lord's kingdom, to the honor of his name for all peoples.

RDC Mandate

The mandate for the RDC was to clarify structural and operational relationships between and among regional expressions of IAPCHE and the Secretariat, with special attention given to: a) the unique and common features of IAPCHE in each region, b) the nature of interregional relationships, c) the relationship between each region and the board of directors, and d) the two-way relationship between regions and the Secretariat.

Background

The RDC consulted foundational documents and individuals in preparing its report and recommendations. The following are noted:
1   The mission of IAPCHE, as articulated in the purpose statement.
2   Proceedings from the 2000 Conference that emphasized decentral-

ization of IAPCHE's planning and activities as much as possible.

3   The Long Range Plan as adopted at the 2000 Conference and updated by the Board in June 2003, with special focus on the following section:

ORGANIZATION. We will build and maintain a structure that recognizes the need for a central office, regional representation on the board, and resources to insure needed networking.

OBJECTIVE 1. Enhance the identity and functionality of the five IAPCHE regions: Africa, Asia/Oceania, Europe, Latin America, and North America. Action steps:

 1.1 Consider the relationships between the secretariat and IAPCHE's regional committees.*

  1.1.1 Consider subdividing Asia/Oceania.

  1.1.2 Develop a set of principles, which would guide and clarify the relationship between regional committees and the secretariat with reference to the proposals developed within each region.

  1.1.3 Support regional associations, such as AIPESC and CPCHEA, as they develop committees to conduct conferences and publish proceedings.

  1.1.4 Consider extending IAPCHE membership to individual members in all organized regional expressions.

 1.2 Set policy for selection of regional coordinators.

 1.3 Continue to work with ARIHE as one regional organization that promotes CHE in North America.

*Regional committees are referred to as "regional councils" in the recommendations that follow. This term more accurately reflects the permanence of this structural entity.

4   Profiles and Dues Analysis documents were distributed earlier. Profiles were prepared, with valuable assistance from the Secretariat, for each region. Anne Maatman prepared the Regional Dues Analysis.

5   The RDC also considered the membership dues structure approved by the IAPCHE board of directors.

6   In preparation for the recommendations below, John VanderStelt met several times with members of the Secretariat (Nick Lantinga, John Hulst, and Anne Maatman). He also met locally with James Koldenhoven, who served as IAPCHE's strategist advisor at Conference 2000, and Emmanuel Ayee, who serves as an IAPCHE board

member and member of the RDC.

RDC Membership
1. African region, Dr. Emmanuel Ayee, IAPCHE board member, communication professor at Dordt College (USA). Since Professor Bennie van der Walt (regional advisor to the Secretariat) was not able to serve, Dr. Ayee has agreed to serve. Professor van der Walt will be copied in on all RDC correspondence.
2. IAPCHE Secretariat, Dr. John B. Hulst, senior advisor
3. IAPCHE Secretariat, Dr. Nick Lantinga, executive secretary
4. IAPCHE Secretariat, Mrs. Anne Maatman, office manager
5. European region, Dr. Natalia Pecherskaya, regional advisor to IAPCHE Secretariat, rector of St. Petersburg School of Religion and Philosophy (Russia)
6. Latin American region, Dr. Sidney Rooy, regional advisor to IAPCHE Secretariat, professor emeritus of Church and Mission History at *Instituto Superior Evangélico De Estudios Teológicos* (Argentina)
7. As counsel, Dr. Jim Skillen, president of Center for Public Justice (USA); Dr. Skillen has background as a political theorist and experience in a parallel service organization (Center for Public Justice).
8. Asia/Oceania region, Dr. Bong-Ho Son, regional advisor to IAPCHE Secretariat, professor at Seoul National University (South Korea)
9. North American region, Dr. John C. Vanderstelt, RDC Chair, regional advisor to IAPCHE Secretariat, professor emeritus of philosophy and theology at Dordt College (USA)

Recommendations
The following guidelines are adopted for implementation of 1.1.2, 1.1.3, and 1.1.4 in IAPCHE's Long Range Plan. (Two items to be considered at a later date are subdividing the Asia/Oceania region and establishing a policy for selection of regional coordinators.)

Purpose of Regional Councils
We recommend the implementation of regional councils to enhance networking among IAPCHE members in the region and worldwide. Regional councils, selected by the members in the region, as are the IAPCHE Board members from the region will enhance the identity of IAPCHE and coordinate the efforts of IAPCHE members in the region.

Recommendation #1: that the following guide the development of a Regional Council in each identified region.

1. A regional council shall consist of no fewer than three members, including the two IAPCHE board members.
2. Each regional council shall determine the maximum number and representation, preferably not to exceed seven members. Geographical representation by country is preferred, but not required. The goal is to have as many countries represented as is feasible.
3. The third and additional members of the regional council shall be selected either by individual members of that region (if practical), or by appointment by the two IAPCHE board members.
4. Normally, one of the two IAPCHE board members in each region shall serve as chair. Selection of a chair and a vice chair shall be decided regionally. The chair and vice chair shall provide leadership commensurate with their offices.
5. One member of the regional council shall be elected or named by the chair as secretary/treasurer. A regional council may decide to separate these offices. Either way, duties are commensurate with their offices:
   - The secretary shall record minutes of meetings and share proceedings with all participants and the secretariat.
   - The treasurer shall hold, disburse, and account for operational program funds allocated by IAPCHE, as well as funds raised regionally.

Recommendation #2: that the following duties outline the work of the Chair and Vice Chair of the Regional Council.

As IAPCHE Board Members:
1. Stay familiar with the IAPCHE networking tools: website, directory, *Contact*, and the Christian Academic Studies Certificate.
2. Maintain regular contact with the IAPCHE Secretariat.
3. Report regularly to IAPCHE's board.
4. Encourage stewardship and efficiency by utilizing the services the secretariat provides for each region, e.g. dues collection, worldwide database, website

As Regional Council Officers:
1. Maintain regular contact with members of the regional council.
2. Report regional news for publication in *Contact*.
3. Develop conferences and other programs.
4. Encourage networking among Christian scholars.

Recommendation #3: that the following guide the activities of regional councils.
1. Engage in long range planning for the region. Long-range plans shall be developed within the context of IAPCHE's long-range plan, be projected for 3-5 years, and be kept current.
2. Develop, encourage, and maintain IAPCHE membership of all types: institutional, individual, associate, affiliate.
3. Encourage and support regional conferences and consultations.
4. Communicate with other regions and with the secretariat regarding long-range planning, relevant networking conversations, papers, presentations, and news for *Contact*.
5. Prepare budgets for the regional council and proposals for consideration by the IAPCHE board.

Recommendation #4: that the following guide the fiscal operations of regional councils and IAPCHE's financial support of regional councils.
1 IAPCHE's regional councils are encouraged to
   - Engage in regional fundraising to support their regional programs
   - Work within IAPCHE's membership dues structure, the resource normally used to fund regional operations (see #2 below).
   - Provide fiscal accountability according to procedures acceptable in each region.
2 IAPCHE will
   - Allot up to $1,000 (US) annually per regional council for operational expenses. Allocations shall be made on written request from the regional council after consideration of demonstrated activity and need.
   - Establish a regional program fund from which regional councils may request funds for regional programs. Awards shall be based on criteria suggested by the following questions:
     a   Is the regional proposal detailed and carefully reasoned?
     b   Does the regional council have a current long-range plan?
     c   Can the regional council provide local support for the anticipated program?
     d   Is there sufficient money available in the program fund?

CONTRIBUTORS

José Ramón Alcántara-Mejía
Rev. Dr. José Alcántara received a MT from Regent College, Vancouver, B.C; a MA in romance literature from the University of Washington, Seattle; and a PhD from the University of British Columbia, Canada. He has worked with the Christian Student Movement in Mexico, with the Intervarsity and Lutheran University movements in the US, and with Christian service groups to Latin American immigrants in Vancouver. Alcántara co-founded various social service and theological education associations in Mexico. He has also taught at a number of seminaries and is currently teaching classes at the Theological Community of Mexico. Since 1983, he has been professor at the Iberoamerican University, serving in research and as director of the Department of Literature. He was ordained as pastor in the Lutheran Church of Mexico on August 11, 2002.

Samuel P. Ango
Dr. Samuel Ango was born in 1960 in Zuru, Kebbi State of Nigeria. He began his university education in 1980 and obtained a BA in English language at Bayoro University, Kano, Nigeria, in 1984. Ango obtained a Masters degree in literature from Ahmadu Bellow University, Zaria, Nigeria in 1994; a Master of Arts in Christian education at ECWA Theological College, Igbaja, Nigeria, in 1997; and a PhD in religious education at the Nigerian Baptist Theological Seminary, Ogbomoso, Nigeria, in 2004. Ango has worked as a clerk and teacher at primary, secondary, and tertiary schools. He has been the provost at UMCA Theological College, Ilorin, Nigeria since 2000.

Doug Blomberg
Dr. Blomberg is Senior Member in Philosophy of Education, Institute for Christian Studies, Toronto. After researching the implications of a Christian theory of knowledge for curriculum, Blomberg worked at Mount Evelyn Christian School from 1977 to 1991. He was also the principal of the (now National) Institute for Christian Education from its inception in 1978 until 1998. In 1990, he was elected a fellow of the Australian College of Education for his contribution to the theory

and practice of Christian education. Blomberg has published widely on Christian schooling, Christian education, and other themes.

M. Elaine Botha

Dr. Elaine Botha was born and raised in the Republic of South Africa. She studied social work and philosophy at the Potchefstroom campus of the University of the North West. She has earned two PhD degrees, one from Potchefstroom University and a second from the Vrije Universiteit of Amsterdam. In 1975, Botha became a full professor in the Department of philosophy of science and interdisciplinary studies at Potchefstroom, was appointed head of the Department of philosophy in 1990, and retired in 1995. She served as academic Vice-President at Redeemer College from 1995-2000 and director of research and faculty development, director of the Dooyeweerd Centre, and professor of philosophy at Redeemer University College from 2000-2004.

Jeffrey P. Bouman

Dr. Jeffrey Bouman is a member of the faculty and Director of the Service-Learning Center at Calvin College, in Grand Rapids, Michigan. He received a BA in sociology from Calvin College in 1987, an MA in student personnel from Slippery Rock University in Pennsylvania, in 1989, and a PhD in education from the University of Michigan in 2004. His research interests include: the role of religion in the history of American higher education; the role that experience, service, and reflection play in the learning process for college and university students; and a redefinition of Christian activism to include both piety and social action. Bouman has been at Calvin since 2002 and is interested in collaborating widely in the area of college students and their making connections between intellectual, spiritual, and physical dimensions of their lives.

Cristian Buchiu

Professor Cristian Buchiu is assistant professor at Hyperion University in Bucharest, Romania where he has been teaching religious and cultural studies since 2003. Before that, he had received his BA in theology from the University of Bucharest and continued his theological studies receiving a Master of theology degree from St. Vladimir's Orthodox Seminary in New York. He is interested in issues regarding the church and modern society, focusing especially on the relationship between Christianity and democracy. Buchiu received a Master's degree in political science from the University of Bucharest with a research paper on this theme. While still working towards finishing his PhD, Buchiu has developed a parallel interest in ecumenical issues and has been elected as a board member of the Ecumenical Youth Council in Europe, a Brussels-based fellowship of national youth councils with members in 26 countries, which trains and educates young adults on ecumenical issues.

Ken Bussema

Dr. Ken Bussema serves the Council for Christian Colleges & Universities as the Vice-President for Student Programs. His responsibilities include oversight and leadership for the CCCU's eleven semester-long/summer-long culture crossing and cultural shaping programs. Bussema brings thirty years of experience in Christian higher education and a decade of experience in study abroad to the challenges of program development and enhancement, assessment of student learning and cultural engagement. With a background in psychology and counseling, Bussema is particularly interested in the impact of student programs on students' emerging sense of identity and calling. Before joining the CCCU staff, Bussema was Professor of Psychology at Dordt College.

Douglas G. Campbell

Dr. Douglas G. Campbell is a professor of art at George Fox University in Newberg, Oregon, where he teaches art history and art studio courses. His paintings, prints, drawings, and mixed media artworks have been included in over one hundred fifty juried and invitational exhibits in New York City, Portland, New Orleans, Pocatello, Montreal, and other cities. His book, *Seeing: When Art and Faith Intersect*, was published by University Press of America in 2002. Campbell's articles, book reviews, exhibitions reviews, poems, and reproductions of his artwork have appeared in *Artweek, Christian Scholar's Review, The Other Side, Mars Hills Review, Liberal and Fine arts Review, Atlanta Review, Windhover* and other publications.

Joel Carpenter

Dr. Joel Carpenter is the director of the Nagel Institute for the Study of World Christianity at Calvin College. From 1996 to 2006, he was provost of Calvin College. Prior to that, he was director of the Religion Program at the Pew Charitable Trusts, a position he took in 1989 after 12 years of teaching at Calvin College, Trinity International University, and Wheaton College. While at Wheaton, he was the director of the Institute for the Study of American Evangelicals. A graduate of Calvin College,

Carpenter received his PhD in history from The Johns Hopkins University. His special expertise is in American religious history, and he is the author of the award-winning study, *Revive Us Again: The Reawakening of American Fundamentalism* (Oxford, 1997). His latest work, which he co-edited with Lamin Sanneh, is *The Changing Face of Christianity: Africa, the West, and the World* (Oxford, 2005).

Premalatha Dinakarlal
Dr. Premalatha Dinakarlal has taught English language and literature at Holy Cross College, Nagercoil, India for over three decades and currently heads the Department of English. She holds masters degrees in English literature and also in journalism and mass communication, and a MPhil in comparative literature. She has won a gold medal from Indira Gandhi National Open University for creative writing in English. She has served as resource person in many national seminars and has published several articles on literature in reputed journals. She has directed and presented quite a few radio programs. Her area of specialization is feminism, and her PhD thesis is on the feminist themes in the fiction of Sylvia Plath, Alice Munro, and Arundhati Roy.

Margaret Edgell
Professor Margaret Edgell teaches and researches as an associate professor of business at Calvin College in Grand Rapids, Michigan in the United States. Her work experience includes nine years as an international economist in the U.S. Treasury Department in Washington, DC, analyzing and enacting US policy in international finance and trade. She is currently conducting research, which she began as a Lilly Faculty Scholar, on the faith formation of business students. Edgell is a doctoral student in higher education at Michigan State University. Her teaching areas are management and macroeconomics. Before she moved to Michigan four years ago, Edgell taught international business and macroeconomics at Seattle Pacific University. She also established an economics course at Bellevue Christian High School. She holds a MA in international affairs from Columbia University, and a BA in international relations from Stanford University.

Musa A. B. Gaiya
Dr. Musa Gaiya is a professor of church history at the University of Jos. He has been teaching in this institution since 1990. His major area of research and publication is in mission history in Africa, especially the

impact of Christian mission in the transformation of African societies. Presently Gaiya is conducting research regarding Muslim/Christian relations globally and in Nigeria.

R. Ruard Ganzevoort

Professor R. Ruard Ganzevoort (b.1965), an alumnus of Utrecht University, is professor of pratical theology at VU University Amsterdam and professor of theology at Windesheim University of Applied Sciences in Zwolle (NL). Previously, he taught for eleven years at Kampen Theological University and served ten years as a reformed minister before his teaching career. His research focuses on life narratives and pastoral care, and on the interface of violence, trauma, and religion. Ganzevoort has published and edited 13 books and over 80 scholarly and professional articles, and he has lectured in Suriname, Belgium, Canada, and South Africa. He has participated in the development of several programs in theological education, focused on student-centered learning strategies, distant learning, and the integration of knowledge and personal experience. Ganzevoort is president of the International Academy of Practical Theology and member of the board of the Dutch Research School in Theology and Religious Sciences.

Nelly García Murillo

Mrs. Nelly García received a scholarship of qualification in Christian education from Mount Hermon Missionary Training College in London, England. Since graduation, she worked four years for the Community of the International Estudiantes Evangelicos (IFES). García has developed the IFES programs in Mexico, Guatemala, and El Salvador. She has taught in a secondary education school, spent three years as a professor of Spanish in the Independent National University of Nicaragua, and four years at the University on Costa Rica. She has written articles pertaining to education, literature, and Latin American culture, which have been published in Central American periodicals. García has been a member of the IAPCHE and IFES boards and currently serves on the Latin American Biblical University and the Ecumenical Department of Investigaciones (DEI) boards of directors.

Perry L. Glanzer

Dr. Perry L. Glanzer is an associate professor at Baylor University. He teaches courses addressing issues related to religion, politics, morality, and education in the Department of Church and State and the School of

Education. His scholarly work addresses these topics in both the United States and the former Soviet Union. His first book, *The Quest for Russia's Soul: Evangelicals and Moral Education in Post-Communist Russia* (Baylor University Press), covered this topic in the Russian context. Glanzer's scholarly articles have appeared in journals such as *Journal of Moral Education, Educational Policy, Journal of Church and State, Christian Scholars Review, Religious Education, Journal of General Education, Journal of Education and Christian Belief and Religion*, and *State and Society*. He received his BA from Rice University in religion, history, and political science, a MA from Baylor in church-state studies, and his PhD from the University of Southern California.

Susan S. Hasseler

Dr. Susan Hasseler is the Associate Dean for Teacher Education and a professor at Calvin College in Grand Rapids, Michigan. She completed her BS in special education at Calvin College; her MA in special education: learning disabilities at the University of South Dakota; and her PhD at Northwestern University, where she focused on social policy and teacher learning. Dr. Hasseler taught for 13 years in elementary and middle schools before pursuing her PhD. Her scholarly interests include anti-racist multicultural education, educational leadership, and international education. She does research on multicultural teacher preparation in South Africa and has worked with Christian school leaders in South Africa and the Democratic Republic of the Congo.

Adrian A. Helleman

Dr. Adrian Helleman has spent most of his professional life teaching cross-culturally. For nine and a half years, he taught philosophy and theology in several schools in the Philippines. He was a member of the Faculty of Philosophy at Moscow State University for six and a half years and taught courses in philosophy and theology at various schools in Moscow and St. Petersburg. He is currently teaching in Nigeria at the University of Jos in the Department of Religious Studies, as well as in several seminaries in that country. He serves there with Christian Studies International, the Canadian affiliate of the International Institute for Christian Studies. Helleman received his BA from Calvin College and his MDiv and ThM from Calvin Seminary. He earned his PhD at St. Michael's College, which is affiliated with the University of Toronto.

John Hiemstra

Dr. John Hiemstra is professor of political science at The King's University College in Edmonton, Canada. He has taught at The King's since 1991. Hiemstra completed a BA in secondary education at Dordt College in 1978. He earned an MPhil from the Institute for Christian Studies in Toronto, and completed a PhD in public policy and political philosophy at the University of Calgary. Hiemstra has been researching plurality, policy, and school choice in Alberta for 4 summers. This has yeilded articles such as 'Calvinist Pluriformity Challenges Liberal Assimilation: A novel case for publicly funding Alberta's private schools, 1953-1967,' in the *Journal of Canadian Studies* (Fall 2005). He has written on many public policy issues as well as faith and multiculturalism in Canadian schooling. He is currently initiating a comparative study of Christian approaches to the analysis of public life and policy, with a special emphasis on the "public justice approach."

Darrel W. Hilbrands

Dr. Darrel W. Hilbrands (b.1949) is the son of a Reformed Church in America pastor. He received a bachelor's degree in education in 1971. After several years of teaching in public schools, he received a MEd in 1979. He went to Atlanta, Georgia, where he started a street ministry. Feeling a stronger call from the Lord, Hillbrands went to study theology, and in 1981 initiated his career in México receiving a MDiv in 1985 and a PhD in 2004. He has served as a pastor and teacher in several churches and Bible institutes and has helped to establish several Christian schools, including ILMES (Free Institute of Mexico for Higher Learning), where Christian teachers are trained. He has worked for more than fifteen years in children's homes. Presently he serves as the general director of the Ministerios Pan de Vida children's home and as rector and professor of ILMES, both institutions in the city of Queretaro, Mexico.

Elisabeth Hulscher

Ms. Elisabeth Herma (Lieske) Hulscher received her MA degree from Amsterdam Free University. She is a registered super-visor/coach/counsellor and teaches in the Departments of human resource management and business administration at Ede Christian University, The Netherlands. Her specialisations are cross-cultural communication and management, supervision, coaching, and counselling.

John Hulst, IAPCHE Executive Secretary Emeritus

Dr. John B. Hulst is President Emeritus of Dordt College, Sioux Center, Iowa. Even though Hulst is an ordained pastor in the Christian Reformed Church, he has spent most of his professional life in the field of Christian education and, since his retirement, has continued working for that cause. He has served as Executive Secretary of the International Association for the Promotion of Christian Higher Education (IAPCHE), as Senior Fellow of the Council for Christian Colleges and Universities (CCCU) in Washington, DC, and as Chair of the Board of the Institute for Christian Studies (ICS) in Toronto, Ontario, Canada. As advisor to IAPCHE, Hulst has also worked with organizations such as the Center for Educational Services, Christian Schools International, Worldwide Christian Schools, and the Youth and Christian Nurture Commission of the Reformed Ecumenical Council, in an effort to assist Christian elementary and secondary schools throughout the world.

J. Emmanuel Janagan

Dr. J. Emmanuel Janagan (b. 1964) is working as the principal of Kaypeeyes College, Kotagiri. He also has worked as the head of the Department of social work in Bishop Appasamy College since June 1996. Before that he worked as a Project Officer in an International Funding agency, "Ceyrac," at Chennai for eight years. Janagan has a BA in English literature, MSW, and MPhil in social work and a PhD in social work. His areas of specialization are human resource management, community development, and social work research. He is presently a member of the Board of Studies in Social Work, Bharathiar University, a member of Salim Ali Naturalist Forum, Annaikatty, and the Citizens Voice Club, Coimbatore. He has published several articles in Indian Express and has presented papers at various universities. He has been the recipient of many awards and certificates of appreciation for his work.

Henk Jochemsen

Dr. Henk Jochemsen (b. 1952) studied molecular biology and completed a PhD in the same field at Leiden University. From 1980-1986 he worked with the International Fellowship of Evangelical Students in Paraguay, at the same time holding the chair in molecular biology at the National University in Asunción. Back in the Netherlands, in 1987, he became the director of the newly founded Professor Lindeboom Institute, a centre for medical ethics. He has published and been consulted nationally and internationally about medical ethical issues such as euthanasia, predictive genetics, and cloning. For the Institute for Culture Ethics, Amersfoort, he worked among other things on the ethics of sustainable development and business ethics. Currently he holds the Lindeboom chair for medical ethics at the Free University medical centre in Amsterdam and is an advisory board member of the Center for Bioethics and Human Dignity, Bannockburn, IL and a Fellow of the Wilberforce Forum, Washington DC.

Lizette F. Knight

Dr. Lizette Knight recently completed her sabbatical leave from the Philippine Baptist Theological Seminary and the Asia Baptist Graduate Theological Seminary where she holds the positions of full professor and associate dean. She has worked as a youth minister at Calvary Baptist Church, University Touch Center, Trinidad Baptist Church, and Cornerstone Church of Los Angeles, USA. Knight has a BS in chemical engineering, a MDiv in religious education from PBTS, a DMin from ABGTS, a MA and PhD in religious education from Southwestern Baptist Theological Seminary, Fort Worth, Texas. Her goal is to equip the equippers in the areas of education, evangelism, mission, and discipleship. Following her sabbatical, Knight was promoted from associate professor to full professor. Her current administrative positions are seminary education by extension director and field education director.

Nick Lantinga, IAPCHE Executive Director

Dr. Nick Lantinga received his BA in political science from Calvin College, and his MA and PhD from Loyola University, Chicago. His dissertation research, *The Miracle that Saves the World: Augustine and Hanna Arendt's Politics of Redemption* relates the religious assumptions of these two thinkers to their social theories. While working as a teaching fellow and instructor at Loyola from 1993 to 1995, he helped develop the first community policing strategies in Chicago. From 1995 to 1997 he served as editorial assistant to the Department of medical education at the University of Illinois, Chicago. He has provided radio political commentary, and has published articles in *Christian Scholar's Review, Regeneration Quarterly*, and in the proceedings of IAPCHE conferences in Sao Paulo, Chennai, and Moscow. Nick was appointed Executive Secretary of IAPCHE in July 2002.

Tom Larney

Professor Tom Larney was born in Ventersdorp in the North-West Province of South Africa in 1946 and studied at the Potchefstroom University for Christian Higher Education (presently the Potchefstroom Campus of North-West University). He obtained qualifications in political science, librarianship and philosophy (the latter uncompleted). After working in military intelligence for five years, he returned to his alma mater in 1976 as lecturer in international politics. Larney transferred to the library in 1980 and was responsible for the library's successful implementation of a variety of digitization projects. Since 2000, he has been director of Library Services. He is currently working towards a PhD in practical theology with a thesis on the family as primary unit for the forming and transfer of faith, which he hopes to complete in 2009.

Stan L. LeQuire

Rev. Stan L. LeQuire is the instructional designer for Eastern University's School of International Leadership and Development and an adjunct faculty member. In addition, he researches the best practices of community-based ecotourism as a model for development. From 1994-1999, LeQuire directed the Evangelical Environmental Network (EEN). In this position, he designed curriculum for churches and Christian organizations, pioneered networks among 19 national evangelical organizations, consulted with these organizations for programmatic change, and developed many strategies to engage evangelicals in environmental issues. LeQuire has served as a pastor, associate pastor, church planter, and missionary in Africa, Asia, and Europe. From 1976-1978, LeQuire was an associate staff member with the International Fellowship of Evangelical Students. He has served as the editor of *Creation Care* magazine and of an anthology of sermons on creation care called *The Best Preaching on Earth*. In addition, LeQuire is also certified in web design and instructional technology.

George A. Lotter

Dr. George Lotter is professor in practical theology at the North-West University (Potchefstroom campus) in South Africa and holds doctorates in pastoral counseling (USA) and New Testament (SA). He was a minister of the Reformed Churches in South Africa for 5 years before leaving to study in the USA. Since 1993, he has read papers at 12 national and 10 international conferences and guided 21 doctoral and 34 masters students who completed their studies successfully. He also authored or co-authored 20 peer-reviewed articles in accredited journals and three books. Lotter is on the National Board of the Association of Christian Counsellors (ACC) in South Africa and a ruling elder in the Reformed Church Potchefstroom-Noord. He was also director of the Pastoral Counselling Centre in Potchefstroom for 5 years.

Anne Maatman, IAPCHE Director of Operations

Mrs. Anne Maatman (b. 1954) was born in North Carolina (USA) to Dutch immigrant parents. She graduated from Dordt College in 1976 with a BA in mathematics. Maatman began serving in the IAPCHE Secretariat in October 2001. Working with a Sioux Center travel agency and serving on the hosting committees of two international conferences in Sioux Center, Maatman became acquainted with the work and membership of IAPCHE. Since 2001, she has assisted with the planning of IAPCHE conferences in Budapest, Hungary; Barranquilla, Colombia; Manila, Philippines; Sao Paulo, Brazil; Chennai, India; Nairobi, Kenya; and Moscow, Russia. As IAPCHE membership grows, she appreciates the variety of scholars and personalities that make up the IAPCHE network. Maatman also works part-time for an Iowa-based organization of Christian school teachers, CSI Heartland Christian Schools, planning an annual convention and other training events; and for Dordt College as the coordinator of their Netherlands off-campus study program (N-SPICE).

David MacPherson

Mr. David MacPherson was born in 1965 in Lima, Peru to missionary parents. His elementary schooling was in Colegio San Andres before the family returned to Scotland where he concluded high school before studying economics and international relations at Aberdeen University. Subsequently he studied theology at the Free Church College in Edinburgh and is an ordained minister of the Free Church of Scotland (Presbyterian). MacPherson currently serves as pastor of the Moyobamba Presbyterian Church and on the board of the Annie Soper Christian School. He is president of a newly formed educational association (Asociación Educativa Reformada del Alto Mayo) formed with a view to establishing a Christian University in Moyobamba, Peru.

Samson Makhado

Mr. Samson Makhado was born in 1948 in the Northern part of South Africa. His father had 6 wives and 23 children. He attended elementary school under a tree, but continued secondary education at Rambuda Secondary School. Makhado was studying to become a sangoma (witchdoctor), but the year he was to be inaugurated as a national witch doctor, was the year in which he accepted the Lord as his personal saviour. In 1973, he went to the Tshisimani Teachers Training College. He worked in public schools as a teacher, vice principal, and principal. In 1986 Makhado and three of his Dutch friends, after dreaming and planning for five years, started a Christian school and in 1990, he was called to move from a public school to Tshikevha Christian School. In 1992, Makhado went to Canada to complete his Masters in Christian education. In 2001, he accepted the post of associate director at ACSI. Makhado has almost completed his doctorate. His studies are based on using education as an instrument for forgiveness and reconciliation.

Peter Tze Ming Ng
Professor Peter Tze Ming Ng is a professor at the Department of cultural and religious studies and concurrently the director of the Centre for the Study of Religion and Chinese Society, Chung Chi College, the Chinese University of Hong Kong. His recent publications include: *The Necessity of the Particular in the Globalization of Christianity: the case of China* in Studies in World Christianity, vol. 12, pt. 2, 2006, pp. 164-182; *Christian Education in China– Some Reflections on Globalization* in Tripod, vol. 26, no. 142, autumn 2006, pp. 25-37; *Teaching Christianity in a Global Context in China* in Quest, vol. 4, no. 1, November 2005, pp. 111-129; *A New Mission for Open Dialogue with Non-Christians in Higher Education Today* in Christian Higher Education, vol. 4, no. 3, autumn 2005, pp. 169-182; and *Changing Paradigms of Christian Higher Education in China*, 1888-1950, in collaboration with Philip Leung, Edward Xu and Jinghuan Shi. New York: The Edwin Mellen Press, 2002.

Faith W. Nguru
Dr. Faith W. Nguru received her BA in communication from Messiah College, Pennsylvania; her MA in Christian ministries from Wheaton College, Illinois and her MA and PhD in mass communication from Bowling Green University, Ohio. She is currently director of research publications and consultancy at Daystar University, Kenya. She has served as dean of the Faculty of Arts, chairperson of Postgraduate Studies at Daystar University, and chairperson of the National Council of Churches of Kenya Communication Advisory Committee. Nguru has worked as a radio scriptwriter and presenter for Transworld Radio, Nairobi, a screenwriter and presenter for Maturity Audio Visuals, Nairobi, and a regular contributor to *Step Magazine*, a monthly national youth publication in Kenya.

Moshe Rajuili

Dr. Moshe Rajuili is the current principal of the Union Bible Institute located in Pietermaritzburg, South Africa. Trained initially as a chemist, he later graduated with a MA degree in theology from London Bible College and a PhD from the University of KwaZulu-Natal. He has been a travelling secretary and later general secretary of the Students' Christian Organisation (formerly known as SCM of South Africa); principal of the Evangelical Seminary of Southern Africa; and area director of Scripture Union. Rajuili is a member of the Uniting Presbyterian Church of Southern Africa. He grew up in Soweto and came to faith in Christ through the ministry of Youth Alive.

Sergio Saavedra Belmonte

Mr. Sergio Saavedra received his BA degree in sciences of education from the Autonomous National University of Mexico. He has a diploma in communications, is a specialist in curricular design and in development of software applied to education. He is author of diversified didactic materials for pre-school, primary, and secondary education. His experience includes work in transcultural missions in a Muslim country, coordination, and assessment of educational organizations and universities in his own land—Bolivia—developing of courses, workshops, and study materials for teachers's training, based on a Biblical worldview. At the present, he is finishing the Ph.D. program PRODOLA of UNELA, and working as coordinator of the Graduate School of the Bolivian Evangelical University and virtual education of the same university.

Daniel S. Shishima

Dr. Shishima (b. 1962) studied religious studies at the University of Jos, Nigeria, and graduated with a Second Class Lower Division. He became the principal of NKST Secondary School, Hom Mbagen, Benue State, Nigeria. Later he was appointed as the agriculture head of the department of religious studies at the Institute of Christian Studies (now the University of Mkar). Shishima returned to the University of Jos where he obtained his MA and PhD degrees in 1992 and 2004 respectively, both in the area of traditional medicine and healing among the Tiv of Nigeria. In 1992, Shishima accepted a job at Benue State University Makurdi as a lecturer and continues to teach there. He has published one book, over twenty research papers, and has supervised more than 15 MA dissertations. His hobbies are football, farming, and traveling. He is highly dedicated to community service. Shishima is a devoted Christian and married to Rose Shishima; they have two children.

Clinton Stockwell

Dr. Clinton Stockwell is the Executive Director of the Chicago Semester, an off campus urban internship program sponsored by 12 Christian colleges. At Chicago Semester, he teaches the Metropolitan Studies Seminar, which is an introduction to the city and current trends in urban studies. He received a MA in history, a MUPP in urban planning and public policy, and a PhD in American urban history from the University of Illinois-Chicago; and the Master of Liberal Arts degree from the University of Chicago. His dissertation at the University of Illinois-Chicago was entitled *A Better Class of People? Protestants in the Shaping of Early Chicago, 1833-1873*.

T. Stephen Tangaraj

Mr. Stephen Thangaraj has been librarian at Bishop Appasamy College of Arts and Science, Coimbatore since 1995. Before that, he served in libraries at Kodaikanal public school and Bishop Heber College. He has completed his Master of library and information science degree and is presently working on a PhD from Vinayaga Mission Deemed University. He is conducting research in the area of information seeking behavior among pastors in the Church of South India, Coimbatore Diocese. He has worked as a technical consultant for LIPSINET (library software) and has attended many seminars, conferences, and workshops.

B. J. van der Walt, IAPCHE African Advisor

Professor B. J. (Bennie) van der Walt is a philosopher-theologian. Until 1999, he was professor of philosophy and director of the Institute for Reformational Studies at Potchefstroom University. Presently he is research fellow in the School of Philosophy of the North-West University, (Potchefstroom campus), South Africa. He has served on the Board of IAPCHE and helped to organize the first international conference in 1975. He has also attended all five international as well as many regional IAPCHE conferences.

Susheila Williams

Mrs. Susheila Williams is the secretary and director at CSI Bishop Appasamy College of Arts & Science. She has a BA in general and rural economics, a MA in English literature, a diploma in office organisation and management from Punjab University, a post graduate diploma in interior design from Sri Avinashilingam Deemed University, and is presently registered in a PhD program at Mother Teresa University for Women in Kodaikanal. Williams was director and principal of CSI Industrial Training Centre for women from 1983-1995; and project manager from 1988-1998 of the Development Programme for Rural and Urban women, dealing with health education awareness and skill training for women, and schools for dropout children. She is presently working with the rehabilitation of women prisoners and sex workers. Williams has attended many conferences for Christian educators and artists.

www.ingramcontent.com/pod-product-compliance
Lightning Source LLC
Chambersburg PA
CBHW020729160426
43192CB00006B/168